# BEHAVIOR PRINCIPLES

## third edition

charles b. ferster

stuart a. culbertson

prentice-hall, inc.
englewood cliffs, new jersey 07632

Library of Congress Cataloging in Publication Data

FERSTER, CHARLES B. (date)
    Behavior Principles.
    Includes index.
    1. Operant conditioning.   2. Reinforcement (Psychology)
3. Behaviorism (Psychology)   I. Culbertson, Stuart (date)
1943-        II. Title
BF319.5.06F45      1982      150.19 '4        81-15424
ISBN 0-13-072520-X       AACR2

editorial production/supervision
    and interior design: barbara kelly
cover design: wanda lubelska
manufacturing buyer: edmund w. leone

Printed in the United States of America

10  9  8  7  6  5  4  3  2  1

ISBN 0-13-072520-X

PRENTICE-HALL INTERNATIONAL, INC., *London*
PRENTICE-HALL OF AUSTRALIA PTY. LIMITED, *Sydney*
PRENTICE-HALL OF CANADA, LTD., *Toronto*
PRENTICE-HALL OF INDIA PRIVATE LIMITED, *New Delhi*
PRENTICE-HALL OF JAPAN, INC., *Tokyo*
PRENTICE-HALL OF SOUTHEAST ASIA PTE. LTD., *Singapore*
WHITEHALL BOOKS LIMITED, *Wellington, New Zealand*

To

# F. S. Keller
whose teaching and writing have been our model

# contents

# 8

## stimulus control in verbal behavior　264

# 9

## complex human conduct viewed from basic behavioral processes　299

# 10

## applications of behavior principles to practical problems　334

# preface

Charles Ferster died of a heart attack shortly after he completed the manuscript of this book. He was 58 years old and at the peak of an illustrious career—writing, teaching, working daily in his laboratory, practicing behavior therapy on occasion, and exercising all those functions that accrue to eminence in one's chosen field.

He was especially concerned with the production of this third edition of *Behavior Principles.* The first edition had been written with Mary Carol Perrot, who worked with him in the development of his "interview technique" of teaching. The second edition was primarily a collaboration with Stuart Culbertson, his colleague at the American University. This one was to be his own, almost completely, and to represent the main objectives of his professional career. He worked intensely on it and brought it to the point of near fruition.

In this book the author brings together his systematic knowledge and his laboratory know-how in the service of analysis and interpretation of individual human conduct in the clinic, the classroom, and everyday behavior. The basic concepts, the critical experiments, the vivid examples, and the special insights all are there for the reader to discover. More than any introductory text I know, this book sheds light upon the "human nature" that we would like to understand, and the means whereby this understanding can be gained. Mastery of its content will provide not only an acquaintance with the structure of behavior science, but an analytic tool for lifetime use within the sphere of human growth and interpersonal relations.

In the preface to an earlier draft of the present text, the author dealt with two important issues with which he had been occupied in recent years and which account in part for both the form and content of the third edition. The first is what he thought of as the widening gap between the science of behavior and its applications. Thirty years ago, the experimentalist, the theoretician, and the technologist were commonly embodied in one person. This was perhaps to be expected when experimental scientists with a systematic bias discovered that their principles and methods could be usefully applied to everyday affairs and the possible improvement of the human lot. But today there is a large and growing province of applied behavior science (behavior modification, behavior therapy, and the like) which seems to be increasingly remote from both the theory and the research out of which it grew and, we may suppose, on which its healthy future will depend. Such considerations led the author to change the focus of the present text from "extended expositions" of practical achievement to the "basic principles" of behavior science and specific instances of their application.

The second and related issue, exemplified within this text, comes from the author's efforts to bring laboratory concepts to bear on therapeutic practice. In this he learned a great deal from other workers in the field who had already faced its problems, with little more than common sense to guide them, or with orientations other than his own—psychoanalytic, for example. He found that similar practices could stem from different theories, or from none at all. He was thereby led not only to appreciate the work of others, but to reinterpret some of their conceptual formulations in a manner that permitted good practitioners to understand each other better. To some behavior analysts, this appeared to be surrender to an alien viewpoint, but Charles Ferster saw it only as an exercise in the application of his science.

The form of this edition of *Behavior Principles,* unlike the two preceding, is not intended to accord with any special teaching system. Its chapters and their parts, however, can be easily adapted to conventional group instruction by the lecture method or to individualized instruction in several of its forms. The author himself, in the last semester of his teaching, was using "personalized instruction," a student-paced system he had indirectly helped to formulate back in 1963. Lecturing had little part to play within this course, but demonstrations were employed to illustrate the principles that were dealt with in the textbook. A co-worker describes the quality of the course as a "continuous change in behavior as a result of a continuously changing environment," which seems to summarize the goal of all good teaching, as well as all good textbooks.

Fred S. Keller
Chapel Hill, N.C.

# acknowledgments

Charles Ferster never left anything alone, from his name which became variously Charles, C. B., Charlie and most recently Boris, to *Behavior Principles,* which evolved from a book of annotated readings in the first edition to a complete Ferster text by the third edition. His life and career embodied successive approximation toward a goal of perfection which no one could have achieved, but his efforts and progress never ceased.

But some things about Charlie never changed. For example, his devotion to his students in general, the teaching and research assistants in particular. A close relationship with his colleagues was important to him, especially with Alan Silberburg who reviewed some of the copy-edited chapters of the book.

Another characteristic which didn't change was that his hand once given in friendship never was withdrawn. Two of those friends had considerable influence on his work. Charles' friendship with Dr. John L. Cameron began with the Linwood Project and lasted until his death. Ian Cameron undoubtedly heard every thought about psychology Charlie had during the past seventeen years. Besides his contributions as a thoughtful listener, Ian contributed substantially to his education in and appreciation of psychoanalysis. Their interaction was a constant stimulus to Charles' attempts to improve our understanding of human behavior by synthesizing and explaining the relationship between principles of behavior and psychotherapy.

The other close relationship from his graduate student days to his death was with his teacher, mentor, and friend, Fred Keller. With all the changes in the various editions of *Behavior Principles,* one item never changed— the dedication—neither the words nor the feeling that inspired them.

Charles died after the final manuscript had been sent to Prentice-Hall but before any of the production work was completed. I would like to thank the reviewers M. Ray Denny, Michigan State University; James G. Holland, University of Pittsburgh; Daniel F. Johnson, Virginia Polytechnic Institute and State University; Margaret Lloyd, Drake University; John W. Renfrew, Northern Michigan University; C. G. Screven, The University of Wisconsin, Milwaukee; and Ben A. Williams, University of California, San Diego; whose comments on the first draft of the manuscript Charlie found most helpful. The contributions of Barbara Kelly, who was responsible for the production of this manuscript, should not be underestimated. No one could have been more helpful, considerate, or conscientious.

The Preface had not been written nor the Glossary updated when Charles died. Fred Keller did them as well as helping me with the innumerable chores—reviewing the copy-edited manuscript, the galleys, and the page proofs. Frances Keller, during these last months, heard more about Behavior Principles than anyone really wants to know and, as usual, was an inexhaustible source of warmth, moral support, and understanding. To Charles it was always Fred *and* Frances—and so it is.

Elyce Zenoff Ferster
Washington, D.C.
October, 1981

# where does behavior come from?

## study guide

This chapter deals with principles that govern the behavior of an organism—animal or human—in its environment. The emphasis will here be placed on *operant* behavior, so-named because it *operates* on the environment. The fundamental principle involved is that of *reinforcement*. Reinforcement deals with all those factors that increase the frequency with which *operants* (instances of operant behavior) may appear. Reinforcement also bears upon the question of where the behavior of an organism comes from, and the way in which behavioral repertories are created.

Our treatment deals initially with simple items of animal performance, wherein the fundamental principles are more readily perceived than they would be in complex examples. Once the basic dimensions are established for operant behavior and the reinforcement process, they may be extended to describe and clarify more complex instances of human conduct. Later on within the book, two remaining issues will be developed: (1) that of *intermittent* reinforcement, which deals with the way in which behavior is maintained after it is once a part of an organism's repertoire; and (2) that of *stimulus control* (how environmental features that are correlated with reinforcement will come to govern the organism's behavior). When both these issues have been treated, *verbal* behavior will be considered.

# technical terms

contingency
deprivations
differential reinforcement
differential reinforcement of other behavior (DRO)
experimental space
extinction
forgetting
frequency
key

striated muscles
lever
magazine
operant
reinforce
reinforcement
reinforcer
successive approximation
token
topography

# outline

Part I:  Reinforcement and Extinction
What is operant behavior?
The use of animals to study the reinforcement of operant behavior
Conditioning an operant performance in a pigeon and a rat
The distinction between extinction and forgetting
Negative reinforcement
Successive approximation
Technical as opposed to common language descriptions of operant performances
Accidental contingencies of reinforcement

Part II:  Some Technical Aspects of Operant Behavior
Performance rather than response
Reinforcement and extinction as procedures rather than changes in behavior
Reinforcement as a consequence of performance
The operant as a class of performances
Examples of environmental reinforcement
Extinction, identification of a reinforcer, and proof of conditioning
The DRO procedure
Reinforcement and extinction in the human natural environment

Part III:  Demonstrations of Operant Conditioning
Laboratory conditioning procedures with a pigeon
Training an animal in the natural environment
Using a token procedure to reinforce behavior in a clinical setting
The practical modification of behavior by token procedures
Accidental reinforcement in human behavior

## part I: reinforcement and extinction

### what is operant behavior?

Operant behavior refers to a broad class of an organism's activities involving the actions of the striated muscles. These actions influence or alter the organism's environment, including the behavior of others. For example, the foraging bird in the natural environment overturns leaves on the ground, thereby exposing larvae, insects, worms, or seeds underneath. Overturning a leaf is an operant performance because it alters the environment by exposing the food underneath. The rat moves from one plant to another, eating the fruit or grain that appears as a result of the movement. In each of these natural examples of operant behavior, the activity exposes food or changes the animal's location, thereby enabling it to eat.

Frequency is a major aspect of most operant behavior. When a performance changes the environment, its frequency increases. When the performance is no longer effective in altering the environment, its frequency decreases. In laboratory research, procedures were developed to increase the frequency of a response. These procedures are known as reinforcement. For example, a pigeon pecks at the wall of its cage infrequently, and a rat only occasionally will press a small horizontal bar. But pecking and bar pressing will increase to a stable and high frequency when the peck or the lever press produces a small portion of food. In this case, food is used for reinforcement.

In contrast with operant behaviors are reflexes, such as the flexion of the leg in resonse to a tap on the knee, the closing of the pupil of the eye in response to a bright light, or fixed-action patterns, such as many grooming or fighting patterns of dogs. Like operant performances, the form of the reflex is relatively fixed and occurs in reaction to the environment. Operant performances, on the other hand, are formed by the way they alter the external environment. The significance of these differences will be elaborated later after we have had a chance to learn more of the technical characteristics of operant behavior.

### the use of animals to study the reinforcement of operant behavior

As we have discussed, a simple activity such as a pigeon pecking at a small illuminated disc on the wall of its cage can be maintained by producing food. This arbitrarily chosen sample of laboratory activity can represent other activities that could be similarly maintained. The generality of the principles which emerge from intensive, laboratory study of this simple, easily repeated and objectively recorded performance has been extended with similar experiments using dogs, cats, monkeys, baboons, chimpanzees, snails, rats, lions, and many other species. These animal-laboratory investigations give a view of the basic processes by which behavior is created in a repertoire, how it comes under the control of environmental stimuli, how it is maintained when its reinforcement is intermittent, and how factors such as emotion and punishment can alter its flow.

The proper study of humankind may well require humans as subjects. Yet, it is useful to take advantage of the findings of laboratory research with animals so that we can see processes of operant reinforcement in their purest form. An important advantage of animal research is that it allows us to study behavioral processes that are common to a wide range of species—that is, principles which are phylogenetically general. Against such general principles, we can take into account special characteristics of humans and other species. Actual experiments with humans and observation of human behavior in the natural environment can then test the usefulness and the generality of these principles.

## conditioning an operant performance in a pigeon and a rat

Since the behavior of a laboratory pigeon pecking is the basis of so many of the principles of behavior that will be described in this book, it will be useful at the start to describe the procedure and the related equipment in some detail. The experiments using rats, dogs, monkeys, chimpanzees, and humans are similar in concept.

**The experimental space** The pigeon experiments are carried out in a small box called an *experimental space.* Figure 1-1 shows a typical space for the study of the behavior of pigeons.[1] A ceiling light indicates when the experimental procedures begin and provides the bird general illumination. It is turned off when it is necessary to interrupt or end the session. The bird eats from a food tray that it can reach through the aperture in the front wall of the cage. The food tray is out of reach except when it is raised by an electro-mechanical device. A light inside the food aperture illuminates the food, as well as providing a clear stimulus that can be presented instantly as a reinforcer for the performance that is to be conditioned. The performance most frequently studied is that of pecking the key, which is an illuminated disc on the front wall. Behind the key is a switch that the bird's peck closes mechanically and that can operate the food dispenser automatically.

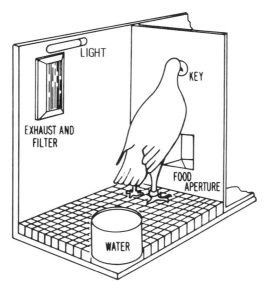

Figure 1-1

**Reinforcing head raising**   The frequency of any performance that is in the bird's repertoire may be increased or decreased. It is instructive to begin by considering a simple act, raising the head, which has a high natural frequency of occurrence. Another term for this is unconditioned frequency or operant level. Pecking at the key will be considered later.

We can increase the frequency of raising the head (condition it) by arranging that the performance produces food. A food-deprived bird, after remaining in the experimental space until the unfamiliar surroundings no longer generate disruptive emotional behaviors, is exposed to the operation of the food dispenser. The food tray is periodically raised for a few seconds, signalled by a light over it. When the bird eats from the food magazine as soon as the magazine light comes on and does not approach it otherwise, the reinforcement procedure can begin. The experimenter operates the food dispenser the instant the bird's head moves in an upward direction. Thus, the light illuminating the food tray follows an exactly specified performance. A moment or so later the bird eats from the raised food tray. As a result of this first reinforcement, the bird will raise its head more frequently. If this performance continues to operate the food magazine, it will continue to occur at a high frequency, so long as the bird is not satiated. If the food magazine does not operate when the bird raises its head then head raising will occur with decreasing frequency. With continued nonreinforcement of head raising, its frequency will eventually fall to the initial level observed before the reinforcement procedure was begun. The same experiment could be carried out with other simple acts such as turning in a circle, nodding, or lifting a leg.

**Conditioning bar-pressing with a rat** This conditioning procedure is parallel to that described for the pigeon. To reinforce a rat's performance, the experimenter deprives it of food and places it in a familiar experimental space which does not evoke disruptive emotional behaviors. The experiment can begin when the animal walks to the food tray and readily eats a food pellet, prompted by the sound accompanying its delivery. The rat, in moving about the cage, soon presses the lever down enough to actuate the food dispensing mechanism and eats the food pellet that is discharged. The lever-press performance will increase in frequency immediately and will occur repeatedly so long as it continues to operate the food-pellet dispenser, or until the rat is satiated.

**Extinction** When a performance no longer changes the environment (produces a reinforcing stimulus), it occurs less frequently. The procedure of discontinuing reinforcement is called *extinction*. When the operant performance occurs sufficiently often without being reinforced, its frequency may drop to the original unconditioned level. For example, if the food magazine no longer operates when the pigeon raises its head, the pigeon will raise its head less often until eventually it raises its head about as frequently as it did before the conditioning procedure was begun.

## the distinction between extinction
## and forgetting

The procedure of withholding reinforcement (extinction) is the most important way of reducing the frequency of a previously conditioned performance. The way it weakens behavior will be clearer by contrasting other ways in which the frequency of an operant performance may be decreased. Some of these influences, such as punishment, intermittent reinforcement, and stimulus control will be presented in a later chapter. A factor that can be usefully discussed at this point is the decrease in the frequency of a performance as a result of time passing since it was last reinforced. If there is any loss in the frequency of some previously conditioned behavior simply due to the passage of time, then we say that the performance has been forgotten. There is evidence, however, that the passage of time, of itself, has little influence on operant behavior.

Skinner, working with pigeons, undertook a long-term experiment to measure the amount of behavior loss due to forgetting.[2] Several birds that had been trained during World War II for guiding missiles were kept for seven years without any further training or experience with the experimental equipment. Birds are ideal subjects for this kind of experiment because they often live at least fifteen years. The birds had been trained to peck at a small detail, a crossroad, from a scene in an aerial photograph. Seven years later they were once again deprived of food and placed back into the original apparatus, reinstating all the original conditions. All three of the birds immediately began pecking at the precise feature where they had been previously conditioned to peck, with surprisingly little loss. Naturally, no food was delivered this time since reinforcement would have made it impossible to determine whether new conditioning was taking place or whether the birds were pecking as a result of their past conditioning. The reduced amount of pecking after a lapse of seven years was the measure of forgetting.

If we ascribe forgetting to losses of behavior caused by passage of time alone, we need to set apart other behavioral processes, also occurring over long periods of time, that might also decrease the frequency of a performance. The person who says, "I forgot to make a dental appointment," demonstrates a reduced frequency of an operant performance (calling the dentist). But the reduced frequency is likely to be due to the history of pain rather than the period of time that has elapsed since the last visit. This kind of forgetting, functionally different from either passage of time or extinction, is similar to the classical Freudian "repression." A more detailed consideration of this kind of interference will be possible in Chapter 5, after there has been a discussion of avoidance, escape, and conditioned aversive stimuli. Another contributor to weakening a performance during a long lapse of time could be competing performances, conditioned during the interim, which are dominant over or interfere with the originally conditioned behavior.

## negative reinforcement

In contrast to reinforcing stimuli that increase the frequency of performances they follow, there are aversive stimuli that are so defined because they increase the frequency of performances that terminate or postpone them. If, for example, a set of metallic bars on the floor of a rat's cage is electrified and if this electric grid is deactivated for a period of time when the rat presses a lever, the frequency of lever pressing will increase. The termination of shock (the aversive stimulus) is the negative analogy to the delivery of a food pellet (a reinforcing stimulus). Spitting out a bitter tasting substance is an operant performance negatively reinforced by the removal of the noxious taste. *Negative reinforcement* is so called because the reinforcer for these operant performances is the removal of a stimulus rather than its presentation. The process is operant because the performance alters the environment. Both positive and negative reinforcement increases the frequency of an operant performance.

Electric shock, while frequently used in the laboratory because of its convenience, is only one of many possible aversive stimuli that can reinforce operant performances. Bright light, loud noise, and the pinching of the animal's tail are other aversive stimuli which have been used in laboratory experiments. For example, if a bright light over a rat's cage is turned off for 30 seconds each time the rat presses a lever or the rat postpones a pinch of its tail for 30 seconds each time it turns a wheel, the performances of lever pressing and wheel turning will be maintained because they avoid the bright light and tail pinch respectively.

Any time there is an aversive stimulus, there is potentially some performance which will terminate it. In bright sunlight we put on sunglasses, shade our eyes with our hands, turn away from the sun, shut our eyes, or squint, all performances which reduce the intensity of light reaching the retina. Each of these performances is reinforced because it terminates or reduces the aversive effects of the bright light. Conversely, we define the bright light as an aversive stimulus because its removal increases the frequency of the operant performance.

Aversive stimuli embrace a wide range of physical trauma in which aversiveness increases with the intensity of the stimulus. Thus, tangible irritants to the body and extremes of temperature, odor, taste, or noise are all aversive stimuli that can increase the frequency of a performance that terminates them. In the vicinity of a shrieking jet airplane the line mechanic puts on ear protectors. Children promptly learn to put their fingers in their ears at the threat of a loud noise. The youngster in the schoolyard says "uncle" when his arm is twisted and the schoolyard bully reinforces the vocal performance of "uncle" by releasing the victim's arm. A performance commonly reinforced by the removal of unpleasant visual stimuli is simply turning the head, as we do at the sight of an injured victim of an automobile accident. Confronted by an irritating television commercial we may turn off the set, go into another room, or turn our attention to another source. Performances such as opening a window, removing an article of clothing, turning on air conditioning, or starting a fan increase in frequency because they reduce the temperature of the air around the body. In winter, going into a heated area, shutting a window, putting on gloves, or otherwise dressing warmly are reinforced by escaping or avoiding low air temperatures on the body. When we remove a shoe to discard a pebble inside, the aversive stimulus is the pebble pressed by the shoe against the foot. The performance (removing the pebble) terminates the pressure on the foot surface. We may pinch our nostrils to prevent noxious odors from entering the nose.

## successive approximation

Because operant behavior is an integral unit combining performance and the immediate reinforcer maintaining it, the form of a performance will vary from one time to the next. For example, if we deliver food when the pigeon raises its head, we observe that occasionally it raises its head slightly higher than would be needed to meet the criterion for reinforcement. Because the conditioned operant's form varies, it is possible to reinforce successive approximations to complex or large magnitudes. When a bird pecks at a key, for example, it will sometimes strike one part of the disc and sometimes another part; some pecks will barely deflect the key, while others will displace it forcefully. Those pecks that do not deflect the key enough to operate the switch that activates the food magazine decrease in frequency because they are not reinforced, while the more forceful pecks continue to operate the food dispenser and hence are maintained. The physical properties of the key provide the differential reinforcement that shapes pecking. The same process of differential reinforcement that occurs naturally can be used to shape new, complex forms that are not currently in the bird's repertoire. The process is called *successive approximation* or *shaping*. At first, performance that approximates the desired behavior is reinforced. For example, when the bird raises its head slightly, reinforcement is given. When the bird raises its head higher than it had before, the reinforcement requirement is shifted to a higher level of head raising. The process, by successive approximations to the performance that is targeted, continues until the bird's physical limit is reached. Thus, through differential reinforcement, the bird's behavior can be shaped into a new form, far beyond that occurring naturally.

Note that two procedures operate at the same time. One is the reinforcement of the successive approximations to the targeted performance. The other is the nonreinforcement of other performances, previously reinforced, that therefore occur less frequently. It is for this reason that the experimenter does not reinforce a particular approximation to the targeted performance for too long. In that event, that performance will become so persistent that considerable extinction would be required before the successive approximation procedure could go forward.

Successive approximation occurs in many natural environments, particularly during early childhood development. The variations in the size of the hole in the nipple in the infant's bottle will reinforce magnitudes and topographies (that is, patternings of the response) of sucking appropriate to the flow of milk that results. Large holes differentially reinforce small, paced, careful magnitudes of sucking, while small holes reinforce larger muscle movements. The infant learning to crawl and walk illustrates the same differential reinforcement of complex forms. Once movement from one location to another is a reinforcing outcome and the requisite anatomical development has occurred, the movements of the legs and arms and their coordination are differentially reinforced. Those movements that result in a change in position increase in frequency, while those that are ineffective decrease. As simple an activity as moving the fingers in front of the eyes is probably differentially reinforced by the sight of them (the fingers) and is most likely an activity that produces considerable development of the child's control of its hands and arms.[3] The position of the hand in the child's field of vision will differentially reinforce those movements that bring the hand there, and the sight of the moving fingers is a reinforcer that develops control of the individual fingers. The case of a child learning to put its fingers or a breast in its mouth, which will be discussed in Chapter 2, is another instructive example of how the natural environment in interaction with the maturing child successively approximates the performances that we see in early development.

## technical as opposed to common language descriptions of operant performances

The technical descriptions of the behaviors of the rat and the pigeon may seem labored when contrasted with common language. For example, one could say that the rat pressed the lever because he wanted food, because he was hungry, or because he knew that in order to get food he had to press the lever. Each of these expressions seems intuitively reasonable and refers to the same events as the technical descriptions. Yet, there is an advantage to using the technical descriptions because they describe the same facts using simple, objective, easily identifiable and measurable events. For example, in common language, "he wanted food" refers to an inner state of which we can have no direct information. But in the technical description of this phrase ("he wanted food"), food is referred to as the critical event in maintaining lever-pressing.

The objective description of conditioning has a practical and theoretical advantage over the use of metaphors of the animal's internal state. Behavioral descriptions detail specific, objective, and tangible conditions of which the behavior is a function. When we infer the rat's inner state of hunger, we still need to know what produces the inner state and what is the effect of it on the behavior. Very little is gained by talking about the animal's inner state except to infer observable variables. But going back to our common language examples for a moment, we can see that the second phrase ("because he was hungry") implies the rat has been deprived of food and is likely to eat if food is set out. However this may not be the case. The rat may have been deprived of food, the reinforcer food may have been a preferred one that the rat will eat even when not deprived, or it may be that eating the food leads to some other reinforcing event such as drinking water. Saying the animal was hungry only describes the first of these possibilities. In fact, it usually doesn't matter *why* the reinforcer increases the frequency of a performance so long as the event maintaining it has been identified.

There is some temptation to speak of giving a child candy as a reward for good behavior or throwing a fish to a seal as a reward for completing an elaborate performance. Unlike this colloquial use of the term *reward,* the technical analyses of the reinforcement process exposes the details of the interaction. Technically, the term *reinforcement* would refer to the event which occurs instantly following a specific act. We note, for example, that in all the applications of reinforcement developed so far the reinforcer is seldom described as the food itself. Rather, some signal such as the click of the food dispenser or the onset of a light preceding the delivery of food is described as the reinforcer. The concept of reinforcement as a stimulus that is the immediate consequence of a performance has important practical applications to tasks such as animal training. The clicker provides an unambiguous stimulus that can be easily presented following an exact performance.

## accidental contingencies of reinforcement

The phenomenon of reinforcement is essentially temporal since all that is required for a reinforcer to be effective is that it follow the performance closely. For example, if a pigeon is trained to eat from the food dispenser, some performance will be reinforced each time that it operates since the bird is continuously emitting one performance or another. When reinforcement increases the frequency of some performance, even though it was not intended, it is described as *accidental, adventitious,* or *superstitious.*

Skinner carried out an experiment in which he demonstrated the temporal aspect of reinforcement. Using untrained pigeons that were deprived of food, he attached a food hopper to the bird's cage, similar to the automatic food dispenser described earlier. Without any further training, the food magazine was raised for 5 seconds every 15 seconds with no reference whatsoever to the bird's behavior. He reported the results as follows:

> One bird was conditioned to turn counterclockwise about the cage, making two or three turns between reinforcements. Another repeatedly thrust its head into one of the upper corners of the cage. A third developed a "tossing" response, as if placing its head beneath an invisible bar and lifting it repeatedly. Two birds developed a pendulum motion of the head and body, in which the head was

extended forward and swung from right to left with a sharp movement followed by a somewhat slower return. The body generally followed the movement and a few steps might be taken when it was extensive. Another bird was conditioned to make incomplete pecking or brushing movements directed toward but not touching the floor. None of these responses appeared in any noticeable strength during adaptation to the cage or until the food hopper was periodically presented. In the remaining two cases, conditioned responses were not clearly marked.[4]

In other words, the birds repeated whatever performance happened to occur at the moment the food dispenser operated. Since a single reinforcement can increase the frequency of a performance, for example, raising its head, there is a high probability that the same performance will occur at about the time that the food magazine operates again. Thus, once a performance is conditioned, it continues to occur, reinforced intermittently on a fixed-interval schedule (such as those that will be described in Chapter 5). The interval between food deliveries will have a significant bearing on whether a specific performance will be conditioned because the previously reinforced performance decreases in frequency without reinforcement during a long interval and therefore is less likely to be occurring at the time the food magazine operates next. If an observer watched two experimental subjects, one whose performance had been deliberately reinforced and the other whose behavior had been accidentally reinforced, both animals would be seen to be engaging in repetitive stereotyped acts followed by the operation of the food magazine. The two kinds of reinforcement procedures could eventually be distinguished because the topography of the accidentally reinforced performance would drift as there is no guarantee that the reinforcer follows a particular topography of performance.[5]

## questions

1. Why are animals useful for studying the reinforcement process?
2. Why is a specific, immediate stimulus necessary to serve as a reinforcer?
3. Describe the procedure of extinction.
4. Describe the features of the experimental space used to demonstrate the reinforcement of head raising or pecking in the pigeon.
5. What did Skinner discover upon putting conditioned birds back into an experimental space after a time lapse of seven years?

6. Describe how to increase the frequency of a performance using an aversive stimulus.

7. Give several examples, including some not in the text, of human performances maintained by negative reinforcement. Describe the aversive stimulus, the performance, and the change in frequency.

8. Describe the procedure of successively approximating the performance in a pigeon of raising its head higher than it ordinarily does.

9. Discuss how the shaping procedure produces a continuous change in the behavior, rather than the sudden emergence of a new performance.

10. Give some examples of successive approximation of human behavior that occur in the natural environment.

11. Why is a behavioral description more useful than explanations such as "the rat pressed the lever because it was hungry"?

12. How does accidental reinforcement illustrate that reinforcement is a temporal phenomenon?

13. Describe Skinner's experiment about accidental reinforcement.

---

## part II: some technical aspects of operant behavior

### performance rather than response

Operant behavior acts on and changes the environment rather than occurring in response to it. The altered environment may consist of a change in the animal's position as a result of the animal's movement or as a result of operating it instrumentally by stepping on a treadle that closes the switch that is mounted underneath it. The magazine stimulus and the food delivery that follows is a further change in the environment resulting from the performance. Operant performances have been traditionally called responses probably because of the enthusiasm of early behaviorists who wanted to extend Pavlov's experiments on conditioned reflex response to a broad range of human activities. However, the term "response" for describing operant behavior has been avoided here because it has misleading connotations. For example, to call an act such as a pigeon raising its head a response implies that it is evoked or elicited by some prior event. In fact, the performance occurs first and results from the reinforcer which follows it. It *is* appropriate, however, to describe a leg movement as a response to a tap on the patellar tendon of the knee.

Even though a certain level of food deprivation may be necessary for reinforcement to be effective, it is not useful to speak of the performance, such as raising the head or pressing a lever, as a response to the deprivation. Nor is it useful to say that the light behind the key produces a response, even though, like deprivation, the key light may be an important condition influencing whether or not or how frequently a bird pecks at the key.

## reinforcement and extinction as procedures rather than changes in behavior

Colloquial English can describe the events of reinforcement and extinction as accurately as the technical terms. We can say that the frequency of raising the head increases when it is followed by the operation of the feeder. When the performance, previously occurring at some frequency, is extinguished, we mean that we have discontinued the operation of the food dispenser. The result of this procedure is usually a decline in the frequency of the performance. It is important to note that *extinguish,* as a verb, has as its object the reinforcer and not the performance. Perhaps it would be better usage to talk about "extinguishing a reinforcer," but this term has not found general acceptance.

Beginning students often speak of extinction as a reduction in the frequency of a performance rather than as a procedure. It is important to remember that extinction refers to the withdrawal of a reinforcer rather than the resultant effect on the animal's performance. Using the term *extinction* to describe a change in the frequency of a performance omits a specification of *how* the performance was weakened. Procedures other than discontinuing reinforcement can decrease the frequency of a performance. By this distinction, we can avoid confusing conclusions such as, "We extinguished bar pressing, but the performance didn't extinguish or extinguished slowly." A procedural description would be of the form, "Although reinforcement no longer followed bar pressing, the frequency of the performance did not decrease." In that event, we can conclude that the reinforcer we discontinued was not the one maintaining the behavior. Similarly, reinforcement as a procedure and reinforcement as the increase in frequency that may occur when a reinforcer follows a performance are confused frequently. Such confusion can result in statements such as, "Reinforcement occurred, but the reinforced performance was not reinforced." A clearer, operational usage would be, "We delivered a reinforcer, but it didn't increase the frequency of the performance."

## reinforcement as a consequence
## of performance

*The stimulus that immediately follows the performance is the reinforcer.*

The reinforcer that actually forms lever-pressing or key-pecking is the specific and immediate consequence of those behaviors—the sound of the pellet dispenser and the light that accompanies the raised food tray. These stimuli maintain the performances because they, in turn, are the occasion on which the animal approaches the food tray and may eat. Food is a necessary condition if the magazine stimulus is to be a reinforcer, but it is not the immediate consequence of the performances.

The concept of reinforcement as the instant immediate consequence of a performance allows a much finer grain analysis than would be possible if we viewed the actual eating of the food as the reinforcer for the performances that are created. The physical properties of the lever and its mechanical connection to the switch that activates the magazine stimuli will reinforce lever presses that have sufficient force to depress it. Presses that are not forceful enough go unreinforced, and therefore their frequency decreases. Thus, the mechanical properties of the lever differentially reinforce magnitudes of performance that are effective. It is the switch on the lever that closes following lever-pressing and thereby forms its topography rather than the food.

Teaching a seal to balance a ball on its nose illustrates the same concept. The fish, thrown to the seal after it has balanced the ball or achieved some approximation of balance, may be necessary to maintain the seal's continued engagement in the activity. But the reinforcer that shapes and maintains the behavior of positioning the ball is the pressure exerted on the seal's nose as it adjusts its head by movements of the neck muscles. There is an exquisitely fine interplay between the pressure of the ball on the seal's nose and the movements of the neck muscles. Such fine-grain interaction, a result of the interplay between gravity, the seal's movements, and the position of the ball, could not possibly be duplicated by the actions of a person who presented food contingent on similar movements.

Riding a bicycle also illustrates how the immediate consequences of performances are the reinforcers that determine their form. The performances are those of adjusting the position of the body as the bicycle tilts. The reinforcer is the maintenance of an upright position. Like the example of the seal with the ball, there is an interplay between the cyclist's body movements and the balance of the cycle. The ultimate outcome of the riding activity, reaching the destination, only serves to keep the rider engaged, like the fish thrown to the seal. The relation between gravity, the rider's position, and the way body movements alter the balance define the detailed behavior of the rider.

## the operant as a class of performances

An operant is a class of performances. The common quality of the performances that make up an operant is that they all produce the same reinforcer. Lever-pressing is a class of movements, all of which move the lever far enough to actuate the switch that operates the food dispenser. The closure of the switch, because it connects electrically with the food dispenser, has a one-to-one relation to the sound of the pellet dispenser —the immediate reinforcer following the performance. The rat could press the lever by sitting on it, pressing it with its feet, grasping it in its teeth, or jumping on it. All of these performances are *functionally* equivalent because they all close the switch and therefore produce the same effect on the environment. The physical properties of the lever in relation to the switch define the operant performances which will be generated in the rat's repertoire.

Describing an operant as a performance operating on and altering the environment has the advantage that it emphasizes the change in the environment that has generated the performance. Consider, for example, the operant behavior of shaking a tree, reinforced by the apples that fall. The relation between the behavior of the man shaking the tree and the physical properties of the tree define the performance that will be reinforced and sustained. Whether an apple will fall depends on how vigorously the tree is shaken, how thick the branch is, and how firmly the apples are attached to their stems. Those performances that make the tree move sufficiently vigorously and cause an apple to fall will increase in frequency. Other performances that do not will not increase in frequency. A tree that has apples firmly fixed to their stems will reinforce more vigorous shaking than one on which apples are loosely connected. Thus, like the lever-press and its relation to the switch that operates the pellet dispenser, the physical properties of the tree and the stem from which the apples hang define the performances in which frequency increases.

The behavior of a pigeon pecking a key illustrates the same concept. The movement of the key is the immediate environmental change produced by the performance and the presentation of the light over the grain hopper is a reinforcer that parallels the key movement. The bird eats the food later. We can consider instances of key pecking by describing the activity topographically or as a class of behaviors—called key-pecking— that have in common that they all move the key. The operant is a class of behaviors because the bird never pecks the key in exactly the same way. It may hit the key hard or softly, in different places, from different angles, with its upper or lower beak, and so forth. It is conceivable, though not likely, that it could strike the key with its food or the back of its head. Each of these performances change the environment in the same way even if their forms differ—they move the key and raise the illuminated food hopper. The operant class may be thought of as a continuous flow of behavior, generated by the reinforcer, rather than a discrete performance.

The performance and the stimulus that reinforces it are related in negative as well as positive reinforcement. The performance and the aversive stimulus it removes are an integral behavioral unit in which each part defines the other. Just as the apple tree will reinforce all topographies of the behavior that loosens the stem of the apple from the tree when it is shaken, an aversive stimulus is also terminated by a class of performances. A bright light may increase the frequency of shading of the eyes, wearing sunglasses, moving to a shaded area, or turning off a switch. All these performances have very different forms, but they are functionally equivalent because they all terminate the bright light.

Reading and studying illustrate how an operant is specified by the change it produces. Reading is a complex activity that is hard to specify and perhaps not completely understood. Advanced study requires a special kind of reading from a student beyond rotely saying the words in one-to-one correspondence with the text. An educational procedure described as an "interview method" illustrates how the special kind of reading that is required of an advanced student can be reinforced by attending to the expected outcome that is the behavioral result of the reading. In the interview procedure, a student is required to tell another person about what he has just read from a limited portion of a text. Study questions may be used to better specify the desired outcome. If the student can say what she has read, then there is evidence that she has read in that special way that converts a rote statement, closely controlled by the text, to a fluent account of the sort that we describe as "being able to talk understandingly about what was read." The reaction of the listener, to whom the student is telling what she has just learned, is the reinforcer analogous to the sound of the pellet dispenser in the rat experiment. Just as we refer to bar-pressing as a class of varying behaviors, defined by the reinforcer they produce, we can also say that the reaction of the listener has reinforced that kind of reading activity that converts rote reading to a fluent account spoken in the student's own words.

## examples of environmental reinforcement

To describe the reinforcement of complex human behavior, it is even more important than with animals to consider the reinforcer as a definition of a class of operant behavior. Suppose, for example, the parent of a 12-year-old child decided to use positive reinforcement to shape and maintain the behavior of the child cleaning his or her room. One procedure that has been suggested is the use of tokens which the youngster could accumulate and spend for food, treats, special outings, and privileges. First, the performances in which frequency is to be increased by tokens need to be defined. Those performances are sweeping with a broom, folding and storing clothes, removing dust with a cloth, changing bed clothes and arranging the cover, washing windows, and so forth.

It would be difficult to break down each performance into its component muscular actions, however, we can view the operant as a class of behaviors defined by the change that they produce on the environment. The specific movements with the broom that are required are exactly defined if we think of a class of activities with a broom that results in a clean floor. The movements of the broom on the floor are equivalent to the topographies of performances on the lever and the clean floor is the equivalent of the sound of the pellet dispenser. In the case of the rat, the food dispenser stimulus is an occasion on which it can eat the food pellet that was signalled. In the case of the child cleaning its room, the clean floor is the occasion on which a token is received, in turn allowing the child to get its treat or special privilege. At a more advanced level, the parent might just inspect the room and deliver the token when the entire room has been cleaned. Of course, implied in the successful application of such a procedure are many collateral conditions. One is the presence of the component behaviors in the youngster's repertoire. For example, a child must be able to lift the broom. A second condition is a history that allows such a long chain of performances (all the activities involved in room-cleaning) to be emitted without weakening the performance. Also required would be a level of self-control on the part of the child that would permit withholding other performances that would be dominant over cleaning the room in the near term.

Practically, the instatement of such a procedure would require a behavioral control, parallel to food dispenser training, where the clean room becomes a conditional reinforcer because of the subsequent contingencies of positive reinforcement or aversive control that the child encounters in the presence of cleaned and uncleaned rooms. It is in this area that the practical limits of such a procedure's usefulness become clear. In the absence of a consequence related to a clean room (and sufficiently connected to the child's repertoire), the result is likely to be that the child does not perform at all. Instead, a power struggle occurs as a result of the arbitrariness of the reinforcer.

## extinction, identification of a reinforcer, and proof of conditioning

If we observe a performance, such as a pigeon raising its head, and wish to determine whether the stimulus that follows this performance is responsible for it, we simply discontinue food delivery (extinction) and observe whether the frequency falls. If the frequency decreases, then we know that head-raising is being maintained because it produces food. We may then speak of food reinforcement as the cause of the behavior. The applicability of extinction for this purpose is based on the premise that a performance has already been conditioned. If the reinforcer responsible for a head-raising performance had not been identified, we could not talk about decreasing its frequency by extinction.

The relation between extinction and the identification of a reinforcer becomes critical when we analyze behavior in the complex natural environment where more than one influence operates at a time. Consider, for example, a situation in which a teacher, assuming that a child's misconduct is reinforced by the attention it evokes from her, attempts to reduce the frequency of the misconduct by not reacting to it. It might be the case, however, that the reinforcer maintaining the child's misconduct is the favorable reaction received from other students as well as her own reaction. If we described her activity as "extinguishing" misconduct, it would be misleading because that would imply that it was, in fact, maintained by her attention. This kind of example gives further reason for restricting the use of the term "extinction" to the procedure of discontinuing reinforcement rather than a decrease in the frequency of the performance. In the present example, the failure to limit the use of extinction to the procedure of discontinuing reinforcement would lead to paradoxical conclusions, such as, "I extinguished misbehavior but it didn't extinguish."

Research workers who have experimented with behavior modification techniques by the use of tokens to reinforce grooming and self-care behavior of patients in institutions for the mentally ill and retarded have taken the responsibility of proving that the reinforcement aspect of the token procedure was the factor responsible for the improvement of the target behaviors.[6] Experiments typically record the frequency of the target behaviors before the token program is initiated, measure the increase in self-care when it is reinforced by tokens, and measure its disappearance when the delivery of tokens is discontinued for a period of time. The three changes in procedure, no tokens, tokens, no tokens, make up *ABA design* and prove that there was an increase in self-care and that the tokens were in fact responsible for patient's self-care actions.

## the DRO procedure

The DRO procedure is a way to continue to deliver a reinforcing stimulus while at the same time carrying out extinction of a previously conditioned performance. The DRO procedure is *differential reinforcement* of *other* behavior; it can be demonstrated in its simplest form in a laboratory experiment with a pigeon that had been conditioned to peck at a key, reinforced by the operation of a food dispenser. The DRO procedure is arranged by having each peck postpone the operation of the food magazine by 15 seconds. So long as the bird continues to peck the key, the food magazine does not operate. In the absence of pecks, the food magazine operates every 15 seconds. Whatever performance the bird happens to be emitting when the 15-second period elapses will be followed by the food magazine operation and hence may increase in frequency, but we cannot be certain what these performances will be. Thus, the DRO procedure guarantees that pecks will not be followed by food magazine operations and maintains the continued operation of the food dispenser following performances other than pecks.

Two aspects of the DRO procedure reduce the frequency of pecking. First, pecks occur without producing food (extinction). Second, as the food magazine operations follow other behaviors, their increased frequency preempts pecking the key. Furthermore, the DRO procedure will have a different impact on the performances that are most incompatible with pecking. If the food magazine operation follows raising the head in front of the key, that performance will not preempt key pecking as much as, say, turning to the rear of the cage. Thus, the "other behavior" that is reinforced is more likely to be turning to the side of the cage opposite to the key than raising the head in front of the key. The DRO procedure proves that the contingency between the performance and reinforcer produces the operant as distinct from giving the animal an opportunity to eat.[7]

The DRO has been used in behavior modification research in lieu of simply carrying out extinction (as described for the token economy experiments in the preceding section) to verify that the reinforcement, apart from the receipt of a token, actually produced the behavioral change. A behavior modification experiment[8] that set out to reinforce the speech of mute mental hospital patients, diagnosed as schizophrenic, illustrates this use of DRO. A program was designed, using imitation and instructional procedures, to reinforce voicing of simple sounds with small parts of a meal. After 79 training sessions the subjects said the word "food," and occasionally the name of the food, reliably enough to receive their entire meal. The experimenters used the DRO procedure to prove that it was actually the contingency between the food reinforcement and speaking (the experimenter said "good" as he gave the patient a bite of his meal) responsible for the increment, independently of simply getting food or some incidental aspect of the interaction.

The outcome of the experiment was the disappearance of speaking when food was given for behavior other than speaking and its reappearance when speaking was reinforced by food. Thus, the experimenters could validly conclude that speech was maintained because it produced food. On the other hand, the experiment also showed the limited therapeutic usefulness of such performances since the patient did not speak outside of the arbitrary features of the experiment. To be clinically useful, the patient's vocal behavior would need to be reinforced and maintained by the social commerce it achieved. The experimenters did prove, however, that these mute schizophrenic patients were still as capable of speaking as they had been prior to their psychosis.

The DRO occurs as a matter of course in many human social situations where the issue is not whether the reinforcing stimulus will occur but that the particular desired performance will occur. The teacher in the classroom needs to pay attention to individual students from one time to the next during the course of normal class events. We know from many experiments, as well as casual observation, that the teacher's attention is an important reinforcer in the typical classroom situation. Student performances which produce the teacher's attention cull an increase in frequency. Ideally, a teacher would attend to students when they are studying or otherwise educationally productive, rather than when they are disruptive, idle, or doing things not relevant to the educational task. Experiments have been carried out (see Chapter 10) in which teachers attempted to eliminate disruptive classroom behavior by ignoring the students when they are disruptive and otherwise maintaining a high frequency of attention to educationally productive activities or approximations to them. The procedures of these experiments is essentially that of the DRO. The DRO procedure refers to the previous history of reinforcement, whereby the teacher's attention had reinforced disruptive activities.

## reinforcement and extinction
## in the human natural environment

The laboratory instances of animal behavior, reinforced with food, show the process of reinforcement in its purest form and provide the concepts and principles that can be extended to human behavior. The behavior of young children, in simple interactions with their physical environment, provide other simple, easily observed activities that illustrate the essential features of reinforcement as it operates in the natural environment.

Consider the activity of a child, between one and two years old, sitting on the floor, reaching for a large ball, pushing it away, picking it up, or rolling it around under the palm of its hand. Pushing the ball refers to the performance—the movement of the child's arm and hand. It is reinforced by the motion of the ball as it rolls away. When the child crawls to the new position of the ball, the reinforcer that follows the crawling movements is the sight of the ball close up. When the child reaches for the ball, the reinforcer is the immediate tactual contact of the hand on the ball. The performances are the movements of the arm and hand. Those movements of the hand and arm that produce extended stimulation of the child's palm increase in frequency apart from those movements which do not. When the child's palm is in contact with the ball, movements of the fingers which fix the ball to the child's hand increase in frequency. Lateral movements of the child's hand result in a rolling motion of the ball. The fine-grain relation between the magnitude of the hand movements and the extent of the lateral displacement of the ball arises naturally from the physical properties of the ball, which differentially reinforce a repertoire in which the extent of the arm movement is controlled by the resulting movements of the ball.

An infant eating from a spoon offers other examples of simple, naturally occurring performances. When the mother holds a spoonful of cereal in front of the infant's mouth, the movement of the mouth to an open position prompts the mother to place the spoon inside the mouth. Thus, the opening of the child's mouth is reinforced by bringing the spoon inside it. The closing of the mouth when the spoon is inside is another operant reinforced because it induces the mother to withdraw the spoon against the closed lips, leaving the food inside the child's mouth. Swallowing the food is another operant reinforced by the entrance of the food into the esophageal tract.

A slightly older child, feeding itself with a spoon, may strike the spoon against the bowl producing a clanging sound. The performance is reinforced by the noise it makes. Those movements resulting in louder sounds increase in frequency over those which miss the bowl or strike it with less force. Thus, the behavior is defined by the relation between the physical properties of the bowl and spoon and the performances that result in the sounds. In all these examples it is important to note 1) that the reinforcer is the immediate consequence of the performance; 2) that the operant is a class of performances; and 3) that the performances which comprise the class have in common the fact that they all are equally effective in producing the change in the environment that increases their frequency.

Although the procedure of extinction is an inherent counterpart of reinforcement, it is difficult to separate them when the reinforcer has a physical connection to the performance that produces it. The tactual stimulation from hand movements to the ball is virtually inevitable so long as visual control of the child's behavior by the ball is intact. Extinction could occur if a second person were present who quickly moved the ball out of reach or who restrained the child's hand whenever he reached out. Although such extinction seems extraordinarily difficult to arrange, it is occasionally seen in the natural environment. Clinical studies[9] have observed parents who attended to a child so persistently that they are able to prevent almost any kind of interaction with the ordinary objects of the home. When the child reaches for an ash tray or dish, the parent picks him up, restrains his movement, or displaces the china out of reach. When the child attempts to touch something that appears dirty, the movement is prevented. Even such immediate and natural reinforcers, such as the tactual contact with an object on the floor, the noise made by banging two objects together, or the movement onto a piece of furniture, can be prevented.

## questions

1. Why is the term *performance* recommended for operant behavior and *response* reserved for reflexes?

2. Why is it more useful to talk about *extinction* as a verb describing the procedure of discontinuing reinforcement, rather than as a noun describing the change in the animal's behavior when reinforcement is discontinued?

3. Describe the close relationship between an operant performance and the critical effect on the environment that increases its frequency.

4. How does the mechanical arrangement between the switch and the lever define the class of operant behaviors that will be reinforced in the rat experiment?

5. Why do we need to describe an operant as a class of performances relative to the reinforcer that maintains them?

6. Give some examples of negatively reinforced operants that illustrate the relationship between the reinforcer and the class of performances that results from it.

7. How do reading and studying illustrate how an operant is specified by the change in the environment that it produces?

8. Say how cleaning a room illustrates performances maintained by a common reinforcer and how this concept allows us to specify the performance.

9. How may extinction be used to prove that a reinforcer is in fact maintaining the frequency of a performance?

10. How can the DRO procedure verify that a performance is maintained by the stimulus that follows it?

11. How was the DRO procedure used in the classroom situation to determine the relationship between the teacher's attention and its effect on the student's behavior?

12. Give some examples of reinforcement and extinction in the human natural environment and analyze the performances in detail using the necessary technical language.

*part III: demonstrations of operant conditioning*

## laboratory conditioning procedures
## with a pigeon

A live demonstration of reinforcement will give first-hand experience with principles of reinforcement that have been presented in the preceding parts of the chapter. The techniques described here are standard laboratory procedures which have generated much basic research about operant conditioning. Where a live demonstration or laboratory experiment is not practical, several films are available which demonstrate the processes clearly.[10]

There is a great advantage in a live experiment where the student can personally arrange the contingencies of reinforcement for creating performances in an animal's repertoire. The experience of reinforcing the behavior of a pigeon is a dramatic one in which the student experimenter, contacting the animal only through a button which operates a food delivery mechanism, increases the frequency of an act almost instantly and shapes it into a more complex form within a few minutes. The experience illustrates the practical importance of viewing behavior and its reinforcement as separate events, and emphasizes a theoretical view that deals with the behavior of organisms as primary data controlled by the way it interacts with the environment. The process that is observed illustrates the fundamental principle in the analysis and control of operant behavior. This principle answers the question, "Where does behavior come from?"

Three kinds of experiments can be usefully carried out. In the first, the frequency of a performance that the animal is already emitting is increased. In the second experiment, the reinforcement is discontinued and the decrease in the performance is observed. In the third experiment, a new performance, not yet in the animal's repertoire, is created by reinforcing successive approximations.

**Preparing the animal** To complete a demonstration in one class period, the bird must be sufficiently familiar with the apparatus and the surroundings so that observers and other events will not disrupt it. This may be accomplished by placing the bird and apparatus in a busy hallway, office, or classroom where it may adapt to the sounds similar to those it will experience during the experiment.

**The apparatus** The essential features of the apparatus are a small experimental space and a device for using food as a reinforcer. Such equipment may be purchased commercially, or constructed almost without cost from cardboard. Manuals such as *Experiments in Operant Be-*

*havior* by Ellen Reese give detailed instructions in the purchase or construction of apparatus and in the care and training of the birds.[11] *Laboratory Studies in Operant Behavior* by Jack Michael[12] provides similar information about rats. Whatever the particular details of the apparatus that is used, the essential characteristics of the experimental space are as follows:

1. It should be large enough so that the animal has room to engage in the performances that the student tries to condition. If head raising is to be reinforced, the vertical dimension of the cage must accommodate the maximum neck stretching of which the bird is capable. Too large a cage may make the demonstration difficult because many performances will compete with the one being reinforced.

2. The conditioned reinforcer needs to be applied quickly. With automatic equipment, for example, the experimenter pushes a button to activate a light, a sound, and the food dispenser. With manual equipment, the same effect can be arranged in two steps. First, the experimenter turns on a sound and light, and then the food is put in the tray or raised within the animal's reach. As long as the sound and light follow the behavior immediately, the presentation of food may be delayed slightly. The most important condition is that the light and sound follow the exact performance that the experimenter intends to increase in frequency. The illustration shown in Figure 1–2 is a side-view diagram of the apparatus typically used in operant-reinforcement experiments.[13]

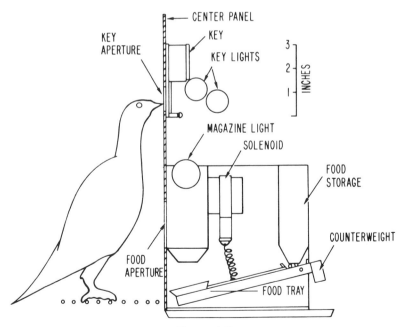

Figure 1-2

A translucent disc or key is mounted on one wall of the experimental space. The pressure of the peck on the key operates a switch which sends an electrical pulse to operate the food magazine automatically. The electrically activated solenoid raises the food tray so that the bird can reach the grain through the food aperture. A lamp over the food aperture is lit whenever the food tray is raised, providing a clear view of the grain. It is also a clear signal (along with the sound of the solenoid) that can follow a performance exactly.

### Increasing the frequency of an existing operant performance

Some behavior which the bird is already emitting may be increased in frequency (conditioned). Following are examples of kinds of performances likely to occur at some unconditioned level: 1) going to one corner of the cage; 2) raising the head; 3) lifting a leg; 4) pecking the floor. Once the frequency of a performance has been counted for 5 to 10 minutes, it may be reinforced. After a number of reinforcements, the conditioned performance will be well established. The student might now wish to record its frequency again for 5 to 10 minutes and compare this with the initial frequency. This difference is the effect of the reinforcer. To decrease the frequency of the performance that has been conditioned, the experimenter simply counts the behavior without reinforcing it. The effect of extinction will be clearer if a simple record is kept.

### Successive approximation of a performance not currently in the repertoire

The same bird can serve as a subject for an experiment on successive approximation if it is sufficiently deprived of food before starting. Beginning with some performance already in the animal's repertoire, the pigeon's behavior is differentially reinforced when it varies in the direction of the targeted performance. Some suggestions for successive approximation are:

1. Turning a somersault
2. Walking in a circle
3. Hopping from foot to foot
4. Pecking a spot on the floor
5. Standing on a cardboard box.

To condition a bird to walk in a circle, the first performance to reinforce would be a slight turn in the desired direction. When the frequency of this performance increases, reinforcement can be shifted in favor of larger rather than smaller turns. Thus, some performance is reinforced that is already occurring with a high frequency. If the procedure is gradual enough, the intervals without reinforcement are not likely to exceed 5 to

30 seconds. If the reinforcement requirement is held constant for too long, some intermediate performance might be conditioned to such a degree that it would be difficult to shift to the next step in successive approximations. Conversely, if an attempt is made to shift too rapidly, there will be few opportunities to reinforce an emitted performance, and the behavior will disappear.

**Conditioning key-pecking** This performance is of special significance because so much of the basic research in operant conditioning involves the pecking movements of pigeons. Although a pigeon will occasionally peck at a key without special training, the frequency is so low that for practical purposes successive approximation of the performance is necessary. Any movement of the bird's head in the direction of the key is reinforced. Since the pigeon is eating from the food dispenser, it is of necessity in a position facing the key. Later, only performances that bring the bird's head close to the key are reinforced. Eventually, an exploratory peck is reinforced. At this point the trainer can continue to reinforce pecking or, if the apparatus permits, allow the automatic operation of the food magazine to take over.

An alternative method of instating key-pecking is to glue several grains on the key. A bird will almost always peck at them, thereby operating the switch. Then the grains can be removed. Such a procedure essentially shifts the control of pecking from its elicitation by the sight of grain to operant control.[14]

**The characteristics of key-pecking that make it a useful operant for studying behavioral processes in the laboratory** In many laboratory research ventures, the key-peck serves as an arbitrary performance, selected to stand for any other item that might be maintained in the animal's repertoire. It is chosen because of certain desirable properties. It is a prominent, naturally occurring part of a pigeon's repertoire because it is a component in so many of its activities. The bird's beak may be thought of as having an analogous function to the human hand. Its action is easily conditioned and readily maintained for long periods. The bird's head is light relative to the weight of the muscles for moving it. This creates the possibility of very high rates of pecking, up to 40,000 pecks per hour, providing a dependent variable, like disposition or inclination to act, which can take values over an extremely wide range. A second advantage is that the reinforcement contingency specified by the key and the switch behind it generates a relatively homogeneous class of behavior. The variations in the topography of pecking simplifies the interpretation of the data. The fact that pecking moves the armature of the key to make an electrical impulse defines a standard class of pecking topographies that makes it possible to program and record the experiments automatically.

## training an animal
## in the natural environment

The same successive approximation procedures can be used to train an animal, such as a dog, in the natural, home environment. Food will be an effective reinforcer for a dog if the training is carried out just before meal time and in a place without distractions that will compete for the dog's attention.

**Establishing the conditioned reinforcer**   A clicker or saying "good" serves as a conditioned reinforcer that can instantly follow any performance that is to be conditioned. To establish the clicker or "good" as an effective reinforcer, it is necessary to have the dog's food in some form that can be given easily, such as a cracker, or ball of meat. The trainer keeps the food in a covered container and sounds a clicker each time he drops a piece of food into the dog's bowl. The pieces should not be too big or the dog will become satiated; but if they are too small, they will not be effective reinforcers. It is necessary to wait perhaps a half minute or minute between each feeding, so the dog may experience going to the bowl without finding food in the absence of the clicker. Each time the dog approaches the food in the absence of the clicker, the frequency of this behavior will decrease. Conversely, when the clicker is sounded and food is found in the bowl, the frequency of going to the bowl, prompted by the clicker, will increase.

**Eliminating begging**   Most dogs have been given food from the trainer's hand at some time in the past and therefore are likely to beg for food. To eliminate this, food is withheld whenever the dog is begging or looking at the trainer. Systematic reinforcement of a particular operant during this phase of training also needs to be avoided, since such performances, unintentionally reinforced, will interfere with the target of the shaping procedure. The shaping procedure can begin when the dog approaches the food bowl as soon as the clicker is sounded, does not approach the bowl otherwise, does not remain in the vicinity of the trainer, and does not consistently emit one particular operant.

**Successively approximating a performance already in the dog's repertoire[15]**   A simple training objective might be going to a corner of a room or touching a wastepaper basket with the nose, performances that would sooner or later occur without intervention, even if the frequency is low. The process could be speeded up by reinforcing successive approximations. When the dog turned its head in the direction of the wastepaper basket, walked, or took a step in that direction, the clicker would be sounded *immediately following* the exact performance. The result would be an increase in the frequency of this movement relative to other performances. The trainer can then shift the contingency of reinforcement to include a step or two in the direction of the wastepaper basket and continue the process until the approximations culminate with the dog walking to the wastebasket and touching it with its nose.

**Successively approximating performances which do not occur naturally**   Retrieving a newspaper, set some feet away from the trainer, is a possible target repertoire. The initial performance that is reinforced is sitting near the trainer with the newspaper nearby. The next step is to reinforce glances at the newspaper rather than looking at the trainer. When the dog turns its head, that movement is reinforced. Once reinforcement has increased the frequency of looking toward the paper, the trainer now sounds the clicker or says "good dog" only after larger rather than smaller head movements toward the paper. When the dog takes a small step in the direction of the paper, that performance is reinforced in place of looking. When the dog is taking steps regularly, reinforcement is discontinued for just looking. Next sniffing or biting the paper, perhaps lifting it off the ground slightly, might be reinforced. Once the dog picks up the paper and this is occurring regularly, movements back toward the trainer, with the paper in its mouth, can be reinforced. When the dog is reliably bringing the newspaper back to the trainer, he places it in varying locations and at varying distances.

The process of successively approximating a complex activity, such as fetching a paper, takes considerable time and patience since there are so many steps required to approximate the target repertoire and it is only possible to reinforce those performances which the dog is already emitting. If the dog wanders off at some stage of training, it is necessary to return to an earlier performance where the frequency of reinforcement will be high enough to sustain it. The immediacy of the reinforcement is a critical feature of the procedure. If the stimulus is delayed from the performance, it will follow some behavior other than what was intended. In practice, delays in reinforcement as short as a fraction of a second can cause difficulties in training an animal. For example, if it were intended to reinforce raising the head but the reinforcer was delivered one-half second following the performance, the reinforcer might actually follow lowering the head, a performance incompatible with the behavioral target. Note that the dog returns to the trainer for the food after each conditioned reinforcer (clicker or saying "good dog"). This guarantees that food can be eaten, even though the conditioned reinforcer is temporarily removed from the food delivery, and even though the animal is a distance away from the place where the food is delivered.

**Jumping in the air**   Another target for reinforcement by successive approximation might be jumping high in the air. Since dogs do not frequently jump into the air, some behavior which the dog currently emits, such as lifting its head or any movement of the front feet off the ground, is a necessary starting point. As each reinforcement increases the frequency of a performance in the direction of the intended one, it becomes possible, subsequently, to reinforce a closer approximation to the target.

**Heeling** Training a dog to heel is a common objective of persons who regularly walk with their dogs. The performance desired of the dog is to walk at the owner's side, either with or without a leash. Consider first how food might be used as a reinforcer for heeling. The dog should be fed its regular meal following the training sessions, which are best kept to about 15 minutes daily. When the dog is neither lagging behind nor pulling at the leash, the trainer says "good" and delivers a bit of food. "Begging," a complication discussed earlier, is likely to occur. The procedure reinforces a large class of activities other than lagging behind and pulling ahead (differential reinforcement of behavior other than lagging or leading). Performances such as lagging behind, sniffing, or pulling ahead will decrease in frequency because they do not produce food, while walking in the vicinity of the trainer continues to be reinforced and therefore maintained. Successive approximations of heeling are adjusted carefully. If the requirement for food delivery is too strictly defined, there will be too few opportunities to reinforce. If the class of performances to be reinforced includes performances where the dog has wandered off, then not enough extinction and differential reinforcement will occur. As the performance of "walking close by" increases in frequency and all the others decline, the contingency of reinforcement can be made more stringent. After training has progressed to the stage where the reinforcer is clearly effective, the food as well as the conditioned reinforcer can be delivered intermittently (see Chapter 8).

**Other reinforcers** The dog's behavior in the natural environment is controlled much more complexly than with food. Furthermore, food is so arbitrary and so little connected in any naturally occurring relation to the performance that the control that emerges is likely to be quite restricted. If the dog spends a great deal of time indoors, the opportunity to exercise and experience the sights and smells on a walk will be powerful reinforcers. The attention and approval of the trainer, who makes possible and accompanies such walks or pets and plays with the dog, will also be a powerful reinforcer. Attention and approval are often more effective reinforcers than food and are durable over long periods of time, if the training is carried out carefully with a collaborative rather than an adversary approach. Heeling performances maintained by such reinforcers are stable parts of the dog's social environment. Such stable, natural control means that the behavior of the controller is reinforced naturally and will be sustained by reinforcers inherent in the interaction.

## using a token procedure to reinforce behavior in a clinical setting

A token procedure for psychotic children who had very minimal behavioral repertoire illustrates how a complex interaction between a child and staff members has simple components that are examples of principles of operant reinforcement.[16] The therapeutic intervention involved the child's interaction with the staff over giving and taking a token, a requirement before being able to sit at the dining room table. Food is the final link maintaining the whole chain of activities, but the component behaviors, preliminary to eating, provide examples of specific performances followed by specific reinforcers.

The staff person at the entrance admits the child only if he or she has a token. Later, a token of the correct color might be required. Someone else, fifteen feet or so from the dining room, gives out the tokens. Any child that comes to the door without a token is sent back for one. The procedures are adjusted so that the requirement is clearly within the child's capability. In practice, the child's entrance into the dining room is simply delayed, so that no one actually misses lunch. Almost without plan, the requirement advances in small increments until the child is under the close control of the token and all the related procedures. Occasionally a child shuffles back and forth between the two people who give and receive the token because he or she does not accept the token, or give it up. This experience subsequently conforms the child's behavior to the requirements of the token procedure.

The first performance reinforced was to take the poker chip offered by the staff member. With a poker chip in hand, the next performance would be reinforced—giving it up to another staff person standing nearby. The initial part of this activity is reaching out for a token. The performance is extending the hand and the reinforcer is the contact of the token in the child's palm. The next performance is closing the fingers around the token (holding it) and the reinforcer is the pressure of the token in the hand.

The next performance, walking to the entrance of the dining room, is reinforced because it changes the child's location. The performance which can be reinforced in the new location is extending the arm and opening the fingers. This performance is reinforced by the next event in the chain, the receipt of the token by the staff person, a reinforcer because it is the occasion on which the child can enter the dining room. Entering the dining room is a performance reinforced by the sight of the food, seats, tables, etc.

Successive approximation was accomplished initially by giving collateral support to the behavior of taking or giving up a token. For example, if a child didn't grasp the token when it was given, the staff person would cover the child's hand with his own and walk with him to the other staff person who was ready to receive it. There would be chatter and cheerfulness, perhaps with the staff person's arm around the child as they walked. In extreme cases, the staff person might carry the poker chip for the child as a first approximation.

Some children did not give up the poker chip when they reached the staff person who was to receive it. In that case, the child might be held comfortably until the grip on the poker was relaxed. There would be generous verbal acknowledgement instantly when the token was released and the child would be quickly escorted to a place in the dining room. In this application, the reinforcement procedure amplified a wide variety of social interactions which would otherwise have not occurred, such as when a more able child, distressed at the difficulty someone was having, offered help. Although the token procedure was temporarily interrupted, there was the added gain that a child ordinarily isolated from others benefited from a social interaction, as did the one who offered the assistance. We don't ordinarily think of these small acts as performances and reinforcers because they are usually so regular and reliable. But with psychotic children, whose repertoires are so meager, we have a chance to see the development of small details of conduct that are so important if such children are to be taught.

## the practical modification of behavior by token procedures

Tokens have been used in mental hospitals to induce chronic schizophrenic patients to carry out activities such as combing their hair, making their beds, washing themselves, using face makeup, and feeding themselves neatly. It is not feasible to give tokens following the actual performances—for example moving a comb through the hair—so the tokens were given on the basis of ratings of neatness and cleanliness when inspection of the patient showed grooming or self care. Such a token procedure is an example of the generic definition of operant behavior. Even though it was not possible to observe the actual behaviors in which frequency needed to be increased, the performances could be still be reinforced by observing the environmental changes that defined the behaviors. Thus, cleaning oneself is a group of activities that results in the removal of dirt from the skin by a wash cloth and a sink basin, a shower, or a bath. Combed hair is, in fact, a product of combing the hair with a brush. The presentation of a token, after an inspection that reveals combed hair, guarantees, with a high degree of assurance, that it was preceded by the performances with the hair brush.

Even if the patient got someone else to comb her hair, the performances are clinically productive and related to the outcome. Getting someone's help to fix one's hair and doing it one's self are functionally equivalent performances because they are maintained by the same outcome. In colloquial terms we would say that both activities indicate the patient's decision to have combed hair and an inclination to do whatever he or she can to achieve it. The same outcome is described behaviorally when we say that the token procedures have established a groomed appearance as a reinforcing outcome, which in turn reinforces those performances that produce a groomed appearance. The analysis is parallel to that of the simple pigeon or rat performance. The occurrence of the magazine sound is a guarantee that some kind of performance, whether pressing the bar with the paws or sitting on it, has occurred just previously. The intervening period of time between the grooming performances and the receipt of the token is of course equivalent to the delay in the rat experiment, since the lapse of time between the receipt of food and the rat's performance it is designed to reinforce is too long for the food to influence the performance directly.

Behavioral experiments have attempted to induce overweight patients to participate in a weight-loss program by giving tokens daily when the patient's weight met the criterion set by the therapy program. The rationale that guided the experiment was similar to that of the token procedures described above. By giving a token on the occasion of weight loss, the patient's weight could be a reinforcer that would shape and maintain whatever performances that would lead to weight loss. The experimenters anticipated that the reinforced performances would be the self-control activities such as choosing less-caloric foods or doing activities incompatible with eating. It turned out, contrary to their plans, however, that performances such as vomiting, taking diuretics, enemas, and total fasting increased in frequency—performances which are detrimental to a therapeutic weight control program.[17] Both this and the preceding examples illustrate a class of performances defined by the outcome that reinforces them. In the former examples of grooming and self care, there was a natural relation between the neat hair and the performances that will produce it. In the weight control example, the performances that increased in frequency all produced weight loss, but their connection to the reinforcer was too variable and included performances that were not therapeutically productive.

## accidental reinforcement in human behavior

Many human behaviors are accidentally reinforced because of the complexity of the natural environment and the multiple determination of events there. Gambling situations, such as card games, generate superstitious behavior by accidental reinforcement because taking in money on a winning hand occurs frequently, even though the person may actually lose money over a longer period of time. Given this high frequency of winning, it is likely that it will follow behaviors such as rubbing a lucky coin before betting. The dice player who shouts "come seven" just before the throw of the dice and then rolls a seven, will be subsequently disposed to say "come seven" even though the speech had no influence on the outcome of the throw. The fact that seven appears on the dice only intermittently does not nullify the effect of the reinforcement. It simply specifies a schedule (see Chapter 8) that may even increase the persistence of the behavior. Pitchers in baseball games commonly carry out rituals such as rubbing the ball, making a stereotyped foot movement, or some other unrelated gesture. These performances are likely to be prone to the same kind of reinforcement as with the gambler, accidentally reinforced by the outcome of the pitch that follows. The ritual dances of primitive cultures, a rain dance for example, also illustrate accidental reinforcement. Rain, as a reinforcer for the praying and chanting, occurs variably. Sooner or later rain will fall, reinforcing praying and dancing. Once the "rain maker" has a strong disposition to pray for rain, its high frequency will make it likely that the behavior will occur when it finally rains. Both doctor and patient are susceptible to accidental reinforcement in the treatment of certain diseases. Many diseases have a natural course of progression regardless of treatment, and the application of therapies will be reinforced by the patient's improvement. Pityriasis rosea, a skin disorder, is such a disease for which only symptomatic treatment is presently possible. Although very uncomfortable for the patient, it has a fixed time course and ends with complete recovery and lifelong immunity. Patient and doctor are susceptible to accidental reinforcement in such a situation.

Avoidance behavior is especially susceptible to accidental reinforcement because it is reinforced when the aversive stimulus does *not* occur. The person who knocks on wood when there is a possibility of an aversive event and the person who avoids a black cat or walking under a ladder are successful in their avoidance so long as there is some initial conditioned aversion. The fact that no harm occurs serves to strengthen rather than weaken the avoidance behavior. To eliminate these accidentally reinforced behaviors, extinction would have to occur in the form of punishing the avoidance behaviors. Alternatively, there would be no avoidance or escape behavior if there were no aversive or conditioned aversive stimuli to motivate them. Tics, phobias, or compulsive activities, when analyzed by their functional relation to the environment, often turn out to be avoidance behaviors that may no longer be directly reinforced (negatively). These performances continue to occur because the person does not test the environment by withholding avoidance. The maintenance of avoidance behavior in experiments with primates for hours at a time without the occurrence of the aversive stimulus that is maintaining the avoidance is evidence of the extreme persistence of this kind of behavior. The notion of reality testing in therapy reflects an awareness on the therapist's part of the persistence of avoidance performances that may no longer be functional in the patient's current environment.

Whether a series of random reinforcements has any cumulative effect depends on the accidental fit between the schedule of the random reinforcement and the repertoire it comes into contact with. Social customs may provide collateral factors that will influence the superstitions that are conditioned. There is a temptation to think mentalistically about accidental reinforcement to convey how an initial disposition or predisposition to engage in the activity influences its conditioning. It might seem convenient to say that the "pigeon thinks it is operating the feeder." But such reference to the bird's mental state can be no more than an indirect way of referring to the objective factors that have been described behaviorally. The objective factors have the obvious advantage that they are measurable and manipulatable.

## questions

1. Describe the experimental arrangement recommended for demonstrating operant conditioning.
2. Describe the procedure for preparing the pigeon for the operant conditioning demonstration.
3. Describe the successive approximation procedures.
4. What are the characteristics of key-pecking that make it a useful operant for studying behavioral processes in the laboratory?
5. Describe how to apply operant conditioning principles to training an animal such as a dog in the natural environment.
6. Describe how conditioning procedures may be applied using conditioning procedures with naturally occurring reinforcers rather than food or tokens.
7. Describe how the token procedure used with psychotic children in the dining room increments the child's repertoire by the natural reinforcement of small items of conduct that accumulate.
8. Describe how the token procedures used in the mental hospital illustrate the generic reinforcement of classes of behavior.
9. How did the concept of generic reinforcement explain the failure of the token reinforcement system to be of use in the weight reduction program that was described?
10. Why are gambling situations such as shooting dice especially susceptible to accidental reinforcement?

*11.*   Why is avoidance behavior especially susceptible to accidental reinforcement?

---

 notes

[1]Ferster, C. B. and Skinner, B. F. *Schedules of Reinforcement.* Englewood Cliffs, N.J.: Prentice-Hall, 1957.

[2]Skinner, B. F. Pigeons in a pelican. *American Psychologist* 15:28–37, 1960.

[3]See Watson, J. S. Memory and "contingency analysis" in infant learning. *Merrill-Palmer Quarterly* 13:55–76, 1967, for a discussion of how infants' actions are controlled by their consequences.

[4]Skinner, B. F. Superstition in the pigeon. *Journal of Experimental Psychology* 38:168–172, 1948.

[5]For an alternative view on Skinner's classic superstition study see Staddon, J. E. R. and Simmelhog, V. L. The "superstition" experiment: A reexamination of its implications for the principles of adaptive behavior. *Psychological Review* 78:3–43, 1971.

[6]Allyon, T. and Azrin, N. H. *The token economy: A motivational system for therapy and rehabilitation.* Englewood Cliffs, N.J.: Prentice-Hall, 1968.

[7]Reynolds, G. B. Behavioral contrast. *Journal of the Experimental Analysis of Behavior* 4:57–71, 1961.

[8]Sherman, J. A. Use of reinforcement and imitations to reinstate verbal behavior in mute psychotics. *Journal of Abnormal Psychology* 70:155–164, 1965.

[9]Ferster, C. B. Positive reinforcement and behavioral deficits in autistic children. *Child Development* 32:437–456, 1961.

[10]Lovaas, O. I. (Technical Director) Reinforcement therapy (film). Smith, Kline & French Laboratories, 1966; Reese, E. P. Behavior theory and practice (film). Englewood Cliffs, N.J.: Prentice-Hall, 1965.

[11]Reese, E. P. *Experiments in operant behavior.* Englewood Cliffs, N.J.: Prentice-Hall, 1964.

[12]Michael, J. *Laboratory studies in operant behavior.* New York: McGraw Hill, 1963.

[13]Adapted from Nurnberger, J. I., Ferster, C. B., and Brady, J. V. *An introduction to the science of human behavior.* Englewood Cliffs, N.J.: Prentice-Hall, 1963, p. 240.

[14]Another procedure for the "automatic" shaping of key-pecking has been described by Brown, P. L. and Jenkins, H. M., Autoshaping of the pigeon's key-peck. *Journal of the Experimental Analysis of Behavior* 11:1–8, 1968.

[15]Skinner, B. F. How to teach animals. *Scientific American* 188:27, 1951.

[16]Ferster, C. B. The use of learning principles in clinical practice and training. *The Psychological Record* 21:353–361, 1971.

[17]Mann, R. A. The behavior-therapeutic use of contingency contracting to control an adult behavior problem: weight control. *Journal of Applied Behavior Analysis* 5:99–109, 1972.

# the reflex and its relation to operant behavior
2

In this chapter, the control of the reflex through conditioning by the environment will be described. The reflex is included in the study of operant behavior because physiological responses alter the state of the entire organism and hence influence the operant repertoire. Conversely, many operant performances actually produce eliciting stimuli for reflexes. The detailed study of the reflex and conditioned reflex offer an opportunity to compare and contrast it with the operant in several ways and to focus attention on the important properties of each.

A functional differentiation between operants and respondents is required when they have the same topography. For example, crying and sucking are discussed as activities in which the topographies of operants and reflexes overlap. In Part III, the interaction between reflex and operant behavior is examined by investigating how reflex or instinctive aspects of an organism's repertoire contribute to reinforcers that in turn generate operant behavior. Also discussed are auto shaping and adjunctive behavior. Autoshaping describes a reinforcer that appears to derive from the inherent reflexes, and adjunctive behavior describes activities collateral to operant reinforcement procedures.

## technical terms

conditioned response
conditioned stimulus
neutral stimulus
ontogenetic history
Pavlovian conditioning

phylogenetic history
respondent conditioning
unconditioned response
unconditioned stimulus
autonomic nervous system

## outline

Part I:  Reflexes
What is a reflex?
The reflex as a stimulus and a response
Descriptive examples of reflexes
The reflex as a behavioral unit
The classical Pavlovian experiment—conditioned salivation
The range of internal reflexes may be conditioned
Conditioned reflexes in the natural environment

Part II:  A Comparison of Operant and Reflex Conditioning
Confusion of terminology
Contrasting and comparing operants and reflexes
Different measurement of results
Distinguishing between operants and reflex of similar forms
Piaget's observations of the overlap between operant and reflex behavior
Biofeedback and the operant reinforcement of reflexes

Part III:  The Behavior of Operant and Reflex Behavior
Simultaneous control by a stimulus
How an operant performance produces a conditioned stimulus for reflexes
Fixed-action patterns
The interaction between fixed-action patterns and the processes of operant reinforcement
Fixed-action patterns as building blocks for infant development
Constraints on responses and stimuli
Autoshaping
Why does a reinforcer increase the frequency of a performance?

what is a reflex?

The environmental control of operant behavior is of primary concern in the study of behavior. The major questions concern how the interaction between an operant performance and the environment shapes its form and alters its frequency. But the reinforcement of operant behavior is in a context of inherited patterns of action—determined by species-specific stimuli. We need, therefore, to understand the substrate out of which operant behavior develops because its emergence in an organism's repertoire is a complex interaction of the two kinds of influences.

The reflex seems remote from the larger aspects of human conduct and unrelated to the reinforcement of operant behavior. It is less sensitive to environmental control, less plastic in its form, and, more than operant behavior, it is a reflection of phylogenetic rather than ontogenetic history, in other words, more a product of evolution of the species than of development of the organism. The main reason for introducing the reflex at this point is to provide a contrast with operant behavior. Even though the two systems interact with each other, as will be discussed in Part III, the reflex, of itself, is a behavioral unit that will illustrate a different kind of functional relation between the environment and a response of the organism.

A reflex is a fixed and relatively unchangeable relation between a stimulus and a response. When a light is shined in the eye, the pupil constricts. When food is placed in the mouth, saliva is secreted. When the knee is tapped, the leg jerks. When the temperature around the body increases, glands in the skin excrete sweat. A hot surface evokes a quick withdrawal of the hand. A sudden loud noise evokes contraction of the blood vessels (blanching). An object in the entrance to the trachea evokes coughing (movement of the diaphragm), and a finger in the esophagus elicits vomiting (contraction of the stomach). In contrast to the reflex, operant behavior is less dependent upon the animal's inherited, genetic history (phylogenetic) and more dependent on its interaction with the environment (ontogenetic history). As discussed in Chapter 1, we use the term *performance* rather than *response* when speaking of operant behavior because the form of the operant, relatively independent of prior stimuli, may vary, depending on the change that it produces in the external environment. Although traditionally the term *response* has been used to describe both operants and reflexes, its use in this book has been limited to reflexes. Use of the term *response* for reflexes seems descriptively relevant because the topography of a response is mostly determined by a specific eliciting stimulus.

The term *elicit* refers to reflexes and the term *emit* to operants. The term *elicit* refers to the close, one-to-one correspondence between the unconditioned stimulus and the occurrence of an unconditioned reflex response. An operant is spoken of as "emitted" because the change on the environment produced by it is the critical factor determining its form. In the reflex, the emphasis is on the unconditioned stimulus which precedes and evokes (elicits) the unconditioned response. In operant behavior, the focus is on the stimulus (reinforcer) that follows the performance.

## the reflex as a stimulus and a response

In each of the reflexes described earlier we say a stimulus elicits a response. Food in the mouth elicits the secretion of saliva. The tap on the knee elicits a muscular jerk of the knee and warm air elicits secretion of sweat. We speak of the stimulus as the eliciting stimulus and the altered condition of the organism as the elicited response. The two parts of the reflex are also called the *unconditioned stimulus* and the *unconditioned response.* The term *unconditioned* is used because the elicitation of the reflex does not depend on any prior experience with the stimulus. The animal is born with the reflex, and all that is necessary to evoke it is the eliciting stimulus. The magnitude of the unconditioned stimulus controls the magnitude of the reflex response (unconditioned response) very closely. The greater the magnitude of the eliciting stimulus, the greater the magnitude of the unconditioned response that is elicited. When the magnitude of the unconditioned stimulus is small enough, no unconditioned response will be elicited. The magnitude of the unconditioned stimulus below which the reflex is not elicited is called the *threshold* of the reflex. No such correlation exists with operant behavior. The frequency of the rat's bar pressing performance will not be higher or lower whether the stimulus that controls it discriminatively is loud or soft sound.

We owe the laws of the reflex mainly to the work of Sherrington in his classic experiments reported in his lectures on "The Integrative Action of the Nervous System."[1] Even though the work was intended to provide a neurophysiological basis of the reflex, the main findings are a description of the relation of the eliciting stimulus and the correlated response. It is interesting to note that as with Sherrington, Pavlov's experiments on the conditioned reflex, which will be presented in the next section, were presented as investigations of the activity of the brain. Actually, Pavlov's references to the central nervous system were almost entirely inferential.

The brain is necessary for the integrated activities of the organism, but the actual technical analysis carried out by Pavlov measured environmental interactions rather than cerebral events.

## descriptive examples of reflexes

Ann blinks as a result of an intense puff of air blown into her eye. Air is an unconditioned stimulus that elicits the unconditioned response of eye-blinking. This is an example of a reflex, since Ann was born with the response produced by the air puff. We notice that the topography of the response is exclusively determined by the unconditioned stimulus. Let us suppose that we deliver a very light, a medium, and a very intense puff of air. The very light puff might not elicit an unconditioned response at all, in which case we are likely to say that it is below threshold. If the reflex occurrs at all, however, its form will be the same as with other air puffs. When we compare the medium and intense puffs of air, we note that the blink elicited by the medium puff took longer to occur (longer latency) and was not as large as the blink elicited by the more intense puff of air.

Bob is peeling onions in the kitchen and his eyes tear. The vapor from the onions is an unconditioned stimulus that elicits the unconditioned response of the secretion of the lachrymal glands of the eye. The response to the onion vapor is a reflex because the form of the response (secretion of tears) is fixed by the innate characteristics of the eye and occurs in response to the onion vapor. The amount of tears elicited depends on the amount and concentration of the onion vapor stimulating the eye. An amount of vapor that is not sufficient to elicit tearing is said to be below threshold. The time between the exposure to the onion vapor and the tearing is the latency of the response and is shorter with a large amount of onion vapor than with a smaller amount.

## the reflex as a behavioral unit

Even though most reflexes alter the organism's internal state (this change is often identified with the science of physiology), it is still a behavioral event because it can be studied by describing the relationships (laws) between the eliciting stimulus in the external environment and the elicited response. The behavioral unit called "the reflex" encompasses both the stimulus and the response and, as such, it is defined generically just as with operant behavior. The generic definition arises because the stimulus eliciting the reflex will vary slightly from time to time and still be effective. Correspondingly, the elicited response, although relatively invariant compared with operant behavior, changes its form slightly from elicitation to elicitation. Thus, the reflex is a definitional unit—apart from any one instance that is observed—that alludes to a class of stimuli and the correlated class of responses that is functionally connected.

The behavioral laws of the reflex are:

1. *Magnitude:* The magnitude of the unconditioned response increases when it is elicited by stimuli of larger magnitude. For example, the greater the force with which the patellar tendon is struck, the greater the deflection of the leg.
2. *Refractory phase:* After a reflex is elicited, there is a short period during which further stimulation will not produce the unconditioned response.
3. *Threshold:* The intensity of the stimulus must reach or exceed a critical value in order to elicit a response.
4. *Temporal summation:* Prolongation of the stimulus, or repetitive presentation within certain limiting rates, has the same effect as increasing the intensity.
5. *Adaptation:* The strength of a reflex declines during repeated elicitation (habituation) and returns to its former value during subsequent inactivity (spontaneous recovery).

These relations between properties of the eliciting stimulus and the elicited response can be described without reference to the underlying physiological mechanisms.

## the classical Pavlovian experiment— conditioned salivation

A neutral stimulus that would ordinarily not elicit a reflex may come to do so when it is paired with the unconditioned stimulus. Reflexes then, like operant behaviors, may be influenced by the individual organism's unique experiences with the environment (conditioned). This discovery came from the work of I. P. Pavlov, the Russian physiologist. While studying the dog's digestive system, he discovered that dogs would salivate not only when food was placed in their mouths but also when they were placed in the room where the feeding occurred. He called this salivation "psychic secretion" to convey the common-sense connotation that the animal "remembered the surroundings in which he was fed." Behaviorally, however, all we can say is that the reflex now occurred in response to the conditioned stimulus, apart from the unconditioned stimulus that originally elicited it. The dog salivated initially in response to food in its mouth; later it salivated in response to the visual stimulus (the room) that was present when the food was placed in its mouth.

Pavlov developed methods for measuring the exact increases and decreases in the magnitude of salivation. The duct from the gland which produces saliva was transplanted outside the dog's cheek by a surgical procedure so that the saliva could be collected, drop by drop, into a graduated flask. A typical experiment began with an unconditioned response (salivation) elicited by the unconditioned stimulus (food in the mouth). A neutral stimulus was next paired with the unconditioned stimulus by presenting it just before the unconditioned stimulus. The neutral stimulus, a metronome, had no influence over salivation prior to the pairing. Pavlov discovered that the sound of the metronome, occurring at the same time that food was placed in the dog's mouth now elicited salivation much as the direct action of the food in the mouth. Pavlov called the metronome a *conditioned stimulus* because it was a previously neutral stimulus that now elicited salivation conditional on its pairing with introduction of food into the dog's mouth. The term *conditioning* has the same connotations as in operant behavior. It implies that some feature of the external environment now controls the behavior as a result of the organism's interaction with it.

The conditioned reflex may be eliminated if the metronome is presented repeatedly without being followed with food introduced into the dog's mouth. This procedure is call *extinction.* In Pavlov's experiments, each time the metronome was sounded without being paired with food, the amount of saliva elicited decreased and the latency of the conditioned response increased. Eventually, no more salivation occurred when the metronome was sounded. The operation by which conditioned reflexes are eliminated is different from operant behavior. Unlike operants, which are emitted freely, a conditioned reflex needs first to be elicited by the conditional stimulus in order to weaken it.

A great deal is known of the details that influence the formation of conditioned reflexes. The temporal relations between the stimuli and responses, the interaction among the compound of elements of the conditioned stimulus, and the nature of the reinforcer all influence respondent conditioning. Since our emphasis will be on the operant repertoire and respondents are of interest to the extent that they influence operants, we will need to consider only the broad outlines of the processes by which respondents are conditioned.

Although the procedure of the conditioned reflex was said to begin with a previously neutral stimulus, it is unlikely that a truly neutral stimulus exists. A particular person may never have fed a dog, but his appearance or sound may control other important events, such as when he plays with, pets, or grooms the dog. Such a person might be neutral in respect to food and at the same time have an important function in the dog's life in other respects. A neutral stimulus might elicit reflexes other than the one that it is intended to condition. It might also elicit a startle response, an orientation reflex, or a change in skin resistance and contraction and relaxation of the small blood vessels. Pavlov frequently referred to the animal's head movement in the direction from where the stimulus originated as an orienting reflex. In the natural environment, which of the myriad stimuli around the organism acquires control over a reflex and thereby becomes the conditioned stimulus as the result of the periodic occurrence of an unconditioned stimulus? The answer lies in a determination of what other performances these stimuli control through other behavioral processes.

## the range of internal reflexes
## that may be conditioned

Although many of Pavlov's experiments dealt with salivation and the flexion reflex (in response to electric shock), a large number of reflexes have been studied and their scope is limited only by the naturally occurring physiological responses of the organism. It seems fair to assume that reflexes may be conditioned to any organ activity mediated by the autonomic nervous system.

Many unconditioned stimuli may elicit a number of unconditioned responses. A noxious stimulus, such as an electric shock, may elicit simultaneously constriction of the blood vessels, an altered breathing pattern, and sweating. Thus, there are three separate reflexes that can be described. If a neutral stimulus, such as a buzzer or tone, is paired with the electric shock, it will elicit much the same physiological changes as the shock. We may elicit diuresis (the excretion of urine) in an animal by injecting water into its rectum. If we now sound a buzzer prior to the injection of water, we soon find that the buzzer alone will elicit urination. The excretion of bile has been elicited by pressure on the gland and conditioned under the control of a previously neutral stimulus. Heart rate changes have been elicited by injections of nitroglycerin and by electric shock, or loud noises, for example.

Reflex conditioning has been demonstrated in such a large number of organ systems of the body that there is little doubt that it represents one of the major avenues of change in the internal economy of an organism as a result of its interaction with the external environment. Even though the long-term body effects of conditioned autonomic changes are only beginning to be demonstrated, they represent a major class of variables that are likely to have relevance to many medical specialities. In cardiovascular disease, for example, the systemic change in heart rate and arterial diameter may well be part of the disease's etiology, and hormonal and digestive processes may well interact with conditioning as a factor in the causes, treatment, and prevention of ulcers.

## conditioned reflexes
## in the natural environment

The dentist's office is a frequent source of large-magnitude conditioned reflexes. The sight and sound of the dentist's drill becomes a conditioned stimulus that will elicit many of the same reflexes that occur as a result of the actual penetration into the tooth and the trauma to the pulp and nerve. All the physiological correlates of the pain experienced by the patient during drilling will now be elicited by the sight and sound of the drill. The fundamental process, although complicated by the operant performances, such as talking and thinking about the impending appointment, are those of the conditioned and unconditioned reflex. The action of the drill on the pulp is the unconditioned stimulus eliciting vasoconstriction, breathing patterns, heart rate, and other reflexes associated with noxious stimuli. The conditioned stimuli are those that occur contiguously with the elicited reflexes and, hence, come to evoke them. The anxiety produced by the waiting room and the verbal behavior and thoughts anticipatory of the appointment are a more complex matter involving the issues of negative reinforcement and other aspects of aversive control (Chapter 4).

The conditionability of the stomach glands and their secretions was described more than one hundred years ago by a physician, Dr. William Beaumont,[2] long before it could be seen technically as Pavlovian conditioning. A man treated by Dr. Beaumont had received an accidental gunshot wound that tore open a part of the chest and perforated the stomach. The man survived, but it was impossible to close the stomach perforation so it could heal. As a result, Dr. Beaumont could directly observe the reflex changes in the walls of the patient's stomach because part of it extruded through the wound.

Anger and excitement disrupted the normal action of the stomach wall The lining of the stomach became sometimes dry and red and at other times pale and moist. This is opposed to the normal condition, which is a pale pink surface covered with mucus and with irregular folds when the stomach is without food and a bright red color and discharge of stomach fluids when food enters. With disruption of an emotional sort, the stomach secretions diminished greatly or even disappeared. The mucous coat was scarcely perceptible. When there was also dryness of the mouth or accelerated pulse, no gastric juice could be extracted even when the stomach wall was physically stimulated. Liquids that were swallowed were immediately passed on, but food remained undigested for 24 to 48 hours.

In his account of the subject's reaction to anger and disease, Beaumont described the conditions conducive to the formation of gastric ulcers and, at least implicitly, how such reactions might be conditioned. Disruption of the stomach mucosa as described by Beaumont was a conditioned response parallel in form to those produced in Pavlov's salivation experiments. Clearly Dr. Beaumont anticipated, over one hundred years ago, the psychosomatic causes of stomach ulcers that are recognized today. *Psychosomatic illnesses* are those caused by a combination of physical and psychological factors. Experiments will be described in Part III of this chapter concerning somatic residues of behavioral processes and the evidence that they contribute to diseases such as ulcerative colitis.

A case similar to that of Dr. Beaumont's occurred one hundred years later when a young boy swallowed boiling soup and closed off his esophagus. In order to feed himself, the boy chewed his food and then inserted it into his stomach through a fistula (hole) that had to be made in the abdominal wall so that he could eat. As a result, it was possible to observe the stomach mucosa directly and measure the acidity of the stomach glands. The "stomach blushed with rage" when the boy was annoyed and hemorrhages appeared under extreme conditions.[3]

## questions

1. Using the terms *stimulus response, elicit reflex, threshold,* and *latency,* discuss "gooseflesh" that occurs in the cold.
2. Based upon your knowledge of human biology, list three other reflexes and designate the stimuli and the responses that they elicit.
3. What is the latency and threshold of a reflex?
4. What is the refractory phase of a reflex?
5. Discuss why the stimulus that is paired with the reflex and that becomes a conditioned reflex had never been literally neutral in its control of the individual's behavior.
6. How may a conditioned response he eliminated or reduced in magnitude?
7. Give some examples of conditioned reflexes in the natural environment and describe them using the technical terms of the reflex and conditioned reflex.
8. Describe the reflexes that Dr. Beaumont was able to observe in the patient he was treating for an accidental gunshot wound in the stomach.
9. In what way are the reflexes observed by Dr. Beaumont suggestive of the conditions that lead to the formation of gastric ulcers as a psychosomatic illness?

## part II: a comparison of reflex and operant conditioning

### confusion of terminology

The use of the terms *conditioning* and *reinforcement* originally came from Pavlov's experiments dealing with salivation of dogs in response to food powder placed in their mouths. The extension of these terms to operant performances causes difficulty because the two types of behavior, as will be seen in this section, have very different properties. Initially, the term *conditioning* was used with both operant and reflex behaviors because both were seen as a modification of the organism's activity that came about from its experience with the environment. The differences between these two kinds of behaviors, however, have turned out to be as important as their similarities.

The discovery of the conditioned reflex caused great excitement in the United States during the early part of the twentieth century, because it appeared to answer the question of how man's behavior became modified by its interaction with the environment. As a result, Pavlov's experiments were taken as a model for all modifiable behavior. The confusion was compounded because the results of early laboratory research on conditioned reflexes were thought to explain how fear and anxiety developed. However, with the discoveries of the technical properties of operant behavior by Skinner and others, it becomes useful and necessary to distinguish between the conditioning of reflexes and their resultant disruption of the ongoing behaviors. In the case of the reflexes, the conditioning process involves a pairing of two stimuli so that a reflex is now evoked by a new stimulus rather than the unconditioned stimulus that originally elicited it. Conditioning an operant, as we have seen, refers to the establishment of a new repertoire that usually opens a way of acting on a new or preexisting environment.

A common source of confusion between reflex and operant behavior occurs because of the colloquial language that we conventionally use to describe the effects of depriving an organism of food. Certainly, a few hours of food deprivation make possible very prominent gastric reflexes such as salivation, secretion of gastric juices in the stomach, and increased blood supply to the lips and mouth. Usually when someone has not eaten for some time, the events that are described most prominently are gastric reflexes such as those mentioned above. From the point of view of the operant behavior of feeding, however, the significant dimensions are the frequency of behaviors that reinforced when food is produced. Conditioned gastric reflexes may appear in maximum magnitudes within a period of hours after ingesting a meal. The inclination to engage in activities reinforced by food (that is, to eat), however, increases continuously, far beyond the point where gastric reflexes have peaked. Laboratory experiments have shown that the disposition to eat increases continuously with loss of body weight. Thus, a person's disposition to engage in behaviors that are reinforced, operant-wise by food, may increase long after digestive reflexes have stabilized. Since the disposition to eat, or the potential frequency of performances reinforced by food, is an event that is much less prominent than the profuse secretion of saliva or gastric juices or the vigorous contractions of the muscles of the stomach, we are much more attentive to the latter. The distinction between the operant and reflex aspects of food deprivation is of great importance, practically, when we attempt to teach children and others how to control their own eating activity. The conditioned reflex concomitants of eating can be reduced by bringing the reflexes under discriminative control (Chapter 6) if eating is restricted to particular circumstances without any reduction in weight. Other measures are required, however, once food intake is reduced to bring about a loss of body weight.

The same confusion occurs with noxious stimuli that elicit reflexes at the same time that they may negatively reinforce operant performances or disrupt ongoing operant activities. When a person reports that he is fearful, some events that he cites as evidence of his fearfulness are likely to be occurrences such as increased heart beat, dry mouth, and changes in breathing patterns—the reflex effects of aversive situations. Yet, parallel to the operant and reflex aspects of food deprivation, there are profound changes in the frequency of operant behaviors that for practical purposes may be more important than the physiological changes. A person who is acutely aware of his or her heart beat in a threatening situation may fail to notice the complete cessation of the operant activities that otherwise would be ongoing.

## contrasting and comparing operants and reflexes

The reflex and the conditioned reflex, as well as the operant, have been described in sufficient detail that there will be considerable benefit from comparing and contrasting these two kinds of behavioral control. There is still theoretical argument in the psychological literature about whether it is necessary to have two separate formulations to describe operants and reflexes. The issues and experiments have largely concerned a search for a concept that would subsume these two kinds of behavioral control. Yet, the factual details of the differences between these two kinds of behavior are important practically even if it turns out that there is a common process underlying them. A further advantage for the student is the fluency and facility that is gained by a detailed understanding of how the two kinds of conditioning differ. The comparison will also serve as a review of the behavioral processes that have been presented so far.

**Internal state versus the environment**   The reflex influences the internal state while the operant alters the external environment. The reflex can be thought of as a one-way interaction with the external environment—an eliciting stimulus (unconditioned stimulus) in the external environment produces a specific change within the organism. The significance of most reflex changes is mainly for its internal economy. Salivation is a clear example. This reflex produces secretion which makes the organism's digestion possible. The main result of constricting the pupil is a decrease in the amount of light entering the eye. Coughing clears the trachea from obstruction. The dilation and constriction of blood vessels alter the flow and amount of blood to the various parts of the body.

Reflexes where the response is the action of striated muscles are intermediate between operants and respondents, because the same topography of response, as, for example, the withdrawal of the hand from a hot surface, can also function as a negatively reinforced operant. The fixed-action patterns, which will be discussed later, also present a category intermediate between performances that are clearly operants and reflexes. Reflexes consisting of actions of striated muscles, such as when an eye-blink protects the eye from intrusion by a foreign object, represent the action of the external environment on the internal economy of the body by closing of an opening. The respondent behaviors represent involuntary control in the sense that full control of the behavior is in the eliciting stimulus that, in turn, is determined almost completely from the phylogenetic rather than ontogenetic history of the organism.

**Successive approximation**   In the case where raising the bird's head was reinforced by food, it was possible to increase the frequency of a performance not initially in the bird's repertoire. The final result was the conditioning of an operant performance that had not occurred naturally before, even as an unconditioned operant. In contrast, the reflex's unconditioned response is fixed by the inherited (phylogenetic) history of the animal. In the salivation reflex, for example, we may alter the latency with which saliva follows the placement of food in the dog's mouth and the amount of saliva secreted, but the form of the response remains fixed. No matter what the outcome of the controversy about the liability of reflexes to operant conditioning, the behavioral outcome is a relatively fixed response, such as salivation. The tap on the patellar tendon of the knee, although involving striated muscles in which movements are potentially modifiable as operant performances, elicits a rather stereotyped action that varies only in magnitude and latency.

In contrast, a crucial characteristic of operant behavior is that the topography of the operant performance may take any form, largely determined by the reinforcer maintaining it. In the laboratory, the experimenter determines what performance will increase in frequency by selecting the one that the reinforcer follows. We can arrange to deliver food to an animal following virtually any performance, and the behavior that becomes conditioned will be the one followed by food. The topography of the reflex, on the other hand, is determined entirely by the unconditioned stimulus and is limited to the particular responses that are part of the animal's physiological inheritance.

**Autonomic and central nervous system involvement**  Reflexes other than the patellar, such as eye blink, heart action, breathing movements, and startle, involve the action of the striated rather than the smooth muscles. Nevertheless, the actions of these muscle movement patterns are very limited in their function as reflexes as compared with the complexity of the relations with the environment that emerges when they are reinforced as operants. The special characteristics of operants whose topographies overlap those of reflexes, such as a sneeze that could be produced by an allergen in the nose or as an operant that is emitted, will be discussed in the next section.

**Behavior and the environment as separate**  Both reflex and operant behavior may be said to describe the behavior of the organism apart from the stimulus causing it to occur. The reflex is described as an unconditioned response elicited by an unconditioned stimulus and the operant is described as a performance that increases in frequency because it is followed by reinforcement. Our colloquial language often does not make it clear that there are two distinct components—the behavior and its counterpart in the environment. An expression such as "food-getting behavior" describes the performance, the reinforcer, and their functional relation to each other, all in one term. It omits details such as the form of the performance and the explicit way that it produces the food. A behavioral description has the advantage of a factual, objective account of all the events in a way that allows them to be described accurately and in detail. Colloquial descriptions of reflexes also do not usually specify the eliciting stimulus, as, for example, when we refer to a salivatry reflex or an eye blink.

## different measurement of results

The measurement of respondent conditioning does not involve the frequency of the behavior, because the reflex occurs only when it is evoked by the unconditioned stimulus. Therefore, the frequency of the reflex is arbitrary. Furthermore, a specific unconditioned stimulus always elicits a specific unconditioned response, and the larger the magnitude of the unconditioned stimulus the larger the magnitude of the reflex that is elicited. For example, the knee jerks more to a forceful tap than to a weak one, the pupil of the eye contracts to a smaller size in a bright than in a dim light, and more sweat is excreted at higher than lower temperatures. The elapsed time between the presentation of the unconditioned stimulus and the occurrence of the unconditioned response (the latency) of the reflex also depends on the magnitude of the unconditioned stimulus. With small magnitudes of unconditioned stimuli, a longer time elapses (longer latency) before the unconditioned response is evoked than with an unconditioned stimulus of larger magnitude. Thus, when a very hot object is placed on an animal's foot, it will be withdrawn more quickly than in response to a moderately hot object. We could say the latency of the withdrawal reflex was shorter with the very hot object (large magnitude of the eliciting stimulus) than with a cooler one. As noted earlier when a weak unconditioned stimulus does not elicit an unconditioned response, we say that it is below *threshold*. The threshold indicates the stimulus magnitude above which the reflex is likely to be elicited and below which it is not.

No such relation exists between a prior stimulus and operant performances. The important dimension is the frequency of the performance because the performances are emitted and maintained by the way that they alter the environment. Thus, with operant behavior the question is not whether the performance will occur or how vigorously it will occur, but how disposed the individual is to carry out the activity. There is a superficial resemblance between operants and conditioned reflexes when a discriminative stimulus exerts close controls on operant performance. For example, if we reinforce a pigeon's peck only when the light behind the key is on and arrange a "trials procedure" whereby the key light comes on for a short time when a peck in its presence operates the food dispenser, it may appear that the key light is evoking the peck, just like Pavlov's metronome evoked salivation. The similarity, however, is more superficial than significant. The latency between the appearance of the metronome and the evocation of the salivation measures the extent of conditioning. In the pigeon experiment, the latency of the peck to the light is long or short depending on whether the operation of the food dispenser is contingent on a fast peck. The latency, therefore, does not give any indication of the bird's disposition to peck the key. In the conditioned salivation response, the amount of saliva secreted is the important indication of conditioning. In the case of the operant behavior, key-pecking, conditioning could as readily increase the frequency of a soft as a hard peck, depending on which topography is required by the reinforcement contingency.

In the topography of the operants typically studied in laboratory experiments, key-pecking and lever-pressing are chosen to provide a performance in which frequency can vary over a wide range. This is because the most important questions we ask about operant behavior concern how frequently the operant will be emitted. It is an operant's frequency that we look to when we try to observe the data that is responsible for observations that occur with comments such as "she is enthusiastic about her new job," "he is a football fan," "she is lazy," "he is timid," "he is highly sexed," "she is enthusiastic about politics." All these descriptions refer, at their core, to the frequency of the class of activities that are designated. The football fan reads and watches football frequently, an enthusiast engages in the preferred activity at every opportunity, a highly sexed person emits a high frequency of performances that allow sexual interactions.

We have difficulty in these colloquial accounts because the performance that has a potentially high frequency can only occur under particular circumstances. Where is the disposition to eat when no food is available? It is a potential frequency of action that can be emitted only in places where food is available. Otherwise, the action is potential, quiescent, and in the repertoire. Terms like *habit* and *motivation* and *disposition to action* are mentalistic ways of referring to the potential frequency of the action if the person were in an environment that could support it. Yet, it is possible to make judgments about whether and how vigorously someone will eat before he or she has an opportunity to do so. Thus, when we say someone is hungry, we are predicting that there is a high probability that he or she will eat if food were available. We observe a high frequency of talking about food and a probability that performances reinforced by food will occur any time they are not preempted by competing performances.

It is important to realize that if terms like *hunger, habit,* or *attitude* are to have any useful meaning they need to refer to external conditions, such as length of the period of food deprivation, the history of reinforcement in the case of the habit, and an indication of the items of action that have a higher frequency of occurrence than others in the person's repertoire.

## distinguishing between operants
## and reflexes of similar forms

Because performances involving the striated musculature may be either emitted or elicited, operant or respondent, it is sometimes difficult to classify a single instance. If we saw a student suddenly remove his hand from a surface, we would have no way of knowing whether the performance was elicited by an electric shock or whether it was an operant performance occurring in a reaction time experiment. Yawning elicited by oxygen metabolism, the knee jerk elicited by a tap on the patellar tendon, the eye blink elicited by an object moving toward the eye, a cough in response to a foreign object in the trachea, the withdrawal of the hand from a hot surface can all be emitted as operants, although of slightly different form.

Such is the case when a cough brings someone's attention or a wink serves as a collateral stimulus to a verbal interaction. When the knee is flexed as if the patellar tendon were tapped, the operant form may resemble its reflex counterpart very closely. But the control of such performances, despite the very similar topographies, is clearly different depending on whether they are emitted or elicited. An infant's cry could be elicited by an open diaper pin puncturing its skin or because the parent comes when the child cries long and hard enough to provide an aversive stimulus whose termination for the parent is a reinforcer. The newborn infant's crying, like the legendary protest against leaving the mother's womb, is reflexive, elicited by loud sounds, trauma, extremes of temperature, or food deprivation. Early in infancy, crying ceases to become solely reflexive and is shaped by the specific consequences that follow it. The child who has not eaten in several hours cries both because such crying has led others to give it food in the past and because crying occurs as a reflex produced by the food deprivation. As with sucking, there is the possibility of differential reinforcement of more intense and finely differentiated crying patterns because the parent reacts to those forms of crying that are especially aversive. This paradox, where the parent inadvertently reinforces those forms of crying that are uniquely aversive, will be discussed in more detail in Chapter 4.

When crying is simultaneously elicited as in a reflex and reinforced as in an operant, which is the major source of the behavior may not be clear. An infant crying because it has not eaten in several hours could be exhibiting a response elicited as a reflex because of the state of the gastrointestinal system. Simultaneously, however, food deprivation increases the frequency of all those operants, such as crying, that have produced food in the past. We have very little objective knowledge about how these two systems of behavior interact with each other. Furthermore, it is often difficult to distinguish between them. It seems probable that operants such as crying and sucking that overlap topographically with reflexes or fixed-action patterns are more persistent, durable items in a repertoire than performances without this second source of control.

To prove that a given instance of crying is reinforced as an operant, it is necessary to identify some immediate consequence of the performance and determine whether it is the reinforcer that is maintaining its frequency. If we suspect that an infant cries because it produces the parent's attention and a subsequent interaction, the hypothesis can be tested by withholding attention when the child cries. If crying occurs less frequently, then there is evidence that it was being reinforced operant-wise. A better test of the control of the child's crying could be accomplished by the procedure described in Chapter 1. In this test, the parent continues to feed, pay attention, and otherwise tend to the child but without any contingency between crying and these events. If the frequency of crying falls, there is evidence that the operant consequences of the crying had been maintaining it. In practice, however, such experiments are difficult to carry out since crying is likely to be very persistent because of its intermittent reinforcement (Chapter 5) in the past. The persistence of crying creates an aversive situation that makes it difficult to withhold attention because any activity that terminates the crying will be negatively reinforced.

An examination of the topography of the performance may be another way to distinguish reflex and operant crying. If the topography of the crying is relatively fixed and the major changes from time to time and from person to person are in its loudness, then the best presumption is that it is a reflex. However, crying that is maintained because it induces changes in the behavior of the parent is subject to successive approximation by the particular sensitivities of that parent. The reinforcement of crying by its influence on the parent is another illustration of the generic nature of operant reinforcement that was discussed in Chapter 1. The operant is specified as accurately by the reactivity of the parent that generates it as by the topographies that actually occur.

## Piaget's observations of the overlap between operant and reflex behavior

Piaget's description of an infant sucking[4] provides an example, like crying, of a performance that begins in the child's repertoire as a reflex but is later reinforced operantly when it becomes a way of altering the environment rather than a reflex action to it. Piaget described the momentary sucking that occurred when the newborn infant's finger acidentally entered its mouth. The contact lasted only for a moment because the infant can neither keep the finger in its mouth nor pursue it with its head. The eliciting stimulus for the reflex is some pressure on the infant's mouth and the reflex response is the sucking. When the child is about three days old, it is apparent that the contact of the child's open mouth with the nipple is a reinforcer that gradually shapes the head movements that bring about the required contact and provide the discriminative stimulus that controls sucking reinforced by food as an operant. Careful observation of such a young infant discloses many instances of differential reinforcement, such as the extinction that occurs when the child turns in the direction opposite to where the breast or bottle is. Such instances of nonreinforcement are crucial elements in the successive approximation that is responsible for the final, well-developed competence of the older infant that never "misses."

Piaget described two experiments prior to the fourth day after birth showing the emergence of operant sucking from the original reflex. The mother's breast was given to the infant about two inches from the nipple. The infant sucked the skin for a moment and then let go, moving the head about two inches from the first position. The contact with the skin at the second location and the movements continued after a moment of sucking the skin. Then one of the movements accidentally resulted in contact between the mucosa of the upper lip and the nipple (the infant's mouth is wide open) and he immediately adjusted his lips and began sucking and drinking the resulting milk. When the experiment was repeated a second time, the infant began to cry after sucking the skin some distance from the nipple and withdrew to another location one-half inch away. Similar random movements were repeated until one of them brought the mucous tissues of the infant's open mouth into contact with the nipple, thereby evoking sustained sucking.

By this process, sufficient differential reinforcement of the movements of the neck and head had occurred so that by the fourth day after birth, the infant turned to the breast directly rather than finding it as a result of random movements, or being dependent on the mother to place the nipple in its mouth. The process represents differential reinforcement in which unsuccessful movements go unreinforced and alternate with effective movements which are reinforced. With continued experience, the sucking performance in infants becomes more narrowly under the control of its reinforcing consequence, milk in the mouth. Unreinforced performances decrease in frequency. Thus, within four days of birth, what was initially a reflex response to pressure on the lips becomes an operant performance that is maintained by its contact with the nipple of the mother's breast.

Piaget observed the same differential reinforcement in the emergence of sucking reinforced by its interaction with the infant's thumb in its mouth. At one time, the pressure of the quilt on the infant's mouth, as a result of the undifferentiated movements of its head, elicits sucking, but neither the sucking nor the maintenance of the head position persists. When the infant finds its hand in its mouth by further random movements of the head and arms, the infant continues to suck it without turning away. At this stage, however, the movements are not coordinated enough for sustaining the contact very efficiently or for very long. Unlike the previous experience with the quilt, however, the infant immediately begins movements whose frequency is presumed to be a result of the previous contact of the finger in the mouth. At this stage of development of the repertoire, however, the finger slips out of the mouth again.

## biofeedback and the operant reinforcement of reflexes

Biofeedback experiments appear to be in a boundary position between operant and respondent behavior because the performances that are of concern are physiological activities such as heart rate, blood pressure, or skin resistance. Changes in the activities of these organ functions are ordinarily elicited reflex-wise or altered through physiological processes. Their connection to operant conditioning arose when it was discovered that many stimuli that can reinforce operant performances will also change the magnitude of these physiological activities. Biofeedback experiments in the clinic and laboratory are designed to give the subject some control over his physiological reactions. Physiological responses, such as heart rate or blood pressure, are monitored moment to moment by appropriate instruments, and a reinforcing stimulus occurs contingent on the increased or decreased magnitudes of response. Usually the subject sees or hears a tone, light, or meter reading that changes in pace with the changes in the physiological response. When conditioning occurs, it is seen as a change in the heart rate or blood pressure. The data seems clear that many such procedures do influence the physiological responses.[5] The mechanism of the changes, however, is still open to discovery. The obvious differences between operants and reflexes remain. Reflexes have a form that is largely fixed phylogenetically; the important measurement of the reflex is its magnitude and latency; and the reflex has its major effect within the individual's internal economy. This is in contrast to the operant, which has a form shaped fluidly over a wide range of topographies by the way it acts on and alters the external environment.

Research in this area received impetus from two directions. The first, essentially practical, concerned the applications of the biofeedback as a way to improve health and prevent disease. The discovery of biofeedback in the human and animal laboratory is connected with the clinical observations and theories of how psychological factors contribute to diseases such as heart failure and high blood pressure. If it is indeed possible to alter physiological activity markedly by reinforcement—and the evidence in that direction appears overwhelming—then some part of human suffering, such as allergies, circulatory diseases, psychomotor tension, headache, pain, and ingestive dysfunction, must be so caused. Thus, the biofeedback research has focused on its potential for selectively controlling patterns of physiological response that can contribute to the management of psychophysical disorders.

The second theoretical area of impetus for research concerns whether or not operant and respondent conditioning could be subsumed under a common process. Historically, no differentiation was made between operant and respondent conditioning by either Pavlov, who first discovered conditioning, or Watson, who extended the concept from Pavlov's experiments on dogs to human problems. Even the complex theoretical formulations of Clark Hull described operant and reflex conditioning by the same formula. Thoughts about their different properties did not begin until Skinner elaborated the technical properties of operant behavior. Yet, for many psychologists the tension remained and the drive to achieve a common formulation of the two kinds of conditioning received encouragement from the experiments showing it was possible to increase the magnitude of a reflex response by following it with a reinforcer. But to prove that the reinforcement mechanisms were identical, it needed to be shown that the conditioning of the reflex was not mediated by some operant behavior. For example, it is possible to influence one's heart rate by holding one's breath, exercising, or even talking to oneself. If a change in physiological activity is a positively or negatively reinforcing outcome, then such a change will increase the frequency of operants that produce or avoid them. Such mediating operant behavior may be very difficult to observe because there are often important factors that reduce their magnitude, perhaps even to covert levels. The mediation of operant reinforcement of reflexes was dealt with in animal conditioning experiments by paralyzing the animals with curare and maintaining their respiration artificially.[6] It was presumed that the curarized animals could not emit operant performances. Unfortunately, the curare preparations involved so many difficult methodological problems that these experiments were neither replicable nor easily interpretable.[7,8] Thus, despite the original rush of enthusiastic reaction to them, it was not possible to rule out the possibility that operant reinforcement of reflex reponses was complicated by some performance that occurred incidentally. The mechanism by which the reflexes could be maintained through interactions with operants could be a chain of behaviors like those mentioned above in which the eliciting stimulus for the reflex reinforces an operant performance. The reinforcement of reflexes in a chain of operant behaviors will be covered in Chapter 6.

## questions

1. Explain the historical circumstances that encourage the tendency to equate operant and respondent behavior.
2. Describe how the colloquial language about reflex and operant behaviors confuses them.
3. Discuss why the distinction between operant and reflex aspects of food deprivation is of great importance in describing how people

control their own eating activities, particularly in respect to dieting.

4. Why is successive approximation a procedure unique to operant performances and inappropriate to reflexes?

5. How do the significant measurements in the reflex differ from those of operant performances?

6. In what sense do reflexes and operant behaviors operate in different directions?

7. In what sense is the reflex a behavioral event despite the prominence of the action of physiological organs?

8. How do the significant measurements in the reflex differ from those of operant performances?

9. What are the indications of a strong reflex and how does this compare with the parallel variations in operant behavior?

10. Describe some of the conditions where operant performances superficially appear to be like respondent behavior.

11. Why is it difficult to determine whether crying is reflex or operant behavior?

12. What data would be necessary to determine whether crying were operant or reflex behavior?

13. Describe how sucking changes from a reflex to an operant.

14. Describe how Piaget's experiment with the newborn infant's feeding illustrates how an initially reflex performance changes its function to that of an operant.

15. How do biofeedback experiments illustrate the relationship between operant and reflex behaviors?

16. Why is it difficult to interpret the results of experiments that attempt to reinforce reflex responses operant-wise?

---

## part III: the behavior of operant and reflex behavior

### simultaneous control by a stimulus

It is useful to keep in mind the differences between operant and reflex behavior because these two types of behavior frequently occur simultaneously and are often interrelated. Movements bring an individual into contact both with stimuli that are conditioned and unconditioned reflexes. For example, a person's performance of walking about is reinforced operantly by changes in location. Such operant activity also brings about the possibility of stepping on a tack. Thus, when a person steps on a sharp tack, a reflex is elicited as a result of an operant behavior that brought the foot down on the tack. An actor might deliberately expose himself to onion vapors (an operant performance), in which case the eliciting stimulus for the secretion of tears (onion vapors) is the product of an operant performance.

Operant performances also produce conditioned reflexes. In the examples of a rat pressing a bar or the pigeon stepping on a treadle, conditioned reflexes were incidentally established when the operation of the food dispenser produced a light and sound paired with the delivery of food. Since these stimuli occurred simultaneously with the delivery of food, and within a second or two of ingestion, the necessary elements for establishing a condition reflex were present. The light and sound accompanying the delivery of food were analogous to the conditioned stimuli that elicited conditioned responses, in Pavlov's classic experiments. Food is the unconditioned stimulus and salivation and other digestive reflexes are the unconditioned responses. Therefore, the light and sound of the feeder had two simultaneous functions. First, they served as the instant and immediate reinforcer for the operant performance they followed, such as stepping on the treadle. In addition, these stimuli elicited salivation and other digestive reflexes because they were also paired with food being present in the dog's mouth.

## how an operant performance produces a conditioned stimulus for reflexes

Lying is an example of an operant behavior that becomes closely connected with reflex responses. The basis for the elicitation of reflexes arises when, for example, a child is spanked after he or she lies. The spanking elicits a wide range of reflex responses including changes in heart rate, breathing pattern, skin resistance, blood pressure, and hormone secretions. At first, these reflexes will also come under the control of the place where the spanking took place and the person who did the spanking. If lying is repeatedly punished, instances of the verbal performance (the lie) will assume the properties of a conditioned stimulus eliciting the same responses that occur when the person is punished. The pairing of the verbal performance with the unconditioned responses elicited by spanking establishes it as a conditioned stimulus.

The lie detector is a physiological recorder. It gives a graphic record of breathing pattern, blood pressure, and heart action while the person is being interviewed. The effectiveness of the lie detector is predicated on a conditioning history where the subject's verbal behavior functions as conditioned stimuli because it has been previously paired with events that elicited strong reflexes. It is presumed that most people have been punished frequently enough when they have lied in early life so that the emission of verbal performances similar to those that have been previously punished will elicit the reflexes associated with the aversive stimuli that occurred with punishment. Thus, a verbal performance that has the characteristics of a lie becomes a conditioned stimulus because it has been paired with the occurrence of an aversive stimulus, or punishment. The conditioned stimuli in lie detector tests differ from those, say, of the Pavlovian type of experiment because the conditioned stimulus is the individual's own behavior, rather than an external stimulus such as a buzzer or metronome. This difference need not cause any special problem, since once an individual emits a performance it is an event that the person (or anyone else) can react to. In fact, one is in a unique position to react to one's own behavior, since contact with the stimulus is closer.

The usefulness of the lie detector depends, of course, on whether the individual has had the required history of punishment. Many people without this history of reflex conditioning will be able to "fool" the detector. The records are also difficult to interpret since almost any kind of emotional disruption, such as anger, surprise, anxiety, or a special reaction to the interviewer, will influence the record as much as lying.

## fixed-action patterns

*Fixed-action patterns* are a bridge between behaviors such as the reflex that operates mainly on the internal environment, and operant behavior. They share with reflexes their relatively fixed structure and their elicitation by a narrowly specified stimulus, called a *releasing stimulus* by ethologists. Fixed-action patterns function like operants because they alter the external environment substantially, often complexly, and in ways that are important for the individual's and the species' adaptation and survival.

Some examples of these fixed-action patterns will clarify how they are different from both operants and reflexes. Red squirrels have a complex pattern of hiding nuts by scratching a hole in the ground with their paws, tamping the nut into the ground with the snout, covering the nut with the earth and then packing the earth down. An experiment was carried out that showed the relatively fixed structure and elicited nature of these behaviors.[9] Squirrels, raised in wire mesh cages on a liquid diet and without nesting materials, were tested two months later by giving them nuts in their cages. They went through all of the movements of burying the nuts even though there was no earth with which nuts could be buried in a normal manner. When exposed to an earthen floor, the animals buried the nuts in the soil and, with further practice, learned how to cover them efficiently. In another experiment, squirrels, isolated at birth from an experience with nuts, gnawed them when first exposed to them later in life, even though the meat inside had been removed.

Let us look at other examples. When the herring gull lays eggs for the first time, it uses its long curved bill to roll eggs back into the nest that have fallen out. From the very start, the bird carries out a scooping motion with its long curved bill that appears to strike the eggs in such a way as to move them toward the nest. The action pattern is elicited by "eggs out of the nest" and it ceases when the eggs are once more in the nest. The aggressive response of the male robin to another male is a fixed-action pattern elicited by the red feathers on it. If presented with a stuffed bird with the red feathers removed, the male robin does not attack. But it will attack a stuffed robin to which red feathers have been added.[10]

In another example, described by Tinbergen[11] the male three-spined stickleback fish will attack other males who have the bright red underbelly that members of the species develop during the mating season. The response is so specifically evoked by the stimulus, that even a wax model of a stickleback will evoke attack so long as its underbelly is painted red. These examples illustrate that not only is the fixed-action pattern inherited but also the effectiveness of the specific stimulus that elicits it.

In a procedure called imprinting, releasing stimuli do not evoke specific performances. Imprinting, originally described by Konrad Lorenz[12] in naturalistic studies of ducks, describes the circumstances by which the newly hatched ducklings come to follow their mothers and how they distinguish their mothers from other adult ducks. Lorenz discovered that ducklings who normally follow their mothers away from the nest within a day or two after they are hatched will also follow another adult duck if it is substituted for the mother. He then reared ducklings himself and discovered that they will follow whichever object is present at hatching, whether the mother, a moving object, or Lorenz himself. Further experimentation uncovered the information that there is a critical period of a few hours just after the duckling is hatched in which the duckling will follow any moving object present during the critical period, just as the duckling followed Lorenze when he was present at the time of hatching. Although imprinting has been studied mainly with birds, it also occurs with mammals of various species.

These fixed-action patterns are the field of ethology that deals with largely inherited behavioral patterns in the animal's natural environment. Not only are organisms born with relatively fixed-action patterns, but these complex sequences of activities are often elicited by specific, highly configurated stimuli, the releasing stimuli, rather than being emitted in the manner of the operants of Chapter 1.

The same kinds of action patterns described above that had important biological consequences, such as sex, feeding, and defense, can occur "for their own sake" in play. Dogs, for example, play-fighting each other, carry out the fixed-action patterns of fighting except that they never bite each other. Their tails wag and the pattern can shift at any moment to some other form of play. The playful fighting will occur until physical exhaustion sets in, as contrasted with sexual, defensive, or feeding patterns that end when the aggressor is fended off, the sexual behavior consummated, or the food eaten. Primates have been shown to work for an opportunity to be able to look about them or to observe novel visual scenes.[13] Ordinary events, such as a view of another animal or the normal kaleidoscope of visual stimulation that is incidental to daily experience, were powerful reinforcers that could maintain a high frequency of pressing a key. Similar experiments also showed that an opportunity to do a puzzle is also an effective reinforcer.[14] Pigeons will peck a key a large number of times when pecks are reinforced by an opportunity to spend time in a larger rather than a smaller space. All these types of behavior illustrate activities in which reinforcement is a direct byproduct of inherited patterns of responses.

Because so many behavior principles were discovered with simple operant performances of animals, such as rats and pigeons, it might be thought that all of an organism's behavior is derived from food reinforcement or other consequences that maintain the organism's physiological equilibrium. Clearly, the kinds of behaviors described above also involve substantial portions of many organisms' repertoires.

## the interaction between fixed-action patterns and the processes of operant reinforcement

Fixed-action patterns and physiological mechanisms are adaptations to the environment just like operants. Both avenues of adaptation accomplish reproduction, digestion, rearing of the young, escape from predators, and so forth. Virtually all fixed-action patterns illustrate the interaction of behavior and the environment. The fixed-action pattern of gnawing a hole in a nut offers one example of such an interaction.[15] To start with, most squirrels gnaw a round hole in the nut. The fibers of the shell run parallel to each other, however, and the shell is more easily fractured and penetrated if the squirrel gnaws along these natural lines of fracture. Squirrels whose only experience was with nuts that had been emptied of meat still learned to split the nut efficiently, reinforced by access to the inside of the empty shell. The physical characteristics of the nut constituted a natural reinforcer that shaped topographies of gnawing that split the nut most efficiently. The splitting activity is another example of an operant performance defined by the effect on the environment that is its reinforcer. The inherited fixed-action pattern determines that the squirrel will gnaw the nut, but the physical makeup of the nut is a natural reinforcer that shapes the final most efficient performance. Eventually, of course, the meat inside the nut will be the major consequence that will maintain the gnawing behavior.

The fixed-action pattern of the herring gull, described in the previous section, is shaped operant-wise by its immediate reinforcer—the movement of the eggs toward the nest. The movements will become more efficient because those beak movements that contact the egg most securely and move it most efficiently in the required direction increase in frequency and the others decrease. In other words, given the movement of the egg toward the nest as a reinforcer, the operant principles of successive reinforcement will shape an efficient form of the behavior. That the bird scoops the eggs at all is determined by the inheritance of the fixed-action pattern. The maintenance and refinement of the repertoire is determined by the operant principles of successive approximation, chaining, intermittent reinforcement, and so forth.

Nest building is another example in which the phylogenetic and ontogenetic influences on behavior are complexly and closely intertwined. The reason why building the nest in the first place is reinforcing is to be found in the animal's inherited history, including hormonal influences. But, given the particular species and hormonal influences, the actual behavior of building the nest is determined by the principles of reinforcement. The species determines *what* outcome is reinforcing and some of the forms of behavior that are involved. But the actual behaviors that are emitted are maintained by their immediate consequences. A bird grasping a straw in the beak is reinforced by the straw's change in location. Given a disposition to build a particular kind of nest, the bird still requires a repertoire that allows it to grasp straws of various sizes lying in various positions on the ground and to adjust its orientation so that it is inserted so as to produce the required shape and size. Although the final reinforcer, the completed nest, is phylogenetically determined, the principles of operant reinforcement control the moment-to-moment constituent activities.

A bird swooping on its prey illustrates the same component processes. That a particular prey at a distance should evoke swooping is determined by the phylogenetic history. The adjustments of the course of flight continuously with the position and direction of the prey are components of operant behaviors already acquired by the bird.

The basic phenomenon of imprinting is present at birth without benefit of postnatal experience. Yet, the process still involves the operation of operant reinforcement principles in important ways. Once the newborn organism follows the mother, the process of behavioral control described in the preceding and following chapters becomes operative. For the repertoire of following the parent to be functional, the imprinted animal needs to learn to recognize its parent from other individuals, at different distances, and from various perspectives. Environmental obstacles will require adaptive patterns of following reinforced by the maintenance of proximity to the parent. Thus the two kinds of behavioral influence operate in complement to each other. The imprinting process establishes a particular individual as a reinforcer that will shape and maintain activity that keeps the newborn in proximity to the adult. The operant processes involving the current influence from the environment account for *how* the required performances are shaped and maintained.

Despite the equal importance of biological and experiential factors, a behavioral analysis has a temporal priority. Before we determine that hormonal factors, actions of the nervous system, or inherited behavioral dispositions have importance for the animal's adaptation, we need to know how the animal's behavior brings it into contact with the relevant parts of the environment that have reinforced it. Thus, the processes of mating, care of the young, escape from predators, and feeding are the ultimate expression of the total biological structure. But the maintenance of these behaviors, despite their dependence on physiological substrates, depends on the environment that poses the demands for the adaptive responses.

## fixed-action patterns as building blocks for early infant development

Fixed-action patterns supply the groundwork for normal development in human as well as in animal behavior. The playful fighting of the dogs described earlier provides the basis for the development of complex behavioral interaction between male and female dogs that is an essential component of the courting behavior required for adult mating.

For the human infant, behavioral development begins with the activity of the mouth, such as the emergence of sucking as an operant as exemplified in Piaget's observations presented earlier in the chapter. Behaviors such as sucking, which emerge initially as reflexes and shift their function to operants, are aptly thought of as building blocks from which the later operant repertoire emerges. The child's initial repertoire consists of two innate components. The first, a rooting response of moving the head side to side, is evoked by tactile stimulation around the mouth area. The second is a sucking reflex evoked by touching the lips. These reflexes serve the important function of energizing movements of the head until the lips contact the nipple where sucking can produce milk.

Given an inherited behavioral pattern of sucking the breast or fingers, what begins as reflexive behaviors or a fixed-action pattern soon comes under the discriminative control of the environment and is shaped by its effectiveness. To begin with, the infant begins sucking when its cheek is stroked by the parent's hand or by the mother's breast in the vicinity of its mouth. The behavioral pattern is rapidly subject to differential reinforcement, as the contact of the mucosa of the mouth with the nipple differentially reinforces those movements of the head that bring about contacts that in turn elicit sucking.

Beginning with the innate tendency to suck when a finger enters the mouth, the natural relation between the arm and hand movements and the contact of the mouth differentially reinforces those movements that bring about sucking. At a later stage, the movements come under the discriminative control of the visual observations of the hand. The result is a repertoire of hand movement, coordination, and a fine-grain adjustment of the hand to the sucked object. The repertoire that is achieved constitutes a general one that can change the child's environment in other ways, such as moving the hands over the blanket, reinforced by the tactual stimulation from touching the smooth texture of the blanket hem. Even the actual fixed-action pattern becomes differentially reinforced as the flow of milk from the breast or bottle differentially reinforces the manner and magnitude of sucking.

Smiling, like sucking, represents a shift in the control of a performance from reflex to operant. Initially, smiling is evoked as a reflex response to the stroking of the infant's cheek or to moving objects in the child's field of vision, such as the movement of the features of the mother's face, or to other moving stimuli. The mother's face, however, has a special salience for the infant and very early in its development evokes a more extended smile in the infant than the fleeting one that appears soon after birth. Almost without exception, the pleasurable gurgling and smiling are an especially effective stimuli for the parent who will emit whatever behavior that will make the infant smile. We cannot assume, however, that the parent's reaction reinforces smiling operant-wise. It is likely that the child's smile is being evoked as a reflex, particularly during early infancy. Whether elicited as a reflex or emitted as an operant, the infant's smile will increase the frequency of all those items of the parental repertoire that induce smiling. Thus, the first maintenance of smiling does not require that the parent's reaction reinforces smiling as an operant performance. From the mother's part, putting her face close to the infant's face and moving her facial features in a lively manner will be reinforced because it evokes a smiling response, however reflexive, from the child. The child, relaxed and positively engaged with the mother, will be in a state where smiling is not likely to be preempted by more compelling activities.

The kind of behavioral analysis set out above confirms the importance of close parenting during the child's first year. Relationships in which smiling is prominent for the parent will also be ones where there will be lots of interaction involving positive reinforcers. Thus, the child's disposition to smile later in adulthood may not be so much a result of its direct reinforcement in infancy as it is a byproduct of a pattern of child-parent interaction that involves much "playful" reinforcement.

The importance of childhood patterns of playful interactions with the parent for the development of the complex, adult repertoire was shown in experiments where monkeys were raised in isolation from the normal and social and physical environment.[16] Not only were they denied an opportunity to interact with other monkeys, but they were deprived of all visual and auditory stimulation except a diffuse light. It was found that their behavioral development was permanently deficient. They lacked motor and perceptual development, failed to mate, and could not develop social relations with other animals.

Ethological observations of the early development of the polecat illustrate the same debilitating effects of early deprivation.[17] In normal development, polecats play with each other by grasping each other by the neck in a way that immobilizes the playmate. This pattern of behavior occurs later in sexual activity and in killing prey. Animals deprived of an opportunity for this kind of play during early development turned out to be retarded in both sexual behavior and in the activity of hunting prey.

## constraints on responses and stimuli

Fixed-action patterns from the animal's inherited history provide some serious constraints on the assumption that behavior is determined solely by the reinforcer maintaining it and that topographies of one performance or another are equivalent.

Certain performances do not appear to be as susceptible to operant reinforcement as others. Observations by psychologists who undertook the practical task of training animals for advertising displays provide dramatic examples.[18] For one advertising display, they attempted to train a pig and a raccoon, by food reinforcement, to insert coins into a piggybank. They discovered that the raccoon persistently rubbed the coins together and the pig repeatedly dropped and rooted them instead of inserting them into the automatic food dispenser. Here, fixed-action patterns from the animals' evolutionary history preempted the behavior for considerable periods of time despite high levels of food deprivation. Attempts to reinforce the grooming behaviors of cats with food encountered similar results. Experimenters observed that either the grooming response was perfunctory and minimal or the normal species-specific behavior patterns of grooming took over at the expense of ignoring the food delivery. Attempts to reinforce a bird's preening behavior with food encountered a bias such as those above. The topography of the preening behavior that emerged was very different from the inherited fixed-action pattern, reinforced by the amelioration of the condition of the feathers. Attempts to reinforce fighting behavior in pigeons and rats have similar constraints. In these experiments, as with grooming, the fighting behavior was either perfunctory or developed into a full blown attack pattern, more than what was needed for reinforcement. As with the attempts to operantly reinforce grooming, the fixed-action pattern that emerges often preempted eating the food from the automatic dispenser.

At the other extreme, it proved virtually impossible to reinforce yawning through operant reinforcement procedures with a dog.[19] Opening the mouth increased in frequency, but the specific character of yawning, including the complex pattern of mouth and face movements coupled with the large intake of air into the lungs, was lacking. Electric shock appears to reinforce some performances more readily than others, particularly topographies such as running and jumping, which are similar to the elicited patterns. Pressing a lever, negatively reinforced by terminating an electric shock, in comparison, is much more difficult to instate than these other performances that are related more naturally to shock.[20] The experiments suggested that the major control by electric shock was specific performance, such as running, jumping, and crouching. Pressing a lever, even though reinforced by the termination of the shock, is conditioned with greater difficulty because it does not have a natural relation to the behaviors elicited by shock.

These observations show not all muscle movements are equally susceptible to conditioning through operant reinforcement, particularly those with strong connections to phylogenetically determined fixed-action patterns. The preceding examples show that there is a continuum of modifiability for a performance by the environment, depending on the predominance of the fixed-action patterns relative to the operant processes that the changing environment imposes.

The phylogenetic history of the particular species also provides constraints on the way in which individuals are more readily controlled by one aspect of the environment than another. This is in contradiction to an assumption that it is not crucial in a psychological learning experiment whether we prompt reinforcement contingencies by a light or tone. Both assumptions, however, are essentially correct. It *is* possible to study the process of learning with one stimulus or another. At the same time, however, it is self-evident that the inherited characteristics of an individual of a particular species influence the sensitivity, preference, and utility of various stimulus modalities. Birds are attentive and sensitive to visual stimuli, including color and form. In contrast, rats and dogs lack color vision and build most of their repertoire on smell and other nonvisual stimuli. Obviously, if we present a dog with a compound stimulus having a visual and olfactory component, it is the odor that will control its behavior, while in the case of the bird the visual stimulus will overshadow the olfactory one. The reinforcer also determines the predominance of one stimulus modality over another. There is evidence with pigeons[21] and rats[22] that when performances controlled by a tone-light compound are negatively reinforced by avoidance of shock, the tone element dominates. In comparison, when the performance is positively reinforced by food, the light element gets attention.

## autoshaping

The phenomenon of *autoshaping* presents another blurring of the distinctive processes of operant and reflex conditioning. In autoshaping, carried out mostly with pigeons pecking a key with food reinforcement, the response key is illuminated periodically and followed by the operation of the food magazine.[23] It was discovered that pigeons will peck the key if the key light illumination preceded food delivery, even though the food presentation does not follow and is not dependent upon the peck. The similarity of the procedure to Pavlovian procedure has led many theorists to the view that the pecking there occurs as a result of reflex conditioning. This view is further strengthened by the phenomenon of omission training.[24] In that procedure, a peck on the lighted key prevents the presentation of food so that the operant reinforcement of key-pecking cannot occur. Even with this procedure, key-pecking is reliably maintained.

The procedure and process described by autoshaping conforms exactly to the paradigm for reflex conditioning. The lighted key, paired with the presentation of grain, elicits the same response, pecking, ordinarily occurring to the grain. Experiments comparing pecks that are autoshaped by food and water provide further evidence of the connection of the pecking response to fixed-action patterns elicited by food and water.[25] It was discovered in these experiments that with food delivery, birds pecked sharply, vigorously, and with their beaks open, while with water they made a slower, more sustained contact with the beak closed, often accompanied by swallowing movements. These are the response patterns that occur when a bird eats and drinks respectively. Whatever the outcome of the theoretical questions about whether autoshaping can be explained as instances of Pavlovian conditioning, it is very clear that the pigeon's peck is a basic part of its biological inheritance. As such, it has many of the attributes of fixed-action patterns with important connections to its phylogenetic origin. The pigeon's peck is basic to its daily existence. It feeds, fights, defends itself, and carries out various manipulations of the environment, such as overturning leaves, uncovering seeds, and preening by pecking. Furthermore, it has the status of an observing response since pigeons tend to look close up at objects, by pecking at them. That the same performance is amenable to two kinds of conditioning has led to the adoption of autoshaping as a way to instate pecking for operant conditioning experiments with pigeons. The autoshaping method has the advantage

of being a standard specifiable procedure in place of the skillful adjustment required for operant shaping.

## why does a reinforcer increase
## the frequency of a performance?

One reason that explains why particular events are effective reinforcers
is the animal's phylogenetic (inherited) history. For example, the phylogenetic history of a cow disposes it to eat grass. Thus, to reinforce a cow,
we give it grass. The phylogenetic history of a pigeon disposes it to eat
grain, which is therefore an effective reinforcer of pigeon behavior. However, the particular behavior the grain will reinforce depends on the bird's
current environment. If we have the appropriate reinforcer for each animal, however, functionally identical environments may be used to reinforce functionally identical behavior.

Whatever the reasons for a reinforcer increasing the frequency of a
performance, such as the neural and physiological events that occur internally, the reinforcer is an environmental cause of the behavior because it
is a manipulatable event by which the behavior is created, strengthened,
or weakened. Naturally, all the behavior of an organism is ultimately
rooted in its phylogenetic history, but it is convenient to distinguish between those variables that are largely determined by the inherited history
of the animal (phylogeny) and those that are determined by its interaction
with the environment (ontogeny).

We may also inquire about the physiological factors within the individual's internal biological system, which are the substrate for the reinforcement processes. For example, one might investigate the point in the chain
of digestive events at which reinforcement occurs when a pigeon eats
grain or a rat a food pellet. Experiments have been carried out to separate
the reinforcing effect of the receipt of food from its subsequent digestion
and metabolism by surgical procedures that prevented food from reaching
the stomach. This was done by disconnecting the esophagus from the
stomach so that food that is eaten can be chewed and swallowed but
cannot enter the stomach.[26] In general, however, it is difficult to separate
the reinforcing effects of food from the digestive, metabolic, and neural
events that follow. The prevailing evidence is that these questions are of
more use and interest for physiologists in relation to their attempts to
understand the functions of the physiological organ systems than it is for
psychologists who are interested in describing and understanding the
interaction of the individual with his environment. Physiological psychologists have also tried to simulate the neural correlates of reinforcement by
directly stimulating the brain electrically.[27] It is not clear, however, that
the reinforcing effects of brain stimulation applied directly to the cortex

are related to the neurological effects of reinforcers such as food, escape from bright light, or an opportunity to exercise or play.

We cannot assume that all human behavior is based on events that have a homeostatic physiological effect, such as eating, defense against aversive consequences, or sex. There is ample evidence that many simple, direct effects on the environment, completely unrelated to important physiological regulatory mechanisms may maintain behavior significantly. Just as we do not have any useful answers to the question about why food is an effective reinforcer, we can ignore *why* the movement of a ball forms and shapes the corresponding movements of the child. The question is best bypassed by viewing the complementary ways that we can understand these behaviors. The one set, involving the organism's developmental and phylogenetic history, are matters outside the scope of a psychological analysis, regardless of their importance. Given an intact organism of a given phylogenetic history, the answer to questions about where its behavior comes from can best be answered at present by indicating the environmental interactions that generated it.

Other reinforcers that do not appear to be connected to a person's metabolic equilibrium are access to space, play, an opportunity to exercise, attachment of infants to parents, and stimulation from viewing new scenes.

# questions

1. How may an operant performance serve as a conditioned stimulus for a reflex?
2. State what properties of operant behaviors associated with lying make them susceptible to Pavlovian conditioning.
3. What is a fixed-action pattern? Give an example.
4. Describe how the squirrel's behavior, splitting nuts, was controlled by the fixed-action pattern rather than by the meat inside the nut.
5. Describe how the egg-retrieval behavior of the herring gull represents the combined effect of an inherited behavior and reinforcement of the constituent operant performances.
6. Describe how imprinting and fixed-action patterns represent the combined operation of inherited behavioral patterns and operant reinforcement principles.
7. Contrast a playful activity with its topographically similar counterpart that is physiologically important.

*8.* How does play serve an adaptive function in the growth and development of the young?

*9.* Describe the behavioral deficits that occur when there is a restricted opportunity to play.

*10.* How does nest building illustrate the combined influences of operant behavior, fixed-action patterns, and phylogenetically determined factors?

*11.* Describe the reflexive and operant aspects of smiling in the newborn infant's interaction with its parent.

*12.* What observations did the Brelands make in training pigs and raccoons that challenge the assumption that operant performances were equivalent in their modifiability to reinforcement?

*13.* What are other examples of topographies of behavior that have limited modifiability by operant reinforcement?

*14.* Describe autoshaping.

*15.* What place do physiological explanations of behavior have in psychology?

*16.* How do we answer the question, "Why does a reinforcer increase the frequency of the performance that it follows?"

# notes

[1]Sherrington, C. S. *The integrative action of the nervous system.* New Haven: Yale University Press, 1906.

[2]Beaumont, W. *Experiments on the gastric juice and the physiology of digestion.* Plattsburgh, N.Y., F. P. Arlens, 1833.

[3]Wolf, S. and Wolff, H. G. *Human gastric function.* New York: Oxford University Press, 1943 and 1947.

[4]Piaget, J. *The origins of intelligence in children.* New York: W. W. Norton, 1963, pp. 25–27.

[5]Pomerleau, O. F. and Brady, J. P. *Behavioral medicine: Theory and practice.* Baltimore: Williams and Wilkins, 1979.

[6]Miller, N. E. and DiCara, L. V. Instrumental learning of urine formation by rats: changes in renal blood flow. *American Journal of Physiology.* 215: 677–683, 1968.

[7]Pomerleau, O. F. and Brady, J. P. *Behavioral medicine: Theory and practice.* Baltimore: Williams and Wilkins, 1979.

[8]Mackintosh, N. J. *The psychology of animal learning.* London: Academic Press, 1974.

[9]Eibel-Eibelsfeldt, I. Concepts of ethology and their significance in the study of behavior. In: Stevenson, H. W., Hess, E. H., and Rheingold, H. S. *Early behavior: Comparative and developmental approaches.* New York: Wiley, 1967.

[10]*Lack, D. The life of the robin.* London: Penguin Books, 1953.

[11]Tinbergen, N. *The study of instinct.* London: Oxford University Press, 1951.

[12]Lorenz, K. *Studies in animal and human behavior, Vol. 1.* London: Methuen, 1970.

[13]Butler, R. Curiosity in monkeys. *Scientific American* 190: 70, 1954.

[14]Creed, T. L. and Ferster, C. B. Space as a reinforcer in a free-operant environment. *Psychological Record* 22: 161–167, 1972.

[15]Eibl-Eibesfeldt, I. *Ethology, The biology of behavior,* 2nd edition. New York: Holt, Rinehart & Winston, 1975.

[16]Harlow, H. F. Social deprivation in monkeys. *Scientific American* 207: 136–146, 1962.

[17]Breland, K. and Breland, M. The misbehavior of organisms. American Psychologist, 16: 681–684, 1961.

[18]Eibel-Eibelsfeldt, I. Concepts of ethology and their significance in the study of behavior. In: Stevenson, H. W., Hess, E. H., and Rheingold, H. S. *Early behaviors: Comparative and developmental approaches.* New York: Wiley, 1967.

[19]Konorski, J. *Integrative activity of the brain.* Illinois: University of Chicago Press, 1967.

[20]Bolles, R. C. Species specific defense reactions and avoidance learning. *Psychological Review* 73: 32–82, 1970.

[21]Foree, D. D. and LoLordo, V. M. Attention in the pigeon: Differential effects of food-getting versus shock-avoidance procedures. *Journal of Comparative and Physiological Psychology* 85: 551–558, 1973.

[22]Schindler, C. W. and Weiss, S. J. The influence of positive and negative reinforcement on selective attention. Presented at meetings of the Eastern Psychological Association, Washington, D. C. 1978.

[23]Brown, P. L. and Jenkins, H. M. Autoshaping of the pigeon's key-peck *Journal of the Experimental Analysis of Behavior* 11: 1–8, 1968.

[24]Williams, D. K. and Williams, H. Automaintenance in the pigeon. *Journal of the Experimental Analysis of Behavior* 12: 511–520, 1969.

[25]Jenkins, H. M. and Moore, B. R. The form of the autoshaped response with food or water reinforcers. *Journal of the Experimental Analysis of Behavior* 20:163–181, 1973.

[26]Hull, C. L., Livingston, J. R., Rouse, R. O., and Barker, A. N. True, sham and esophageal feeding as reinforcements. *Journal of Comparative and Physiological Psychology,* 44: 412–422, 1951

[27]Delgado, J. M. R., Roberts, W. W., and Miller, N. E. Learning motivated by electrical stimulation of the brain. *American Journal of Physiology,* 179: 587–593, 1954.

# aversive
# control

## study guide

The topic of aversive control was introduced in Chapter 1, where negative reinforcement was described as a way to increase the frequency of an operant performance. Negative reinforcement will be elaborated in this chapter by describing some procedures and results of animal studies to illustrate details of the processes involved. After this, we will extend these principles to circumstances that occur in human behavior.

Besides increasing the frequency of performances that terminate it, an aversive stimulus may also be used as punishment, a term used both technically and in the common language. Punishment, technically, is limited to those situations where an aversive stimulus *follows* a specific performance. Shouting at a child when he picks up food with his fingers is punishment of eating with the fingers. We describe an electric shock following each of the rat's presses of the lever as punishment, whereas electric shocks occurring periodically regardless of what the animal is doing is not so described.

A stimulus may influence an organism's behavior in several ways, depending on how it is related to the specific activity. When a stimulus following a performance increases its frequency, we call it a positive reinforcer. When an aversive stimulus follows a performance, it may decrease the frequency of the performance, and we call it punishment. When a performance brings an aversive stimulus to an end, the frequency of the performance may increase, and we describe the action of the stimulus as negative reinforcement. Presenting an aversive stimulus may elicit reflexes in addition to its influence on behavior through punishment or negative reinforcement, since many aversive stimuli are the unconditioned stimuli for reflexes. Electric shock, for example, will elicit changes in breathing, heart rate, and blood pressure. Conditioned reflexes will occur also since many incidental stimuli, such as the place, will come to elicit the same reflexes as the electric shock. Because one kind of stimulus, such as an electric shock, can have such diverse influences on behavior, it is important to describe the exact manner in which an aversive stimulus influences particular items of conduct.

Aversive stimuli are sometimes derived from an individual's experience and they are of two basic kinds: 1) stimuli that are aversive because they precede or set the occasion for a primary aversive stimulus; and 2) stimuli that are aversive because they signal a reduction in positive reinforcement. Most instances of aversive control in human behavior involve such derived aversive stimuli.

The most influential kinds of aversive control in the natural environment occur in social interactions. Despite the complexity of these situations where two persons are involved in an interaction, it is possible and useful to describe the component activities as positive and negative reinforcement of specific activities.

## technical terms

aversive stimulus
avoidance
conditioned aversive stimulus
contingency
escape

free-operant avoidance
pre-aversive stimulus
punishment
time out

## outline

Part I: Derived Aversive Stimuli
Conditioned aversive stimuli
Aversive stimuli derived from the withdrawal of positive reinforcement
Interrupting a chain of behavior as an aversive stimulus
Withdrawal reinforcement as a component in aversive control
The form of the aversive stimulus
Interruption of a chain of positively reinforced performances
Distinguishing between extinction and punishment

---

## part I: derived aversive stimuli

### conditioned aversive stimuli

The aversive stimuli that have been described in earlier chapters primarily have been those in which the aversive effects do not depend on the animal's special history or experience with the stimuli. In other words, the stimuli are aversive simply because the animal was born a member of a particular species. Bright lights are aversive stimuli for rats, and darkness is aversive for most birds, for example. Loud noises are especially aversive for most people, whereas birds are relatively insensitive to noise. Without any prior experience, turning off a bright light or an electric shock can reinforce a rat's lever-press; presenting the light and/or the shock after the performance would be punishment.

A buzzer preceding an electric shock can acquire the properties of an aversive stimulus through conditioning. This is the principle of *conditioned aversive control*. A stimulus that is paired with a primary aversive event or precedes it will also come to function as an aversive stimulus. Not only will the buzzer negatively reinforce an operant, it will exhibit all the other properties of aversive stimuli. It can be used as punishment to suppress a performance and it will influence the overall state of the organism in the sense of emotional disruption, just like primary aversive stimuli.

An important element in the process whereby a stimulus acquires conditioned aversive properties was presented in Chapter 2 when the conditioned reflex was discussed. The procedures for establishing a conditioned reflex and those for establishing a conditioned aversive stimulus are very similar. The conditioned reflex describes the way that the control of a reflex, frequently a physiological response, shifts from the original eliciting stimulus to a previously neutral stimulus. Blood pressure elicited by electric shock comes to be evoked by the buzzer that precedes the shock.

The behavioral control, on the other hand, concerns the frequency of an operant, negatively reinforced by the conditioned aversive stimulus, punished by it, or disrupted by the emotional state that is generated by it. Although we frequently do not measure the reflex and physiological changes elicited by conditioned aversive stimuli in ordinary day-to-day activities, we can presume that they are occurring. Our common language descriptions of behavior often confuse these two different effects of an aversive stimulus. We may especially notice our pounding heart or some-one else's pale face in a dangerous situation, yet the major effects are on operant behaviors. Performances that escape from the aversive situation increase in frequency and a general suppression or disruption of the ongoing operant repertoire will occur. Such broad changes in operant behavior that are caused by aversive or conditioned aversive stimuli will be discussed in the section on emotion in Chapter 4.

Most control by aversive stimuli in human behavior tends to be exercised by conditioned aversive stimuli, rather than the aversive event itself. The shift from primary aversive stimuli to conditioned aversive stimuli tends to occur because most aversive control is fairly predictable and occurs under special circumstances that tend to repeat themselves. A traffic light is a conditioned aversive stimulus partly because the performance of stopping is negatively reinforced by the avoidance of the impact with another car. The dentist's office serves as conditioned aversive stimuli. The sound of the drill that precedes a painful attack on the tooth nerve is an especially powerful conditioned aversive stimulus. Police attempt to control traffic accidents by using pictures of serious accidents. The sight of potentially noxious stimuli such as speeding cars, hot objects, high places, or sharp knives, acquire aversive properties because they occur contiguously with primary aversive stimuli. Demands or commands tend to be conditioned aversive stimuli because they specify an aversive event that will occur if some particular behavior is not emitted. The parent who makes the demand, "Pick up your toys," is an example. If the toys are not picked up, the child might be spanked. Subsequently, the child terminates such a threat (pre-aversive stimulus) by picking up the toys because the threat now has properties of the aversive event from which it derives its effect.

The effectiveness of such conditioned aversive stimuli as threats depends in large part on how closely they are correlated with the actual aversive event. With many parents, the conditioned aversive stimulus is a progressive event, the form of which changes continuously until the aversive event is finally delivered. The parent, for example, will first say, "Pick up your toys" in a mild voice. If the avoidance performance is not emitted, the demand is repeated a second or third time. Then the intensity increases, along with some change in the form and quality of the voice. Finally, at a high intensity, the spanking may occur if the child has not yet picked up the toys. The effectiveness of such a threat, of course, depends upon the stage at which it is actually followed by the aversive event. Eventually, the child distinguishes among the different forms of the threat. The early threats lose their conditioned aversive properties (extinction) because they are never followed by the aversive event. Hence, the avoidance or escape performance is postponed until the threat reaches a form that is consistently related to the spanking.

An animal experiment offers a useful analogue of this kind of interaction with a child. A bright light decreases slowly in intensity until a shock is delivered when the light goes out. Although the rat could restore the light to full brightness by pressing a lever, under most conditions the rat waits until the light was almost out before pressing. As with the buzzer and the rat, the effectiveness of the threat to the child depends on following it periodically with the aversive stimulus.

When we observe someone who frequently makes threats without actually achieving the intended control, it is likely that the threat is not followed by the aversive stimulus often enough. If the threat is never followed by the aversive consequences, it ceases to serve an aversive stimulus at all. As with conditioned positive reinforcers, the topography of the threat is arbitrary. This is illustrated by the aphorism, "Speak softly and carry a big stick." Most often, threats are emitted in anger or under other strong emotional states, but this correlation is not a necessary condition for the effective function of the threat. The emotional tone of most threats is probably a secondary factor that comes from a heightened disposition to punish under strong emotional states. Parents who are indisposed to punish a child may even consciously goad themselves into escalating their emotional state to make it possible to deliver the aversive stimulus that is intended to generate the avoidance or escape performances by which the child is controlled. From the child's point of view, the parent's extreme emotional state sets the occasion for when to act, as the dimming light that signaled the shock in the rat experiment described earlier.

Such phrases as "You should have warned me" or "There should be a stoplight there" indicate the usefulness and function of conditioned aversive stimuli in the natural environment. "It's cold outside" is a conditioned aversive stimulus that reinforces putting on a coat to avoid freezing. Conditioned aversive stimuli are also useful if they occur reliably in the environment. Since their absence signals safety, there is no likelihood of the occurrence of the aversive stimuli they are paired with. Given a choice, however, one would prefer to have someone provide this stimulus in the environment and will even seek it out as, for example, stationing a lookout. For example, "the boss is coming" is likely to be a conditioned aversive stimulus and will be terminated by the employee appearing to be working hard, thus avoiding the boss's wrath. Avoidance of potentially aversive events in the natural environment occurs by the same process, as for example, when we put our hand up to our face at an approaching object, handle a sharp knife or razor in a special way, or do not step off the curb into the street in heavy traffic.

## aversive stimuli derived from the withdrawal of positive reinforcement

Both the primary and conditioned aversive stimuli that have been described so far have a close connection with the phylogenetic history of the particular organism. Stimuli such as shock, extremes of heat and cold, light, loud noises, and physical trauma require no special history before they may negatively reinforce an operant performance, elicit general systemic reflexes, or influence the individual's emotional state. The kinds of aversive control that are derived from primary aversive stimuli occur mostly in interaction with the physical environment involving avoidance of sharp objects, extremes of temperature, loud noise, collisions with objects, injury from sharp tools, and hazards of high places. Despite the commonplace occurrence of these naturally occurring aversive stimuli, the most pervasive and disruptive kinds of aversive control in human behavior are based on a loss or reduction in positive reinforcement. Human social situations, in which one person can influence the reinforcers supporting the behavior of another person, are the places where such aversive control will be especially prominent.

The general form of the process is most simply illustrated by the animal experiments in which a stimulus correlated with extinction or a reduction in positive reinforcement is used to punish errors or to negatively reinforce some operant. In experiments with chimpanzees, for example, the aversive stimulus is established by reinforcing key-pressing with food in the presence of a tone and withholding reinforcement during intervals when the tone is turned off. As a result of the nonreinforcement of key presses during the silent periods, the frequency eventually falls to zero. The aversive properties of the silent periods derive from the chimpanzee's inability to obtain food by pressing the lever during the silent periods. Once the silent periods control a cessation of the key-pressing activity, they can be used to negatively reinforce or punish other activities. For example, if we provide a second key and arrange that pressing it postpones the next appearance of a silent period, we discover that we can condition a stable, persistent rate of avoidance behavior. The rate at which the chimpanzee will press the second key will be governed by how long it postpones the appearance of a silent period. The responsiveness of the avoidance key-pressing to the length of the postponement of the extinction period is evidence that its avoidance is a reinforcing consequence, that the removal of the opportunity to press the lever for food is indeed an aversive event, and that the stimulus indicating the extinction period is an aversive stimulus. The silence functions as an explicit stimulus that can be used as a reinforcement contingency to follow a specific performance exactly.

**Withdrawal of positive reinforcement in human behavior**  The withdrawal of reinforcement results in the conditioning of many aversive stimuli in human behavior. If a child is kept in her room for the afternoon, the incarceration is aversive because the confinement prevents the reinforcement of those behaviors that might otherwise occur, such as playing with other children, going outside, and having normal interactions with adults. The confinement and stimuli of the room are functionally analogous to the loss of reinforcement and the silent period of the chimpanzee experiment. Some parents use confinement as a negative reinforcer for picking up toys. If the child is incarcerated every time he fails to pick up his toys, the announcement of the incarceration is functionally parallel to a conditioned aversive stimulus based on the silent period. Both are aversive stimuli because their occurrence occasions a reduction or stopping of positive reinforcement. The performance of picking up the toys is negatively reinforced by the avoidance of incarceration and the escape from threats of it.

Fines, incarceration, anger, and ostracism are aversive stimuli because they prevent or preempt many performances that produce important reinforcers. Since money reinforces performances such as buying things in a store, its loss through a fine signals the loss of these reinforcers, and is functionally analogous to the period of nonreinforcement of key-pressing in the chimpanzee experiment. Prison incarceration has a similar effect because a person locked in a cell and restricted to a prison environment cannot go to a restaurant, buy clothes, have normal relations with the opposite sex, maintain a house or apartment, drive an automobile, walk in the country, or visit a nightclub. Incarceration in prison over a long period of time, however, might produce a different result from that of a brief stay. Over a protracted period of time, the behaviors and reinforcers within the prison environment would become the baseline for increases or decreases in positive reinforcement. Its aversiveness derives from the contrast between prison life and a realistic alternative of a richer environment elsewhere. Therefore, in actual practice, long-term incarceration might not be functionally parallel to the procedure in the chimpanzee experiment where there was a constant interaction between the avoidance performances and the opportunity to emit performances positively reinforced by food. This would be especially true for persons whose opportunities in the community were little better than prison life, and may be true also for the institutionalized mentally ill, mentally retarded, chronic offenders, and others who spend the larger portion of their lives in prison.

**Criticism as a derived aversive stimulus**   An especially prominent form of aversive control in human affairs is criticism. It is a powerful form of aversive control because nearly all the major reinforcers that maintain an individual's behavior involve interactions with other persons. In most cultures there is a broad correlation between a person's facial expressions, the general tone of his voice, and the likelihood that he will reinforce some behavior. An individual who frowns, shows anger, or criticism is, in general, one who is disinclined to provide positive reinforcement. In contrast, a person who is smiling is likely to reinforce rather than to extinguish or punish. When we criticize someone, we are essentially presenting a stimulus that specifies behavior that will produce a withdrawal of reinforcers from others. Thus, when we tell someone that his clothes are unpresentable, this statement is equivalent to saying that with these clothes the individual's interaction with the social environment will not be as effective in producing the reinforcers inherent in social interactions as it would be if he were better dressed. An applicant for a job is less likely to be successful if poorly dressed than if she is well dressed. A salesperson is more likely to make a sale if well groomed than if disheveled.

## withdrawal of reinforcement as a component of other aversive stimuli

There is an implication from ordinary observation of human behavior that aversive stimuli derived from a broad withdrawal of reinforcers inherent in social interactions have much greater impact than primary aversive stimuli. In fact, it is tempting to speculate that the higher one goes on the phylogenetic scale of development, the more prominent are the derived aversive stimuli as compared to primary ones. While it is possible to demonstrate that a period of time out from positive reinforcement may be used to punish errors in a discrimination procedure in pigeon experiments, it is only in experiments with primates that very much sensitivity to control by withdrawal of reinforcement has been demonstrated. Dogs appear to be an exception, perhaps because of the special breeding that has taken place as a result of their domestication. That there should be a correlation between the prominence of such derived aversive stimuli and the level of behavioral development seems reasonable since there needs to be an extensive repertoire maintained by a wide variety of reinforcers before their withdrawal can be a significant factor in an organism's daily life.

The relation between primary aversive stimuli and aversive effects derived from the withdrawal of reinforcers is exemplified when a parent spanks a young child. In such a situation, the effective aversive stimulus may be the discontinuation of positive reinforcement rather than the spanking itself. The parent who is disposed to punish a child is also indisposed to smile, show approval and affection, or interact positively. The function of the withdrawal of reinforcement as opposed to the spanking itself can be demonstrated in an experiment that can be carried out easily and informally with most children. The experiment consists of spanking the child vigorously but playfully, as in a game—smiling and indicating in every way that there is no disapproval of any aspect of the child's conduct. Under these conditions, most children may be spanked with sufficient force to sting the hand without any reaction from the child other than mild surprise and some confusion as to what the game is all about. The same or even a lesser degree of corporal punishment administered in other circumstances will produce crying, fear, and anxiousness.

The same issues bear on the analysis of why a child's crying is so aversive to parents. While part of the aversiveness of a child's crying may be derived from its loud noise, its important and extensive influence comes from more complicated interactions between the larger aspects of the child's and the parent's repertoires. First, the child's cry is aversive because it may indicate that the child is injured or ill. Not only do injury and illness present a situation where there is threat of loss of the child during the period of its incapacity, there is also the child's demand for relief of pain, the threat of the loss of the child, as well as the possible expense and trouble of treatment. More immediately, the child's crying interferes with the current reinforcers maintaining the parent's behavior. The interruption is functionally parallel to the discontinuation of reinforcement in the animal experiments. When the child cries, the parent may be forced to interrupt activities such as watching television, cooking, or sleeping. Crying children often generate elaborate avoidance behaviors in parents who carry out whatever attention is necessary to the child by ways of toys, feeding, or play in order to prevent the crying. The parents' actions are evidence of the aversiveness of a child's crying to a parent.

## the form of the aversive stimulus

The actual form of the stimulus is quite arbitrary when the aversiveness of a stimulus comes from the reinforcement contingencies associated with it. In general, a given culture is consistent about the occasions that signal reinforcement or extinction. Smiling individuals are inclined to reinforce, and frowning ones are not. The correlation is not, however, inevitable, and almost any form of a stimulus may be correlated with practically any condition of reinforcement. As an example, consider a social situation, such as a poker game, where all the usual correlations between reinforcement practices and facial or postural features are distorted. A smile on a player's face will have the contingencies associated with an aversive stimulus if a player smiles because he has a winning hand. In that case, the smile is an occasion when betting behavior of the other players is not likely to be reinforced. Persons in authority sometimes smile and assume a genial manner when they criticize or withdraw reinforcers. Because smiling and a genial manner usually occur with positive reinforcement, they reduce the emotional impact of the reinforcement withdrawal and hence minimize the disruptive effect of the emotional upset that might otherwise have occurred. The administrator can continue such practices without losing the effectiveness of his smile if he deals with people for brief periods. Ultimately, the aversively controlled person will distinguish between stimuli correlated with the actual reinforcement conditions and those that are irrelevant.

The form of aversive stimuli may vary markedly even from family to family. For example, in one family the phrase "dear" may signify a mood of a speaker in which there is a disposition to reinforce, but in another family it may be used to soften a criticism and hence have the correlations with reinforcement and extinctions characteristic of punishment. Its function there is to soften the impact of an aversive stimulus. In extreme cases, the correlation between social form and reinforcement practice may break down completely. Some parents may take very harsh action with children in an even, genial tone of voice, while in another family a parent who shouts, screams, and shows great anger and emotion may actually not interfere at all with the major reinforcers supporting the child's behavior.

Conversely, stimuli that are normally aversive may come to serve as positive reinforcers in situations where they precede or set the occasion for positive reinforcers. A simple animal experiment illustrates the properties of this process. The experiment begins with a rat that is pressing a bar because each performance is followed by food. The procedure is changed so that pressing the lever produces food only when the rat has received a very mild electric shock. The shock is mild enough that it simply sets the occasion for reinforcement rather than functioning aversively. Since the delivery of a food pellet occurs only after a shock, the frequency of pressing the lever soon falls to zero in the absence of shock. At this stage of the development of the process, the shock could be used as a reinforcer for some other performance, such as going to a rear corner of the cage.

A chain of behaviors occurs as follows: going to the right side of the cage leads to a very mild electric shock and this in turn is the occasion when pressing the lever can produce food. In this circumstance, the shock serves as a conditioned reinforcer similar in function to the click of the food dispenser in animal conditioning experiments. If the intensity of the shock is now slowly increased, it may reach intensities which would ordinarily generate a severe emotional disruption and generate avoidance and escape behavior. However, because its intensity has been gradually increased and because it sets the occasion for positive reinforcement with food, it remains a positive reinforcer. The operant behaviors, reinforced by food and occasioned by shock, become prepotent over the reflex and emotional effects of the shock. In a manner similar to the behavior described in this experiment, the functional effect of a parent spanking or shouting at a child may be reversed when the spanking or shouting set the occasion for the reinforcement of important behaviors. The dynamics of such a reversal may involve a parent who experiences guilt after punishing or shouting at a child and "makes up for it" by being especially supportive. Often the child collaborates in the process if he or she can generate sufficient guilt in the parent to produce the conflict of emotions. Clinical cases have been described where the attention of the parent is such a strong reinforcer that the parent's displeasure or even anger is preferred to no reaction or interaction. Such "masochism" becomes even more dramatically established when a parent reinforces positively *only* after a spanking.

## interruption of a chain of positively reinforced performances

Some kinds of derived aversive control are nonsocial. These occur because reinforcers that involve changing the physical environment occur in proportion to the number of performances that are emitted. Reaching a destination, for example, proceeds in proportion to the number of steps that are taken. Taking a wrong turn or direction is punished by the lengthening of the journey. More complex activities are chained to each other so that each provides the conditions for the next. The typist who makes an error must restart the page. The inappropriate performance of hitting the wrong key or typing the wrong line is punished by the resetting of the response requirement when the page has to be redone. The machinist making a complicated piece on a lathe or milling machine faces the same contingency of reinforcement. When he or she makes an error while working on a complicated pattern of machining, he or she will have to begin all over again. Children's games often have an aversive event of this form as part of the play. The aversive event is a physical displacement toward the start of the game in the form of taking several steps backward or moving a marker to the start position on a game board.

As in other behavioral processes, animal experiments have the essential features of this mode of aversive control. A pigeon matching-to-sample provided the baseline performance. A stimulus appeared on the center of three keys. When the bird pecked it, the two side keys lighted and food was delivered when the bird pecked at the side key that corresponded to the center one. At issue is the accuracy with which the bird pecks. If pecks at an incorrect key are punished by a brief period of darkness during which the bird cannot proceed with the activity, the accuracy improves. The bird matches to sample at a still higher level of accuracy when the food magazine operates after a fixed number of correct matches. But the highest level of accuracy occurs when each mismatch puts the bird back to the start of the fixed-number requirement.

## distinguishing between extinction and punishment

Punishing a performance by following it with an aversive stimulus is not the same as a situation in which a performance is simply not reinforced and hence decreases in frequency because of the extinction. There is a tendency in ordinary conversational language to refer to a parent that does not attend to a crying child as punishing it. Even though the nonreinforcement of an operant performance may function as an aversive stimulus, it is misleading to refer to it as punishment, a term in which the meaning is strictly reserved for describing an aversive stimulus that occurs following a specific performance. Extinction creates a potentially aversive stimulus, and punishment is the application of that aversive stimulus following some operant behavior that it is intended to suppress. A stimulus that controls a low frequency of a performance because it has not been reinforced on that occasion creates the potential of punishment or avoidance. We tend to speak of a student who receives a low grade as a result of insufficient study as being punished for "not studying." The situation is better described, however, as simply reduced reinforcement. It is true that a low grade is an aversive stimulus, but the situation is more analogous to deprivation than punishment. The low grade is simply an outcome of the lack of an effective repertoire and there is no performance that is punished.

## questions

1. Give some examples of conditioned aversive stimuli in human behavior.
2. Explain why the control of operant performances by conditioned aversive stimuli is more prevalent than with primary aversive stimuli.
3. Describe how conditioned aversive stimuli that frequently occur in human conduct are effective.
4. Explain how the red light was established as an aversive stimulus in the chimpanzee experiment.

5. Describe how fines, incarceration, anger, ostracism, and criticism derive their aversive properties.

6. Why might incarceration in prison for a long period of time not be as effective an aversive stimulus as a shorter period?

7. Why is criticism an especially aversive stimulus for humans?

8. Why is the aversive effect of a parent spanking a child likely not to be limited to the direct physical results of the spanking?

9. Describe under what conditions a smile could serve as an aversive stimulus and a frown as a positive reinforcer.

10. Describe the animal laboratory analogue of masochism and compare it to the descriptions of the arbitrariness and the form of the conditioned aversive stimuli that control much of human behavior.

11. Describe how a parent would be sure that the terms "dear" or "honey" did not become aversive for the child.

12. Describe how the properties of a chain of positively reinforced operant performances create a possibility of an aversive stimulus.

13. Why is there some tendency to refer to extinction as punishment?

---

## part II: laboratory studies of negative reinforcement and punishment

### negative reinforcement

The common sense meaning of the word *negative* as synonymous with aversive or undesirable confuses negative reinforcement with punishment. Whether an aversive stimulus functions as a negative reinforcer or punishment is determined by the contingency between the performance and the aversive stimulus. If the aversive stimulus follows a performance, the procedure is called *punishment.* If the aversive stimulus is present and the performance terminates it, the procedure is called *negative reinforcement.* Punishment usually decreases the frequency of the punished performance and negative reinforcement will usually increase a performance's frequency. Technically, *negative* has the meaning of the removal or absence of the aversive stimulus rather than the favorableness or unfavorableness of the stimulus. The confusion, in part, stems from the practice of some writers who have designated punishment as negative reinforcement.

Many different performances, maintained by various aversive stimuli, have been studied with animals. If a rat presses a lever to terminate an electric shock, we describe this colloquially and technically as escape. The animal's performance actually leads to the removal of the aversive stimulus. The escape from or removal of the aversive stimulus is the event that is responsible for the frequency of the behavior. In other experiments, a buzzer sounds and is followed by an electric shock several seconds later. A lever press while the buzzer is on turns it off and hence postpones the shock that would otherwise follow. The buzzer, because it precedes the shock, is called a *conditioned aversive stimulus* (or sometimes a *pre-aversive stimulus*). By escaping the buzzer, the rat avoids the shock; hence, this kind of behavior control is called *avoidance*.

As with positive reinforcement, the form of the performance is arbitrary and depends on what behaviors actually terminate (escape) or postpone (avoid) the aversive stimulus. The relationship between the performance and the shock is frequently referred to as a *contingency*. The contingency refers to the connection between the performance and its effect on the environment—in this case, whether it terminates or postpones the shock and the topography of action that is required.

**Free-operant avoidance** Even when there is no pre-aversive stimulus, a performance may be maintained by postponing an aversive stimulus. For example, when each lever-press postpones the occurrence of shock for 20 seconds, a rat will press at a high steady rate. So long as the rat never pauses for more than 20 seconds no shocks will occur.[1] Or, the performance might be running in a wheel, leaping from one platform to another, or stepping on a treadle. Such avoidance is called *free operant avoidance.* This kind of avoidance is difficult to think about, as compared with positive reinforcement or negative reinforcement of the escape kind, because there is no immediate consequence of the behavior that reinforces it similar to sound and light of the food magazine operation that is the immediate reinforcer for key-pecking in the pigeon experiment. In avoidance behavior, it is the absence of the stimulus rather than its occurrence that is responsible for the avoidance behavior.[2] The need to think of a specific stimulus that the avoidance behavior terminates, as the buzzer that precedes the electric shock, leads us to assume that some aspect of pausing or doing things other than pressing the lever becomes paired with the electric shock. These performances become conditioned aversive stimuli as a result of these pairings. Pressing the lever, then, is reinforced because it preempts or interrupts these other activities that tend to be followed by shock.

**Accidental reinforcement** Avoidance behavior is especially susceptible of accidental reinforcement because it is reinforced when the aversive stimulus does *not* occur. As we discussed in Chapter 1, persons who knock on wood when there is a possibility of an aversive event and persons who avoid a black cat or walking under a ladder are successful in their avoidance so long as there is some initial conditioned aversion. The fact that no harm occurs serves to strengthen rather than weaken the avoidance behavior. To eliminate these accidentally reinforced behaviors, extinction would have to occur in the form of punishing the avoidance behaviors.

**Extinction**  The behavior that occurs during extinction after avoidance conditioning has special properties because the reinforcer maintaining it is the absence of the aversive stimulus. Nothing happens when reinforcement of avoidance occurs, so that extinction does not expose the animal to a condition that differs from the actual avoidance situation. Since well-conditioned avoidance behavior frequently is very persistent, with few failures to avoid the aversive stimulus, the performance is likely to occur for a very long time before the behavior diminishes or disappears.

This property of avoidance behavior gives a clue to clinical problems such as phobias and other compulsive activities that are so often debilitating. It is reasonable to surmise that phobic avoidance of foods, places, animals, as well as compulsive activities such as hand wringing, tics, pacing, and even complaining or crying have the same basic characteristics as the avoidance behaviors described previously. The problem in psychotherapy and clinical diagnosis is to determine what kind of aversive events these activities preempt and how they are connected with the performances.

Some behavioral therapists have proposed a therapy called "flooding" as a way to eliminate phobic and compulsive activities. These therapists assume that the performances are avoidance activities that have not decreased in frequency by extinction because the person never experiences situations when the phobic activity is *not* emitted and no aversive event follows. The rationale, therefore, in this kind of therapy is to restrain the organisms so that the phobic act can be prevented. Flooding may or may not be a workable therapy but it is described here because it illustrates the relation between compulsive phobic activity and extinction of avoidance behavior. The effectiveness of flooding, clinically, would depend on whether or not the aversive events underlying the phobia were still operative. If the aversion represented in the phobia were somehow connected to or derived from the overall social maintenance of the person's repertoire, then the clinical problem would be defined as how to lessen the aversive control by broadening the positive reinforcement of the underlying repertoire.

## definition of punishment

The definition of punishment, like positive reinforcement, negative reinforcement, and extinction, refers to a procedure. It involves the behavioral control that results when a performance is followed by an aversive stimulus—usually a decrease in the frequency of the punished performance. The processes involved in punishment are inevitably complex because several behavioral processes interact. First, the performance has to occur with some frequency before it can be punished. Therefore the variables governing the emission of the performance, its positive reinforcement, will be a major factor that will determine punishment's influence. Persistently maintained performances will be affected by punishment very differently than weakly maintained ones. A person on a driving trip, for example, will be more inclined to speed under time pressure of arriving at a destination than someone riding leisurely with interesting company. The aversive events that may function as punishment for speeding include the fine, inconvenience, and the embarrassment of being stopped and charged by a policeman. The performance is driving and the reinforcer maintaining it is progress toward, and arrival at the destination. The aversive event is punishment because it occurs following the performance. Also to be considered is the negative reinforcement of performances incidental to the punished performance, as well as the emotional by-products that usually result from exposure to an aversive stimulus. Because of this potentially complex interaction of the aversive stimulus with three different avenues of behavioral control, it is important to define punishment as a procedure. Although the procedure of punishment is simple, its effects are complicated so that its influence on a performance needs to be analyzed case-by-case.

## does punishment remove or suppress behavior?

With severe enough punishment, such as the tetanizing shock used in an animal experiment, the frequency of the punished performance will be reduced to the point that it no longer occurs. It was thought that the punishment of dogs using a very strong shock in a shuttle box experiment eliminated the performance irreversibly.[3] Present evidence, however, indicates that the effects of even a tetanizing shock may be reversed and the punished performance at least partially reinstated. The predominant evidence from laboratory studies is that punishment "suppresses" the punished behavior in the sense of temporarily "holding down" the performance.[4] More important than a categorical statement about whether or not punishment weakens behavior or whether its effect is temporary or permanent is our knowledge about the details of the complex processes that occur.

**Skinner's punishment experiments**   An early animal experiment demonstrating the general effect of punishment on an existing operant performance was carried out by B. F. Skinner.[5] His purpose was to determine how and to what extent mild punishment influenced the frequency of a rat's food-reinforced bar-pressing. The aversive stimulus was a rapid upward motion of the lever that slapped the rat. Reinforcement that had occurred after each lever-press was discontinued (extinction) and the shock delivered in its place.

When each bar-press was punished, Skinner discovered that the rat stopped pressing the bar almost immediately. Otherwise, it would have pressed 200–400 times—the number that typically occurs in extinction after continuous reinforcement. The period of punishment was limited to 10 minutes and the rat began to press as soon as the punishment stopped. In fact, the rat compensated for the lever-pressing behavior that was suppressed during the period of punishment by pressing more frequently when it returned to the lever. As a result the number of bar presses following punishment approximated the number that would have occurred had there been no punishment. Thus, mild punishment, sufficiently strong to almost completely stop the performance, was effective only so long as it was applied. Figure 3-1 describes, in graphic form, what happened. The graph depicts a cumulative record of the rat's bar-pressing during two consecutive daily experimental sessions of 2 hours each. Both curves show the result of extinction of lever-pressing after the previous continuous reinforcement. The bottom curve depicts the performance of those rats that were punished and the top curve provides a control that

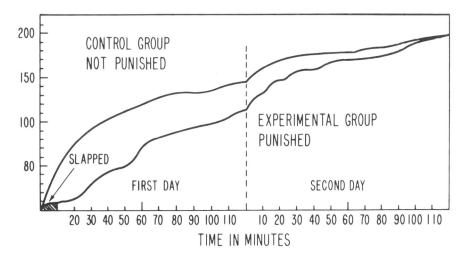

**Figure 3-1** Effect of punishment upon extinction. The two curves are from groups of four rats each, with the same experimental history. All responses made by one group during the first ten minutes of extinction were slapped. The rate is depressed for some time but eventually complete recovery is made. (Skinner, B, F. *The behavior of organisms.* Englewood Cliffs, N. J.: Prentice-Hall, Inc., 1966, p. 154.)

shows what might have been expected following extinction without any punishment.

A cumulative curve depicts the total number of times the rat pressed the bar at any given time. During the first 10 minutes of the experimental session depicted in the graph, the rats that had been punished pressed the lever only about 25 times compared with almost 100 presses for the rats in the control group that had not been punished. By the end of the second hour, the punished rats had made up some of the difference having pressed about 100 times compared with about 145 presses for the rats that had not been punished. By the end of the second 2-hour period on the following day, the punished rats had caught up completely. Although the punishment had initially depressed the rate of lever-pressing, it did so only temporarily.

Skinner suggested that the effect of punishment is more correctly described as the suppression of behavior, rather than its elimination. It was clear that punishment cannot be considered the opposite of positive reinforcement. The result of mild punishment, (the magnitude that predominantly occurs in human affairs) is aptly described by the aphorism, "When the cat's away the mice will play." Only extinction can decrease the frequency of pressing the lever in the sense of removing the performance from the animal's repertoire.

**Punishment reinforces incompatible behavior** The mechanism by which moderate punishment decreases the frequency of a performance is clearer when we consider that the aversive stimulus can, whatever our intention, serve as a negative reinforcer. Any performance other than pressing the lever is reinforced by postponing or avoiding the shock. Thus, if the rat walks to the rear of the cage, it cannot press the lever because this performance is incompatible with lever-pressing. Walking to the rear of the cage increases in frequency because it postpones the shock that would occur if the lever were pressed. There are two conflicting inclinations: The rat has some disposition to press the lever because food has reinforced this behavior; but walking to the rear of the cage avoids the shock which now follows the lever pressing. The incompatible behavior is an inevitable result of the procedure, since the punishment specifies that the aversive stimulus will not occur following any performance other than the punished one.

A description of the effect of punishment in colloquial terms might be that the "rat has learned not to press the lever." Actually, this phrase is not meaningful in a behavioral sense. One cannot talk behaviorally about "not acting" as a performance that is reinforced by terminating an aversive stimulus. We describe the same process more accurately by specifying the reinforcement of other performances such as going to the back of the cage. While thus engaged, the rat cannot press the lever. The more durably these incompatible behaviors are reinforced, the more likely that they will continue to be prepotent over the tendency to press the lever. The child, previously mentioned, who puts his hands behind his back when faced with the temptation of the fragile dish, avoids the censure or spanking that will surely occur if he plays with it. Such behavior is termed "self-control" because it is incompatible with reaching for the dish and hence preempts that risky action. A child who has been punished for giggling in class may bite his lip or clamp his hand over his mouth in order to prevent the punished behavior from recurring. The behavior of holding the hand over the mouth is incompatible with speaking or laughing aloud and is reinforced by avoiding the aversive consequences that would follow if the child were to laugh or speak. Some children may actually inflict pain on themselves so as to create a behavioral state incompatible with laughing.

## punishment by extreme magnitudes
## of aversive stimuli

Despite evidence that punishment is not, in any fundamental sense, simply an opposite of positive reinforcement and that it suppresses rather than eliminates behavior from an organism's repertoire, common experience supplies examples where it does seem to do so effectively. For example, children have been observed to become phobic in the presence of dogs as a result of a single experience of being attacked. The shuttle box experiments with dogs described earlier produced large decrements in performance. Animal experiments in which performances were punished with extreme magnitudes of electric shock have shown large decrements in performance. Often punishment completely eliminates the behavior for long periods of time.[6]

Such prolonged disruptions may not contradict the view that punishment merely suppresses performance. Long-term suppression may simply mean that avoidance behaviors, such as those described in the preceding section, do not permit the aversive stimulus to occur.

## reinstating punished performances

Although we describe a performance as an action that changes the environment, it is also, of itself, a stimulus. An individual can attend to the fact that she is acting or has just acted. Thus, an operant performance is at once a performance or a stimulus, depending on which of its functions we are talking about. Therefore, when a performance is punished, the conditions are those for generating a conditioned aversive stimulus. The performance, as an event that can be discriminated, will acquire the properties of a conditioned aversive stimulus because its punishment has consistently been followed by the primary aversive stimulus. This conditioned aversive elicitation by the punished behavior is a major factor in the suppressive effect of punishment. The mechanism is the negative reinforcement that is generated when there is some inclination to emit the punished behavior. These conditioned aversive stimuli will be terminated by any performance incompatible with the punished one (negative reinforcement). Thus, any incipient movements toward pressing the lever will evoke conditioned aversive stimuli that will be terminated by anything that the rat does that is incompatible with pressing the lever, such as going to the rear of the cage.

This aspect of punishment explains why it is so difficult to reverse the effects of punishment even though it no longer occurs. This characteristic of punishment is analogous to the inertia that occurs when we attempt to reduce avoidance behavior by carrying out extinction. Unless the animal witholds the avoidance behavior in the presence of the buzzer, it never experiences a prolonged period in the presence of the buzzer without the shock following. The buzzer will lose its conditioned aversive properties only if the rat remains in its presence without emitting some performance that turns it off or escapes from it. Punishment has the same inertial characteristics as avoidance behavior and for the same reasons. Punishment's inertia is caused by the negative reinforcement of the performances incompatible with the punished behavior. In order for the punished performance to cease functioning as a conditioned aversive stimulus, it needs to be emitted without the shock following it. If the animal does not emit the previously punished performance then the performance itself, as a clearly discriminable conditioned aversive stimulus, will continue to reinforce avoidance behavior.

**Punishment of verbal behavior**  The punishment of verbal behavior illustrates this process in areas of human conduct that are crucially important for mental health and psychotherapy. A substantial part of human behavior is reinforced through the mediation of other persons rather than by a direct effect on the environment as in the animal experiments that have been described. Since verbal behavior, whether vocal or in other modes, is the way that people influence each other, it is in this area that we need to examine the major effects of punishment in human interactions. Freud's concept of psychological defenses that he formulated as repression, denial, and reaction formation, illustrate how punishment interacts with complex human verbal behavior. In these psychological defenses, the performances are predominantly verbal. Most are in vocal form because Freud collected his clinical observations in face-to-face interviews. Reaction formation provides a convenient example of how punishment results in such defenses. As will be seen, the term *defense* is a metaphor related to the negative reinforcement that is involved.

In reaction formation, the speaker who has been severely and consistently punished for criticizing persons important to him, may find himself praising them—not because he is positively disposed to praise them but because, by praising them, he is able to withold criticism. Hence praising is reinforced because it preempts, and therefore avoids, the aversive consequences that might occur if he criticized. The verbal behaviors of criticism are reduced in frequency because they have been followed (punished) by an aversive stimulus. As a result of this pairing, any tendency to speak or think critically generates a conditioned aversive stimulus severe enough that the punished thoughts are completely preempted by the negative reinforcement of incompatible behaviors. The critical statements still tend to be emitted because they are suppressed rather than eliminated, even though they do not appear in overt form.

If particular forms of speech are regularly punished, they will serve as aversive stimuli just as a motor activity or the buzzer preceding an electric shock. The results are probably even more pronounced in speech than in overt motor behavior because the speaker is in even more intimate contact with his own speech than the rat is with the buzzer in the laboratory avoidance experiments described earlier. The result is that the person whose activities are controlled by the dynamics of reaction formation, denial, or repression is constantly emitting performances whose only result is to ward off parts of his ongoing repertoire. It is in this sense that these defense mechanisms are described as *covert processes.* Therefore, the goal of psychotherapy is characterized as "bringing the covert to the overt." The phenomenon is referred to as "unconscious process" by psychodynamically oriented psychologists, but the main data is intraverbal and behavioral, involving the negative reinforcement of verbal performances that preempt those producing aversive stimuli.

## questions

1. Describe escape and avoidance as negative reinforcement.
2. Describe free-operant avoidance.
3. Why is avoidance behavior especially susceptible to accidental reinforcement?
4. What happens when an operant that previously was negatively reinforced now is punished?

5. What are the special characteristics of extinction of avoidance behavior? How do these relate to clinical problems about phobias and compulsive activities?

6. How does adventitious punishment affect avoidance behavior? What are the implications of this for clinical problems?

7. Why is it important to define punishment as a procedure?

8. Why did Skinner positively reinforce bar-pressing when the rats were slapped? What did Skinner conclude from the results of the experiment?

9. Why is reducing the frequency of a performance by punishment different from reducing it by extinction?

10. How may the decreased frequency of a punished performance be due to the emission of another one?

11. Discuss why the changes in the frequency of an operant performance that is punished often appear permanent even though we presume that punishment suppresses rather than eliminates behavior.

12. Describe a procedure for curing a rat who was so severely punished after pressing a lever that he has never returned to it even though it now delivers food without any shock.

13. Give some examples from children's conduct where punishment reduces the frequency of a performance by negative, indirect reinforcement of another behavior incompatible with the first.

14. Describe some Freudian defenses in terms of the negative reinforcement of behaviors incompatible with the punished performance.

15. Why is a phrase like "the rat has learned to not press the lever because he has been punished" not a useful way to describe the phenomenon?

---

## part III: aversive control in interactions between persons

### how social interactions can result in aversive consequences

The previous section has described many forms of aversive behavioral control where the aversive event was derived from a reduction or loss of positive reinforcement. The aversiveness of these stimuli arises because the organism is prevented from emitting performances that would produce positive reinforcers. Human relationships produce many circumstances where the interactions between the persons are seriously influenced by the way the conduct of one person interferes with the normal reinforcement of the other person's behavior.

For example, when a child cries, the aversiveness for the parent is not simply derived from a reaction to loud noise. It is a complex reaction that is determined by the properties of the crying as a conditioned aversive stimulus. Part of the aversiveness of crying comes from its interference with the parents' ongoing operant repertoire in other areas of their life than the interaction with the child. In order to attend to the child when it cries, the parent may have stop activities such as watching television or working on a project. It is for this reason, as will be shown in the next section, that the cry of the parents' own child is likely to be far more aversive than someone else's child. The performances of attending to the child are reinforced, negatively, by stopping the crying. As we discussed earlier, the aversiveness of the crying for the parent is seen in the elaborate avoidance performances that are so often generated, such as providing the child with toys, a bottle, or a pacifier.

Similar derived aversive stimuli operate in the reverse direction when a mother tries to get a child to pick up his or her toys by screaming, nagging, or otherwise showing displeasure. The loud voice is not only innately aversive but it derives additional effects because the child is interrupted; the parent preempts the child's attention to other activities and there is the possibility that the parent might interfere even more seriously in the child's routine.

A child's conversation, ordinarily a positive reinforcer, may function as an aversive stimulus for a parent because it interferes with a telephone conversation or preempts talking to another person. Whey we say that conversation with someone is boring, the implication is that the control of one's behavior by that person is preempting other activities that *are* effective reinforcers. The maintenance of the boring conversation suggests that the interpersonal activity is being maintained by aversive control that is so strong that the alternative positively reinforced behavior cannot compete.

## analyzing the aversive control of a parent by a child

Many examples of negative reinforcement in human behavior occur in interactions between two persons where each exerts aversive control over the other. Although such interactions are more complex than the episodes that have been dealt with so far, they are a useful way to elaborate the reinforcement process as it operates in human social activity. This section will set out the behavior of a parent and child as the child exerts control of the parent to produce positive reinforcement by negatively reinforcing the parent's behavior.

The struggle may center around simple demands such as "I want a cookie," "I want to go outside to play," "Read me a story," or "Pick me up." In its simplest form such episodes may not involve aversive control if the child's performance, eating the cookie for example, is sufficient in itself as a positive reinforcer that maintains the parent's compliance. Frequently, however, the parent may be indisposed to comply. The child's request might be refused because the parent is busy or is annoyed with the child, because no cookies are conveniently at hand, or because the parent sees harm for the child in eating sweets. The child who is refused a cookie might scream and cry, while repeatedly requesting a cookie. At some point, the cumulative result of the tantrum might become so aversive that terminating it becomes prepotent over any other consideration. The child stops crying because eating the cookie is prepotent over the tantrum. Giving the cookie in that case is negatively reinforced by the ending of the annoying behavior. When the parent gives a cookie because the crying and tantrum is annoying enough, the effect is an increase in the frequency of tantrums. The events of the interaction are illustrated diagramatically in Figure 3-2.

The letter P denotes a performance and S a change in the environment stimulus that is produced by the performance. The arrow stands for the phrase "is followed by" and indicates the contingency between the performance and the change in the environment it produces. The control of the child's behavior is shown in the top line. The verbal performance of saying "cookie" is reinforced by the receipt of the cookie. On the bottom line, the reinforcer maintaining the parent's behavior is diagrammed. In the presence of the screaming or nagging child, giving a cookie stops the screaming and nagging.

It is in the interaction between the two repertoires, indicated by the arrows that go between the top and bottom line, that the important dynamics of the interaction occur. The behavior of giving a cookie is reinforced by the termination of the child's crying ($S^{-av}$) and caused by the cumulative aversive impact of the crying ($S^{av}$) on the parent. As a result, there is a fine-line, continuous relation between the severity and persistence of the child's crying and the parent's escape from it by giving a

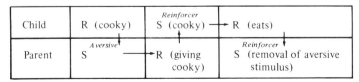

| Child | R (cooky) | Reinforcer<br>S (cooky) → R (eats) |  |
|---|---|---|---|
| Parent | Aversive<br>S ——→ | R (giving<br>cooky) | Reinforcer<br>S (removal of aversive<br>stimulus) |

Figure 3-2

cookie. The more severe and annoying the child's behavior is, the greater will be the negative reinforcement of the parent's escape. As a result there is, inherent in the interaction between the two repertoires, a process that will differentially reinforce the child's crying in the direction of more persistent and aversive forms. If the parent is more likely to give a cookie when the child screams louder, then the interaction is tantamount to the differential reinforcement of loud screaming. If the child stops screaming only when the parent gives a particular kind of cookie, then that behavior will be reinforced.

## unique aversiveness of the child's demand

When the child first asks for a cookie, there is nothing to encourage the development of nagging. The problem arises when the child's demands go unreinforced because the parent doesn't comply. Since such demands or requests have been reinforced before, they can continue to be emitted for some time even without reinforcement. The process is that of extinction, and if the parent does not comply at all, the frequency of the demands eventually falls off. However, a characteristic of behavior during extinction introduces a complicating element. There is usually an emotional by-product of extinction in the form of an increase in the magnitude or intensity of the performance and an increase in the frequency of aggressive behavior.[7] As a result, the more intense, emotional behavior characteristic of extinction increases the aversiveness of the child's demands and makes it more likely that they will evoke the negatively reinforced compliance by the parent. If the parent does not comply with the first instance of annoying speech, the repetition of the child's demand cumulates its aversiveness until it can evoke the negatively reinforced "cookie-giving."

The paradoxical reinforcement of those forms of crying, nagging, and verbal assault that are maximally and uniquely aversive illustrates the generic relation between the child's performance and the parent's reaction to it. The events particularly aversive to a parent are likely to be unique, depending on the particular person. Just as the mechanical relation between the microswitch that operates the food dispenser and the physical properties of the lever shapes exactly how the rat presses the lever, the reactivity of the parent determines the kinds of performances the interaction will reinforce in the child's repertoire.

The difference between the parent as a reinforcer and the switch on the lever in the rat experiment is that the switch has a stable characteristic while the reactivity of the parent varies in complex and subtle ways from one time to the next. For example, when the parent is ill or has a headache, she or he will comply after a lesser level of assault than when feeling well.

To overcome a depressed parent or one pressed by many competing demands, a child will have to escalate its demands to a much higher level than would be the case normally. The result is, therefore, an escalation in the level and kind of assault uniquely tailored to the particular parent.

## effect of intermittent reinforcement

The child's demand is reinforced intermittently because the parent's compliance depends on so many variables. How long the child's nagging will persist without reinforcement depends on the schedule of intermittent reinforcement. The persistence of behavior following different schedules of reinforcement is a topic that will be presented in chapter 5. Nevertheless, some of the essential facts about intermittent reinforcement can be anticipated because they are so germane to the analysis of this kind of interpersonal interaction.

A performance is least persistent after it has been reinforced continuously and most persistent after it has been reinforced intermittently. This difference is seen in how long the performance persists after reinforcement is discontinued completely and by the fact that it can be emitted at a continuous high rate even though only occasional instances are reinforced. The child whose request for a cookie has always been successful will be less persistent in its requests than one whose requests have sometimes been reinforced. Thus a parent who reinforces the child's nagging only after the child accumulates an annoying effect by crying a certain number of times, will increase the child's persistence on later occasions. This aspect of the schedule of reinforcement is a natural consequence of the parent's reactivity. The actual schedule of reinforcement is called a "number or ratio schedule" because the reinforcement of the child's crying depends on how much the child cries. Behavior is very persistently maintained under such ratio schedules and can be altered only with difficulty. After such intermittent reinforcement, the child's disposition to repeat a demand may become so strong that the child will be able to overcome any degree of the parent's lassitude or preoccupation.

## behavioral vignettes
## of childrens' playground activities

The following vignettes provide an opportunity to analyze the contingencies of reinforcement inherent in naturally occurring social arrangements. Following each vignette is a behavioral analysis, keyed to it.

situation #1:

A group of children were playing in the playground. John snatched a marble from Frank and ran away (1). Frank immediately chased after him (2). When Frank caught him, John put the marble in his mouth (3). Frank sat on John on the ground, twisted John's arm behind him, and said "Give me that marble (4). Tears came to John's eyes before he finally spit out the marble and ran away (5).

*Behavioral analysis.* (1) John's snatching the marble from Frank was the withdrawal of a positive reinforcer. John's running away was a performance reinforced by escape from an aversive stimulus: Frank would take the marble and/or hit Johnny if he stayed. (2) A performance maintained by positive reinforcement. For John: Running was a negatively reinforced performance that prevented the loss of the marble. (3) A further example of avoidance. (4) An aversive stimulus was applied with an instruction that its termination depended on giving up the marble. (5) Giving up the marble was reinforced by the termination of the aversive stimulus—the twisted arm. Frank's application of aversive control to John was positively reinforced by regaining the marble. Elicited reflexes were evoked by the aversive stimulus in addition to the negatively reinforced operant performance.

situation #2:

Timmy was waiting his turn to get onto the slide but Susan tarried on top, preventing him (1). Timmy first said, "Come on, Susan. I'd like to have my turn" (2). Susan paid him no heed (3). Timmy then climbed on the first rung and spoke again, this time a louder voice; he began whining a little (4), and Susan said, "Don't bother me" (5). Finally, Timmy began to cry and shout and Susan slid down the slide and walked away (6).

*Behavioral analysis.* (1) An aversive stimulus derived from the impossibility of playing with the slide with Susan blocking the way. (2) A performance reinforced in Timmy's past, relevant to behaviors that have a high frequency in his repertoire. (3) Extinction. (4) Application of an aversive stimulus to induce a negatively reinforced performance that would provide the positive reinforcer. (5) Extinction. (6) The aversive stimulus is increased sufficiently to produce the negatively reinforced performance. The overall result has been differential reinforcement by Susan of Timmy's demands into forms that have an increased aversive effect.

situation #3:

Bill had talked to his neighbor instead of doing his assignment and the teacher had scolded him repeatedly (1). Finally, the teacher got angry and made Bill sit in the corner (2). Even after Bill was allowed to return to his seat the teacher remained upset about his conduct (3). For example, when the teacher gave children assignments that they liked, such as cleaning erasers, going on errands for her or serving as monitor, she ignored Bill completely (4).

*Behavioral analysis.* (1) Bills' behavior was an aversive stimulus for the teacher because his conduct prevented her from accomplishing the work she was hired to do. This is also an example of extinction where the performance is teaching and the reinforcer is the engagement of the student. (2) The teacher's anger and aggressive behavior to Bill is an example of the by-products of extinction. (3) An example of an emotional state, in the sense of continued inclination to act agressively. (4) The punishment and evidence of aggressiveness to Bill consisted of withdrawal of support for important items of conduct that would otherwise have been supported by the classroom environment.

## aspects of psychotherapy involving aversive control

Descriptions of simple interactions between a therapist and a mute, autistic child provide applications extending the behavioral analyses that have been developed so far. The following is a trained observer's account of such an interaction.[8]

One time, taking off K's sweater, the therapist stopped with one hand still in the sleeve and said, "Now *you* take your hand out of the arm." K withdrew her hand. This contingency reinforced undressing because it actually "took the sweater off." On later days, K did more as the therapist did less of the work of taking off the sweater for her and K became able to emit the performances farther back along the chain of behaviors leading to the sweater coming off.

Although removing the sweater eventually may become an intrinsically reinforcing outcome, to start with it is a product of an aversive stimulus applied by the therapist. With the sweater partially off, the child is immobilized and cannot initiate or engage in any other activity. Such an action takes great clinical skill and experience to avoid a destructive fight with the child. Sensitive judgments need to be made about how much can be realistically required of the child at a particular time. In this case, for example, little more than random squirming was asked. In any event, the therapist could have adjusted the requirement to meet any momentary difficulties. In practice, the interaction—even though based on negative reinforcement—involved a continuous interaction between the two.

Let us turn to another example, in which the therapist attempts to eliminate crying:

The therapist placed K on a rocking horse where she stayed without crying as long as the rocking and singing continued. After a few minutes, the therapist stopped rocking the horse for brief periods but kept on singing. She carefully sensed how long she could stop rocking the horse without losing control of K's behavior by the horse play. The return to rocking always followed some behavior other than crying.[9]

The aversive control here involves the disruption of the child's normal activities by placing her on the unfamiliar environment of the rocking horse. In any particular instance, it would be difficult to judge whether crying were a reflex elicited by the aversive situation or an operant performance that was effective in the past in inducing others to remove the child from such aversive situations or from related situations. Opposed to the escape from the rocking horse are the positive reinforcements by the rocking movements and the singing of the therapist in rhythm to them. The interaction shows a sensitive interplay between the positive consequences of playing on the rocking horse and the reflexes and escape performances engendered by it. The clinical skill in the interaction involves the careful adjustment and balance of these two aspects of the child's experience. Let us look at another situation in which the therapist tries to end the child's compulsive relation to a doll:

Next, the therapist took the plastic doll from K's hands, set it on the table and quickly moved the table to K who promptly picked up the doll. One would guess that under any other circumstances taking the doll away would have led to screaming. Although K was without the doll only for a few seconds, it allowed for the reinforcement of a constructive behavior—reaching for and regaining the doll. For a period of time, K and the therapist interacted over rocking the horse and singing, and then the episode with the doll was repeated but this time the movements were a little slower so that K was without the doll for a few seconds longer than before.[10]

Although picking up the doll might be thought of as a positive reinforcement, the fact that it was carried by the child compulsively and that the therapist arbitrarily took it away makes its description as aversive control more correct, technically. By carrying out the maneuver deftly and rapidly, the therapist insured that the performance of reaching for it and recovering it would be prepotent over the behavior that might be evoked by the aversiveness of its withdrawal. The doll's removal was aversive because it supported significant activities in the child's repertoire. The sensitive clinical balance is between the behaviors controlled positively in the form of body movements reinforced by the change in the horse's position, the singing that occurred contingent on the rocking, the aversive aspects of the disruption of normal routine, and the loss of the doll.

As K rocked more vigorously and continuously, it became difficult to clutch the doll and operate the handles of the horse. As a consequence, she placed the doll on the table herself. K continued rocking without the doll while the therapist sang along. Next the therapist kept silent for a brief period while K rocked. At this point, when the therapist's singing was no longer paced with the child's rocking, K's activity on the horse diminished and she reached for the doll. But it dropped to the floor accidentally, and for the first time the child cried. The therapist asked, "Do you want to pick up your doll? I'll help you," and extended her hands. When K touched the therapist's hands, she clasped them; the therapist helped K from the rocking horse in the direction of dismounting to reclaim the doll. But the child did not lift her foot to clear the saddle. The therapist simply held K in this position until she made some movement. When K didn't move at all, the therapist prompted the required action by moving the foot partially over the saddle, allowing the child to complete the final part of the action. She then held K in the vicinity of the doll until the child picked it up.[11]

The aversive control is here clearly a product of the competition between the two repertoires. As the frequency of engagement in rocking increases, it becomes prepotent over the control by the doll. When the rocking diminishes, however, the absence of the doll becomes an aversive state of affairs. The behaviors of regaining it are examples of negatively reinforced operants. Note how the therapist approximates the required behavior by collateral support of the child's movements based on a judgment of what the child could carry out independently. The incident where the child is held over the saddle until she moves her foot is another aspect of the aversive control. For the moment, she is immobilized and the escape from the immobilization would appear to be one of the reinforcers supporting the movement.

## questions

*1.* Why is the aversiveness of a child's crying to a parent not simply derived from the reaction to a loud noise?

*2.* Analyze an interaction between a child and a parent in which the aversive control of each over the other escalates.

*3.* How does the parent's sensitivity to aversive control by the child shape the child's demands into a form that is uniquely aversive to the parent?

*4.* How does the parent's reactivity to the child's demands result in intermittent reinforcement that increases the persistence of the child's demands?

*5.* Recount several behavioral vignettes of children's playground activities you have observed and give a behavioral analysis of the aversively controlled behaviors.

*6.* Give several examples of negative reinforcement of the child's behavior by the therapist during the therapeutic interaction on the rocking horse.

*7.* How did the therapist avoid a fight with the child when attempts were made to control the child's behavior aversively?

## notes

[1]Sidman, M. Two temporal parameters of the maintenance of avoidance behavior by the white rat. *Journal of Comparative and Physiological Psychology* 47: 145–147, 1953.

[2]There is argument about whether the reinforcement of avoidance behavior is mediated by the reflex or the conditioned aversive effects of the primary aversive stimulus, or whether the negative reinforcement of the operant does not require an event immediately contingent on the avoidance performance. Mowrer, O. H. and Lamoreaux, R. R. Fear as an intervening variable in avoidance conditioning. *Journal of Comparative Psychology* 39: 29–50, 1946. Herrnstein, R. J. Method and theory in the study of avoidance. *Psychological Review* 76: 46–49, 1969.

[3]A shuttle box is a pivoted runway with a chamber on each end. Shock could be delivered through the floor. When the dog escaped the shock on one end it could be turned on in the other compartment so that it had to shuttle back and forth. Solomon, R. L. and Wynne, L. C. Traumatic avoidance learning: Acquisition in dogs. *Psychological Monographs* 67: No. 354, 1953.

[4]Waters, G. C. and Grusec, J. E. *Punishment.* San Fransisco: W. H. Freeman, 1977.

[5]Skinner, B. F. *The behavior of organisms.* Englewood Cliffs, N.J.: Prentice-Hall, 1966.

[6]Azrin, N. and Holtz, W. C. Punishment. In: Honig, W. K. (Ed.) *Operant behavior: Areas of research and application.* Englewood Cliffs, N.J.: Prentice-Hall, 1966, pp. 380–447.

[7]Hutchinson, R. R. By-products of aversive control. In: Honig, W. K. and Staddon, J. E. R. (Eds.) *Handbook of operant conditioning.* Englewood Cliffs, N.J.: Prentice-Hall, 1977.

[8]Ferster, C. B. Transition from animal laboratory to clinic. *The Psychological Record,* 17: 145–150, 1967.

[9]Ibid.

[10]Ibid.

[11]Ibid.

# evaluating control by aversive stimuli

## study guide

In this chapter, we discuss the multiple effects of aversive stimuli. These effects include emotional factors, in addition to changes in the frequencies of the specific performances that are reinforced or punished. Aspects of the disruptive process that may result from aversive control are exemplified by Watson and Rayner's classical experiment in which a child was made fearful.

In Part III, the efficacy of positive reinforcement is compared with that of negative reinforcement. Also discussed are the relative advantages of punishment and extinction as ways of reducing the frequency of performances. Some of the reasons why aversive control is so widely used despite its obvious disadvantages are discussed. The technical properties of positive and negative reinforcement and punishment suggest ways that positive reinforcement can be substituted for aversive control. Positive reinforcers can also involve aversive control, particularly in some social applications. These are discussed in the context of reinforcers that are generically related to the behaviors that they maintain compared with those with arbitrary connections.

---

## technical terms

pre-aversive stimulus
systematic desensitization
arbitrary control
power struggle

emotion
reciprocal inhibition
natural control

---

## outline

Part I:　Measuring the By-products of Aversive Control in Animal Experiments
　　　　The multiple functions of an aversive stimulus
　　　　The effects of a pre-aversive stimulus
　　　　The Watson-Rayner experiment
　　　　Extinction of conditioned aversive stimuli by approximations
　　　　What is emotion?
　　　　Somatic by-products of aversive control

Part
　II:　A Comparison of the Control by Positive and Aversive Stimuli
　　　　Increases in frequency due to positive and negative reinforcement
　　　　Conditioning a performance not yet in the individual's repertoire
　　　　Reduction in frequency of positively reinforced performances by extinction and punishment
　　　　The DRO procedure as an alternative to punishment
　　　　Reasons for the use of aversive control despite its undesirable by-products

Part
　III:　Substituting Positive Reinforcement and Extinction for Aversive Control
　　　　Aversive control without undesirable by-products
　　　　Distinguishing between benign and malignant forms of aversive control
　　　　Positive reinforcement with aversive and other undesirable effects
　　　　Arbitrary restrictions of positive reinforcement from social control
　　　　Power struggle
　　　　Alternatives to the punishment of "not performing."
　　　　Collateral support as a way to substitute positive reinforcement for arbitrary aversive control
　　　　Psychotherapy
　　　　The goals of psychotherapy and behavioral control

*part I: measuring the by-products of aversive
control in animal experiments*

## the multiple functions
## of an aversive stimulus

The different ways that an organism's behavior can be functionally related to an aversive stimulus were presented in the preceding chapter. As we discussed previously, an electric shock may increase the frequency of an operant performance that terminates it (negative reinforcement), decrease the frequency of a performance that it follows (punishment), elicit unconditioned reflexes, or establish new reflexes to previously neutral stimuli (conditioned reflex). Many of these occur simultaneously, such as when a rat's bar-press is followed by an electric shock; unconditioned reflexes are elicited such as jumping, changes in heart rate, blood pressure, or skin resistance. Conditioned reflexes develop when incidental features of the room come to elicit the same unconditioned reponses because they are paired with the unconditioned reflex. One of the conditioned stimuli that will elicit these same reflexes is the punished performance itself in its function as a discriminable event, because it is inevitably paired with the shock. Alternately or concurrently, the animal might be able to avoid or escape from the situation entirely. Such performances as jumping out of the cage are negatively reinforced by terminating all of the situational stimuli that are present when the shock occurs. Other performances— negatively reinforced by reducing the electric shock by limiting the physical contact with it—might include jumping in the air the moment the shock comes on, climbing the walls of the cage, or lying on the back with the thick of the fur in contact with the electric grids. In addition to the specific performances that are negatively reinforced or punished, there are broad changes in the frequencies of other items that might be disrupted or simply preempted by the high frequency of the negatively reinforced operants. These broad changes in the overall repertoire are the topic of emotion that will be taken up in the next sections.

The same complex ramification of the aversive stimulus, with all of the elements of an animal's repertoire that occur with punishment, are also present when a performance is maintained by avoidance of electric shock. Occasional shocks occur when avoidance fails. These shocks will reinforce conditioned reflexes in which features of the room are conditioned stimuli. They will punish the performance that the rat happens to be engaging in when it is not pressing the lever, and in conjunction with the conditioned stimulus mentioned above, it will affect the ongoing repertoire emotionally.

## the effects of a pre-aversive stimulus

Even though an aversive stimulus such as an electric shock clearly disrupts almost anything that an animal might be doing at the time a shock occurs, such effects are likely to be over quickly. A much more extended disruption occurs by the stimuli that regularly precede the electric shock. The core of the process is best illustrated by an animal experiment. The experiment begins with some operant emitted at a stable, continuous rate such as occurs when a rat's lever-presses are reinforced on a variable schedule, say every three minutes on the average, but unpredictably. Under such a schedule of reinforcement, the rat will press the lever at a fairly constant rate of about a lever press every second or two. The lever-pressing, reinforced by food, provides a baseline level of activity to assess the disruption by the shock; the lever-pressing could stand in place of any other operant activity maintained by positive reinforcement that might be ongoing in the rat's repertoire. We would expect that the result would be the same whether the rat were stepping on a treadle, pulling a chain, or building a nest. An occasional shock delivered independently of the food schedule disrupts the rat's ongoing operant behavior very little. The rat may jump or even defecate after the shock, but it would resume whatever it had been doing almost immediately. If, however, 2 minutes preceding each shock a pre-shock stimulus such as a buzzer or a red light appears, the disruption in the ongoing operant repertoire is magnified. Almost all operant activity, including the food-reinforced performance such as pressing the lever, is likely to cease as soon as the pre-shock stimulus appears and not resume until after the shock has occurred. The major effect of the shock occurs with the stimulus preceding it. The rat begins pressing the bar and doing whatever activities were ongoing or supported by that environment almost immediately following the shock.

The pre-shock stimulus is likely to produce reflex effects as well as disrupt the ongoing operant activity. The animal may defecate, urinate, show reflex erection of the hairs on its back, as well as internal reflex changes such as heart and blood pressure. Because both operants and reflexes change, there is often confusion between physiological responses and the behavioral disruption by the pre-aversive stimulus. We tend, conversationally, to identify emotional changes in behavior, such as those caused by the pre-shock stimulus, with the disturbances in heart rate, blood circulation, and breathing. But the psychological changes in the operant repertoire that occur concurrently are the real focus of our concern from a behavioral point of view.[1]

Parallels in the human natural environment of the control by a pre-aversive stimulus are easily found. In all of these examples, physiological changes are likely to be seen in the person's skin color, breathing, or in less observable changes such as heart rate and blood pressure. Nevertheless, the changes that are important psychologically are in the overall interaction with the social and physical environment. Students just before an examination, patients in the dentist's waiting room, the job candidate preceding an important interview, the actor before curtain on opening night, the athlete waiting for a match to begin or the errant child facing its parents to account for misdeeds, all exemplify control by a pre-aversive stimulus. There is an aversive event preceded by a clearly defined and discriminable event in all of these situations. For example, in the first case, examinations sometimes are failed, and the consequences of failing are important losses of reinforcers. The dentist's waiting room is often the prelude to painful operations on teeth. The failure to qualify for a job is an important loss of income and professional or job support. The audience's reaction to the actor's performance signifies either continued employment and success or the play's closing down. The athletic event is the prelude to winning the prize or its loss, and the child facing the angry parents has probably experienced in the past physical punishment, withdrawal of approval, and loss of privileges. The control exercised by each of these distinctive circumstances involves a broad change in the person's operant activity. The patient in the dentist's waiting room idly turns pages, unable to read thoughtfully. Conversation is either absent, fitful or of a compulsive nature that appears to have the function of avoiding the nervous agitation generated by the waiting room. The errant child facing a parent is likely to engage in behavior that will avoid, escape, or lessen the punishment. That is, the behaviors emitted will be restricted to a class of operants negatively reinforced by the aversive events that are controlling. Athletes preceding a match will find that the predominant activities will be warming up and mimicking the behaviors that they will carry out in the event. Usually there is a dramatic difference in the overall level and kind of activity seen during the pre-aversive situation and just after it when the aversive event or its threat has already passed. Students, just before an examination, are likely to be depressed, fidgety, or compulsively turning the pages of their book. As soon as the exam is over, conversation may begin, and animated and overall physical activity increases.

The broad disruption of the overall operant repertoire is likely to be a factor that will interfere with attempts to reinforce and maintain behavior by negative reinforcement with stimuli such as electric shock or other highly aversive events. At the same time that an aversive stimulus reinforces an operant performance, it will also elicit physiological and reflex effects that interfere with the very performances that are intended to increase in frequency. There remains the paradox that the aversive stimulus is needed as a reinforcer for the operant behavior that is intended to be conditioned, but that it has side effects that disrupt the animal's ongoing operant behavior, including the performance to be conditioned. The interference will be the most extreme during the performance's initial development before it is well enough established because the shock will be occurring frequently then. Without the frequent electric shock, there would be no reinforcer to increase the frequency of the escape behavior. Yet, the electric shock may disrupt the very performance that would terminate it. Such an interaction between negative reinforcement and the disruptive state of the organism that it generates probably explains why negative reinforcement is a difficult laboratory technique that can generate the target behavior only under very carefully prescribed conditions. The same difficulties would appear to operate in the human, natural environment when attempts are made to shape complex forms of behavior by negative reinforcement.

## the Watson-Rayner experiment

An experiment by John B. Watson and Rosalie Rayner[2] in 1920 was a pioneer attempt to demonstrate experimentally in a human infant that the disruptive by-products of aversive control were conditionable. Their thinking emphasized the conditioning of reflexes more than the general operant repertoire that was disrupted because the behavioral concept of emotion was not then developed. The Watson and Rayner experiment was typical of the work of early behaviorists who sought to understand human behavior through the new discoveries of Pavlov.

The experiment was carried out with a healthy, nine-month-old infant named Albert, who was to be made fearful, experimentally, of stimuli such as a white rat through the process of pairing the rat with an aversive event. The paradigm was that of conditioning a response to a previously neutral stimulus, as Pavlov had, by pairing it with a primary aversive stimulus. Albert was confronted for the first time with a white rat, a rabbit, a dog, a monkey, masks with and without hair, cotton, wool, and so forth. Mostly he reached for or played with the objects without any suggestion of being afraid of them. The primary aversive stimulus that was to be paired with the white rat was a loud noise that the experimenters produced by striking a hammer on a metal bar held over Albert's head. That the sound was aversive was indicated by all of the somatic reactions of fear such as trembling, crying, and startle as well as behavioral reactions of escape. Having tested the aversiveness of the loud sound, it was then introduced in a conditioning paradigm.

The rat was next given to Albert as he played, and the experimenters struck the bar producing the loud noise just as he reached for it. At intervals during the same session, they produced the noise six more times when Albert reached for the rat. In between each of these conditioning trials they tested how much the rat, of itself, evoked the reaction. Albert's reaction to the rat became increasingly severe after each pairing of the loud noise with the presentation of the rat. Eventually, he began crying as soon as the rat was placed on the floor next to him, and he crawled away with some alacrity.[3] Five days later, they tested Albert with the other stimuli to which he had given no reaction prior to the pairing with the loud noise. The rabbit, the fur coat, cotton wool, and a santa claus mask, all evoked a reaction similar to that produced by the white rat. When they tested Albert with blocks that he had previously played with, he played with them normally as he had before the conditioning trials with the noise and the white rat. The play with the blocks indicated that the effect of the conditioning was limited to the white rat and closely related stimuli.

Even though Watson and Rayner used the language of the conditioned reflex, most of the behavior they observed was operant. The statement that the child became fearful came partially from those conditioned physiological reflexes that could be observed such as crying and breathing pattern, but equally prominent in their observations were changes in the frequency of the behavior that the child would normally engage in such as the casual movements of his arms, the exploration of odd items around him, and visual exploration of the room. These behaviors were reduced in frequency considerably and in their place were the elicited response to the loud noise and the conditioned stimuli that come to evoke these same responses. In addition, there was an increase in frequency of operant performances reinforced because they terminate or provide escape from or lessen the exposure to the aversive and conditioned aversive stimuli. Such behaviors were described by Watson and Rayner: Albert turned sharply to the left, fell over to one side, raised himself on all fours, and began to crawl rapidly away. We know of course that the white rat becomes a conditioned stimulus through Pavlovian conditioning for many reflexes that could have been discovered if instruments were on hand to measure them, such as skin resistance, dilation and constriction of blood vessels, reduction in the saliva secretion, changes in adrenalin secretion, dilation of the pupils, and heart rate changes. These are changes collateral to Albert's overall operant activity. The behaviors negatively reinforced by escaping or lessening the loud noise are a more direct and behavioral connection to the disruption that occurs than the conditioned physiological reflexes. The child crouching in the corner, covering his face or attempting to crawl away, is engaged in escape behaviors that are so strongly reinforced that they are prepotent over anything else the child may be doing. As a result, they preempt the operant repertoire that might be normally ongoing.

## extinction of conditioned aversive stimuli
## by approximations

Just as a conditioned aversive stimulus, such as the white rat in Watson and Rayner's experiment, acquired its aversive properties by being paired with the loud noise, its function as an aversive stimulus could be weakened by presenting it alone. Presumably with repeated presentations of the white rat, without the loud noise following, it would soon lose its aversive properties. The procedure is that of extinction of a conditioned reflex described in Chapter 2. (Recall in that chapter that the buzzer no longer elicited salivation when it was presented repeatedly without being followed by the food powder in the dog's mouth.)

Watson and Rayner attempted to carry out such an experiment but could not complete it because Albert's reaction to the conditioned stimulus was too severe. They then tried to carry out extinction more slowly by choosing stimuli which only slightly resembled the white rat. They first showed some object which elicited only reflexes of small magnitude (such as a ball of cotton) and they presented these at a distance. As the conditioned responses to these stimuli diminished through not being paired with the unconditioned stimulus, the experimenter moved the stimulus closer to the child until the conditioned responses if elicited were lessened. Watson and Rayner discovered that although the magnitude of the reflexes fell substantially as a result of nonreinforcement, they did not disappear entirely.

As the following excerpt from their report shows, Watson and Rayner concluded that the results of conditioning may not be reversible.

> A series of experiments with a Santa Claus mask, a fur coat, a set of blocks, a rat, and a rabbit demonstrated conclusively that directly conditioned emotional responses as well as those conditioned by transfer persist, although with a certain loss in the intensity of the reaction for a longer period than one month. Our view is that they persist and modify personality throughout life. It should be recalled again that Albert was of an extremely phlegmatic type. Had he been emotionally unstable, probably both the directly conditioned response and those transferred, would have persisted throughout the month unchanged in form.

The experimenters doubted that the results of conditioning are ever completely reversible. They could have tested this question by repeatedly presenting the rat to Albert after they had stopped pairing it with the loud noise over his head. Had they done so they would have carried out a procedure similar to the flooding therapy described in Part II of Chapter 3. Thus, their conclusion that the conditioned reflex cannot be eliminated may be due to their failure to carry out the extinction procedure for a sufficient time.

Other factors, however, could have prevented extinction. If the child is huddled in the corner with his eyes shut there is little chance that extinction can occur; since extinction presupposes that the child is exposed to the stimulus. The negative reinforcement of huddling, screaming, and closing the eyes removes the very conditioned aversive stimulus—the white rat—whose control was to be diminished by extinction.

More recently, many psychotherapists, notably Dr. Joseph Wolpe,[4] developed a therapeutic technique called *systematic desensitization.* This concept is similar to that operating with Albert in Watson and Rayner's experiment. Both are related conceptually to Pavlov's principle of reflex conditioning rather than to those of operant behavior, as set out by Skinner, for example. Noting that the experiment proved that the loud noise conditioned stimuli that resembled the white rat, the behavior therapists concluded that it would be possible to carry out extinction using stimuli other than the original one that elicited the phobic reaction. To carry out a treatment program with Albert, stimuli resembling the white rat would elicit lesser magnitudes of aversive effect than evoked by the rat itself. Furthermore, the aversive effects could be graded by controlling how far the aversive stimulus was from the child. Presumably a ball of cotton would elicit a reflex of lesser magnitude than the white rat, and a ball of cotton at a distance would evoke reflexes of even smaller magnitudes. Watson and Rayner's failure to eliminate the phobia, they reasoned, was because they failed to carry out extinction systematically. With a graded program of stimulus presentations, continued long enough, they speculated that the aversive control by the white objects, and eventually by the white rat itself, could have been eliminated.

Wolpe's systematic desensitization technique was designed mainly to eliminate phobias such as a fear of airplanes or closed spaces. It was assumed that at some time during the person's life an extremely aversive occurrence established those situations as conditioned aversive stimuli, similar to the influence of the loud noise on Albert's reaction to a white rat. In Wolpe's procedure, also called *desensitization by reciprocal inhibition,* the patient is taught to relax and the pace of the desensitization is adjusted so that the patient always maintains a relaxed state. Thus, the patient's state of relaxation provides a means for controlling the level of the disruption produced by the desensitization procedure. The details of the desensitization procedure will be elaborated in Chapter 10. If the gradations of aversiveness are small enough so that the patient remains relaxed, then it is certain that the desensitization is being carried out at the minimum levels of aversiveness. The term, reciprocal inhibition, refers to a theory of how the patients state of relaxation and the aversive effects of the conditioned aversive stimuli interact.

The therapist makes a list of events that resemble the description of the phobia but are dissimilar enough that the reaction each event evokes is not disruptive of the patient's state of relaxation or does not reinforce escape or avoidance. The list of events is arranged in a hierarchy of similarity to the primary phobic situation. The least provocative step in the hierarchy is presented first and the patient's interaction with it is prolonged until the phobic reaction disappears. The patient is then exposed to the next statement in the hierarchy, portraying a scene slightly more similar to the primary phobic event.

Therapists are not in general agreement about the effectiveness of desensitization therapy, although experiments have been carried out which show significant improvement from it. The arguments for and against are difficult to evaluate but enough evidence has accumulated that it is clear that it is effective for some patients under some conditions. For the purposes of this course of study, however, it is a useful way to think about the by-products of aversive control and the behavioral processes that are involved. For example, it seems reasonable to assume that the same processes are at work in psychoanalytic therapy when a patient, in free association, talks about the events of his or her life. The patient, relaxed and lying on a couch, is not likely to talk about matters that generate large aversive effects. Nor is the therapist likely to force the patient into discussions of events that precipitate large aversive effects. The analyst's influence by way of prompts, confirmations, or questions or interpretations could easily have the same function as the behavior therapist's hierarchy by way of guiding the pace of the patient's entry into difficult topics of discussion or description. We need not be concerned at this point about evaluating the claims, criticisms, and counter claims made by the advocates of one therapy mode or another. The first task is to describe the details of what happens. Behavioral language has the same advantage in clinical work as physiology has for internal medicine. It helps to make the underlying processes identifiable and communicable and directs us to the data we should be gathering.

Even though desensitization therapy purports to deal with objective behavior and even though psychodynamic therapies purport to deal with mental representations of events, behavior principles can be usefully applied to both to analyze how they work. One example could be that of a psychoanalytic therapist, recommending that a child with a school phobia be induced to enter the school building even if he only sits in the principal's or counselor's office to do some school work or to read. The advice is to be kindly supportive but firm.

When we look at the actual practices of desensitization therapy rather than the theory that guides it, some of the more radical differences from other therapies disappear. We notice, for example, that the desensitization occurs with speech about the phobic events rather than the events themselves. Thus, while there are practices called *in vivo therapy* in which a phobia about an airplane is treated by a companion who accompanies the patient in hierarchical approximations to actually going on an airplane trip, the predominant therapy mode is, like psychodynamic therapy, two people talking to each other.

## what is emotion?

Emotion is a word that is widely used in everyday, colloquial talk about human behavior. We say someone doesn't express emotions easily when we refer to someone who is phlegmatic or or whose facial movements are very limited. We say one child hit another because of anger. We sometimes see physiological responses such as trembling, clenched teeth, and blanching, and we say that they occur because the person is angry. We observe someone shouting at another person, and we say the shouter's adrenalin is flowing. In many of our colloquial accounts of emotion, we fool ourselves into thinking that we have explained something. Many of these explanations are little more than tautologies where we say the same thing using other words. When we say that one child struck another in anger we say little more than the observed fact that one child had injured another. When we describe emotion by noting physiological changes, there is the difficulty that these changes are diffuse and do not differentiate among the important experiences and behavioral conditions.

There are significant advantages of a technical, behavioral description of the same phenomenon. These advantages accrue from taking into account the actual behaviors that change and the reinforcers maintaining them. By and large, a behavioral analysis of emotion will deal with changes in the frequency of operant behaviors. The basic format for thinking about emotion has already been presented in the discussion of how a pre-aversive stimulus disrupts the individual's ongoing operant behavior. The significance of emotion, apart from other behavioral conditions, is that it describes a change in many different behaviors simultaneously.

Although the rat had been conditioned to press a bar and did so under the conditions of food deprivation that prevailed, it is clear that the red light preceding the shock would have disrupted wheel-running activity, grooming another animal, sex play, or any food-reinforced operant that had been conditioned. Thus, we describe the disruptive effect of the pre-shock stimulus as emotional because it affects a large part of the animal's repertoire simultaneously. The operation producing the broad, emotional change is the buzzer preceding the electric shock and the change in behavior that is termed emotional is the changes in frequencies that result. In this case we are likely to describe the rat, colloquially, as fearful or anxiously anticipating the shock. The same facts, however, are described behaviorally without recourse to inferences about a mental state.

Albert, the child described in the Watson-Rayner experiment, illustrates changes in the frequency of ongoing operant behaviors that are parallel to the disruption of bar-pressing in the pre-shock stimulus. Albert stopped emitting many operant performances maintained by a wide range of positive reinforcers. He no longer explored the room visually, played with his fingers, experimented with making sounds vocally, or played with his blocks. The same process appears to operate when a person suddenly loses a job or when a close relative dies. One is likely to stop playing sports that one otherwise enjoys, eat less than one customarily does, and be disinclined to talk to people, except about the loss one has just experienced or about one's discomfort.

Some emotional operations cause changes in frequency of a limited class of behaviors, rather than the overall disruption that occurs with a pre-shock stimulus. When we do something to make a person angry we observe an increase in the frequency of a limited class of behaviors that have in common that their function is to injure, attack, destroy, or repell. Punishment, extinction, and restraint are such operations. Although the most prominent result may be an increase in "attack" behaviors, the overall result on the broader repertoire will still be a broad disruption of the ongoing operant repertoire similar to the disruption by the pre-shock stimulus in the rat experiment. It is difficult to determine, *a priori,* how much the "attack" behaviors are elicited, fixed-action patterns[5] and how much they are derived from a history of reinforcement of the perfor-mances as operants. Both probably operate in varying proportions. The high frequency of angry behavior of the person who has been punished or denied something important preempts any other operant activity that might have otherwise occurred. The same kind of interaction occurs when an individual undergoes a period of food deprivation. The result is an increase, selectively, in all those activities that have produced food in the past. As with anger, the emotional aspect of the process is that one operation—a period of food deprivation—increases the frequency of a selective class of activities and that the high frequency of these activities preempts anything else that the child might do.

Special problems, related to emotional effects, arise when an operant performance is acquired by negative reinforcement; these have been described earlier. Before the behavior is well established, the frequent occurrence of the aversive stimulus may suppress the only performance that could reduce its frequency. Without the frequent electric shock there would be no reinforcer to increase the frequency of the escape behavior. Yet, the electric shock may cause large disruptions of the rat's overall repertoire including the very performance that might avoid the shock. These conflicting influences are dealt with in animal experiments, say with a rat, by using a small experimental chamber and a prominent lever. These make it likely that the lever-press will occur with some frequency.

The situation is quite different, however, with more highly differentiated performances than lever-pressing. A student composing a poem or writing a creative essay under the pressure of negative reinforcement also faces the opposing processes of negative reinforcement and emotional disruption. Escape from the the larger situation is the likely outcome in these cases. The same dilemma obtains when we attempt to get children to do their chores by aversive control. The disruption by the aversive control used to negatively reinforce doing the chores will increase the frequency of aggressive activity and will establish the entire situation as a conditioned aversive stimulus that reinforces escape in one form or another. The overall disruption that is engendered may often disrupt the actual behavior of doing the chores. Thus, parental nagging may decrease the likelihood of an adequate clean up. The student who has mastered techniques of memorization and recall may prepare for an examination with a calm, efficient mood and not be affected at all by an overall disruption, like that controlling the rat in the presence of a pre-shock stimulus. But the control by the examination may still be aptly described as an emotional operation. The aversive control by the examination generates study behavior that is maintained by negative reinforcement and the negatively reinforced study activity will preempt almost any activity that the student might otherwise engage in. Furthermore, the emotional control by the negative reinforcement will preempt "playful" learning whose reinforcer is an increment in repertoire that may not contribute to passing the exam.

Other emotional operations are described colloquially as frustration, rage, loneliness, sorrow, and joy. All are collateral to decreases or increases in reinforcement and consist of changes in selected parts of the repertoire that are related to these reinforcers. In frustration, some potentially high frequency activity cannot be emitted because of physical or social restraint or a missing part of the environment, such as when someone loses the key to the house and can't enter late at night. The colloquial term *rage* appears to describe situations where the person applies extreme forms of aversive control that might remove some social restraint or gain a reinforcer that another person is blocking. The fixed-action pattern described earlier may be a component. In loneliness, there is a reduced level of interaction because a person's "critical social supports" are lacking for one reason or another. Sorrow implies a depression controlled by the loss of a reinforcer that maintains a substantial segment of an individual's repertoire. Joy or happiness suggests emotional operations that increase the frequency of behaviors that are maintained by positive reinforcement. For example, news of a windfall or the arrival of a good friend are discriminative stimuli that control a wide range of positively reinforced behavior. Such emotional effects are described as changes in the state of the individual because broad classes of behavior change frequency. With the arrival of the friend thoughts turn to forthcoming activities, plans for spending time together, gossip and news to be shared. News of a windfall prompts plans for buying things and thoughts about all of the new activities that will become possible.

In all of these situations the behavioral changes need to be distinguished from the physiological effects. Collateral physiological and reflex changes occur in most of the circumstances described above. Yet it is patently clear that varied emotional states cannot be differentiated by the physiological changes they produce.

## somatic by-products of aversive control

The field of psychosomatic medicine deals with diseases that do not have a clear cause by pathologies such as an infection, a damaged organ, or an endocrine imbalance. Diseases that are thought to be particularly influenced by stress and aversive control in the patient's past or present life are stomach ulcers, hypertension, asthma, hay fever, hives, back pain, Reynaud's disease (the shut off of the blood supply to the hands or feet), constipation, vomiting, dysmenorrhea, impotence, and frigidity. Paralysis of limbs, loss of vision and anesthesia of large areas of the skin have been described by psychotherapists who have reported success in alleviating the dysfunction with psychotherapy. There is evidence that even diseases such as the common cold or tuberculosis are as much due to the overall level of stress experienced by the person as the cold virus or tuberculosis bacillus. Most of the evidence is epidemiological or in the form of clinical case histories, but the mass of evidence is so large that few are in doubt about the importance of these psychological influences on the presence or absence of disease. Medical writers have estimated that the largest part of patient visits to doctors' offices involve the treatment of diseases or complaints that are mostly due to aspects of their social life and behavioral repertoire. Laboratory evidence of psychosomatic causes of disease is accumulating in many areas of research with animals, particularly with the biofeedback methods described in Chapter 2. While practical treatment methods are not yet available, there is clear evidence that essential hypertension (high blood pressure without evidence of medical pathology) can be controlled by psychological intervention.[6] The conclusion that life histories are an important factor in these diseases appears inescapable.

It is in the ulceration of the stomach, however, that cause by aversive control has been most explicitly demonstrated. The pioneer experiment with monkeys subjected to the stress of long periods of shock avoidance presents evidence that it was possible to induce ulcers as a by-product of aversive control.[7] That experiment exposed monkeys to the free-operant avoidance conditioning described in Chapter 3. The monkeys lived, restrained in a chair, with shock given through the grids on which they sat.

One monkey could avoid the shock by pressing a lever mounted on the chair close to its hand. Another monkey in an adjoining room sat in an identical chair but without a lever with which to avoid shocks. It received an electric shock every time the other monkey did. Thus, shocks were administered to both monkeys the same number of times, but the first monkey could avoid them by pressing the lever, while the "yoked" monkey had to receive the shocks passively. Brady discovered that the "executive monkey" developed ulcers while the yoked monkey did not. Although it turned out to be an artifact of the experiment that the ulcers were caused by the executive monkey's responsibility of the avoidance behavior, the experiment established the fact that exposure to such experiences indeed induced the psychosomatic disturbances. The experimenters discovered, however, that the experiment's result was due to the method of choosing the executive monkeys. Brady placed the first four animals to develop the avoidance behavior in the executive position and the others in the yoked position. Inadvertently, he had placed those monkeys most liable to aversive control and therefore most susceptible to ulcers in the executive position. Further research has clearly confirmed the exposure to the electric shock as the cause of the ulcers, even though it turned out that it was the animal's inability to control the shock that was the major factor producing physiological distress rather than the responsibility for the control.[8]

## questions

1. Describe the various ways that an electric shock as an aversive stimulus can be functionally related to an organism's behavior.
2. Describe the experimental paradigm for studying the function of a pre-aversive stimulus. Describe some situations where it operates in the natural environment.
3. Why are the physiological responses elicited by a pre-aversive stimulus not the central aspect of its behavioral control in emotion?
4. How does the broad disruption of the overall operant repertoire interfere with attempts to maintain and reinforce behavior by negative reinforcement?
5. Describe the conditioned stimuli, unconditioned stimuli, conditioned responses, and unconditioned responses in the Watson-Rayner experiment.

6. Say why, in the context of the data of the Watson-Rayner experiment, the term "fear" is best used to describe a general state of the organism rather than a physiological response.

7. What was the result of presenting the rat to the child after the iron bar had been struck on two previous occasions when the child reached for the rat?

8. How could Watson and Rayner have gone about reversing the aversive control of the child's behavior they had established?

9. How are the procedures of behavior therapy by systematic desensitization related to those of the Watson-Rayner experiment?

10. What is the significance of the reciprocal inhibition in the behavioral desensitization procedures?

11. Describe and give examples of emotion as changes in the frequency of broad classes of operant behavior.

12. What are the special problems related to emotional effects that arise when an operant performance is acquired by negative reinforcement?

13. Describe the details of the behavioral control that are alluded to in common, everyday language descriptions of emotion.

14. Describe how the interaction between operant and reflex behavior may be the cause of psychosomatic illnesses such as ulcers.

---

## part II: a comparison of the control by positive and aversive stimuli

### increases in frequency due to positive and negative reinforcers

The preceding sections have described how we can increase the frequency of a performance by following it with a positive reinforcer such as food, or by having it terminate an aversive stimulus, such as a loud noise or electric shock. Conversely, the frequency of a performance because of reinforcement (either positive or negative) may be reduced by discontinuing reinforcement or by punishment. The extinction procedure for positive reinforcement is to no longer follow the performance with the reinforcing stimulus. In negative reinforcement, the extinction procedure is to no longer allow the operant to terminate the aversive stimulus or, in other words, the performance is followed by the aversive stimulus it had previously terminated. An alternative way to decrease the frequency of a performance is to punish it by following it with an aversive stimulus such as an electric shock or a stimulus correlated with nonreinforcement. Because these different procedures change the frequency of an operant performance in the same direction, it will be useful to compare the characteristics of behavior controlled by them.

Table 4-1 summarizes the functions of positive and aversive stimuli that have been described so far. The column headings describe the two types of stimuli, while the row headings denote what happens to that stimulus when an operant performance occurs. The cells indicate the procedure that describes this relationship between a performance and a reinforcing stimulus.

Cell A of the table deals with positive reinforcement where the presentation of a reinforcer, contingent on an operant performance, increases its frequency. Food as a positive reinforcer following key-pecking increases the frequency of key-pecking. In Cell D the frequency of an operant performance is increased when the operant performance terminates the aversive stimulus (negative reinforcement). The aversive stimulus in this instance may be one such as shock or one derived from a history of nonreinforcement such as the red light in the chimpanzee experiment signalling when a performance will not produce food. We define both the withdrawal of the positive reinforcer following a performance (Cell B) and the presentation of an aversive stimulus following an operant performance (Cell C) as punishment. Note that extinction does not appear in this table even though it is an important procedure for reducing the frequency of an operant performance. In Cell B, the withdrawal of positive reinforcement should not be misinterpreted as extinction. Here, we assume that some stimulus controls a zero rate of performance (as with the red light in the chimpanzee experiment) because of a history of nonreinforcement.

## conditioning a performance
## not yet in the individual's repertoire

If the operant to be strengthened already is occurring at a high frequency, it may be as easily conditioned with negative as well as positive reinforcement. The high initial frequency of the operant terminates the aversive stimuli quickly, and the aversive stimulus is not present. The situation is somewhat different, however, if the performance to be conditioned is not yet in the animal's repertoire.

An examination of how successive approximation of a complex performance would proceed with negative or positive reinforcement illustrates an important difference between the two modes of reinforcement. It will be useful, first, to review the contingencies and procedures of successive approximation. To shape a complex performance with either positive or negative reinforcement, it is necessary to begin with some form of behav-

**Table 4-1** Classification of the Contingencies Between Operant Performances and Reinforcing Stimuli

|  |  | PRESENTATION | WITHDRAWAL OR TERMINATION |
|---|---|---|---|
| STIMULI | Positive Reinforcer | A.  Positive Reinforcement | B.  Punishment |
|  | Aversive Stimulus | C.  Punishment | D.  Negative Reinforcement |

ior already in the organism's repertoire. When a variation in the direction of the required form is emitted, the reinforcing stimulus is presented immediately and the particular form of behavior that is reinforced increases in frequency. After an approximation of the complex performance becomes conditioned, the contingency is shifted toward a slightly more complex form, in the direction of the target.

With an aversive stimulus as the reinforcer, however, it is necessary for the aversive event to occur periodically in order for its termination to provide the basis for the negative reinforcement. For example, consider a case where a pigeon is nodding in the direction of the key and the performance to be conditioned by negative reinforcement is that of pecking at the key. When the experimenter changes the reinforcement contingency in the direction of large magnitudes of nods, he does so by delivering an electric shock when the bird is only nodding slightly or not nodding at all. The delivery of the electric shock is necessary because its removal is the only reinforcer maintaining the performance. Hence, at all times except when the required performance is emitted, it is necessary to shock the pigeon. The delivery of the shock when the pigeon is not performing will elicit reflexes that, in turn, reduce the likelihood that the performance will occur. In addition to the direct effects of the electric shock, the details of the animal's environment will become pre-aversive stimuli whose disruptive effects are even more severe than these of the shock itself. These emotional effects will disrupt and compete with most of the animal's repertoire, including those performances being conditioned. Even worse, however, the experimenter may punish nodding when the topography falls slightly short of the magnitude required for negative reinforcement. If, for any reason, the nodding performance becomes weak, the aversive stimulus must be delivered more frequently and the depressive effects of the aversive stimulus become intensified as more and more aversive stimuli are delivered.

Positive reinforcement, on the other hand, has no such indirect disruptive effects. Should positive reinforcement be withheld temporarily, the behavior will continue at a substantial frequency because, under most circumstances, a positively reinforced operant occurs many times without reinforcement before its frequency falls substantially. Should the behavior become seriously weakened, a single reinforcement will usually reinstate it. With optimal frequencies of reinforcement, the animal will be very disposed to stay in the situation and to continue behaving. To shape complex behavior with aversive control, it is necessary to prevent the animal from leaving the situation either by restraint or by additional aversive control.

## reduction in frequency of a positively reinforced operant performance by extinction and punishment

Punishment and extinction both may decrease the frequency of a positively reinforced operant performance. There are, however, important differences between the two methods of control. One difficulty in understanding the efficacy and characteristics of punishment as a method for reducing the frequency of reinforced performances in normal human behavior lies in the special conditions that are necessary in the laboratory experiments. Those experiments where punishment has suppressed performances employed severe shock—at almost lethal levels unthinkable in the case of human beings. Furthermore, it is possible in these experiments to administer the shock so consistently that there is a certainty that each performance will be punished. Even under these conditions, with only a few exceptions, the performances are reduced in frequency rather than eliminated, particularly if the punished behavior is also positively reinforced.[9]

In contrast, punishment in the human social environment is uncertain, intermittent, and usually delayed. For example, only a small percentage of the crimes that are committed are identified with the person who committed them, and of the small percentage of criminals who are brought to trial, only a portion are convicted and punished.[10] Speeding is an example of a strongly maintained performance whose suppression is effective only so long as there is a visible and comprehensive police presence and vigorous, consistent enforcement. Even naturally occurring punishments may be ineffective in completely suppressing the performances they follow. People continue to smoke, eat excessively, drink to excess, or take harmful and addicting drugs despite their aversive consequences. Work accidents resulting from the improper or incautious use of tools and careless recreational accidents are profitably viewed as instances where punishment is ineffective.

Extinction, then, appears to be a more effective way to eliminate or reduce the frequency of an operant performance than punishment when it is possible to alter the environment drastically enough. Extinction is more effective than punishment because it removes the variable that generates and maintains the behavior in the first place. To use extinction to eliminate behavior is much more complex practically than appears at first glance, however. Consider the interaction that was analyzed in Chapter 3 between the parent and the nagging child. The child nags because the aversive effects of nagging induces the parent to comply with the demand by negative reinforcement. But the nagging might just as likely induce the parent to punish the nagging rather than to reduce it temporarily by complying with it. More likely, however, a parent is likely to punish the nagging one time and negatively reinforce it by complying at another time. Thus the control shifts back and forth between parent and child. One time the child controls the parent by negative reinforcement; at another time the parent controls the child by punishing the nagging. The same performance is alternately reinforced and punished. But even the punishment has complications and by-products that are at cross purposes with its intended effect. A parent who punishes a child is interacting with it and paying special attention. The fact of an interaction, aversive or not, will be a reinforcer for many children under many circumstances. In that case, punishment turns out to be a powerful avenue of control of the parent by the child instead of the parent's intended purpose of reducing the child's nagging. A parent who resorts to such punishment may be in the paradoxical position of punishing and reinforcing the nagging at the same time.

Extinction of nagging, as an alternative to punishment, seems very difficult for most parents in most circumstances. It becomes possible to carry out extinction if the parent can break the connection between the child's nagging and the instant, seemingly automatic annoyance it produces for the parent. So long as the parent responds so immediately and so profoundly to the child's nagging, there is no possibility of reducing its frequency by extinction. The parent's reaction is the reinforcer for the nagging and it takes the form that influences the parent most profoundly. The elimination of the reinforcer that makes extinction of nagging possible requires a basic change in the parents before their reactions can be neutral in respect to the child's attempts at aversive control. The required change is complex and explains why such interactions are so difficult to resolve productively.

## the DRO procedure as an alternative to punishment

The procedure of differentially reinforcing "other" behavior, described in Chapter 1, is an alternative to extinction as a way to reduce the frequency of a performance. The DRO would operate more frequently in social situations, such as the nagging child described in the preceding section, where there are important characteristics of the interaction that make it difficult to carry out extinction. By simply shifting the reinforcement contingency to some other behavior, it becomes possible to maintain a normal frequency of positive reinforcement, yet not allow it to be contingent on the forms of behavior that have unwanted by-products for all of the parties in the interaction. The teacher's attention in a typical classroom is a reinforcer that lends itself to the differential reinforcement of other behavior. Typically, like the nagging child in the interaction described in the preceding section, the student produces the teacher's attention when she or he is disruptive, failing to study, or is inattentive. The reinforcement of study behavior, whether by the teacher's attention or by the increment in academic repertoire, is delayed considerably. In practice, a student's disruptive behavior will be immediately reinforced by the attention that it engenders from the teacher. Or, the disruptive student may get attention from other students in the class should the teacher be able to withhold her reaction. Instead of allowing her attention to be preempted by the students' disruptive behavior, the DRO procedure suggests that the teacher deliberately seek out children and pay attention to them when they do something productive. This procedure suggests a classic maxim in teaching that it is better to tell a student what to do than to tell the student what not to do.

Behavioral psychologists carried out an experiment in a classroom demonstrating the efficacy of the concept of reinforcing other behavior as an alternative to punishing undesirable behavior.[11] The studies were carried out in elementary school classrooms located in an economically deprived area of Kansas City, Kansas. The experimenters stationed observers in the classrooms of teachers who volunteered for the experiment. Several disruptive students were targeted and the observers kept records of class participation, study behavior, and disruptive activity. They recorded a baseline performance that could be used as a reference point for the DRO procedure that was to be implemented after the teachers were trained in the new way of reacting to the students. The observers, seated in the rear of the room where they were not easily seen by the students, held up cue cards to identify when a student was attentive or studying so that the teacher could attend to the child by moving to its desk, addressing some relevant comment, or even just pass by, placing a hand on the child's shoulder. There was evidence of a substantial increase in study activity and a corresponding decrease in disruption. Presenting the actual quantitative records of the changes in the students' performance also served as a reinforcer for the teacher's participation. The details of the interaction with one of the pupils gives a clearer description of how the teachers' and pupils' behavior changed.

Robbie was chosen because he was considered a particularly disruptive pupil who studied very little. Robbie's study behavior was defined as having a pencil on paper during 5 sec. or more of the 10-sec. interval. During baseline, study behavior occurred in 25% of the intervals observed during the class spelling period. The behaviors which occupied the other 75% of his time included snapping rubber bands, playing with toys from his pocket, talking and laughing with peers, slowly drinking the half-pint of milk served earlier in the morning, and subsequently playing with the empty carton.

During the baseline period the teacher would often urge Robbie to work, put his milk carton away, etc. In fact, 55% of the teacher attention he received followed non-study behavior. Robbie engaged in continuous study for 60 sec. or more only two or three times during a 30-min. observation.

Following baseline determination, whenever Robbie had engaged in 1 min. of continuous study the observer signaled his teacher. On this cue, the teacher approached Robbie, saying, "Very good work, Robbie", "I see you are studying", or some similar remark. She discontinued giving attention for non-study behaviors including those which were disruptive to the class. An increased study rate was observed during the first day of the first reinforcement period. Studying was recorded in 71% of the intervals during this period.

Robbie's teacher reported behavior changes correlated with his increased rate of study. During baseline, she reported that Robbie did not complete written assignments. He missed 2 of 10, 5 of 10, 6 of 10 words on three spelling tests given during baseline. By the final week of reinforcement, she reported that he typically finished his initial assignment and then continued on to another assigned work without prompting. Disruptive behavior had diminished and it was noted that he continued to study while he drank his milk and did not play with the carton when finished. He missed 1 of 10 words on his weekly spelling test.

Subsequent follow-up checks made during the 14 weeks that followed (after signaling of the teacher was discontinued) indicated that study was being maintained at a mean rate of 79%.

The question might be raised, along the lines of the discussion of arbitrary and natural reinforcement in the next part of this chapter, of whether the teacher's attention and approval is the most advantageous reinforcer for study behavior. Ideally, if the increment in the child's competence were the reinforcer maintaining its study behavior, then the child would be able to learn for its own sake. To this end, the teacher's attention might also be seen as a way to amplify, for the student, the amount of learning that is taking place.

A state of affairs similar to the teacher's problem in the classroom exists when a child's crying is maintained by the parental attention it gains. If the parent is sufficiently attentive to the child, then the parent would react to smiling and cooing as readily as to crying. In that case when a child's cries are elicited by organic distress, illness, or food deprivation, they would be clearly distinguishable from the situations where crying is maintained by the attention and interaction it gains from the parent.

## reasons for using aversive control despite its undesirable by-products

When reinforcement procedures are used in the animal laboratory, the change in the behavior of the animal is the reinforcer that maintains the behavior of the experimenter. The experimenter is controlling the behavior of the animal by the way reinforcement is delivered or withheld but the animal is controlling the experimenter because the changes in its performance are the consequences that maintain the experimenter's activity. Who is reinforcing whom? Obviously there are important differences between the control in the animal and human situation most involving the greater freedom the experimenter has in manipulating the animal's behavior. But both the animal experiment and the human social environment maintain behavior most strongly when the performance achieves an immediate, large effect.

The immediacy of the aversive stimulus accounts for the importance of escape and avoidance in social interactions. The child who picks up his toys when the parent screams provides immediate reinforcement for the parent's behavior because the aversive stimulus instantly strengthens the required escape performances. If the aversive stimulus is of sufficient magnitude, it instantly generates avoidance or escape that is prepotent over any other behavior in the individual's repertoire. This instant control provides a very strong reinforcement for the controller and reinforces his or her disposition to continue the use of aversive control despite its long term disadvantages. These disadvantages include the necessity of continuing the aversive control if the behavior is to be maintained or to remain suppressed, the possibility of counter-control by the individual who is punished, and the emotional states that are generated in both the controller and controllee. These undesirable by-products of aversive control are often overlooked because they occur a considerable time after the behavior of the controller has been reinforced by an immediate change in the behavior of the controllee.

With positive reinforcement, the state of affairs is usually reversed. The reinforcement of the controller's behavior is usually delayed in contrast to the immediate effects of aversive control. For example, an experiment with a pigeon using food as a reinforcer, cannot begin until the bird has been deprived of food for a week or ten days. With a performance that is negatively reinforced, simply presenting the aversive stimulus instantly duplicates an equivalent to food deprivation. To reduce the frequency of a pigeon's pecking after some schedules of reinforcement, ten to twenty hours of extinction and 80,000 unreinforced pecks need to occur. The same performance could be suppressed almost instantly with a severe enough electric shock or a pre-shock stimulus. The child in the classroom who is scolded for giggling stops during the scolding and thereby provides immediate reinforcement for the teacher's behavior. It is for these reasons that aversive techniques of behavioral control are widely used despite their unfortunate by-products, long-term disadvantages, and frequent ineffectiveness.

Alternatives to punishment almost always involve extinction by withholding the reinforcer maintaining the performance. They are difficult to prescribe because virtually every known behavioral process has some relevance for reducing the frequency of behavior.

## questions

1. Why doesn't extinction appear in one of the cells in the table describing the presentation and withdrawal of a positive reinforcer and an aversive stimulus?

2. In what way are positive and negative reinforcement similar? In what way are they different?

3. Describe how the use of aversive stimuli to control behavior may change the individual's repertoire—including undesirable by-products—beyond the particular performances to be controlled.

4. Compare the reduction in the frequency of a positively reinforced operant performance by extinction and by punishment.

5. How is the DRO procedure an alternative to punishment?

6. Why is an aversive stimulus more likely to reinforce behaviors incompatible with those we are interested in when the relation between the aversive stimulus and the performance is arbitrary rather than natural?

7. Why is the reinforcement of the controller delayed when the control of the behavior of another person is by positive reinforcement?

8. Describe why aversive control is so frequently used despite its obvious disadvantages.

## part III: substituting positive reinforcement and extinction for aversive control

The preceding discussion suggested that it is less harmful for people to control each other by positive reinforcement than aversively. To discover alternatives for punishment, a technical view of behavior was proposed to identify the reinforcer maintaining the performances that are causing difficulty. In that case, extinction can weaken the performance or, alternatively, other performances can be found that achieve the reinforcer without engendering punishment. Because aversive control so often occurs socially we need to understand the variables governing the behavior of the controller and controllee and the interaction between them. To discover the alternatives to aversive control, we first need to be exact about how it arises and what causes the undesirable effects.

## aversive control without undesirable by-products

Many kinds of aversive control occur so naturally that we tend not even to notice them. Many examples of negative reinforcement introduced in Chapter 1 are such stable performances with such predictable results that it is hard to imagine serious sequellae to them. Looking away from an unpleasant sight, putting ones fingers in the ears to block out a loud noise, pinching the nostrils reinforced by the prevention of the noxious odor, turning the wheel of a car or braking to avoid an obstacle, are all movements that terminate or avoid a stable, highly predictable part of the environment. The infrequency with which we bump into pieces of furniture, stumble on an irregularity in the sidewalk or trip on the stairs is evidence of the stability and lack of concern about the observing behaviors that are negatively reinforced by avoiding these accidents.

Extinction is an aversive event that may have undesirable side effects in criticism, incarceration, fining, or anger. Yet, in the natural environment it operates unobtrusively to differentiate performances subtly and without harmful by-products. Many performances are shaped by natural environments that differentially reinforce without stress. For example, given that getting food into the mouth is a reinforcer, there is a natural contingency inherent in the physical characteristics of a spoon that will teach a child to hold the spoon upright and that will punish the child for failing to do so. The performances are shaped by the physical characteristics of the spoon in relation to gravity. Movements of an upright spoon are reinforced by the appearance of a spoon full of food at the child's mouth and movements of the spoon turned over are not. When a parent calmly restrains a child's hand when it reaches for a food with its hand, extinction occurs. So long as the child has a repertoire that is adequate for using utensils and the parents' avoid a power struggle, extinction will be a natural result of the consistent practices. Such restraint, if carried out neutrally, arranges extinction of the behavior of reaching for the food with the hands. We generally do not notice the features of most parental environments that shape eating with utensils rather than with the fingers. Nor are we likely to notice the extinction that is arranged when food is taken disproportionately.

Many other contingencies arranged by the social environment, although applied by other persons, are as consistent as those supplied by the physical environment. We do not, for example, think very explicitly about how we conform to the prevailing modes of dress. This is undoubtedly because the social consequences of going to a theater with bare feet or flatulating loudly with a new friend at a dinner dance would almost as reliably be punished as looking directly into the sun. Nor would one be likely to encounter a member of an audience at a piano recital who would applaud loudly during the middle rather than at the end of a movement even if he was greatly enthused about the performance. Traffic violations such as going through the gate on a toll road without paying are so consistently enforced that it doesn't matter that the aversive consequences are mediated by another person and not generically related, physically, to the performance. The control exemplified in these situations, like eating from a spoon, emerge as a result of innumerable instances where brief and relatively benign occurrences of extinction shape behavior during childhood development.

## distinguishing between benign
## and malignant forms of aversive control

It will be instructive to compare the relatively benign forms of aversive control described above with the situations where there are likely to be serious side effects. The most important difference between benign and malignant forms of aversive control occurs when we restrict how a performance may terminate the aversive stimulus. Consider the arbitrary conditions imposed on the animal escaping electric shock in a laboratory experiment. Left to its own devices, the rat would simply jump out of the box. Without that alternative, it might climb on the lever and sit there. Most experimental spaces have anticipated the alternative ways that the animal might avoid or escape the shock. Some rats may climb the walls of the chamber or lie on the thick fur of its back to minimize the shock. In that case an experimenter who intends to condition bar-pressing as the means by which the shock is to be avoided might lower the height of the ceiling to prevent jumping or shave the fur off the rat's back. Such problems are forestalled in monkey experiments by restraining them in a chair with electrodes fastened at body locations they can't reach.

Thus, the animal that is controlled aversively in an experiment suffers from the experimenter's demand that there be only one way to escape the shock. Without arbitrary intervention by the experimenter, the animal would escape from the entire situation. By comparison, a variety of performances can terminate a bright light in a natural situation. Closing of the eyes, putting on sun glasses, looking the other way, or putting hands over the eyes are generically related performances because they all have in common that they reduce the amount of light entering the eye. When an experimenter or a social controller is concerned about what particular performance turns off a light, special measures are needed to restrict the subject's options. In the natural environment, on the other hand, the various performances that will reduce the intensity of a light are equivalent. Clearly many of the deleterious effects of aversive control are inherent in the social aspects of the control.

There are many examples, in the interactions between parents and children, illustrating how the malignant effects of aversive control are a result of social factors. Consider, for example, a child who starts to go outdoors on a moderately cold day and is stopped by a parent who demands that a coat be worn rather than the sweater. The behavior that is of high frequency in the child's repertoire is playing outside. The function of the coat, anticipated by the parent, if the child were to have it on outside, is to avoid being cold. But other alternatives for staying warm outside exist for the child even though they do not seem satisfactory for the parent. The child could maintain its body temperature by keeping very active or by periodically going indoors to warm up. Alternatively, the restriction by the coat or the social pressure from the other children might be even more aversive than being cold. The parent's concerns, however, involve the contingencies controlling his or her own behavior. The behavior of forcing the child to wear a coat is negatively reinforced by the threat that neighbors would be critical that the child is not properly cared for or by the fear that the child might become ill from exposure to the cold air. The deleterious effects of the aversive control applied by the parent are based on the possibility that the restrictions are arbitrary, that they might not be applied consistently, and that they might lead to escalating levels of aversive control such as the power struggle mentioned earlier (also see p. 133).

## positive reinforcement with aversive or other undesirable aspects

Laboratory experiments maintaining a performance such as a pigeon pecking a key has many parallels to experiments on escape and avoidance of electric shock. Although we describe the pigeons behavior as exemplifying positive reinforcement in the sense of being maintained by producing a stimulus that increases the frequency of pecking, the pigeon's restriction in a small experimental space involves aversive control. The key at which the bird pecks reinforced by the appearance of the food magazine will maintain the bird's behavior only if the usual alternative ways of eating are not present. Given a larger environment where grain and fruit was present on plants and worms and insects under leaves it is unlikely that a bird would confine itself to a small space such as the experimental chamber to eat. The arbitrary action of the experimenter, restricting the bird to the experimental space constitutes aversive control that was a necessary condition before food could be used as a positive reinforcer. The circumstances are similar when food is used as a reinforcer in clinical experiments in mental hospitals or schools for the retarded. Clinical staffs have used tokens to reinforce behaviors such as making beds, attending group therapy sessions, working in the hospital laundry and self-grooming. These patients have a long history of free access to the dining room and continue to observe other patients walking in for their meals without restriction. The aversive control that is applied is inescapable.

A more serious difficulty with applications of positive reinforcement that require such arbitrary restrictions is their durability, permanence, and utility to the person being controlled. The difficulty can be illustrated by comparing arbitrarily restricted positive reinforcement with alternative ways of maintaining the same performance by a reinforcer generically related to it.

Attempts to develop speech in mute psychotic children by reinforcing utterances with food illustrates the disadvantages of creating a reinforcer by arbitrary restrictions. If the speaking that develops is indeed from reinforcement with food we would expect that the child would speak only when food is deprived. Further, the child's speech requires the constant presence of a therapist or experimenter to continue the reinforcement procedure. From the reference point of the child's repertoire, there are simpler ways to get food than to speak for it and we would expect that the child would return to them just as soon as the restrictions are lifted. Normally reinforced speech occurs because of its influence on a listener. Once it is established, its reinforcement will be a natural by-product of the interaction with the listener and will persist as long as there are listeners and an inclination to influence them. To use the reactivity of the listener as a reinforcer to develop and maintain speaking requires that other people mediate enough of the reinforcers supporting the child's behavior. Once speech begins to emerge, reinforced by the natural reactivity of the listener, it will be shaped and enlarged as the child grows. In contrast, speech reinforced by food, requires the continuous intervention of an arbitrary agent.

## arbitrary restriction of positive reinforcement from social control

The ability of one person to control the environment of another poses difficult problems in how behavior is maintained, for whose benefit is the reinforcement procedure and the utility of the resulting behavior. The problem is particularly acute in education where the dilemma is between socially aversive pressures on the student to study and the fear that the student won't study at all if left with the natural consequences of an increased repertoire. George Bernard Shaw posed the dilemma when he said, "Goading a calf down the street is not the only alternative to letting it wander into every china shop."

The examination in the typical formal course represents one such restriction. It reinforces study, negatively, by avoiding the aversive consequences of a low or failing grade. But the goal of school is an increment in competence that will continue to be a part of the student's repertoire after he leaves. In extreme cases, particularly when the threat is serious, the examination will reinforce cheating. Students will seek out old examinations to minimize the amount of study that is necessary. Because the examination specifics a small sample of the competence required, much of the students' activity is concentrated on anticipating what will be tested and in what depth. Corresponding to the students accommodation to the aversive control by the examination, the teacher sets up a proctored situation where the examination is policed. Old examinations are closely guarded and attempts are made to design tests that do not allow the student to do a rote exercise. The dynamics of the interaction between teacher and student are similar to those described earlier between parent and nagging child.

A behavioral view of knowledge is that of an ongoing activity. Its most important aspect is its frequency, subsequently, in the student's life. Thus, an unrestricted reinforcement of educational activity specifies outcomes (reinforcers) that are generically related—that is, a natural outcome to the student's activity. In this vein, the teacher's job is that of one who instructs the student how to increase intellectual competence. If the teacher does not have the position of goading the student to accomplishment, there is the possibility of a repertoire that can be maintained naturally, without restriction. The risk, practically, with an unrestricted, natural reinforcement of learning is that there might not be circumstances in the student's life to support learning. But the alternative has equal disadvantages. A student who learns because of threats of loss will stop learning and stop using the knowledge when the threats cease. Even in those cases where knowledge gained defensively acquires a new function when it is applied after school ends, the extent and depth of its penetration is likely to be limited because of the arbitrary restriction from its negative reinforcement.

Other undesirable sequellae from the use of arbitrary, negative reinforcement are the emotional by-products. The examination, like a pre-aversive stimulus, will disrupt the person's overall activity, including restriction in the range and kind of study. Naturally reinforced learning, generically related to the performances that increase the students' knowledge have no such by-products. Praise is an example of an event that is usually a positive reinforcer but whose arbitrary restriction, because of its social aspects, may make it coercive and manipulative. Praise is nominally a positive reinforcer because, as the opposite of criticism, it is evidence that a person's behavior is affecting others usefully and positively. Arbitrary restrictions on the function of praise occur when one person (the controller) adjusts the contingency between the other person's performance and the praise arbitrarily, in some restricted way. When a skilled carpenter builds a fine piece of furniture, the reinforcer that will maintain his or her skills most productively will be the knowledge of the use the furniture will be put to, the money earned, and the subsequent business that comes from the customers's satisfaction. When a craftsperson is largely controlled by the praise of the work, independent of its use by the customer, the control of the craftsperson's behavior shifts from these stable outcomes to the idiosyncrasies of another person who may give or withhold praise for his or her own purposes.

The support of a student's behavior in school by the teacher's praise raises the same issue. The child who works in school "for his teacher" may lose his behavior when he goes to another classroom with a teacher for whom he is not disposed to work. But the child whose school experience has led to new competences inside and outside of school has a repertoire that will allow her to seek a teacher or that will persist in the absence of the teacher. Although the latter child is called "inner directed," it is important to observe that there are reinforcers (changes in the environment) maintaining the behavior other than the teacher's praise or goading. The inner directed student brings to mind George Bernard Shaw's statement that "things have not happened to me; On the contrary, I have happened to them."

An incident described by John Holt[12] illustrates the greater persistence and durability of behaviors naturally or generically connected with the reinforcer maintaining it. Holt observed a child struggling to assemble a mechanical pen and noticed the intense persistence and involvement in the activity, despite the difficulty of the task and the long road to its mastery. In contrast, he observed the same child in nursery school in an instructional task with a teacher where the slightest difficulty caused distress. The difference in performance occurred because the reinforcer in the classroom was the praise or censure of the teacher and competition with other children rather than the reinforcer with the pen that is intrinsic to the task.

## power struggle

*Power struggle* is a term used by clinicians to describe an interaction where a controller applies aversive stimuli to a controllee to produce a performance that might otherwise not occur. The controllee, in turn, engages in performances (negatively reinforced operants) whose thrust is to escape from the aversive control. One of the reasons why the application of punishment or other kinds of aversive control typically produces a power struggle in social situations is the inherent pressure to escalate the aversive control. The escalation occurs because situations where punishment is applied require restraint to prevent the controllee from simply escaping the aversive contingencies applied by the controller. A parent, for example, who punishes a child for coming home late by incarceration, withdrawal of privileges, or corporal punishment constructs an environment that is likely to negatively reinforce behaviors such as lying or constructing stories about extenuating circumstances. The child confined to its room may simply leave or, in the extreme example, run away from home, and the aversive control then moves to attempts to control the compliance with the punishment by further aversive control.

The interaction between a child and the mother where the child wants to go outside and the mother demands that he wear a sweater is another example of an interaction that commonly leads to a power struggle. The interaction between the two is a relatively simple chain of behaviors. The chain of events can be described from the point of view of either party. For the parent, seeing the child about to go out on a cold day without a coat, the demand "put on your coat" induces the child to dress and the final reinforcer is the sight of the child going outdoors properly clothed. For the child, the final event maintaining behavior is going outside and playing freely. The child terminates the threat of the parent by putting on the coat and, suitably dressed, is allowed to go outside.

The interaction may become complicated, however, because there is no generic connection between putting on the coat and the aversive control applied by the parent. Like the rat that climbs on the bar to avoid the electric shock instead of pressing it, the child might argue, saying "No, I don't want to," or "It's not cold, and the other kids will make fun of me dressed like that." Alternatively the child could start to leave without dressing or cry and whine in complaint. Either of these outcomes is, functionally, nonreinforcement of the parent's performance because the same variables that influenced the parent's behavior are still operative. The parent, therefore, shifts to another, escalated aversive control functionally determined as before by preventing the unclothed child from leaving. At this point the parent might say "You are not going outside without a coat and if you continue to argue and disobey me, I will not let you out at all." At this point, the parent's threats, instead of inducing dressing by negative reinforcement, may reinforce performances whose function is to escape from the parent's aversive control. In that case, the next likely performance might be whining and crying which, as aversive events for the parent, are operants that may be negatively reinforced if the parent escapes them by letting the child out without a coat.

Such a struggle will escalate the magnitude and frequency of the aversive stimuli each applies. The aversive stimuli are applied by negatively reinforced operants. One possible outcome is that the aversive stimulation applied by the child will reinforce "Oh, go outside and let me be through with you." Or alternately, the aversive stimulus generated by the child's attempts at counter control may evoke extreme censure. At this point the parent might end the child's tantrum by corporal punishment, restriction to its room, withdrawal of privileges, or total withdrawal of the parent from interaction with the child. The child, in turn, might continue to escape from the parent's aversive control by giving up its play in favor of a continued struggle.

Putting on a coat would be reinforced naturally if the consequences maintaining the performance was the increase in the temperature of the air around the child's skin. In that event the performance is generically and stably maintained, negatively reinforced by the warm air around the child's skin. Wearing a coat, however, is only a single performance representing a class of behaviors that will avoid chilling. These might be wearing a coat, sustaining vigorous physical exercise, or periodically going to a warm place. Such negative reinforcement is innocent in the sense that there are no by-products such as those from the power struggle described above. Arbitrary reinforcement often leads to power struggles because the control of the situation shifts back and forth between parent and child. Each can obstruct the reinforcement of the other's behavior by withholding the required performance. What begins as a mild command turns into an assault of one on the other. The consequences of such a power struggle may be serious for both the child and parent. The child reinforces behavior in the parent at a level of primitiveness comparable to its own repertoire and vice versa.

Another example illustrates further details of a power struggle. Jim's mother tells him to put on his shoes. He picks them up and throws them across the room.

Mother: Go pick up your shoes.

Jim: You do it.

Mother: You pick them up.

Jim: You do it.

Mother (desperately): Jim, for the last time, will you pick up the shoes?"

Jim: "You do it."

If the parent picks up the shoes, Jim has won a fight easily. To phrase the matter behaviorally, the aversive control implied by the mother's threats did not negatively reinforce the behavior of picking up the shoes. The mother would have had to be more persistent or increase the aversiveness of her action to achieve this result. The mother then takes the child's hand and pulls him over to the shoes. Jim holds back, struggles, and kicks. The level of aversive control by the mother escalates and reinforces new performances. If Jim's struggle thwarts the attempt to drag him to the place where the shoes are, the struggle ends. If the mother is strong and persistent enough to overcome the tantrum, then the struggle reaches a new intensity.

The new magnitude of aversive stimulus will differentially reinforce, by escape, corresponding performances in the boy's repertoire. That is, for each level of aversive stimulus, there is some activity that will escape from it. When Jim is dragged back to the shoes, he can run away as soon as his mother relaxes her grip. If she holds firmly and tries to put Jim's hand on the shoes, he can make a fist. This maneuver shifts the struggle to a new performance—getting Jim to open his hand. Through all of this Jim will lose no opportunity to be as aversive as possible, aimed at preventing the mother from continuing the interaction. He bites, screams, breaks any object at hand, injures himself, or tears or soils his own and his mother's clothes. These actions are counter control in the sense that they are reinforced by generating behavior in the mother's repertoire that in turn preempt her continued control of Jim. At each of these stages of the struggle, the mother is applying aversive stimuli designed to negatively reinforce some behavior in the boy's repertoire. Eventually, the mother, if she has the will to win, finds some level of force that will control the child. In the process, however, she will have shaped, in successive approximations, performances that escape the intermediate levels of aversive control she had applied. What starts out to be a mild command turns into an assault on the child. Corresponding with the mother's escalation of the struggle, the child acquires new ways of acting aversively or defensively with the mother. As in the previous example, arbitrary constriction of reinforcement contingencies leads to a power struggle because the control of the situation shifts over to the child who can tease, obstruct, and otherwise control the mother by withholding behavior.

## alternatives to the punishment
## of "not performing"

Aversive control occurs very frequently in social situations when a person fails to do something required by someone else. For example, a child comes home late for dinner, fails to complete a school assignment, or doesn't cut the lawn or take a bath. A behavioral analysis of these situations points to the delayed aversive stimulus as the critical problem. In getting a child to clean its room, for example, the actual performances that are required are picking clothes off the floor, putting them in drawers, making the bed, sweeping, and throwing out trash. The common sense view is that punishment for *not* cleaning will increase the frequency of the activities that are required. Explanations to the child purport to overcome the long delay and the lack of a specific contingency between the aversive stimulus that is applied when the child is punished and the specific performances that are desired. Such a common sense view of the situation is of little help in achieving a satisfactory resolution of the problem.

Behaviorally, we know that reinforcement is a contingency between a specific performance and a stimulus. Therefore, we need to be concerned about the actual performances whose frequency is low and how some contingency between them and a reinforcer can increase their frequency. One solution is to establish a "cleaned room" as a reinforcer that can increase the frequency of the component activities of cleaning. The advantage of this approach is that "a cleaned room" is a generic specification of the required performances. If a "clean room" is a reinforcer, it will naturally, generically, and stably reinforce those activities that produce it. Conversely, the diffuse presentation of an aversive stimulus is likely to do little more than generate counter control. The basic difficulty that needs to be resolved is that the clean room is a reinforcer for the parent and not for the child. Without this condition, there is little prospect of any satisfactory resolution of the tension.

One basis for establishing the clean room as a reinforcer for the child's cleaning activity is through the parent's approval. If the parent's approval is a sufficient reinforcer, then the cleaning activities serve in a chain of performances in which picking up clothes, and so forth, is reinforced by a "clean room" that, in turn, is the occasion on which there are positive interactions with the parents. The process is functionally similar to the chain of behaviors in the pigeon experiment where the peck is reinforced by the magazine light that in turn provides an occasion when the bird can eat. A complication of using parental approval as a reinforcer occurs when the component behaviors are not in the child's repertoires so that approximations need to be reinforced. But the approximations need to be established as collateral support so that the child's participation results in the final "cleaned room." Otherwise the generic connection between the child's performance and the state of the room would be lost.

Aversive control is another avenue for establishing the "clean room" as a reinforcer. If the untidy room becomes an occasion for restriction of the child and the clean room an occasion when normal activities can be carried out freely, then the untidy room functions as a conditioned aversive stimulus that can negatively reinforce the cleaning activities. In both aversive and positive cases, the specific behavior of cleaning the room is a natural, unrestricted by-product of the reinforcer. However, the interactions with the parent when the child is incarcerated may lead to a struggle.

The behavioral processes that are fundamental to both of these repertoires are chaining and conditioned reinforcement, topics which will be taken up in a later chapter.

Whether or not it is reasonable or productive to demand a clean room of a child is a larger question and beyond the scope of the kind of behavioral analysis attempted here. But the exercise is a useful one because such interactions occur so commonly and they illustrate the technical aspects of reinforcement in practical contexts.

## collateral support as a way to substitute positive reinforcement for arbitrary aversive control

Frequently aversive control is escalated in social interactions because the behavior required by one person, say the parent or teacher, is not in the repertoire of the child or student. For example, the child who spills food may not have acquired sufficient control of the utensils. Or, there may be reinforcers incidental to getting food into the mouth, such as a playful reaction to seeing the food splash or engaging the reaction of the parents, even if it is annoying to them. Support by collateral variables is one way to sustain these performances without resorting to attempts to control them aversively.

Consider the task of teaching a child to eat with utensils without using arbitrary aversive control. Choosing foods that are easily handled with a spoon is one possible form of collateral support, and helping the child to hold the spoon is another. If the food is cut into pieces easily handled with a spoon, and if the spoon is easy to handle, unapproved forms of eating are less likely to occur. Another form of collateral support would be actual physical assistance in handling the spoon. A process of collateral support is possible where the parent supplements the feeding behavior by holding the spoon along with the child, loosely, so that the child's movements can be sensed. The parent moves the spoon only when the child does not or when the movement is inept. Thus, the collateral support guarantees that the performance will be reinforced naturally and regularly and can be gradually diminished, paced with the new repertoire that emerges.

Restraining the child is another form of collateral support by which a parent can carry out extinction of the undesired eating patterns without risking a power struggle from arbitrarily restricted aversive control. By simply restraining a child's hand when it reaches into the jam with its hands in place of a spoon, movements of the spoon from the jam to the mouth are reinforced (by jam in the mouth) while movements with the bare hands are not. Therefore, one is reinforced and the other decreases in frequency by extinction. Alternatively, the jar might be moved out of the way when the child reaches into it with his hand. With very young children who can be restrained without a physical struggle, the parental restraint guarantees that the undesirable behavior will not be reinforced even if it is initiated. The alternative practice of reacting with punishment after the performance will produce the kinds of by-products discussed in the preceding section.

The common practice of allowing the child greater autonomy in self-feeding, paced with its ability to use the eating utensils successfully, illustrates how incompletely developed repertoires can continue to be reinforced with collateral support. In that way, their generic relation to the reinforcer can continue to maintain it and shape it into an effective form. Collateral support, intervention, and physical restraint imply consistent parental practices, moment-to-moment, in which certain topographies of feeding are reinforced because they bring food to the child's mouth while others are not.

## psychotherapy

Although there are many theories and methods of psychotherapy, one aspect of it, behaviorally, concerns the way it presents an experience where the patient is controlled by naturally unrestricted positive and negative reinforcement rather than the arbitrarily restricted aversive conditions that have prevailed heretofore. Some aspects of psychotherapy with autistic children provide a useful transition from the easily understood aspects of reinforcement in animal laboratory experiments and children's development to the complex verbal interactions of adult therapy.[13] The autistic child presents an especially undeveloped repertoire in which all but the most primitive modes of interacting with the environment, both social and physical, are lacking. The following examples describe therapy procedures with mute, severely disturbed autistic children that illustrate how naturally occurring, unrestricted reinforcers can be used to augment their competence. Such reinforcement is therapeutically productive because it is a stable part of the environment that is relevant to the child's current repertoire.

Even food, despite its frequent arbitrary and restrictive use, may be used in a natural, unrestricted relation to the child's current repertoire. For example, a young autistic child lacked the skills for opening a jar by unscrewing the lid. The therapist offered the child some candy from a glass jar with the lid on. But the first time that she did so, the lid was lying on top of the jar so that the child had merely to displace it from the opening to get the candy. The next time the cap was screwed on about half a turn and on successive occasions it was fastened more securely, paced with the increment in the child's competence, until the child learned how to unscrew it completely. The reinforcement was by food but it was natural and unrestricted because the only requirement imposed on the child's performance was by the physical characteristics of the jar and lid. Furthermore, the performance that emerged was one that would be reinforced in many environments since it is common for such candy, as well as other foods, to be kept in similar jars. Other performances, such as asking for food at the table or using a spoon to eat difficult foods such as pudding or ice cream are examples of natural reinforcement despite their dependence on food and food deprivation. Once the child has the competence, the reinforcement of these behaviors does not depend on the arbitrary intervention by the therapist or teacher.

Another example of natural reinforcers that are not arbitrarily restricted occurred when several children who were at a more advanced social level than the children mentioned above, showed interest in a place to hide away from their classroom work. Their wish for a place of their own suggested that building a cabin (with the help of a carpenter) would provide powerful reinforcers for school room activities. They needed to apply for a permit, order materials, compute costs, visit stores, go over plans, and take part in the construction. At every stage, the progress of the construction depended on their collaboration with these essentially verbal, school-type activities. The therapist's role was to fill in some of the intermediate steps so that the children could accomplish something successfully each day. The final goal, as a reinforcer, was neither attainable nor effective with the children's existing repertoires. There was always something concrete for which school work was needed to increase their competence to do the job. It might be computing the amount of nails needed so that they could be ordered, or the number of board feet of lumber. At another stage, they might need to read an instruction. Other kinds of reading, although not essential for the construction, connected with the project thematically.

Natural reinforcers are sometimes puzzling because they seem to reinforce so much behavior yet their effects appear to be evanescent when there is an attempt to use them deliberately. One of the reasons for this is that by their nature, they cannot often be made to happen by a second party's interest. Reinforcement is largely within the child's own repertoire. Cutting with scissors is one such activity often naturally reinforced. The performance is manipulating the scissors against the paper. The reinforcer is shearing of the paper in fine-grain relation to the scissors movements and the shaped pieces of paper that emerge. If a child has never used scissors before, however, there is no possibility of the performance being reinforced enough to increase its frequency. The reinforcer can be amplified, however, by providing enough collateral support for the performance no matter how limited the child's capability might be. For example, the therapist stands behind the child with one arm over each of his.

In this position the therapist will not distract the child and the therapist's arms around the child reduce the possibility of his walking away because of slight distractions. The child's fingers are put into the scissors and the therapist's hands cover the child's in such a way that the therapist can manipulate the child's fingers and at the same time feel the slightest muscle movements. If the child operates the scissors to any degree the therapist withholds support or action in favor of the child's action. Such a procedure reinforces the slightest approximation to cutting behavior. The therapist's support fades out naturally as the child takes over the movements of the scissors. Thus the therapist's activity is collateral to the child's performance and the reinforcer remains effective even after the therapist leaves the situation.

## the goals of psychotherapy and behavioral control

The goals of psychotherapy expressed by the major schools of clinical practice also illustrate the issues of arbitrary and natural control—reinforcers that are naturally and generically related to the performances that produce them. One important issue concerns who is to control whom. Rogers addressed this point when he wrote that the goal of therapy is "that the client will become self-directing, less rigid, more open to evidence of his senses, better organized and integrated, more similar to the ideal which he has chosen for himself. In other words, we have established external control by an individual in pursuit of internally chosen goals."[14] Implicit in Roger's statement is a relation to the client similar to the collateral sources of support described above for therapy with autistic children. The therapist provides collateral support that allows reinforcement to occur that is generic to the patient's repertoire and relevant to his or her current environment. It implies that the therapy is an elaboration of the patient's existing capabilities.

Psychoanalytic treatment has much the same attitude as Rogers when the analyst reacts to what the patient says at whatever level psychological development he or she is at. The basic injunction to "say whatever comes to mind" also expresses the patient's control of the content of therapy. So long as the therapist reacts to the repertoire that is occurring at the moment, including the behaviors controlled by the therapist, there is no possibility of arbitrary control. For this reason, it is frequently considered appropriate to deal with a very limited problem even though the therapist has evidence that the particular incident is only one of very many areas in which the patient is having difficulty. The freedom of the patient to choose can be described as emitted behavior that is reinforced by natural and stable features of the therapeutic environment. Without arbitrary restrictions in the control of behavior, a naturally reactive environment will shape it into forms of activity that are maximally effective for that individual.

The terms controller and controllee have pejorative connotations historically since control has always been for the benefit of the controller. Machiavelli's prescriptions usually emphasized procedures designed to benefit the prince rather than the subject. However, in the broader sense that the term control is used here, it defines the functional relation between a performance and its controlling environment. Hence the use is technical and does not specify either an aversive or a positive stimulus or whether the result benefits the controller, the controllee, both, or neither.

The distinction between arbitrary and natural reinforcement suggests that the term "control of behavior" can be profitably disentangled from the pejorative sense of coercive control. A full description of the complex natural environment requires that we understand the functional relation between conduct and the way it acts on the social and physical environment. Good or bad, this functional relation is best described as control. The full complexity, humanism, or freedom of behavior need not suffer from recognizing that the environment has generated the behavior.

## questions

1. Under what conditions does aversive control not have undesirable by-products?
2. Describe examples of human behavior where extinction of unproductive forms is a natural consistent product of the environment without harmful sequellae.
3. How are benign and malignant forms of aversive control distinguishable?
4. What are the factors in social, interpersonal control that lead to undesirable by-products?
5. How many positive reinforcement have aversive or other undesirable aspects?
6. How would the reinforcement of speech by tokens and food exemplify the disadvantages of arbitrary control with positive reinforcers?
7. Compare and contrast the arbitrary and natural reinforcement of educational activities.
8. How may praise turn into a contingency that is coercive and manipulative?

*9.* Describe the behavioral components of a power struggle. Use the same terms to analyze an example.

*10.* Describes the alternatives for punishing a child for not completing some activity and analyze the behavioral interaction that are indicated by a behavioral formulation.

*11.* Describe "collateral support" as a way to substitute positive reinforcement for arbitrary aversive control. Give an example.

*12.* In what respect may psychotherapy be described as an attempt to shift the control of the patient's behavior from arbitrary to natural reinforcers? Give some examples from therapy with children that illustrate this kind of development.

*13.* How do the concepts of arbitrary and natural control bear on the goals of psychotherapy?

## notes

[1] Animal laboratory research has gone some distance toward demonstrating competing responses such as mechanism of the suppression of ongoing operant behavior during a pre-aversive stimulus. See Blackman, D. E. Conditioned suppression and the effects of classical conditioning on operant behavior. In, W. K. Honig and J. E. R. Staddon (eds.) *Handbook of Operant Behavior.* New York: Prentice-Hall, 1977, pp. 340–363. One mechanism of suppression is simply a disruption in the organism's overall capacity to function as a result of loss of bladder and bowel control, and large scale changes in heart rate, blood pressure and hormonal secretion. Another mechanism includes the elicited skeletal responses such as biting and fighting. See Hake, D. F. and Campbell, R. L. Some relations between classically conditioned aggression and conditioned suppression in squirrel monkeys. *Journal of the Experimental Analysis of Behavior.* 34:149–165, 1980.

[2] Watson, J. B. and Rayner, R. Conditioned emotional reactions. *Journal of Experimental Psychology* 3:1–14, 1920.

[3] The researchers rationalized any possible harm the experiment might produce by noting that similar aversive occurrences would happen outside the nursery in the natural give and take of the child's home.

[4] Wolpe, J. *Psychotherapy by reciprocal inhibition.* Stanford, Ca.: Stanford University Press, 1961.

[5] Azrin, N. H., Hutchenson, R. R., and Hake, D. F. Attack, escape and avoidance reactions to aversive shock. *Journal of the Experimental Analysis of Behavior* 10:131–148, 1967.

[6] Pomerleau, O. F. and Brady, J. P. (Eds.) *Behavioral medicine: Theory and practice.* Baltimore: Williams and Wilkins, 1979.

[7] Brady, J. V. Ulcers in "executive" monkeys. *Scientific American,* 199:95, 1958.

[8]Weiss, J. M. Psychological and behavioral influences on gastrointestinal lesions in animal models. In: Maser, J. D. and Seligman, M. E. P. (Eds.) *Psychopathology: Experimental Models.*, 1977.

[9]Azrin, N. H. Effects of punishment intensity during variable reinforcement. *Journal of the Experimental Analysis of Behavior*, 3:123–142, 1960.

[10]President's Commission on Law Enforcement and the Administration of Justice. The challenge of crime in a free society. Government Printing Office, 1967, pp. 43–44.

[11]Hall, R. V., Lund, D., and Jackson, D. Effects of teacher attention on study behavior. *Journal of Applied Behavioral Analysis*, 1:1–12, 1968.

[12]Holt, J. *How children learn.* New York: Pitman Publishing Co., 1967.

[13]Ferster, C. B. Transition from animal laboratory to clinic. *Psychological Record*, 17:145–150, 1967.

[14]Rogers, C. *Client-centered therapy.* Boston: Houghton-Mifflin, 1975.

# schedules
# of reinforcement

5

## study guide

When every response emitted is reinforced, we call it *continuous reinforcement.* In noncontinuous or intermittent reinforcement, some responses are not reinforced. Since intermittent reinforcement concerns the maintenance of behavior after it has been conditioned in an organism's repertoire, schedules of reinforcement are of special interest. Each kind of schedule produces its unique pattern of behavior that is maintained stably so long as the schedule is continued. An examination of these states reveals many behavioral processes that can be observed in the natural human environment. Intermittent reinforcement of an operant performance profoundly influences how long it will persist in an organism's repertoire after reinforcement is completely discontinued. These properties of intermittently reinforced behavior have relevance to the transition from one schedule to another and clarify many of the phenomena that occur in natural human settings involving changing reinforcement conditions. Four basic schedules are introduced in this chapter and the standard performances generated by them are described.

A fixed-ratio schedule of reinforcement requiring a large number of performances for each reinforcement weakens a performance. This fixed-ratio strain, or abulia (lack of behavior), is a unique property of ratio schedules. On interval schedules the performance tends to be sustained under almost any frequency of reinforcement. In a pigeon experiment, for example, the rate of pecking on interval schedules remains proportional to the frequency of reinforcement, and the animal almost invariably re-ceives food at the maximum frequency. This chapter shows, in technical detail, how the schedules interact with the performances to bring these phenomena about.

One way to lessen the strain that ratio schedules tend to produce is to reinforce variably instead of on a fixed schedule. The chapter presents data demonstrating that variable reinforcement will, in general, sustain more behavior than a comparable fixed schedule. Another experiment explains in some detail why fixed-ratio schedules (at optimal values) pro-duce higher rates of behavior than interval schedules. These experiments are partial answers to such questions as "Why do fixed-ratio schedules often weaken behavior so severely?" and "What is responsible for the sustained high-frequency performances on optimal ratio schedules of rein-forcement?"

## technical terms

| | |
|---|---|
| abulia | multiple schedule |
| acceleration | Schedule of reinforcement |
| dependent variable | strain |
| fixed interval | variable interval |
| fixed ratio | variable ratio |
| independent variable | |

## outline

Part I:   Introduction to Intermittent Reinforcement
          How intermittent reinforcement arises naturally
          The frequency of a performance as a fundamental factor of operant behavior
          Animal-laboratory experiments involving four basic schedules of rein-forcement
          The cumulative recorder
          Reading a cumulative record
          A classroom demonstration of intermittent reinforcement

Part II:  Stable States After Reinforcement on the Basic Schedule of Reinforce-ment
          Fixed-interval reinforcement
          The stable state after reinforcement under different FR schedules

---

## part I: introduction to intermittent reinforcement

### how intermittent reinforcement arises naturally

Far from resulting in a decreased frequency of an operant, the periodic failure to reinforce the operant may increase its persistence and fre-quency. The analysis of nagging and teasing in Chapter 3 involved in-termittent reinforcement as a result of the social interaction. The aversive-ness to the parent of the child's asking for a cookie increased in proportion to the number of times the child made the request or demand. As a result, the child's repeated requests were reinforced intermittently by the par-ents' compliance. The intermittent schedule of reinforcement—the ratio of the child's performances needed to produce parental compliance—was defined by how many requests the child needed to make before the parent escaped the nagging by giving the cookie.

**Intermittent reinforcement in the natural environment**   Intermit-tent reinforcement of animal behavior occurs inevitably in the natural environment. For example, consider our earlier example of a pigeon foraging for grain that is hidden from view under leaves on the ground. The pigeon turns over leaves and occasionally finds a grain under one of them. As we saw in chapter 1, these grains, or an insect or worm, occur only under some leaves, while the performance goes unreinforced when there is no food underneath. So the variation from leaf to leaf determines the schedule by which flicking the leaves over is reinforced. This would be an example of a schedule where the food occurs as a result of the number of leaves that the pigeon turns. The more leaves that are turned, the more food that is found. But the number of leaves that needs to be turned for each food discovery varies from place to place. The behavior of a person shaking a tree, reinforced by the apples that fall, is an example of another schedule of reinforcement that occurs naturally. The number of apples that fall is proportional to how many times the tree is shaken. As we saw in an earlier chapter, it is necessary to shake the tree a number of times to weaken the stems of the fruit. Although the number of shakes may vary from time to time, a certain minimum number will usually be needed to loosen the apples. Thus, the schedule is one in which reinforcement is based on the number of times the tree is shaken and the resulting fall of the apples from the tree.

### Social interaction as a source of intermittent reinforcement

Social situations are the greatest source of intermittent reinforcement in human behavior. There, the behavior of one person has its effect by influencing the action of a second, as in the nagging and teasing interaction mentioned earlier. For example, someone asks a person standing at a window whether the taxi has arrived yet. The performance whose reinforcement schedule is being analyzed is a verbal one, "Has the taxi come?" The reinforcement for the performance is a reply from the person at the window. Whether the person at the window replies depends upon many variables that might influence her behavior. Various factors could interfere with a reply. The person might be preoccupied with concerns completely unrelated to the speaker; she might be disinclined to answer because she has just had an argument with the speaker; or she might be hard of hearing. Whatever the reasons, the result is that the behavior of the speaker may go unreinforced on one or more occasions.

Intermittent reinforcement may occur in such routine behaviors as cooking a meal for a family, reinforced by their eating it. Many factors other than the quality of the food will determine whether members of the family eat the meal. The likelihood of picking up another serving and eating it will be lower if they have just eaten a plate of fudge, or if they are under the influence of an extreme emotional state that is disrupting all of their operant behavior. Other social behaviors, such as persuasion and selling, also exemplify intermittent reinforcement. The amount of activity necessary to influence the other person defines the intermittent schedule. In selling, the performances are going to the vicinity of the client and persuading him or her. The reinforcer is the customer's purchase and the money received for it.

**The prevalence of schedules of reinforcement based on number and time** Most of the behaviors described previously are called *ratio* schedules because there is a specified ratio of performance to reinforcer. They might be described conversationally as "piece work." The ratio refers to the ratio of unreinforced to reinforced performances. Reinforcement based on number of performances is the schedule that occurs predominantly in human behavior. Most of the important consequences of human activity occur as a result of a certain amount of behavior. Climbing stairs is reinforced on a fixed-ratio schedule because a fixed number of steps is required to get to the top of the landing. Similarly, reinforcement for digging a hole, turning a piece of metal in a lathe, writing a letter, shaving, or telling a story all depend on the amount of behavior that is emitted. In each of these cases, the likelihood of the reinforcer increases only with the required amount of behavior. The very nature of operant behavior, defined by how it changes the environment, makes its reinforcement predominantly on a ratio schedule.

In contrast to ratio schedules are *interval* schedules of reinforcement, in which passage of time determines whether or not a performance will be reinforced. In these schedules, the number of performances emitted does not contribute to the likelihood that reinforcement will occur. In general, interval schedules of reinforcement come from temporal events, such as the rising and setting of the sun, the changing of the tides, or the scheduling of television and radio programs. Cooking and baking offer examples of interval schedules of reinforcement. The performances intermittently reinforced are looking at a pot of water on the stove, and the reinforcer is having the boiling water available for use. Looking down the street while waiting for a bus is reinforced on an interval schedule. Looking down the street is reinforced by the sight of the bus, an occasion on which the person can board it. The number of times a person looks at the pot of water on the stove or down the street for the bus has no influence on whether the water boils or the bus comes. The boiling water is determined by the amount in the pot and the heat that is applied and the appearance of the bus by its timetable. Another example of an interval schedule of reinforcement is dialing a telephone number after hearing a busy signal. If the phone is busy, the likelihood of getting an answer increases with passage of time rather than the number of times the telephone number is dialed.

Interval schedules do not occur as frequently in the natural environment as ratios because by its very nature operant behavior tends to be reinforced in proportion to how much it alters the environment. Despite their infrequent natural occurrence, interval schedules are important theoretically. The contrast between interval and ratio schedules of reinforcement will be found useful in later discussions of laboratory methods to analyze why schedules of reinforcement influence behavior as they do.

## the frequency of a performance as a fundamental factor of operant behavior

The frequency with which an organism emits an operant behavior is a theoretical and experimental analogue of such colloquial terms as habit, motivation, and persistence. We say a child who makes his bed every morning is in the habit of making his bed because we notice that it is done regularly. Terms like habit and motivation are potentially troublesome, however. What we actually observe is the frequency with which the child makes his bed. Terms such as *motivated* or *habit* are an inference we draw about the child's future actions from observations that he made his bed in the past.

When we say someone has not acted because she is timid we note a low disposition to act, perhaps because of a history of punishment or nonreinforcement. Timidity, in this case, refers not so much to a current state but to the low frequency of a performance and a history of punishment that may have been observed. It is the history of punishment, not some current state, that is responsible for the low disposition to act. A woman who speaks out because she has a strong opinion speaks freely and persistently. We speak of a high disposition to speak out because there are many occasions in which speaking cannot be reinforced, as for example, in the absence of a listener. So the inference is used to account for where the behavior is when it cannot, at the moment, be emitted. We often invent a current cause for a performance by using a term such as "strong opinion." The causes for the strong opinion, however, lie in the individual's history of reinforcement. What we can measure is the frequency with which the person speaks out under a given set of circumstances and, therefore, the probability of her speaking out under similar circumstances. Other colloquial terms also refer to the frequency of particular actions, as when we call someone a tennis, music, or skating fan; or highly sexed; or an inveterate gambler. In all of these circumstances, it is the frequency with which the person plays tennis, listens to music, skates, has sex, or gambles that is the relevant factor. We speak of the tennis player's interest or enthusiasm for tennis, rather than the absolute frequency of play, because there may be arbitrary reasons for not playing tennis, such as the unavailability of a court or inclement weather.

But it is important to remember that we cannot observe disposition, inclination, or likelihood of action. These are inferences we make when we notice the frequency with which a person acts. The control by inter-mittent reinforcement deals with the issue of disposition to action by creating an experimental situation in which the frequency of a simple operant can vary freely from very high to very low.

## four basic schedules of reinforcement

Table 5-1 is a convenient summary of the main ways that intermittent reinforcement can occur. The capital letters in parentheses are shorthand notations for the schedules.

In the ratio column, reinforcement depends on the number of perfor-mances that must be emitted to result in reinforcement. When the num-ber of performances required for each reinforcer is constant (fixed), the schedule is called *fixed-ratio*. When the number of performances required for each reinforcer varies, the schedule of reinforcement is called *vari-able-ratio*.

In the interval column, the first performance that occurs *after* a desig-nated interval elapses is reinforced. Performances that occur before the interval has elapsed do not produce the reinforcing stimulus and are not required by the schedule. When the interval between scheduled rein-forcers is constant, the schedule of reinforcement is called *fixed-interval*. If the elapsed interval required before a performance results in a rein-forcer varies from time to time, the schedule of reinforcement is called *variable-interval*.

The designation of schedule is usually abbreviated in laboratory de-scriptions of schedules of reinforcement, and a number which follows the abbreviation gives the value of the schedule. Thus, FI 2 is an interval schedule in which a performance may be reinforced two minutes after the previous reinforcement was delivered. Under a VI 2 schedule reinforce-ment is also delivered for a performance occurring after an elapsed time, but the time varies from reinforcer to reinforcer, perhaps from five sec-onds to six minutes, with the average interval between reinforcers being two minutes. For ratio schedules, FR 50 designates a schedule of reinforce-ment in which every fiftieth performance results in a reinforcer, and VR 50 designates a schedule in which the number of performances, averaging fifty, may vary between two and three hundred from reinforcement to reinforcement.

**Table 5–1**  Four Basic Schedules of Reinforcement

|  | *RATIO* | *INTERVAL* |
| --- | --- | --- |
| Fixed | Fixed-Ratio (FR) | Fixed-Interval (FI) |
| Variable | Variable-Ratio (VR) | Variable-Interval (VI) |

Students sometimes erroneously think a reinforcer is delivered after the passage of time on an interval schedule whether or not the performance occurs. A performance *must occur* after the time has elapsed for a reinforcer to be delivered. In animal experiments on interval schedules of reinforcement, a clock stops and does not start again until the performance is emitted and the reinforcement is delivered. This means that the interval is measured from the performance that results in a reinforcer (thus restarting the clock from zero) to the next time the measured interval elapses.

Intermittent schedules of reinforcement eventually produce stable states that will be maintained so long as the schedule of reinforcement is continued unchanged. It is in this sense that intermittent reinforcement is concerned with the maintenance of behavior.

## animal laboratory experiments involving intermittent reinforcement

The frequency with which a pigeon pecks a key or a rat presses a lever has proven to be a useful way to study the fundamental aspects of how behavior is maintained under various intermittent schedules of reinforcement. An arbitrary performance, such as pecking, is useful for this study because it is a simple, easily repeatable act that takes little time to execute. Also, intermittently reinforced pecking is not constrained by time the bird spends eating, since food delivery occurs infrequently. The frequency of pecking can vary continuously over a wide range, since the pigeon is capable of pecking at rates of up to 40,000 pecks per hour (10 pecks per second). The frequency of pecking, therefore, provides a way to continuously record the subject's disposition to carry out the reinforced behavior.

It can be presumed that performances other than pecking, such as pressing a treadle or raising the head, would be similarly influenced by intermittent reinforcement. These other performances would suffer the disadvantage of being constrained by their topography, which decreases their potential rate of emission. Thus the properties of fixed-ratio reinforcement that we discover by studying a pigeon pecking a key will help us to understand the complex and varied kinds of intermittent reinforcement occurring in human behavior. By choosing a model behavior like pecking, however, we have an optimal situation for exposing the frequency of a performance.

Literally thousands of different schedules of intermittent reinforcement are possible by permutations and combinations of possible contingencies. Many of them have been studied in the laboratory and have been found to produce stable and distinctive performances. It is not always possible to know intuitively what kind of performance a particular schedule of reinforcement will produce. Schedules of reinforcement that seem superficially similar may produce different amounts and kinds of behavior.

We speak of the animal's performance as a dependent variable that can change as a result of the influence of an independent variable. When we discuss how behavior is influenced by intermittent reinforcement, the dependent variable is the rate at which the animal performs. The term, variable, is used because we expect the rate of the performance to change (vary) as we alter the conditions that influence it.

The schedules of reinforcement, one kind of influence on the rate of pecking, are called *independent variables.* They are independent in the sense that when they are altered they lead to a change in the bird's performance. They are also independent in the sense that they may be changed independently of the bird's performance. A change in the dependent variable, on the other hand, requires some change in the independent variable. Other dimensions of the animal's performance, such as the force with which the bird pecks, might also be measured as a dependent variable.

It is useful, however, to consider the topography of operant behavior and its frequency of emission separately. When we want to know the probability of a performance, studying the topography is of little value, since it tells little about the independent variables that control frequency. A situation in which a person requires a performance of another, but the performance does not occur, illustrates the relation between frequency and topography. If we want to know why it is not occurring, we need to know first whether the performance was ever in the organism's repertoire. A performance may be missing because it never has been conditioned rather than because it has a low frequency. If we know that the performance has been in the repertoire, then our questions concern the independent variables that may reduce the frequency of the performance. Schedules of reinforcement are concerned with the maintenance of behavior already in the repertoire. Although many independent variables will increase or decrease the frequency of an operant, the schedule of reinforcement is one of the most important determinants.

## the cumulative recorder

The cumulative recorder provides a concise graphic record that summarizes changes in the frequency of a performance so that they can be read at a glance. It is especially useful because experiments on intermittent reinforcement generate many thousands of pecks in a single, daily experimental session. Figure 5-1 is a generalized diagram of a cumulative recorder. Each time the pigeon, for example, pecks the key, an electromechanical device moves the pen a small distance across the paper. At the same time, the paper moves at a constant speed. The combination of these

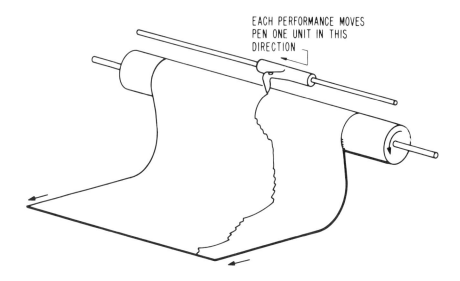

EACH PERFORMANCE MOVES PEN ONE UNIT IN THIS DIRECTION

**Figure 5-1**   Diagram of a cumulative recorder.[1]

two movements produces a diagonal line whose angle with the base of the paper depends on how fast the bird pecks. If the bird does not peck at all, the pen draws a line horizontal to the base of the paper. The pen resets automatically when the pen gets to the top of the paper; the recorder has a sufficient supply of paper and ink so that long experimental sessions can be recorded and the scale—how fast the paper feeds and how far each performance drives the pen across the paper—can be varied. Usually the scale is reduced so that the record concisely summarizes thousands of performances.

### reading a cumulative record

Figure 5-2 illustrates a cumulative performance record from a pigeon pecking at a constant rate. The graph on the left side of the figure illustrates a bird pecking at a constant rate of 20 times a minute. This rate can be determined by reading off the number of pecks that have occurred after any period of time. For example, after 50 minutes, the graph shows that 1000 pecks have occurred and after 30 minutes 600. The graph at the right illustrates a lower rate of pecking, also constant. After 60 minutes the graph indicates that the bird has pecked 600 times, indicating a rate of 10 pecks per minute. The reduction in the record is responsible for the even appearance of the line. Since 1000 pecks move the pen only a few inches, each individual peck is not readily seen. If the record were to be magnified, its steplike character would appear similar to the line in Figure 5-3.

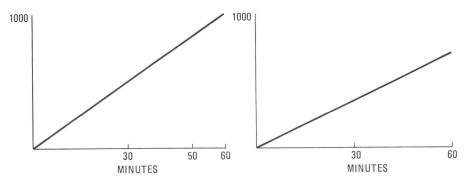

Figure 5-2    Cumulative records illustrating constant rates of pecking.

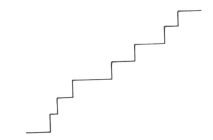

Figure 5-3    Enlarged view of a cumulative record that shows individual performances.

The cumulative record in Figure 5-4 gives further practice in interpreting the performance it depicts. The grid insert, shows the slopes of lines that would indicate 10, 20, or 40 pecks per minute. Intermediate rates are easily interpolated.

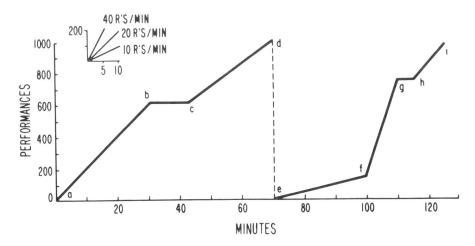

Figure 5-4    A stylized cumulative record showing abrupt shifts from one rate of pecking to another.

The highest rate occurred from f to g, an interval of about 11 minutes, during which the bird pecked about 550 times at a rate of about 50 pecks per minute. There is a pause without any performances from g to h of about 5 minutes and from b to c for about 10 minutes. From e to f the rate of pecking was about 6 per minute for about 30 minutes. The same exercise, completed for the other segments of the graph, gives practice in reading the cumulative record.

### Reading changes in rate of pecking from a cumulative record

The curves in Figure 5-5 illustrate how cumulative records make it easy to observe changes in the rate of pecking. The left part of the figure shows a stylized version of a performance on a fixed-interval schedule in which the bird pauses for a time after reinforcement and then begins to peck slowly. Thereafter the rate of pecking increases continuously, until a constant rate of about 200 pecks per minute is reached. Such an increase in the *rate* of pecking is called *acceleration.* A decrease in rate is called *deceleration* or *negative acceleration.* The dotted line gives the slope of the curve and hence the rate of pecking at that time. The dotted line is the tangent to the curve at the point of the arrow. The increases in the slopes of tangents along the curved part of the record show the positive acceleration. The cumulative record on the right of the figure depicts the rate changes that occur when the rate of pecking is falling, as would occur as a result of extinction. Such rate changes are described as negative acceleration or deceleration. The rate of pecking starts high and then falls continuously until after 10 minutes pecks are occurring about every four seconds. The intermediate rates can be read by drawing a tangent at various points along the curve and reading the rate from the grid. These

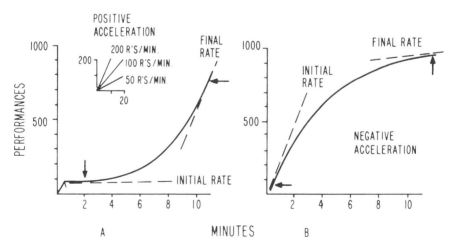

**Figure 5-5** A stylized cumulative record illustrating the recording of continuously accelerated and decelerated rate changes.

graphs show the advantage of a cumulative record as a summary of changes in rate of pecking. At a glance, it can be seen that the rate of pecking increases continuously and smoothly to a final value in the left record and decreases in the same fashion in the right record.

## a classroom demonstration of intermittent reinforcement

A performance alternately maintained under two different schedules of reinforcement may be used either as a classroom demonstration or carried out by individual students. The stable state generated by such a schedule can be achieved in a relatively short time. An opportunity to watch the bird peck at the same time the cumulative record is made is an excellent way to learn how to read the records.

The performance on such a multiple schedule of reinforcement illustrates two of the basic schedules of intermittent reinforcement and gives an opportunity to practice reading cumulative curves that record the performance. Pecks at a key lighted alternately red and green are reinforced. When the key color is red, food is delivered every 50 times the bird pecks. This is the fixed-ratio (FR) schedule that was mentioned previously. After reinforcement the key turns green and the first peck after three minutes operates the food magazine. This is the fixed-interval (FI) schedule described previously. Under such a multiple schedule of reinforcement, the bird effectively possesses two separate repertoires that can be strengthened independently and arbitrarily simply by changing the color of the light behind the key. Figure 5-6 is an excerpt of a cumulative record

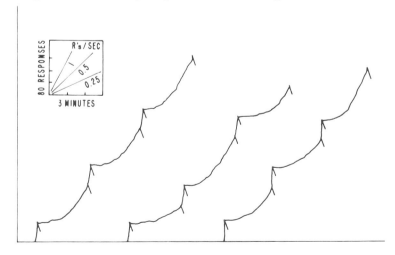

**Figure 5-6** A cumulative record of a pigeon's performance on a multiple fixed-ratio, fixed-interval schedule of reinforcement.

showing the stable state produced by these schedules of reinforcement. The grid in the upper right part of the figure gives the scale of the record. The first reinforcement, indicated by the hatch mark after the first part of the record, shows the performance when the color behind the key was red and reinforcement occurred after 40 pecks. The details of the record are interpreted by using the scale of the grid insert as was done in the preceding example. It only takes a few seconds to complete the 40 pecks. The rate of pecking is about 3 per second. Following the reinforcement on the fixed-ratio schedule, the key color turns green, correlated with the 3-minute fixed-interval schedule, and the bird immediately stops pecking for 10 or 15 seconds; there is only an odd peck or so for the first two minutes and a half. Thereafter the rate of pecking accelerates until a final, asymptotic rate of about 1 peck per second is reached, and it is maintained until a peck operates the food magazine after 3 minutes elapses. A total of about 60 or 70 pecks occur during the three-minute period of the fixed-interval schedule. The pattern of rate changes is similar for the remaining part of the record and provides an opportunity to pratice reading a cumulative record by noting the variations and consistent features of the performance. The cumulative record of such a schedule of reinforcement shows how the orderliness and nature of the rate changes that are generated are summarized so succinctly that they can be read at a glance.

## questions

1. Describe some of the ways in which intermittent reinforcement arises in animal and human behavior in the natural environment.
2. Why are social interactions the greatest source of intermittent reinforcement in human behavior?
3. Describe the relative prevalence of interval and ratio-schedules in the natural environment. What accounts for the differences?
4. How does the maintenance of behavior under intermittent reinforcement accent frequency as the fundamental factor of operant behavior?
5. Describe the four basic schedules of reinforcement.
6. Describe how a cumulative record is made and why it is especially useful for operant reinforcement experiments.
7. Describe the procedure of a multiple fixed-ratio fixed-interval schedule of reinforcement. Draw a sample of a cumulative graph of the type of performance that would be recorded, and interpret the rate changes.

## part II: stable states after reinforcement on the basic schedules

Earlier we stated that intermittent schedules of reinforcement eventually produce stable states that are maintained so long as the reinforcement schedule is maintained. This part of the chapter will be concerned with such stable states rather than the transitions that take place when the organism is first introduced to the schedule or when the schedule of reinforcement is altered.

The sections that follow make a detailed analysis of the behavioral process of intermittent reinforcement, using the pigeon pecking experiment as an example. The sections examine the details of how the frequency of the bird's pecking changes in time as a result of the schedule of intermittent reinforcement that is imposed. The level of behavioral analysis gained from the fine-grain detail of the observations of these orderly processes will be a useful way to learn how to gain facility in observing behavior in complex environments.

### fixed-interval reinforcement

The record in Figure 5-7 was taken after a bird had been reinforced for 66 hours under an FI 4 schedule. On such a schedule, the first peck following a four-minute period since its last reinforcement is reinforced.

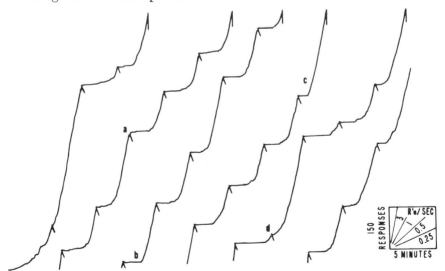

Figure 5-7    A stable state performance on an fixed-interval schedule (4 minutes) after 66 hours of exposure to the schedule.

**159**

A total of 990 reinforcements had been delivered on this schedule before this performance was recorded.[2] The performance described in the cumulative record is called the stable state of this schedule because it continues relatively unchanged so long as the same schedule of reinforcement is maintained. A few comments about individual segments of the record will be of use in giving practice in reading the cumulative records and noting significant details.

The cumulative graph has been collapsed by cutting out the empty part of the record between successive segments that occur as a result of the recorder pen resetting to the bottom of the page. Collapsing the record makes a more compact graph but does not affect how to read it, since the dimensions of the time scale and number of pecks are given in the insert at the top right of the figure. At *a* there is a burst of pecking immediately after the food delivery from the preceding interval. This is in contrast to the more usual pattern that occurred in segments *b* and *d,* where there is a clear pause after reinforcement. The number of pecks that occur during the 4-minute interval varies from about 30 when there is a long pause after reinforcement to over 500 pecks when there is no pause as, for example, in the second interval. Although all of the segments are positively accelerated, the transition to the final rate of pecking is more abrupt in some cases than in others.

The same general pattern of behavior occurs with larger intervals between reinforcements, except that all of the features of the performance are magnified. The bird pauses longer before starting, the period of rate acceleration is prolonged and the terminal rate of pecking is sustained longer and at a lower rate. Figure 5-8 illustrates the kind of performance that may be routinely expected after a bird has an extended history of reinforcement on an FI 45-minute schedule of reinforcement. The number of times a bird pecks for each 45-minute interval varies considerably over a wide range from the 300 to 400 pecks that occurred in the third segment to over 3000 pecks that occurred in the second. Occasional instances will appear in which fewer than 300 pecks occur.

A very large amount of behavior is sustained despite the very low frequency of reinforcement (every 45 minutes) and the small amount of food that is delivered. Because each reinforcement consists of approximately 3 to 4 seconds of access to the feeder, during which the bird can eat approximately one-fourth of a gram of food, it would take approximately 45 hours for the bird to receive a whole day's ration. As a result, the bird would starve to death under this schedule of reinforcement unless its diet was supplemented. Yet under the stable state of this schedule of reinforcement, substantial amounts of behavior are maintained despite the very low frequency of reinforcement. In the sample presented in Fig. 5-8, the bird pecked over 8000 times in slightly less than 4 hours.[3] Well over 1000 pecks occur in every 45-minute period except the third.

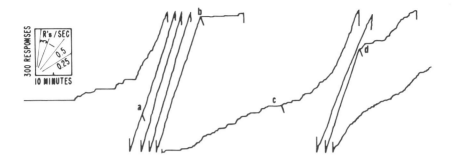

Figure 5-8    A cumulative record of a segment of a bird's performance on an FI 45 schedule of reinforcement after 30 hours of reinforcement.[4]

While a performance such as the one recorded above developed in the stable state after an extended history of reinforcement, no intermediate procedures or approximations of the final schedule were required. The bird was placed on an FI 45 reinforcement schedule immediately following continuous reinforcement without risk of losing the performance. This is in marked contrast to the fixed-ratio schedules that will be discussed later.

The pattern of rate changes becomes much more regular and conforms better to the fixed-interval time pattern when a period of time out separates each of the fixed-interval segments. Figure 5-9 is a cumulative record of a performance on the same FI 45 schedule with an interruption after each reinforcement arranged by darkening the box for 20 minutes, during which the bird cannot peck. With the 20-minute interruption after each reinforcement, the pause after reinforcement occurs regularly and the high sustained rates disappear. The performance with the time out conforms more closely to the temporal schedule. This normalizing effect of the interruption occurs because it prevents the behavior in one interval from influencing that in the next.[5] To have read these records in sufficient detail, you should be able to state the final rate of pecking in each interval, how long before this terminal rate is reached, the variation in the number of pecks from interval to interval, and for how many pecks the terminal rate of pecking is maintained.

**Examples of interval reinforcement in daily life**    Performances associated with waiting are examples of interval reinforcement—for example, a wife waiting for her husband to come home from work or vice versa. Since the appearance of the spouse depends only on the passage of time, the behavior of looking out the window is reinforced on an interval schedule by the sight of the person. The reinforcer (the arrival that in turn occasions the performances of having dinner or talking) is largely unaffected by the frequency of looking. Similarly, food reinforcement on an

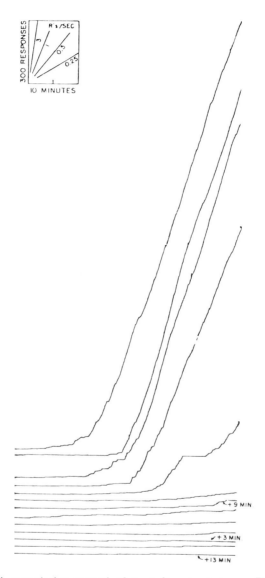

**Figure 5-9** A cumulative record of a performance on an FI 45 schedule of reinforcement with a 20-minute time out after each reinforcement. The fixed-interval segments have been rearranged in order by the number of pecks the bird had made during the 45-minute interval.

FI schedule is not related to how often the pigeon pecks. The result is that the rate of looking out the window is lowest when the person first begins looking and then increases as time passes. There is positive acceleration in the rate of looking because there is a maximum interval, similar to the fixed interval of the pigeon experiment, after which the spouse does arrive.

**162**

A cumulative record of instances of looking would, under some circumstances, resemble the pigeon's cumulative record. The person waiting for a cake in the oven to rise also illustrates an interval schedule. The interval is fixed by the amount of time required for the cake to completely bake. The frequency of looking when the cake is first put in the oven is very low, just as the pigeon's rate of pecking on a fixed-interval schedule is low just after reinforcement. The frequency of looking in the oven increases, however, as the time approaches when the cake is done. To specify schedules of reinforcement such as those described previously, we need to state the specific performance, the exact reinforcer maintaining it, and the relation between the two. In the case of waiting for the husband, the wife's performances are likely to involve looking out the window, pacing, and verbal statements such as "Why doesn't he come?" Some of these are examples of accidentally reinforced behavior, to be described later, but the dynamic effects of the control by the schedule remain identical.

The smoothly accelerated curve, characteristic of the fixed-interval reinforcement, does not occur under all conditions in animal laboratory experiments nor in the natural environment.

With extremely strong behavior, such as waiting for an ambulance, there may be little pausing in nervous pacing or looking, even though the person knows that it will take the ambulance five minutes to arrive. When a pot of hot water is badly needed, the person may hover over the stove continuously in spite of long experience in which water never boils immediately after being placed on the stove ("a watched pot does not boil"). At the other extreme we can observe the housewife who may leave a pot of water on the stove five or ten minutes after it has come to a boil, while she attends to other chores in the kitchen. If, in fact, the pot has a whistle on it, she may not look at the stove at all until the pot signals that the water is boiling. In that case, the housewife's performance is analogous to the pigeon whose rate of pecking is low because there is no substantial amount of food deprivation or because reinforcement is signaled by a discriminative stimulus. All of these are examples of fixed-interval reinforcement, but the way in which the rate of the performance is related to the time since the last reinforcement depends on many conditions secondary to the actual schedule of reinforcement.

## the stable state after reinforcement under different FR schedules

Schedules based on the *amount* of behavior emitted have very different characteristics than the interval schedules described in the previous section. Figure 5-10 shows the performances that occur at different fixed-ratio values that denote the number of performances required to be emitted prior to reinforcement.[6] As with the fixed-interval schedule, fixed-ratio reinforcement generates a patterned rate of performance unique to that schedule. Each segment in Figure 5-10 is an excerpt, typical of the bird's daily performance on that schedule. Each of these records is the final stable state after thousands of reinforcements on the schedule, so these performances will not change, except in minor details, as long as the same conditions of reinforcement are continued.

The major effect of changing the number of pecks required for reinforcement in a fixed-ratio schedule is observable in the varying lengths of time the bird pauses after reinforcement. The more pecks required for reinforcement, the longer is the pause. When 70 pecks are required for reinforcement (the first segment), the pause after reinforcement seldom exceeds a few seconds. When 120 pecks are required for reinforcement, there is a longer pause after almost every reinforcement. When the bird does begin pecking again, however, it starts immediately at the final rate, 3 to 4 pecks per second, which is maintained until the next reinforcement. At larger values of the fixed-ratio schedule the pause becomes even longer, but the performance is otherwise unchanged; that is, once the bird begins pecking it continues to do so at a high constant rate. The overall or average rate of pecking decreases as the bird is required to peck more times for each reinforcement, but this rate is influenced by how long the bird pauses after reinforcement rather than the actual rate of pecking when he is performing. If the number of pecks required is made large enough the bird will stop pecking altogether.

The lack of a recuperative feature is one of the important ways that a fixed-ratio schedule differs from a fixed-interval. No matter how infre-

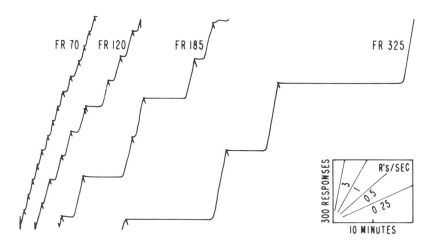

**Figure 5-10** Cumulative records of typical performances recorded at various values of fixed-ratio schedules of reinforcement. The periods of no pecking after reinforcement grow longer as the number of pecks the bird is required to make is increased.

quently a bird pecks under a fixed-interval schedule, a single peck, whenever it occurs after the fixed interval has elapsed, will operate the feeder. The bird may peck a number of times or only once in a fixed interval, but the frequency of reinforcement will be unaffected except in extreme cases. This *recuperative feature* guarantees that some reinforcement will occur even if the bird has a very low disposition to peck. This recuperative feature is lacking in the fixed-ratio schedules, however. Should the performance be weak for any reason, the bird will still be required to emit the same number of pecks.

The predominance of fixed-ratio schedules of reinforcement has already been discussed in the first part of this chapter and examples presented of how it controls animal and human behavior in the natural environment. It will be useful, in addition, to consider some observations by an educator, John Holt, that illustrate the importance of intermittent reinforcement in a child's emerging repertoire. Holt observed an infant trying to fit a piece of a puzzle into place.[7] The piece was in the right location, but turned a little away from a proper angle so that it wouldn't fit. There were no obvious cues, so the child pressed, pushed, turned this way and that, until he gave up by sucking his thumb while sitting on a blanket. After a while the child crawled back and completed the puzzle. Holt's observation illustrates how intermittent reinforcement arises whenever a performance will be reinforced only if it conforms to special requirements such as form or sequence. The performance is grasping a puzzle piece and placing it in the matrix. The reinforcer is the completed pattern. Intermittent reinforcement results when repeated placements of a piece do not contribute to the picture or pattern or form a continuous surface.

Note the emotion and the decrease in frequency of the performance produced by the intermittent reinforcement. The retreat to blanket and thumb and the escape from the puzzle and its location are the emotional effects, perhaps related to the adjunctive behavior discussed in Chapter 4; this is frequently seen in animal experiments when a performance is temporary and would be seen on a cumulative graph as a short pause in the performance. When a pigeon first encounters a fixed-ratio schedule of reinforcement, it pauses, flaps its wings and vocalizes a lot during the initial period. After a while the rate of pecking becomes uniformly high and the emotional behavior disappears.

## establishing a performance on large values of an FR schedule

An important property of fixed-number schedules is that it is necessary to go through small and intermediate values to achieve a performance on a large fixed-number schedule. Consider at one extreme a bird that has been reinforced continuously. Such a bird will peck perhaps one or two hundred times without reinforcement (extinction). If the schedule of rein-forcement were changed suddenly from continuous reinforcement to FR 300 (reinforcement occurring every 300 pecks), the bird would never achieve the first reinforcement on the fixed-ratio schedule, since the num-ber of pecks without further reinforcement would likely be fewer than 300. Nor would prolonging reinforcement on the continuous reinforce-ment schedule help. Beyond a point, prolonged continuous reinforcement is not likely to increase the number of times the bird pecks following introduction of extinction. Fortunately, the number of times an animal will peck without further reinforcement is very large after even small values of intermittent schedules.

To establish a stable performance on a large fixed-ratio schedule we need first to sustain the performances on small fixed-ratio schedules and then gradually increase the number of performances required per rein-forcement. Thus, by pacing the increase in the size of the fixed-ratio carefully, depending upon whether the performance is maintained, it may be possible to maintain a stable high rate of performance under a large fixed-ratio schedule that would not have been sustained if the progression from one requirement to the next had not been made slowly and paced with the stability of the individual's behavior.

## variable schedules of reinforcement

The fixed-ratio and fixed-interval performances that have been de-scribed contrast the major dimensions of intermittent reinforcement— whether the reinforcement occurs as a result of elapsed time or as a result of the number of pecks that are made. The amount of time in the interval schedule may be variable as well as fixed just as the number of pecks required in ratio schedules can be either fixed or varied.

### Stable states after reinforcement on variable-interval schedules

The schedule is described by the average of the intervals between reinforcements as well as how these intervals are distributed about the mean value. For example, there might be an equal number of each of the intervals that comprise the schedule. Or there may be a preponderance of short over long intervals. In each case, the average interval of reinforce-ment could be the same. Figure 5-11 illustrates a pigeon's performance on a variable-interval schedule of reinforcement (VI 3). The intervals that determine reinforcement average 3 minutes, but vary from one interval to the next. Occasionally successive pecks are reinforced, while some of the intervals are as long as 6 minutes. Short intervals are distributed equally with longer ones. There is a fairly steady rate of about 1 peck per second. In contrast to a fixed-interval schedule, the variable occurrence of reinforcement has eliminated the pause after reinforcement.

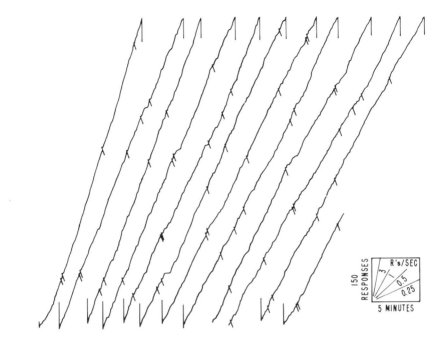

Figure 5-11   Cumulative record of a portion of an experimental session in which pecks were reinforced on a VI 3 schedule of reinforcement. The performance was recorded after the bird had been reinforced on the schedule for 45 hours.

As the mean of the intervals between reinforcements become larger, the rate at which the bird pecks declines. Figure 5-12 illustrates the performance changes that occur when the average frequency of reinforcement decreases in a variable-interval schedule. The graph illustrates variable-interval performances of a pigeon where reinforcement occurs on the average of every 1, 2, 3, 6, and 10 minutes. Each of the segments is a short excerpt taken from the longer record of a daily experimental session and is typical of the stable state that finally emerges as a result of reinforcement on the indicated mean value of the variable-interval schedule.

The most obvious effect recorded in the graph is that the animal's performance remains continuous at all frequencies of reinforcement. The performance does not cease even at much lower frequencies of reinforcement than those shown in the illustration. Thus, in the last segment, where reinforcement occurs every 10 minutes on the average, the pigeon pecks continuously but at a rate of a peck every 2 seconds. In the first segment, where reinforcement occurs every minute, the bird pecks twice each second. In intermediate ranges, the rate of pecking is similarly correlated with the frequency of reinforcement. This continuous change in the rate of pecking is in marked contrast with the character of the performance

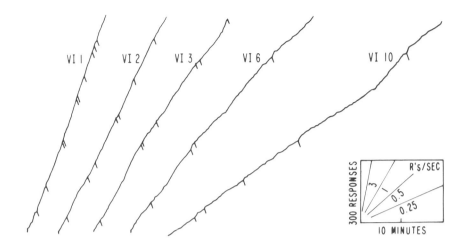

Figure 5-12    Segment of cumulative records taken from experimental sessions when the variable-interval performances were reinforced on the average of every 1, 2, 3, 6, and 10 minutes.

that was described for fixed-ratio reinforcement. There the change in the frequency of pecking occurred as an abrupt cessation of pecking just after reinforcement contrasted with a high sustained rate once pecking resumed again.[8]

**Variable-ratio schedules**    Under a variable-ratio schedule, reinforcement occurs as a result of the number of pecks the bird makes but the number varies from reinforcement to reinforcement. Like the variable-interval schedule, it is specified by giving the average number of pecks that are required per reinforcement as well as a description of how the required number is distributed.

Figure 5-13 is a cumulative record showing a pigeon's high sustained rate of pecking on a variable-ratio schedule where reinforcement occurred every 375 pecks on the average (VR 375).[9] Note the extreme variation in the number of pecks that are required from reinforcement to reinforcement. The reinforcement that occurred in the eighth segment, for example, followed over 3000 pecks. In contrast, the reinforcement in the next-to-last segment occurred after less than 50 pecks. The overall rate is extremely high and the bird frequently sustains its performance for hundreds of pecks at rates of over 5 per second. In general, variable-ratio schedules generate very high rates of pecking as compared with variable-interval schedules.

The comparison is not absolute, however, because the overall rate of pecking on a variable-ratio schedule can be reduced considerably by requiring a large amount of behavior per reinforcement. The result will be

**168**

an increase in the amount of pausing eventually leading to a cessation of behavior, very similar to that previously described for fixed-ratio schedules.

## examples of variable reinforcement in human behavior

Many human behaviors are reinforced variably from one occasion to another. For example, ordinary conversation depends, for its effect, upon the *amount* of speech. However, the amount varies from time to time, ranging from "good morning" reinforced by a reply of "good morning" (continuous reinforcement), to ordinary conversation, where the amount of speaking needed to influence a listener is larger. At one extreme is an extensive verbal interchange of a lecture. Here, the reinforcer for the speaker is a change in the verbal repertoire of the listener. A seasoned lecturer illustrates a large fixed-ratio schedule in which a relatively large and fixed amount of behavior is required for the targeted change in the listener's behavior.

Fly casting, a performance reinforced by catching a fish, is generally reinforced on some kind of ratio schedule since the probability of catching a fish depends upon frequent casting. In certain kinds of fishing the probability of reinforcement is high enough so that the schedule is essentially variable-ratio since two fish may occasionally be caught in rapid succession, for example, when a school of fish is feeding. In ocean fishing, a fish may bite very soon after the line is dropped in the water. In contrast, there

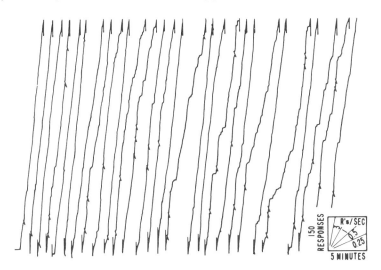

**Figure 5-13**   A cumulative record of a bird's performance on a variable-ratio schedule that maintained a high overall rate of pecking.

is trout fishing where the probability of catching a fish may be so low that there are few instances where successive casts are reinforced. Many variable schedules reinforcing human behavior are of this sort.

Driving a car or walking provide other examples of the contrast between variable and fixed schedules. By and large, a hike or a long driving trip constitute an episode with the dynamic properties of a large fixed-ratio schedule. A certain amount of behavior is required, although it may vary somewhat. On a hike or a cross-country drive, arriving at the destination is the reinforcer. Such a reinforcer cannot occur after only a small amount of driving or walking. Driving about the city or walking about the house, however, are reinforced after small amounts of behavior. The schedules of reinforcement for driving and walking locally are variable because the distances may vary considerably. The patterns of behavior generated by the schedules of reinforcement of local and long-distance driving and walking are parallel to those recorded on fixed- and variable-ratio schedules of intermittent reinforcement.

To analyze how variable and fixed schedules of reinforcement change behavior, it is very important to specify the immediate and specific consequences of the behavior. We may speak of a lathe operator as being on a piecework schedule if he or she is paid in terms of the number of pieces produced. Yet the actual performances intermittently reinforced may be the small operations on the lathe, leading only to a part of a piece for which the worker is paid at piece rate. The actual reinforcer maintaining the performance (turning the handle that drives the cutting tool) is the chip of metal coming off the piece in the lathe. It may take a series of such movements for just one of the operations needed to complete the piece.

## extinction after schedules of intermittent reinforcement

The schedule of reinforcement has a profound influence on how many times the animal will continue to perform when performances are no longer reinforced. Extinction after continuous reinforcement produces the smallest amount and variable-interval reinforcement the largest persistence of the performance. Figure 5-14 is a stylized cumulative performance graph containing two curves that show the number of performances that might be typically expected after continuous and intermittent reinforcement schedules. After continuous reinforcement, a bird will characteristically peck 50 or 100 or even 200 times without further reinforcement, but after intermittent reinforcement 3000 pecks would commonly occur and 10,000 pecks would not be unusual.

Thus there is a paradoxical contrast between what happens when behavior is maintained by intermittent reinforcement and during extinction when reinforcement is discontinued. During the maintenance of behavior

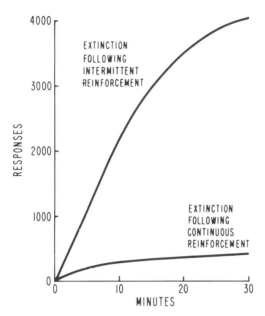

**Figure 5-14** Stylized cumulative records illustrating the magnitude and form of rate changes that occurs in extinction following continuous and intermittent reinforcement.

under intermittent reinforcement we saw how the rate of pecking on a variable-interval schedule decreased when pecks were reinforced less frequently. Under fixed- and variable-ratio schedules, the pausing that develops as increased number of pecks are required indicates the weakening of the performance by the intermittent reinforcement. Yet in extinction, the number of times the performance will occur is almost always larger after intermittent reinforcement schedules. Sometimes, the amount of extinction behavior is larger after more intermittently reinforced performances than after less intermittently reinforced ones.

The extinction performance usually resembles the pattern of behavior that occurred while the behavior was being maintained. Figures 5-15, 5-16, and 5-17 illustrate the connection between extinction performances and the behavior that had been maintained by the preceding schedule of reinforcement. The extinction records also give some picture of the large amount and persistence of the behavior that occurs. Figure 5-15 is a record of a performance that occurred in extinction after a variable-interval performance with a mean of 7 minutes. Figure 5-16 describes extinction after the same variable-interval schedule for another bird whose overall rate of pecking was considerably higher when the performance was being reinforced, and Figure 5-17 describes extinction after a fixed-ratio schedule requiring 60 pecks per reinforcement.

In Figure 5-15, the part of the record up to the arrow shows the performance that was maintained under the variable-interval schedule. The

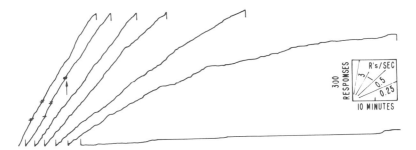

Figure 5-15 A cumulative record of a pigeon's performance during extinction after the bird had been reinforced on a 7-minute variable-interval schedule.[10]

performance continues for almost 1000 pecks before there is any change in the rate of pecking, probably because there were many long periods during the preceding variable-interval reinforcement when the pigeon emitted that number of pecks without reinforcement. Thereafter, there is a gradual and continuous fall in the bird's pecking rate. After 4000 unreinforced pecks, the rate falls to less than a peck every 4 seconds and finally, by the end of the record, 4 hours later, to an even lower value. Even then the performance does not really cease, though the rate of pecking is very low.

Figure 5-16, in comparison, is a record of much more persistent extinction after the same VI 3 schedule of reinforcement. Here, the bird pecks 17,000 times without reinforcement before the rate of pecking falls substantially. It is not until 11,000 pecks have occurred that the bird departs from the rate of pecking that had been maintained under the previous variable-interval reinforcement.

The performance during extinction after fixed-ratio reinforcement (Figure 5-17) is in contrast to those recorded after variable-interval reinforcement. Very high rates of pecking alternate with pauses that lengthen as extinction progresses, rather than the smoothly decelerating rates of pecking that occurred in extinction after variable-interval reinforcement.

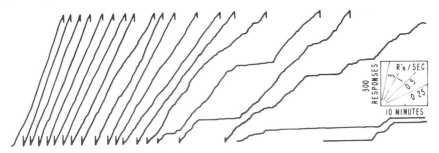

Figure 5-16 A cumulative record of a pigeon's performance during extinction after the bird had been reinforced on two 7-minute variable interval schedules whose reinforcement intervals were arranged in a geometric progression.[11]

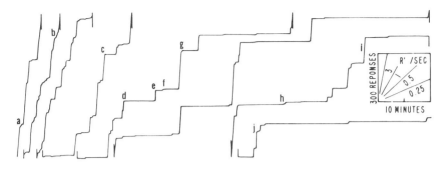

**Figure 5-17** A cumulative record of a pigeon's performance during extinction after the bird had been reinforced on an FR 60 schedule.[12]

The laboratory study of extinction after intermittent reinforcement supplies information that is useful for understanding what happens when the human environment changes. During the interim period when a person's behavior has not yet come under the control of the reinforcement contingencies in the new environment, the previous behavior undergoes extinction. The transition to the new reinforcement conditions will depend substantially on how extinction proceeds. Extremely persistent behavior, despite the fact that it is no longer reinforced, will impede the transition of the control of behavior by the new environment. A parent's attempt to eliminate crying, reinforced by parental attention, is an example of an attempt to change the reinforcement contingencies maintaining the child's behavior. How much and how long the child cries during extinction depends on how the parents had reacted previously. If the parents had appeared each time the child cried (continuous reinforcement) the sudden change in the parents' practices about crying could lead to its easy elimination. On the other hand, if there was a history of inconsistent attention to the child, in which the parents appeared variably, crying would be much more persistent during extinction because of the previous variable-ratio schedule of reinforcement. The dimensions of the analysis are similar to those of the nagging and teasing episode described earlier.

## questions

*1.* Write a moment-to-moment description of the rate changes in one of the illustrations of the cumulative record from a fixed-interval performance in the text.

*2.* What is the effect of a time out after reinforcement of fixed-interval responding?

3. Give examples of fixed-interval and variable-interval reinforcement in daily life.

4. Describe the stable state after reinforcement under different values of fixed-ratio schedules.

5. Describe the effect of a time out after reinforcement on a fixed-interval performance and draw some sample cumulative curves illustrating the types of performance that occur with and without time out.

6. What is the recuperative feature of a fixed-interval schedule?

7. How is a fixed-ratio maintained when the number of pecks required for reinforcement is too large initially for the bird to sustain.

8. Describe what happens on a variable-interval schedule of reinforcement when the mean interval of reinforcement is decreased.

9. Describe what happens under a variable-ratio schedule when the number of pecks per reinforcement is increased.

10. Compare the performances under variable-ratio and variable-interval schedules.

11. Give examples of variable-ratio reinforcement in the human natural environment.

12. Compare a pigeon's performance in extinction after variable-interval and variable-ratio schedules of reinforcement.

13. Discuss why crying is likely to be reinforced on a variable-ratio schedule and why the characteristic performance in extinction makes it difficult to alter the performance.

## part III: how schedules of reinforcement influence the overall maintenance of a performance

The following experiments illustrate how the factor of unpredictability in variable-ratio reinforcement schedules may alter the form and increase the frequency of a performance, as compared with fixed-ratio reinforcement schedules. The effect of variable- versus fixed-ratio reinforcement upon behavior is important, since so much of human behavior occurs under these conditions. Variable schedules are perhaps even more common in the natural environment than fixed ones, because most events in the natural environment are determined in multiple and complex ways. The behavior of the gambler is a simple example of a schedule of reinforcement in which the reinforcing stimulus occurs variably, but still depends upon the amount of behavior. The behavior of a man operating a slot machine is a direct analogue to the behavior of the bird whose pecking performance is reinforced according to variable-ratio schedule of reinforcement. The number of coins delivered is directly proportional to the number of times the machine is played, but the reinforcement occurs variably due to the mechanical properties of the slot machine.

The variable-ratio reinforcement schedule influences the pigeon and the gambler similarly. Both perform at high rates, even with infrequent reinforcement. The gambler may lose in the long run, and the pigeon may not receive enough food at the end of the day to cover the metabolic loss from its activity. The schedule of reinforcement sustains the performance despite the overall lack of economy.

## experiment I: measuring the contribution of the variable schedule to the maintenance of the behavior

The first experiment shows the effect of altering a schedule of reinforcement from a variable- to a fixed-ratio, with the average number of pecks per reinforcement constant. The experiment began with a bird having a long history of reinforcement on a variable-ratio schedule (VR 360). Under the variable schedule the bird pecked continuously at an overall rate of about 2 pecks per second. The bird pecked stably and reliably from 7,000 10,000 times per hour for 8 or 10 hours a day, day after day, as long as the schedule of reinforcement was continued. The plan of the experiment was to alter the schedule in middle of the session to one requiring a fixed rather than a variable number of pecks. The first effect of the change to the fixed reinforcement schedule is shown in Figure 5-18.

The first segment of the cumulative record, marked A, is typical of the stable state on the variable schedule. The bird pecks continuously at a rate of about 2 pecks per second. Beginning at the arrow, reinforcement occurs on a fixed schedule of 360 pecks *per* reinforcement rather than every 360 pecks on the average. The rest of the graph shows the first state of transition to a fixed-number performance.

The following text from the original publication describes the result:

We studied this difference in performance on VR and FR by changing the VR 360 schedule to FR 360 and observing transitional effects.

Figure 5-18 shows a transition from VR to FR. The first excursion of record A is the fourth in the session. The next shows the prevailing performance on VR. At the arrow the schedule became FR 360. The lower rate and acceleration at a and b are characteristic of the variable-ratio performance during the larger number requirements. Record B shows the 11th and 12th excursions, with a further development of the fixed-ratio performance.

Record C shows the 18th through the 21st excursions of the recording pen. A brief period of responding at a high rate follows the reinforcement at c, but 45 minutes is required for the next 360 responses. A long pause also occurs near the start of the fixed-number segment at d.[13]

A fifteen-minute period, during which the bird did not peck at all, is cut out of the graph.

Thereafter, 3 reinforcements are run off at maximum rate, and a remaining segment shows the character of the first excursion in Record C.[14]

Thus, even by the end of this first session on the fixed-ratio schedule, the bird begins to pause more than it did previously on the variable-ratio schedule. Continued reinforcement on the fixed-ratio schedule over the next three sessions (approximately 8 hours each) weakens the behavior even more. The bird's performance does not change immediately to the characteristic performance on a large fixed-ratio schedule because it takes a number of reinforcements on the new schedule before the transition is complete. The intermittent rates of pecking and the pauses at times other than following reinforcement are a carryover from the previous variable-ratio reinforcement, where pecks were reinforced unpredictably.

Figure 5-19 shows the same bird's performance, on the same fixed-ratio schedule, three sessions and some 150 reinforcements later. Pauses after reinforcement become longer. The performance is more characteristic of a fixed-ratio schedule as the effects of the previous variable-ratio schedule are lost and the performance comes under the control of the new sched-

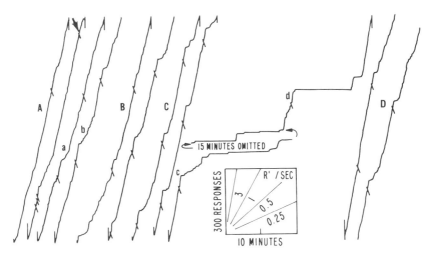

**Figure 5-18**   A cumulative record of a pigeon's performance during the transition from a VR 360 to an FR 360 schedule of reinforcement.

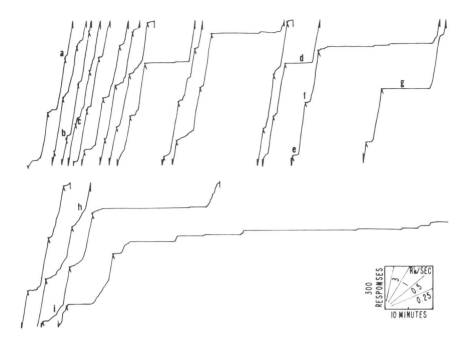

**Figure 5-19** A cumulative record of the performance on the FR 360 schedule of reinforcement showing the transition from the previous reinforcement on the variable-ratio schedule.

ule Even though the number of pecks required per reinforcement is the same as under the previous variable-ratio schedule, the *overall* (though not necessarily the momentary) rate of pecking is lower, and the bird is receiving much less food than before. If reinforcement on the fixed-ratio schedule were continued longer, the pauses would become even longer and reinforcements would occur even less frequently. The bird received fifty reinforcements during this period. In contrast, at the overall rate of pecking that had occurred on the previous variable-ratio schedule (2 pecks per second), this number of reinforcements would have occurred in 2.5 hours as opposed to the almost 4.5 hours required here. Conversely, had the bird been on the variable-ratio schedule during the 4.5-hour period, he would have pecked about 32,000 times and received about ninety reinforcements. Although the rate of pecking falls continuously during the session, the long pause at the end of the session is not intended to suggest that the bird's performance has ceased. Eventually, the number of pecks required for reinforcement would have been completed, although it would take a long time.

The following text from the original publication describes the details of the cumulative record.

The figure shows the entire 3rd session on FR 360. It begins with instances of responding at a high rate immediately after reinforcement before pausing, as at a, b, and c. But these priming runs become less frequent as the session continues. Most of the fixed-number segments now show a pause immediately after reinforcement. The overall rate of responding falls progressively during the session as the pause and lower rate following reinforcement become extended. During the final 70 minutes of the session, only 250 responses occur, and the last fixed-ratio requirement is not completed. Many of the number segments are identical to a standard fixed-ratio performance, as at d, e, f, and g. Toward the end of the session (lower curves), segments begin to show a prolonged acceleration with rough grain, as at h and i. When FR 360 was maintained for 6 sessions, the trend in the figure continued. The overall rate remained low, with substantial pauses following reinforcements.[15]

## reinstatement of the performance
## by a return to variable-ratio reinforcement

The behavior weakened by the change to the fixed-ratio schedule was recovered by returning to the original variable-ratio schedule. The following experiment, with the same bird and the same schedules, describes the

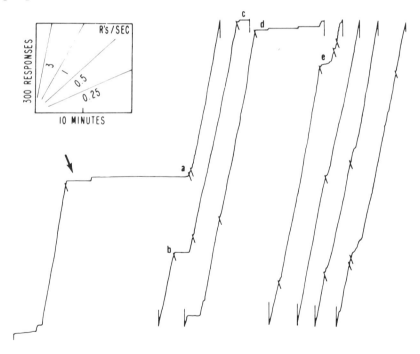

**Figure 5-20** Transition from FR 360 back to VR 360. Changing the schedule back to variable ratio eliminated the longer pauses and reinstated the high rates following reinforcement. The schedule was changed to VR at the arrow and it takes some time for the performance to conform to the schedule change.

recovery of the original high rate of pecking when the variable-ratio schedule is reinstated.

The text and the cumulative record that describe the result are from the original report of the experiment. By chance, two reinforcements on the variable-ratio schedule occurred after only a small number of pecks. Had the variable-ratio schedule programmed a larger number of pecks at this point, the transition to the final performance might have been slower than was the case here.

A second reinforcement occurs immediately after a few pecks. The reinforcement at b occurs after 750 pecks and is followed by a pause of about 2 minutes. A similar pause follows other reinforcements at c and d. But by the reinforcement at e, the transition to the variable-ratio performance is practically complete, with consistent responding, immediately after reinforcement. The rate is not yet as high as will be characteristic of this bird under the final VR.[16]

Figure 5-21 describes a repetition of the first experiment. The first part of the record above shows the continuation of the variable-ratio performance: a sustained high rate of pecking. The fixed-ratio schedule again gradually leads to pausing and to a low overall rate of pecking. Continued reinforcement on the fixed-ratio schedule (not shown in this graph) leads to much longer pauses after reinforcement.

Here, as in the previous experiment, pecking just after reinforcement is a carry over from the previous variable-ratio schedule where pecks were occasionally reinforced for only a few pecks following the previous reinforcement. With further reinforcement on the fixed-ratio schedule, these periods of pecking just after reinforcement give way to pauses.

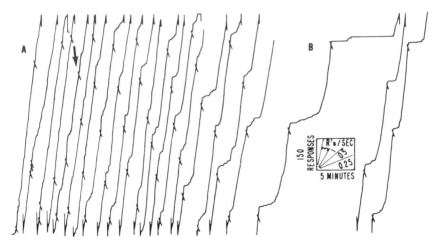

Figure 5-21    A cumulative record describing a second transition from VR to FR 360.

summary

These experiments, comparing fixed-ratio and variable-ratio reinforcement, show that the schedule of reinforcement has a profound effect on how frequently the bird pecks. Only one characteristic of the schedules of reinforcement, the variable versus the fixed character of the schedule, was responsible for the dramatic change observed in the performance. The same number of performances, the same fine-grain contingency between performances and its effect at the moment of reinforcement, the general features of the apparatus, and the level of food deprivation were identical in both schedules.

The change in the bird's performance as the schedules of reinforcement were changed from fixed to variable and variable to fixed suggests the extreme plasticity (susceptibility to change) of much of operant behavior. Operant behavior is adaptable, in that when the contingencies of reinforcement in the environment supporting the behavior are changed, behavior also changes. In addition, operant behavior is often *reversible:* the effect on a performance by one schedule of reinforcement can be removed after the performance has been switched to another schedule, simply by changing it back to the original one.

In the preceding example, the change in the performance when the schedule of reinforcement was alternated between fixed and variable schedules was not immediate. In the first experiment pauses did not develop after reinforcement even after 3 days on the fixed-ratio schedule. Almost 100,000 pecks and hundreds of reinforcements were required before the fixed-ratio schedule produced its typical performance pattern.

Many behavioral processes take time before they produce the stable state resulting from the control of the new environment. This delay, before the schedule of reinforcement has its final effect, makes if difficult to see the effect by casual observation. Psychotherapists encounter the same problem when they do not observe immediate changes in a patient's behavior when the circumstances in his life have changed. This lag between the application of a new reinforcement procedure and the corresponding change in the organism's performance is one of the unfortunate reasons why control of behavior by positive, rather than aversive, reinforcement is not always practiced in the natural environment (Chapter 4). The behavior of a parent in altering the environment that controls the behavior of a child is reinforced by the child's new performance. Such reinforcement is delayed with positive reinforcement because it takes time before the new behavior comes under the control of the new environment.

Aversive control, however, usually results in immediate reinforcement for the parents or another controller. When the parent applies an aversive stimulus, the child's escape from it is an immediate reinforcer for the parent. Unfortunately, the immediate reinforcement produced by aversive control tends to encourage its use despite undersirable by-products, while positive reinforcement procedures are less likely to be applied for this reason despite their long-term effectiveness.

Extinction after variable-interval reinforcement poses a similar problem in the delay of the controller's reinforcement by the change in the performance of the controllee. After certain kinds of VI reinforcement, such as the case of the pigeon that pecked over 20,000 times before stopping, there may be several hours without reinforcement before the frequency of the performance falls enough to be discernible. A parent, for example, who timidly tests the hypothesis that the child's crying is due to parental attention (reinforcement), may never test the hypothesis effectively because the parent does not withhold attention long enough. The parent who has not had experience in weakening crying by extinction may not be able to ignore the child's crying long enough to see that the frequency of the crying is actually falling.

## questions

1. Describe the relative maintenance of behavior under the VR 360 compared with a fixed-ratio performance of the same value.

2. How was the pigeon experiment carried out to show the contribution of the variable-ratio schedule to the maintenance of the performance?

3. Describe the details of the rate changes in Figure 5-2.

4. Describe some of the implications of the experiment showing the transitions between fixed-ratio and variable-ratio reinforcement to human behavior.

5. Discuss why an interval schedule is an indirect way of reinforcing low rates of pecking.

6. Why is a ratio schedule of reinforcement an indirect way of enforcing high rates of pecking.

7. Describe how an experiment in which the reinforcement schedules of two birds were yoked demonstrated the differential reinforcement of high rates independently of the change in frequency reinforcement.

8. Discuss why the frequency of reinforcement and rate of pecking are confounded in a fixed-ratio schedule.

The experiment to be described in this section will provide information as to why ratio schedules of reinforcement, in general, produce higher rates of performance than fixed-interval schedules. Before describing the experiment, however, it will be useful to understand some of the differences between the two schedules. Two properties are confounded (change together) in ratio schedules. First, the faster the animal performs, the more frequently it is reinforced. Such increased frequency of reinforcement can itself increase the frequency of pecking, as is the case with the variable-interval reinforcement schedule where the rate of pecking is high when reinforcement is frequent (say, once every minute on the average), and decreases as the frequency of reinforcement decreases. Second, ratio schedule also differentially reinforces high rates of pecking.

## the shaping of high rates of pecking
## at the moment of reinforcement

The discussion of how ratio schedules differentially reinforce high rates is best introduced by first examining what happens at the moment of reinforcement. Consider the fine grain of the relationship between the two pecks preceding reinforcement in an interval schedule. The longer the animal pauses on an interval schedule, the more likely it is that the *next* peck will be reinforced, since *only* the passage of time, and not number of pecks, increases the likelihood that the next peck could be reinforced. In the extreme case, if the bird pauses for the entire interval it is certain that one peck will produce the reinforcer. One result tends to be stereotyped activity between pecks because of accidental reinforcement. For example, if the bird goes to the back of the cage and preens itself, the time taken in preening makes it more likely that the reinforcement interval will have elapsed when the bird returns to the key. Any performance that takes time has a higher likelihood of preceding the reinforced peck. Interval schedules are therefore indirect ways of reinforcing low rates of pecking because of indirect, accidental reinforcement of competing behavior.

The reverse, however, is true for ratio schedules. The occurrence of a reinforced peck in a ratio schedule depends *only* on the number of times the bird pecks. A peck following a pause is no more likely to be reinforced than any other peck. A peck just following another peck, however, will be reinforced more often because the likelihood of reinforcement on ratio schedules depends on the number of times the bird pecks. This differential reinforcement of high rates is an important contribution to the high rate of pecking that ratio schedules produce.

The argument can be visualized in Figure 5-22, which represents the behavior of a pigeon whose pecks are distributed somewhat randomly before a fixed-ratio schedule is imposed. Each deflection in the record represents a peck. Some pecks follow relatively long pauses. Others occur in rapid succession.

If we classify the bird's pecks in terms of whether they are preceded by a pause or by another peck, we see that in three out of four cases the last peck is preceded by another peck (b, c, and g are examples). In total, there are only 5 cases out of 20 of a peck following a pause (the first peck of each group at a, c, e, f, and h), and 15 cases out of 20 of a peck following another peck. Since the probability of reinforcement on ratio schedules increases only with the number of pecks, the likelihood of any peck being reinforced does not depend on the time from the last peck. This means that in three-fourths of the cases, the peck that is reinforced will have occurred as a part of a group. By contrast, a peck after a pause is reinforced only one-fourth of the time. This result may be restated as the differential reinforcement of a high rate of pecking.

## experiments comparing interval and ratio reinforcement when frequency is identical

Either a high frequency of reinforcement or the differential reinforcement of high rates of performing could contribute to the higher rate of the performance during ratio as opposed to interval schedules of reinforcement. The following experiments were designed to measure 1) how much of the high rate of performance on ratio schedules comes from the differential reinforcement of high rates due to the fixed-ratio requirement; and 2) how much is from the increase in frequency of reinforcement that naturally occurs when the rate of pecking increases.

The question was answered by a yoked-bird experiment. A bird in one experimental chamber is reinforced on a variable-ratio schedule. The performance of a bird in a second experimental chamber will be rein-

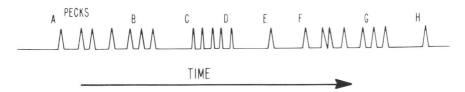

Figure 5-22    A polygraph record showing the details of the time between pecks.[17]

forced *any time* the first bird is reinforced. The second bird is yoked to the reinforcements of the first. The performance of the bird in the first chamber determines when the bird in the second chamber can be reinforced (not when it will peck). The schedule of reinforcement for the second bird is a *variable-interval* since its performances are reinforced only after time has passed *and* it emits a performance. The procedure insures that the overall frequency of reinforcement is equal for both birds and rules it out as a factor that could determine any differences in rate of pecking between the two birds. Thus, if there is a difference, it could only be due to the differential reinforcement of high rates of ratio schedules as opposed to the higher probability of reinforcement after pauses in the interval schedule.

The experiment is accomplished by an electrical connection between the two boxes. When the first bird (on the variable-ratio schedule) is reinforced, an electrical circuit is produced that arranges that the *next time* the second bird pecks, that peck will operate the food magazine. Thus, the first bird's reinforcement is determined by the number of times it pecks (variable-ratio), but the second bird's reinforcement is determined by the passage of time, independent of the number of pecks (variable-interval). The overall frequency of reinforcement is virtually identical for the two birds, but the actual schedules differ. The following text is the original published account of the experiment.

When reinforcement is determined by the number of pecks, as it is on any ratio schedule, the frequency of reinforcement increases with the rate of pecking. We cannot be sure that the high rates generated by variable-ratio schedules are not due to increased frequency of reinforcement rather than to the differential reinforcement of rates or groups of pecks. The following experiment was designed to separate frequency of reinforcement from other factors in the variable-ratio schedule.

The problem was to design a control experiment in which frequency of reinforcement would be identical with a variable ratio, but in which none of the other factors of a variable-ratio schedule would be present. The procedure was to "yoke" two experimental boxes. When a reinforcement occurs in one box, it automatically sets up a reinforcement in the second box. The apparatuses were in separate rooms and hence will-insulated from each other, except for the electrical connection which set up reinforcements in the second box. The bird in the first box was reinforced on a variable-interval schedule. The same schedule was set up in the second box, since every time the first bird was reinforced, a reinforcement was set up for the second bird (Fig. 5-23). We matched rates of pecking in the two situations by varying levels of deprivation. When rates of pecking were approximately the same, the schedule of reinforcement in the first box was changed to *variable-ratio*.

The values of pecks per reinforcement were chosen to match the actual numbers appearing in the performance on the variable-interval schedule. The frequency of reinforcement in the lead bird was thus unchanged at the start of the transition from variable-interval to variable-ratio. Any initial increase in rate

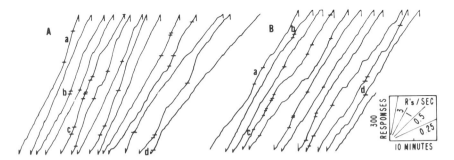

**Figure 5-23** Cumulative records showing the final performances for the experimental bird and its yoked control on the variable-interval schedule. Record A shows the performance of the bird and the variable-interval schedule and Record B is the cumulative record of the pigeon whose reinforcement schedule is yoked to the first bird.

must result from some other factor, such as the differential reinforcement of high rates. As soon as the rate had increased, however, the frequency of reinforcement is increased, and the process may continue in an "autocatalytic" fashion. The bird in the second yoked apparatus, however, still remains on a variable-interval schedule. The actual intervals are determined by the performance of the first bird on the variable-ratio schedule, but have no relation to the number of responses emitted by the second bird. The schedules of reinforcement of the two birds are variable-ratio and variable-interval, respectively, while the frequency of reinforcement is identical. The extent to which the increased frequency of reinforcement in the variable-interval schedule is responsible for the increased rate can be determined from the increase in rate under the variable-interval schedule in the yoked apparatus.[18]

The final result is shown in Figure 5-24. Record A gives the performance on the variable-ratio schedule for the first bird. The performance is ratio-like, where rates of 3 to 4 pecks per second alternate with periods without any pecking. Record B for the yoked bird shows a performance typical of variable-interval schedules of reinforcement. Even though the frequency of reinforcement is identical with the first bird, the overall rate of pecking is lower (about 1 peck per second) than that of the variable-ratio bird, and the fine grain of the record is continuous, typical of interval schedules. The point of contact between the schedule of reinforcement and the animal's behavior is at the moment of reinforcement, and it is here that interval and ratio schedules exert their differential control over the animal's performance. These results clearly show that it is the differential reinforcement of higher rates of performing and not merely the frequency of reinforcement that accounts for these large differences in interval versus ratio schedules. It is a combination of both these variables that contributes to the final performance on the schedule of reinforcement. Although the frequency of reinforcement is higher on the variable-interval schedule in Record B than it was before, the increase is not large enough to increase the overall variable-interval rate. The following text, from the original publication, provides a test of your ability to read the record fluently.

> The VR performance after 11 sessions is shown in A of Fig. 5-24 taken from the middle part of the session. While the local rate of pecking is only 3 per second, pecking is sustained at this rate for longer periods. There are clearly only two rates, the prevailing rate of 3 responses per second and zero. The overall rate is about 2 responses per second.
>
> The corresponding record for the yoked bird (record B) continues to show overall rates of less than 1 peck per second. Also, the rate changes continue to reflect the VI, with smooth transitions from the higher rate following the reinforcement to lower rates elsewhere.[19]

## applying data on intermittent reinforcement in animals to people

In extrapolating the effects of intermittent reinforcement to complex cases, it is important to distinguish between the technical use of the term *reinforcement* and the colloquial use of the term *reward* by specifying the exact performance that is reinforced and the exact stimulus that is the reinforcer. For example, reinforcers maintain the behavior of a salaried worker. Superficially, a salary arrangement might be considered to be a fixed-interval schedule of reinforcement, in the sense that the money is a reinforcing event that is delivered every fourteen or thirty days. In the technical sense of reinforcement, however, money reinforces only the behavior of accepting the paycheck. Although the money may be a necessary condition to maintain all of the behaviors associated with the person's employment, it is only indirectly related to the person's day-to-day activi-

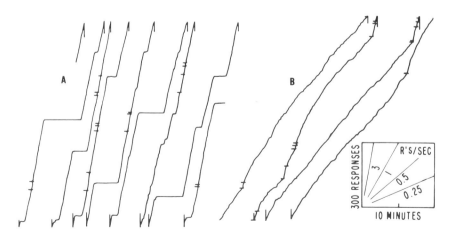

**Figure 5-24**   Yoked pair during the eleventh session of VR.

ties. The bulk of the performances that occur on a person's job have immediate, local consequences. These are the reinforcers that actually follow the performances and whose schedules play the major role in maintaining the behaviors.

A schedule of intermittent reinforcement could occur with the delivery of the salary check, however, if we consider the behavior of looking for the check. For example, consider the situation where the salary checks are delivered somewhat variably and without advance notice. Under conditions where the check may be needed badly, the individual may frequently look toward the desk where the checks are delivered, or telephone to see whether they have arrived yet.

## examples of weakened human behavior
## due to the properties of ratio reinforcement

Nearly all intermittent reinforcement in occupational behavior is on ratio schedules. The salesperson usually sells her product in proportion to the number of calls she makes, rather than to the passage of time. A clear effect of a ratio schedule of reinforcement is in the piecework pay of the factory worker we discussed earlier. This is a fixed-ratio schedule of reinforcement where the employee is paid directly as a function of the amount of behavior he emits. It is well known that this type of incentive produces a high rate of activity compared with any other pay system. Like all forms of ratio reinforcement, however, both the salesperson and the pieceworker may be disinclined to work if too much behavior is required per reinforcement (fixed-ratio). Some of the objections to the use of piecework pay systems are based on the fear that the employer will decrease the amount of pay per unit of work and that the worker will not receive the benefit of extra productivity and will experience considerable strain.

The student is on a similar piecework schedule when she studies for examinations or writes an essay or long report. She must sustain performance for a long time and emit a large amount of behavior in the form of written words, reference material read, and editing. Ratio strain occurs in the form of a low inclination to return to work just after the examination or after completing certain sections of the entire term paper. Typical of the results of ratio schedules in laboratory experiments, the student works in spurts. Once she begins, the behavior is sustained at high rates, but the student is erratic as to when she actually works. The data may be somewhat masked in the natural environment because the student may be doing other things during the pause after reinforcement. Although she sharpens pencils, goes to the movies, talks to neighbors, and cleans her room, she is still not studying or writing. Studying and writing would be prepotent over these other activities if its frequency were not low due to strain from the ratio schedule.

## persuasion as an example of intermittent reinforcement of social behavior

The closest approximation to continuous reinforcement in social behavior is the execution of the social amenities. In our culture, reactions to "Hello," "Good morning," or "How are you?" are almost inevitable. Almost all other verbal behavior, however, involves considerable intermittent reinforcement. Consider, for example, the situation in which a man would like to alter his wife's reluctance to buy a new house. To do so, he needs to elaborate to her all the desirable consequences of moving. He needs to describe their present facilities, compare them with those of the proposed house, and explain how the new facilities will improve her life. He needs to describe the proposed new location, elaborate upon how it will make commuting easier, and describe schools for the children and social contacts with the neighbors. The persuasiveness of the husband depends on a complex and large verbal repertoire. A dimension of such an interaction may add further intermittency when the husband's persuasions are repeated several times, its function changes from advice to nagging. In that case, a fixed-ratio schedule occurs because the nagging accumulates and becomes aversive enough to produce avoidance and escape behavior to terminate the nagging.

When the aversive control, such as nagging or threatening, is used to produce some behavior in another person, the person who applies the aversive stimuli (the nagger) is intermittently reinforced. The reinforcer for the nagger is the compliance of the person he is nagging. The fact that an amount of behavior is required to establish an aversive state of affairs specifies this schedule as a ratio schedule of reinforcement. The schedule becomes variable when different people require different amounts of nagging and threats before the situation becomes aversive enough to terminate it by compliance. Even the same person will vary from time to time in his or her reactions to nagging. The intermittent reinforcement experienced by the instigator of nagging and teasing behavior makes it very difficult to eliminate this kind of behavioral control.

---

## notes

[1]Ferster, C. B. and Skinner, B. F. *Schedules of reinforcement.* Englewood Cliffs, N.J.: Prentice-Hall, 1957, p. 24.

[2]Ibid., p. 107.

[3]Ibid., p. 183.

[4]Ibid., p. 183.

[5]Ibid., p. 185.

[6]Nurnberger, J. I., Ferster, C. B., and Brady, J. P. *An introduction to the science of human behavior.* New York: Appleton-Century-Crofts, 1963, p. 244.

[7]Holt, John. *How Children Learn.* New York: Pitman Publishing Company, 1967.

[8]The relation between rate of pecking and frequency of reinforcement has received much attention in a theoretical account proposed by Herrnstein, called "the matching." Herrnstein, R. J. Formal properties of the matching law. *Journal of the Experimental Analysis of Behavior,* 21: 159–164, 1974. In the matching law Herrnstein attempts a formulation represented by a simple mathematical statement that relates the frequency of a performance maintained under any schedule of reinforcement to the frequency of reinforcement. Whatever the ultimate outcome of Herrnstein's theoretical proposal, however, the empirical description of how various schedules of reinforcement maintain a performance provides data that is needed for understanding how behavior is maintained when it is intermittently reinforced.

[9]Ferster, C. B. and Skinner, B. F. *Schedules of reinforcement,* p. 396.

[10]Ibid., p. 347.

[11]Ibid., p. 349.

[12]Ibid., p. 58.

[13]Ibid., p. 407.

[14]Ibid., pp. 407–408.

[15]Ibid., pp. 408–409.

[16]Ibid., p. 409.

[17]Ibid., p. 410.

[18]Ibid., pp. 399–400.

[19]Ibid., pp. 403–404.

# 6

# stimulus control

This chapter analyzes the different ways that the environment (stimuli) may control a performance. A performance is reinforced or not when a stimulus is present or absent. The environmental control of behavior, traditionally called *discrimination,* makes possible the orderly occurrence of an operant repertoire in the face of the thousands of reinforcers that can maintain an equal number of performances on a wide range of circumstances.

The operant behavior of pigeons, reinforced in the various experiments that have been described so far, would be lost very quickly unless it were controlled by the particular occasion when it was successful. The food-magazine light, for example, controlled when the pigeon inserted its head into the food dispenser to eat. Otherwise the bird might repeat the activity continuously during the periods interposed between food presentations. Not only would the constant emission of the food-magazine activity interfere with the performances that were to be conditioned, but the huge amount of nonreinforced approaches to the feeder would weaken that behavior. This process by which the environment controls when operant performances will be emitted is called *stimulus control.* The first section of this chapter describes the basic data of stimulus control, primarily from animal experiments, to provide a conceptual framework to understand complex human behavior.

Not all stimuli that control operant behavior are single stimuli related to discrete performances. In many cases there is a continuous relation between a range of stimuli that controls a corresponding range of performances. Such a repertoire, called a *fine-grain repertoire,* may be established in animal experiments. It represents an important kind of human stimulus control, as in the case of imitative behavior.

This process provides a way to understand the basic processes that contribute to concept formation, abstraction, or the control of behavior by an abstract or limited dimension of a stimulus.

When an operant performance is brought under the control of a stimulus, it is inevitable that some performances will go unreinforced when they are emitted in the presence of an inappropriate stimulus. One way to reduce inappropriate behavior (and thus excessive extinction) is to develop a systematic program beginning with obvious differences between stimuli and proceeding to subtler ones. Part III describes several techniques. For example, if the stimulus differences are programmed carefully, in procedures called *fading,* an organism's behavior comes under the control of the differences between stimuli without *any* instances of unreinforced behavior.

Part IV discusses two important factors influencing the accuracy by which stimuli control the operant performances whose reinforcement they set the occasion for. One is punishment, by postponing reinforcement of performances that are emitted inappropriately. The other technique stems from the effect of schedules of reinforcement.

## technical terms

abstract property of a stimulus
discriminative stimulus ($S^D$)
discrimination
environmental control of behavior
fading

fine-grain repertoire
matching-to-sample
S-delta ($S\Delta$)
stimulus control

## outline

Part I: How Stimuli Control Behavior
A multiple schedule demonstration of stimulus control
Stimulus control as a 3-term contingency
Stimulus control of reflexes
Examples of stimulus control from the preceding chapters

How a performance may be brought under control of a single property of a stimulus
"Triangularity" as a reinforcement contingency
The advantages of the term "abstract property of a stimulus" over "concept formation"
Establishing complex stimulus control by matching-to-sample

*part I: how stimuli control behavior*

a multiple schedule demonstration
of stimulus control

A pigeon experiment explicitly demonstrates the process by which a stimulus acquires control over a performance. We begin with a bird whose pecks have been reinforced when there have been a variety of colors behind the key. The key-color is then alternated between red and green. The first peck in the green light is reinforced. After the reinforced peck, the key-color turns red for 5 minutes during which time pecks are not reinforced. This is the multiple schedule described in Chapter 5. The two schedules, under the discriminative control of the red and green lights, are extinction and continuous reinforcement. The alternate extinction and reinforcement of the peck on these two occasions brings the behavior under the differential control of the two stimuli before the end of a 60-minute session. As the cycle is repeated, the bird pecks less in the red light while pecking at the green key is sustained. Figure 6-1 gives a graphic record of the result that can be routinely expected when an experiment

NUMBER OF PECKS

ALTERNATING PERIODS OF GREEN ■ AND RED □

**Figure 6-1** The continuous decline in the rate of pecking during a 60-minute session when 5-minute periods of a red key-light (white), in those presence pecks are not reinforced alternate with a green light (black), in whose presence a peck operates the food-magazine.

such as this is performed. The bird pecks steadily when the green light comes on. In the presence of the red key-light, when pecks are not reinforced, the rate of pecking decreases during the successive 5-minute periods until the bird virtually stops pecking.

The process takes considerably longer when the stimuli are not so grossly different as colors of light that are especially prominent stimuli to birds. Figure 6-2 describes the results of an experiment in which the stimuli behind the key are fine vertical or horizontal lines.

Because the process takes a long time and is gradual we know the differences between the stimuli are more subtle than those between the red and green lights. The experimental sessions are about 2 hours long, equally divided between brief periods when the lines are vertical and horizontal. The graph plots the total number of pecks the bird emits, cumulatively, over the 11 sessions that constitute the experiment. When pecks are reinforced in the presence of the horizontal lines, under a variable-interval schedule, there is a constant rate of pecking that is sustained. This rate remained constant during the 11 sessions and served as a comparison for the declining rate that occurred in the other stimulus where pecks were not reinforced. The dotted line indicates the rate of pecking on this schedule when the lines are horizontal and the pecks were reinforced on the variable-interval schedule. The solid curve gives the number of pecks, session-by-session, cumulatively, when the lines behind the key are vertical and pecks are not reinforced. Even during the first session, the rate of pecking in the presence of the horizontal lines becomes less than the reference rate in the presence of the stimuli where pecks are reinforced. The number of pecks emitted in the presence of the vertical lines de-

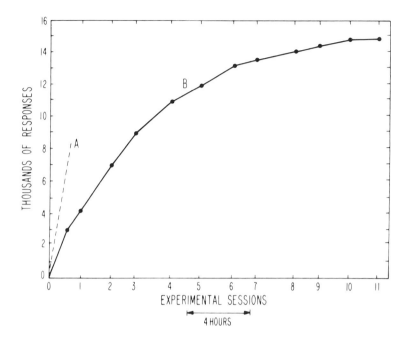

**Figure 6-2**  Overall changes in rate of pecking during eleven sessions during which the bird's performance comes under the discriminative control of vertical and horizontal lines correlated with the variable-interval and extinction schedules that alternate.

creases session-by-session almost continuously. By the eleventh session, pecking all but ceases. Overall, 14,000 pecks over 11 sessions took place in the extinction periods with the vertical lines compared with less than 1000 pecks in a 60-minute experimental session with the red and green light.

## stimulus control as a 3-term contingency

With the development of the concept of the control of an operant by a stimulus that sets the occasion for its reinforcement, the basic definition of an operant as a 3-term contingency is complete. We would describe the operants of the preceding experiments by the paradigm: $S^D \cdot P \rightarrow S^R$. The $S^D$, or discriminative stimulus is the green light or horizontal lines behind the key. The performance is pecking the key and the arrow (which reads "is followed by") indicates that the stimulus it produces maintains its frequency. Implied in the definition of the operant is the differential reinforcement that occurs when it is emitted on occasions when it does not alter the environment by producing the stimulus that increases its fre-

**194**

quency. That contingency is described by the three terms, S$\Delta$·P $\nrightarrow$ S$^R$. S $\Delta$ is read "S-delta" and indicates the absence of the stimulus that sets the occasion for the reinforcement of the performance. The broken arrow indicates that the performance is not followed by the reinforcer in the absence of the discriminative stimulus. Since virtually every operant performance is influenced by all three terms—the discriminative stimulus, the performance, and its relation to the reinforcer—the specification of an operant is not complete unless it includes all three terms.

In everyday conversation we are more likely to describe stimulus control as "noticing a stimulus, discriminating between the horizontal and vertical lines, or perceiving a difference." Yet there are important advantages of the behavioral description. Like so many colloquial accounts of human behavior, terms like noticing, being aware of, and discriminating are mentalistic. That is to say, they imply some faculty or agent, within the person, that is responsible for the fact that an individual may act differently because a new stimulus is present. In actual fact, the colloquial statements arc little more than an assertion that the person acts differently in the presence of the stimulus (notices it) than in its absence. But there seems always to be a tendency to take the next step and attribute causality to a faculty, within the person, that does the noticing. As we have seen, however, a causal analysis requires that all three terms of the operant be taken into account to describe the functional relation of each to the other. Thus, when we say that the red light controls a low rate of pecking we are obliged to inquire further about the reinforcement contingency that brings about such a reduced control of pecking. We then do not have far to look before we discover that the crucial event is the nonreinforcement of pecking when the light behind the key is red. At that point we could say that the pigeon notices the red light because pecking it never produces food while pecking the green light does. But in that case we could as easily substitute "stops pecking the red light" for "notices the red light." The behavioral description turns our attention to the actual operations by which we bring an organism's behavior under differential control of various aspects of the environment.

## stimulus control of reflexes

Just as the reinforcement of an operant increases its frequency selectively on the particular occasions when it is reinforced, conditioned reflexes are also controlled by the surroundings in which they are conditioned. The experiment with conditioned reflexes where Pavlov discovered that the room where the experiment took place became part of the stimulus complex that elicited the conditioned response is an example of the stimulus control of a reflex. When the dog whose salivary reflex had been conditioned was placed back in the experimental room it began to salivate even before the experimental conditioned stimulus, the buzzer, was sounded. The room itself was an effective part of the conditioned stimulus. To narrow the control of the conditioned reflex to the buzzer alone it was necessary to carry out the same kind of differential reinforcement as described for operant behaviors. The dog was left in the room for long periods of time during which no food was placed in its mouth. As a result, the room, as a conditioned stimulus, no longer elicited salivation without reinforcement by the unconditioned stimulus. On these occasions, without reinforcement, the magnitude of the reflex decreased and its latency increased.

Pavlov, in a classical experiment, produced differential control of a reflex deliberately by restricting the control of a conditioned stimulus by differential reinforcement. He put food in the dog's mouth only when the dog was shown an ellipse and not when shown a circle. Eventually elicitation of the reflex by the circle disappeared through extinction.

The interaction of operant and reflex conditioning may interfere with the development of stimulus control of reflexes. There is a classical story about an explosion that occurred at the instant a salesman pushed a doorbell. The result was that all of the circumstances present at the time of the explosion became conditioned stimuli eliciting the reflexes evoked by the explosion. The emotional reaction of the salesman to this accidental pairing was so extreme that it generalized to any approach to any house. His behavior was so disrupted that he could no longer engage in house-to-house selling. As a result, the salesman was never exposed to the eliciting stimuli for the reflex through conditioning because avoidance of doorbells was superstituously reinforced (negatively). So long as there is no exposure to the doorbells and surrounding cicumstances, there is no possibility of weakening the reflex through extinction. In other words, a person cannot be exposed to the conditioned stimulus for a reflex if it immediately reinforces some operant performance that terminates it. The same process may explain why phobic reactions are so resistant to elimination or change. This is the reasoning behind treatments such as implosive therapy that force the patient to remain in the presence of the conditioned stimulus so that the reflex can be elicited without being paired with the unconditoned stimulus.

## examples of stimulus control
## from the preceding chapters

Consider the training procedure for a dog that was described in Chapter 1. The presence of a trainer who controls a dog's behavior by food reinforcement is a discriminative stimulus. The dog's behavior produces food only if the trainer is present to carry out the reinforcement procedure. As a result, the target performances are alternately reinforced when the trainer is present and not reinforced when he is absent. The click of the food dispenser also controls the dog's operant behavior discriminatively. It is the only occasion when the dog finds food when it approaches the food bowl. In the absence of the sound, approaching the food bowl is not reinforced by the sight of food. As a result of this differential reinforcement, the frequency of looking into the bowl remains high when the clicker sounds and becomes very low in its absence.

A child will seldom try to push a chair until he has his hands on it. Younger children, however, may be seen to reach for and push objects that are actually beyond their grasp. Such differential reinforcement is eventually responsible for bringing the child's behavior of reaching and pushing under the control of its distance from the child. Pushing the chair is the performance (P) reinforced by the change in its location ($S^R$). Pushing the chair can be only reinforced on limited occasions, however, such as being in tactile contact with it. The token which a hospital patient can change for food or privileges is also a discriminative stimulus controlling an operant. With a token in his hand a patient can go to the store and buy something. The same performance goes unreinforced without the token. Thus the patient who goes to a store and asks for a package of cigarettes without a token will not receive them. The alternating of reinforcement of asking for a cigarette when the patient has a token and its nonreinforcement without a token brings the behavior of asking for the cigarette under the control of the token. The token is functionally parallel to money in the normal human environment and the same analysis is usefully extended there. The clerk in the store will not give the child candy if money is not offered. The same performance when the child has money makes it likely that the clerk will comply with her request. As a result, not only is the clerk's behavior under the control of the child's money, but also the child's inclination to enter the store is under the control of "having money in hand." The performance of picking up a heavy object requires a different posture and topography than the movement needed for picking up a light one. These performances come under the control of the visual aspect of objects because the appearance of most objects is closely correlated with their weight. Persons unaccustomed to lifting objects of various weights frequently assume the wrong position. With repeated experiences where a heavy object is approached with the posture appropriate to lifting a light weight, the manner of lifting soon comes under the control of the "apparent weight" of the object that is to be lifted. The alternate reinforcement and extinction soon brings the relevant performance topography under the control of the visual aspects of whatever is being lifted.

Stimulus control of "lifting" sometimes breaks down when something to be lifted has a deceptive appearance. For example, when one tries to lift a sandbag filled with fluffy cotton or a small parcel filled with lead, the natural correlation between size and weight no longer holds and the posture taken with the bag of cotton balls would be that appropriate for the small parcel of lead and vice versa.

## how a performance may be brought under control of a single property of a stimulus

The experimenter calls a stimulus "red" because behavior is controlled by the wavelength of the light on the bird's key rather than by other aspects of it. Actually, the naive bird faces a stimulus with many properties, any one of which could potentially control its behavior. Although the wavelength of the light might be more prominent than other aspects of the stimulus, for the bird or the experimenter, it is possible that the higher intensity of the green light or the different patterns of light distribution on the key could control the frequency of pecking in place of or along with the wavelength. In other words, although the language we use to describe the color of the light behind the key implies that the wavelength is the property of the stimulus that controls the bird's peck, the effective stimulus is a compound with several important properties, each of which might exert total or partial control.

For purposes of most experiments or practical situations, it is important only that there be two clear and distinct stimuli that differentially control the bird's performance. In these cases, the exact characteristics of the stimulus responsible for this control are not important. In carrying out such an experiment we would discover that the differential control by a red and green light would develop quickly. However, if we want to be sure that the bird is controlled solely by the wavelength of the key light, we must randomly vary the intensity of the light, saturation of the color, and the distribution of light across the key for both the red and green stimulus. By doing so we are sure that there is no consistent correlation between reinforcement, extinction, and properties of the key light other than wavelength. When the brightness of both the red and green stimulus is varied so that one time the red would be brighter than the green and another time the green brighter than the red, we would discover how much pecking was controlled by brightness. If the bird's pecking had been controlled, even partially, by brightness the bird would begin pecking in the red again even though it had previously been closely controlled by the difference between the two lights. Continuing the differential reinforcement, however, based now only on wavelength and saturation, would eventually reduce the frequency of pecking the red. The control by the saturation of the color and the pattern of light on the key could be reduced in the same way.

## "triangularity" as a reinforcement contingency

The process of control by an abstract property of a stimulus was illustrated in its basic form in the experiments described in the previous section. In colloquial use, we do not usually think of the designation of a light by its color as a concept or abstraction. We come into closer contact with the ordinary colloquial usage, however, when we describe the procedures for bringing a pigeon's behavior under the control of abstract properties of stimuli such as 'triangularity.' If the pigeon's behavior is to be controlled by the property of triangularity, the stimulus that controls the bird's peck must not be a triangle of a particular size and shape, but a form belonging to a class defined by three closed sides forming a figure whose angles total 180 degrees. Such a definition specifies a rule for generating stimuli that can be classed into groups that occasion reinforcement of pecking and those that do not. To bring a pigeon's behavior under the control of the property of "triangularity" we need to generate a large number of triangles that vary in every dimension except their being triangles. The size would vary from small to large and the angles would occur in every possible relation. The colors, the width of the lines, as well as the texture of the surface would vary. Alternating with these triangles would be other geometric forms that would share all the properties of the triangular figures except the essential one. The geometric figures would be projected onto the key at which the bird pecks. The actual stimuli that might be used are shown in Figure 6-3. The first group of figures are all triangles and are the stimuli to be presented when pecks will operate the food magazine. The second group of figures share all of the characteristics of the first group except that they are not triangles. When these forms are projected on the key no pecks are reinforced. The two groups of figures would be identical in every respect such as their area, circumference, width of line, or color. The only difference between the two sets of figures that could set the occasion for when a peck operates the food magazine is whether the figure has three closed sides forming a figure whose angles total 180 degrees.

A step-by-step account of the procedure is a useful way to gain a view of the process. It begins with a stimulus from Group I projected on the key. Pecks at the triangle on the key operate the food magazine. After reinforcement, the stimulus on the key changes or stays the same, randomly, so that the sequence cannot set the occasion for reinforcement. If another triangle appears, the peck is reinforced again. If the stimulus is not a triangle all pecks go unreinforced for a period of 5 minutes. A DRO procedure prevents pecks at the end of the 5-minute interval from being reinforced because they accidentally produce the appearance of a triangular figure. When the 5-minute interval elapses and if the bird has not pecked for a minute (the value of the DRO), the figure that is projected on the key changes again. Continuing the random alternation between stimuli from the two groups eventually decreases the frequency of the bird's pecking in the presence of nontriangular geometric forms while normal rates of pecking are maintained when triangles are present.

Because the stimuli from the two groups share so many properties we can expect that a very large number of unreinforced pecks will need to occur before the bird's pecks come under the differential control of the two classes of stimuli. For example, when a triangle is present it may also be red, large, and boldly outlined. Reinforcement of pecks at this figure will therefore increase the frequency with which the bird will peck at red, large, and boldly outlined nontriangular geometric forms. Because the physical dimensions of triangularity are a constant feature when pecks are reinforced, while all other variations in the stimulus occasion nonreinforcement, the triangular property of the stimulus will eventually control whether or not the bird pecks. The amount of unreinforced pecking that occurs will depend on how many different properties the triangular and nontriangular stimuli have in common. With a large enough selection of triangles varying in every possible dimension, and an equally large selection on nontriangular geometric figures, a great deal of extinction will need to take place before the peck is controlled by the single property of the stimulus.

| Group I | Group II |
|---|---|
| $S^D$'s: Occasions on which pecks are reinforced. | $S^\Delta$'s: Occasions on which pecks go reinforced. |

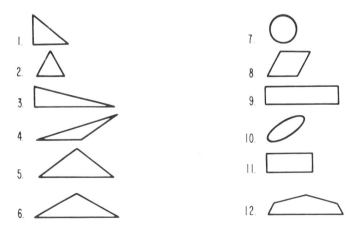

**Figure 6-3** Stimuli used in triangularity reinforcement experiments.

## the advantages of the term
## "abstract property of a stimulus"
## over "concept formation"

Traditionally, the type of behavioral control exemplified by the experimental procedures described above has been designated "concept formation." The phrase "control by an abstract property of a stimulus" is preferable to concept formation because it emphasizes the controlling properties of the stimulus rather than an inner, unreachable mental event or process. When we say that a person has a concept, it implies that the concept is something that resides within him as an agent that reacts differentially to the stimuli. In contrast, the term, abstract property of a stimulus, emphasizes that the control of behavior by a stimulus depends on how reinforcement contingencies are arranged in respect to a particular property of the stimulus. Thus we use the term, *abstract stimulus control,* because it refers to the environmental events responsible for the control of the behavior. The term, *concept formation,* tends to place the control of the behavior inside the organism. There, it has the danger of becoming an explanatory fiction rather than a description of how the interaction with the environment influences the behavior.

## establishing complex stimulus control
## by matching-to-sample

Matching-to-sample, a behavior under more complex stimulus control than that considered so far, is another useful way to study some of the more complex ways that stimuli can control operant performances. In the experiments previously mentioned, stimuli alternated so that a performance was reinforced or not depending on which stimulus was present. Matching-to-sample has the advantage over the previous precedures because there is a very active, fine-grain interaction between the performance and the variations in the stimuli. Rather than having a stimulus present for a period of time, say 5 minutes, stimuli change repeatedly as the bird pecks at them, with the corresponding differential reinforcement. Figure 6-4 illustrates the procedure as it might be applied with a human or an animal subject.

There are three windows that the subjects may touch with a finger or peck with the beak. A switch behind the window gives an electrical signal when it is pushed. Figures, colors, or pictures can be projected on the windows. The sequence begins with a figure, called the sample, in the center window. When the subject pushes the sample window, stimuli appear in the other two windows on both sides of the sample window. One of these stimuli, the matching one, corresponds with the sample. The

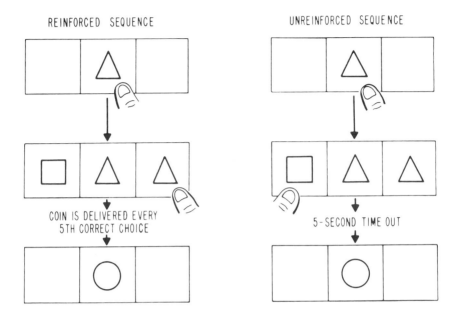

Figure 6-4　Matching to Sample.

other one, the non-matching stimulus, does not. Pressing the window that has the stimulus corresponding to the sample causes the delivery of a coin in the case of a human subject or the operation of the food dispenser in the case of an animal. If the subject presses the window where the figure does not correspond to the sample, the stimuli in the side windows disappear and the subject must then press the sample window to start the sequence again. The procedure also allows for the punishment of non-matching choices by following them with a brief time out when the entire apparatus goes dark and is not operable. Pressing the sample window induces the subject to pay attention to the stimulus projected there because people tend to look where they touch and pigeons look where they peck. Most animals tend to be controlled by those stimuli they point to or manipulate. This control comes from a past history when the beak or the fingers are controlled by the stimuli at the place where they peck or touch. At the very least, the peck at the sample orients the bird in that direction.

All three stimuli—the sample and the two choice stimuli—control the subject's performance in the matching-to-sample procedure. To start, pecking the sample produces stimuli on the side keys. Pecks at the blank side keys are not reinforced. To emit a reinforced peck, the bird needs to be controlled by both the sample stimulus and the choice. It is likely that

**202**

the absence of a peck to the S represents control by it. Thus each peck produces a continuous interplay between the stimuli and the bird's behavior.

**Guaranteeing that the subject is controlled by the identity of the sample and choice stimuli**   If a pigeon can "memorize a list of geometric figures" we could not be sure that the bird is pecking at the stimulus that is identical to the sample. If we are to be sure that the property of the stimulus that controls the performance is the identity between the sample and the choice stimuli, the form of the figures needs to be varied widely. We can be sure that the performance is controlled by the identity between the two figures rather than by their individual features when the addition of a new stimulus does not disrupt the performance. How fine a distinction a bird will make in "identity matching" depends on how similar the stimuli were during the previous matching experiences. If, for example, a large number of geometric forms, all of which differed by one-quarter inch controlled the bird's performance discriminatively, we would expect that some of the control of the bird's behavior would be lost if the differences were made less. On the other hand, the bird's performance would approach being controlled by "identity" if the reinforcement contingencies required finer and finer differences to the limit of the sensory capacity.

**Mismatching**   The matching-to-sample procedure is not limited to the case where the bird's peck is reinforced on the side key that corresponds to the sample stimulus. The procedure for bringing a performance under the control of the mismatch between the sample and choice stimuli follows the same form as when the bird is matching. The bird pecks the sample window as in the previous experiment but a peck at the nonmatching side window is reinforced. Such a repertoire is not functionally different than matching.

**Conditional discrimination**   In a conditional discrimination procedure we approach some of the complexity of the stimulus control found in the natural environment. Consider the first matching-to-sample procedure that was discussed where the subject matched a triangle or a circle depending on which figure was in the sample window. To make the control conditional we add a red and green light to the same and complicate the reinforcement procedure. The subject now matches the sample when the background color is red but chooses the nonmatching stimulus when it is red. Thus, with a red triangle in the sample window, pecks at a circle are reinforced, but with a green triangle pecks at a triangle are reinforced. In the conditional procedure three properties of the stimulus display must be taken into account simultaneously—the background color, the form of the sample stimulus, and the geometric contours of the stimuli on the right and left side keys. A pigeon will readily come under the control of such conditional reinforcement contingency, particularly if the repertoire is developed in approximations. The same kind of conditional discriminative control occurs with reflexes as shown by Pavlov in his original studies.

**Developing control by abstract properties of stimuli by the matching-to-sample procedure**   A complication of conditional discrimination is implied in the reinforcement contingencies implied in terms such as "larger than," "to the left of," "on top of," or "inside of." All of these terms have definite, although complex, relations to a reinforced operant performance. The matching-to-sample procedure usefully illustrates the reinforcement conditions implied in these terms. If we wish to bring a bird's behavior under the control of an abstract property of stimulus such as "larger than" we need a large number of pairs of stimuli. The stimulus in whose presence a peck is reinforced is always the larger of the two. But in all other respects the characteristics of the stimuli vary randomly. Other than size, the characteristics of the two groups of stimuli would overlap each other in line, thickness, color, geometric form, and texture. If the sample stimulus was a circle with an area of 3 square inches, the stimuli presented on the side keys might be a triangle whose area was 5 square inches and a circle whose area was 2 square inches. At another time when the sample stimulus was a triangle with an area of 3 square inches, the side keys would present a choice between a larger triangle and a smaller circle. Thus, the only dimension of the stimuli that is differentially correlated with reinforcement is the area of the figure. The procedure for establishing the other kinds of relational control mentioned above follow the same paradigm.

## questions

1.  Describe how the multiple variable-interval extinction schedule brought about discriminative control of pecking.
2.  How did the development of discriminative control by the vertical and horizontal lines compare with that which occurred with the red and green lights.
3.  What are some of the advantages that are derived from using the 3-term contingency to describe stimulus control rather than colloquial terms such as "noticing a stimulus" or "perceiving a difference."
4.  Describe the experiment by which the discriminative control of a reflex was narrowed.

5.  Give some examples from the preceding chapters of the discriminative control of an operant performance.

6.  How may a performance be brought under the control of a single property of a stimulus? Describe the process in an animal experiment.

7.  How may "triangularity" be described as a reinforcement contingency. Describe the procedure for bringing a bird's pecking performance under the control of this abstract property of a stimulus.

8.  What are the advantages of the term "abstract property of the stimulus" over "concept formation."

9.  Describe how the matching-to-sample procedure may be used to bring a performance under the control of a stimulus.

10. Describe how the discriminative control by the stimuli in a matching-to-sample procedure may be narrowed to a limited number of properties.

11. What are the reinforcement procedures involved in a conditional discrimination?

---

## part II: imitation and the fine-grain repertoire

### introduction to the phenomenon of the fine-grain repertoire

The examples of stimulus control that have been discussed so far are ones where discrete stimuli control discrete performances. For example, in the presence of a red light the bird pecks the key and in the presence of a green light it steps on a treadle. Matching-to-sample, where key lights control pecks as they light up successively, is an intermediate case. There remains another kind of stimulus control that is extremely prevalent in the natural environment. This kind of control involves stimuli that change continuously in time and control a performance that changes correspondingly. The behavior of the reader is in this direction. Vocal performances are under the point-to-point control of the details of a text. Not only does the child say "cat" when she sees the letters *c-a-t* but she also says "at" in the presence of the letters *a-t*. Furthermore, the control of this behavior by the *c* extends to the text *c-a-r*. There is an even finer grain correspondence between a performance and its controlling stimulus when a child copies a letter or a geometric form with a pencil. In copying a letter, the writing performance, moving the finger, produces a stimulus—the letter —that has a point-to-point correspondence of the letter that is being copied. If the child is a skilled artist, the correspondence with the stimulus and the performance it controls is so close that the letter drawn may be indistinguishable from the controlling stimulus.

Steering a car is another example of a fine-grain repertoire. The position of the car on the road is the stimulus that controls the driver's performance with the wheel. As the car's position changes in relation to the road, it controls the driver's movements of the wheel which in turn, bring the car back to the required location. The balancing of a ball on the seal's nose controls fine movements when the ball changes position. The head movements keep the ball firmly in position on the nose. Another example is the child's performance as a function of small changes in the position of the bicycle as he rides. As the bicycle changes position the child emits performances that keep it balanced.

Fine-grain repertoires are especially apt examples of the generic relation between an operant and the reinforcer maintaining it. It is, in fact, almost impossible to specify the actual topography of the seal's balancing behavior. We are more likely to describe the topography as those movements that keep the ball balanced. Here the colloquial description is consonant with a technical behavioral view. The generic reinforcer is the position of the ball on the nose or the balance of the bicycle and it will increase the frequency of those performances that produce it.

## animal procedures for developing fine-grain repertoires

As in preceding instances in the text, animal experiments provide a useful demonstration of the essential details of the processes we are describing because they allow us to actually synthesize the repertoire. In the procedure for developing a fine-grain repertoire described in Figure 6-5, we can see how the correspondence between the performance and the stimulus may be produced without entering all of the complexities of the natural environment. A sample stimulus appears in the window at the top of the figure and an adjustable stimulus appears in the window just below. Pecks at the top key are reinforced if the adjustable stimulus is the same as the sample. If the bird pecks at the top key when the stimuli do not correspond, there is a short time out before the bird can begin again. Following each reinforcement, a different stimulus appears in the sample window and the bird again needs to adjust the form below to correspond with the sample before a peck will again produce food. The bird is copying the stimulus in the sample window in the sense that the adjustable stimulus provides a range of stimuli that correspond in varying degrees to the sample. The relation between the sample and the behavior that produces

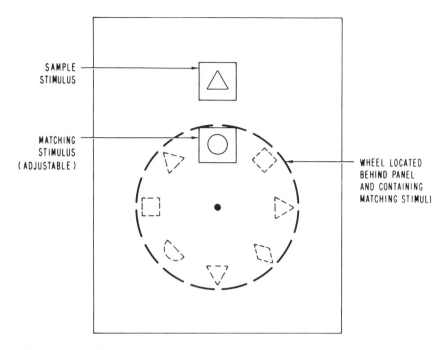

**Figure 6-5**  Correspondence between performance and stimulus.

the adjustable stimulus is not as continuous as in the case of copying a letter or driving a car, however.

An animal repertoire approaches the fine-grain control of driving a car if the bird is made to copy the length of a line rather than to adjust a geometric form in discrete steps. Figure 6-6 illustrates a physical arrangement that might be used to generate such a repertoire. The sample line is fixed for a given trial. The bird can increase or decrease the length of the line by pecking the two round keys. If the bird pecks at the upper window where the sample line appears and the length of the adjustable line is not equal to the sample, its length goes to zero and the sample is changed. If, however, the adjustable line equals the length of the sample line (within specified limits) then a peck at the upper window operates the food magazine.

In actual practice it would be necessary to develop the repertoire in stages by first setting broad limits for the correspondence between the sample and adjustable line and requiring closer correspondence as the performance comes under the control of the stimuli. The adjustable stimulus bears a point-to-point relation to the sample and can take on a continuous range of intermediate values. The process is functionally parallel to the behavior of the child drawing a letter. Instead of a pencil producing a line that can take an infinite variety of forms, the two keys that the bird

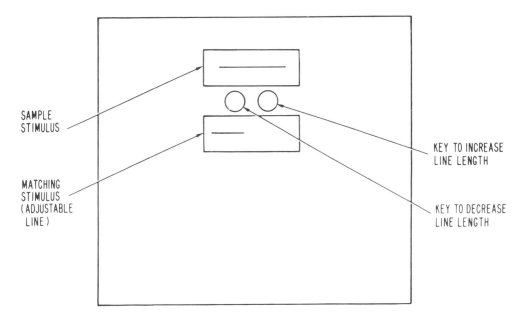

SAMPLE
STIMULUS

MATCHING
STIMULUS
(ADJUSTABLE
LINE)

KEY TO INCREASE
LINE LENGTH

KEY TO DECREASE
LINE LENGTH

**Figure 6-6** Generating fine-grain repertoire.

pecks adjust the length of the line continuously. The two situations differ only in the number of dimensions of the stimulus that can change.

**Progress toward identical stimuli as a reinforcer**    The procedure is actually a chain that is best understood in the context of conditioned reinforcement. The final member of the chain, a peck at the sample key, is reinforced when the adjustable stimulus corresponds to the sample. The same peck goes unreinforced when the sample and the adjustable stimuli do not correspond. Thus, identity between the sample and the adjustable stimulus becomes a conditioned reinforcer that can maintain and shape the performances on the adjustment keys. As a result of the control of this final member of the chain by the identity between the sample and the adjustable stimulus, any behaviors that bring about a change in the adjustable stimulus are increased in frequency.

### examples of fine-grain repertoires in human behavior

There are many examples of discriminative repertoires in the natural environment where an individual's performance is controlled continuously by progressively changing stimuli. Many singers can sing any tune they hear. Some artists will make a drawing that is almost identical with the original. The mimic develops an imitative repertoire to such a fine degree that his or her speaking voice may be indistinguishable from the voice he or she is imitating. The reinforcement for mimicry is a vocal pattern that corresponds in every detail with the speech of the person being imitated. Mimicry is differentially reinforced because there is an audience, partly the mimic him or herself, who reacts to the correspondence between the celebrity's voice being imitated and the actual stimulus that the mimic produces.

Such reinforcement depends on the prior control of the mimic's behavior by the nuances of the speech of the person being imitated, such as the words, the pitch, the accent, and the length of the glide during vowel changes, and so forth. If these nuances do not control the imitator's behavior, then they cannot serve as differential reinforcers to produce the imitative performances. If, to cite another example, a child who is copying the letter *o* is not under the control of variations in the size of letters, there is no basis for adjusting her writing to produce a letter of the size of the copy. To the extent that the child is already controlled by the correspondence between the *o* she has drawn and the sample, there will be immediate differential reinforcement of the performance. As a wider range of stimuli are copied, the child comes under the control of finer and finer details of the stimulus until she can reproduce an entirely new form on her first try. The necessary condition for such a performance is that the child will have encountered such a wide range of forms to be copied that extinction will have taken place in respect to almost every inappropriate performance; each element of the stimulus will narrowly control its appropriate performance. It is in this sense that we describe such repertoires as fine-grain.

## imitation

The use of the term *imitate* has been deferred to this point because it is less apt, technically, than the phrase *fine-grain repertoire.* The technical term emphasizes the procedures that bring the performance under the control of the environment. The terms *imitate* and *imitation,* like the terms *perceive* and *perception,* put the process inside the individual as an unreachable subjective event. When we say that the bird perceives or imitates a stimulus, we still have to find a performance under the control of a stimulus and account for how it came under the control of that stimulus. The words *perceive* or *imitate* serve as colloquial descriptions of some behavior but do not contribute an explanation for that behavior. This explanation is not that the organism "has learned to imitate" but that the behavior occurs in a fine-grain relation between a sample stimulus and a matching stimulus where the correspondence serves to reinforce the behavior.

# questions

*1.* Give some examples of fine-grain repertoires in natural human behavior and describe the nature of the discriminative control.
*2.* Describe animal procedures for developing a performance where the animal adjusts one stimulus so that it matches whatever stimulus appears as the sample.
*3.* Describe *imitation* as a fine-grain repertoire.
*4.* Give some examples from the early development of a child to show how fine-grain repertoires develop and function.

## part III: the weakening of an operant by stimulus control

### extinction due to an abstract property of a stimulus

Since the major process for bringing a performance under the control of a stimulus is differential reinforcement, it is inevitable that reinforcement will be intermittent and that many performances will go unreinforced. For example, if we reinforce all of a pigeon's pecks when the key is green but none when it is red, there will be an intermediate period when reinforcement is effectively intermittent because the bird will peck several hundred times before the rate of pecking in the red color falls to zero. Thereafter, we have effectively two conditions of reinforcement—pecks are reinforced continuously in the green color and never in the red color, which functions as a time out from the experiment. Thus intermittent reinforcement and extinction are a temporary occurrence during the intermediate phase while the performance is coming under the control of the stimuli that determine the reinforcement schedule.

When a performance, already controlled by a stimulus, is brought under the control of a restricted property of that stimulus, intermittent reinforcement and extinction will occur again. Such was the case earlier in this chapter when the multiple aspects of a red light were discussed. More extinction was necessary to bring the bird's pecks under the control of wavelength alone than occurred when all of the properties of the light were correlated with reinforcement. The amount of unreinforced pecking would depend on how much the performance was controlled by the intensity and saturation of the light as compared with the control by the wavelength. The amount of intermittent reinforcement and extinction that occurs depends on how much the behavior controlled by the SΔ occasion correlated with nonreinforcement needs to be weakened.

The details of a chimpanzee experiment illustrate how the development of complex stimulus control generates intermittent reinforcement and extinction. The experiment used the matching-to-sample procedure to teach the animals to identify a binary number that corresponded to a number of geometric forms appearing as the sample.[1] Figure 6-7 illustrates the procedure.

It required the chimpanzee subjects to choose the binary number that corresponded to the number of geometric forms in the center window. The binary numbers were represented by a pattern of three lights that represented the numbers from 1 to 7. In the particular setting represented in the figure, pressing the left key would be reinforced since that pattern of lights represents the binary number "3." If there were four triangles in the center window, pressing the right key would be reinforced. In the repertoire that finally developed, the chimp pressed the key under the binary number corresponding to the number of geometric figures in the center window with great accuracy.

At this point it was uncertain whether the choice of the binary number was controlled by the *number* of geometric figures, triangles in particular, the configuration of their arrangement, or even the sequence of the various stimulus settings. To be certain that the controlling relation was the numerosity rather than specific features of the stimuli, it was necessary to vary the sample in all details except the essential property of the *number* of forms. Thus the form, size, and spatial arrangement of the sample stimuli varied from trial-to-trial, still preserving the relation of number of forms to the reinforcement contingency.

Figure 6-8 describes the result of changing some of these features of the sample stimulus to bring the chimpanzee's behavior more narrowly under the discriminative control of "numerosity." Prior to the change the performance was nearly error free, perhaps some 2–5 errors for each 100 trials. With the change, the number of errors reached levels that would occur if the chimpanzees were reacting by chance—an incorrect choice for

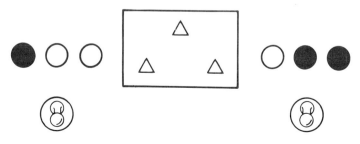

Figure 6-7

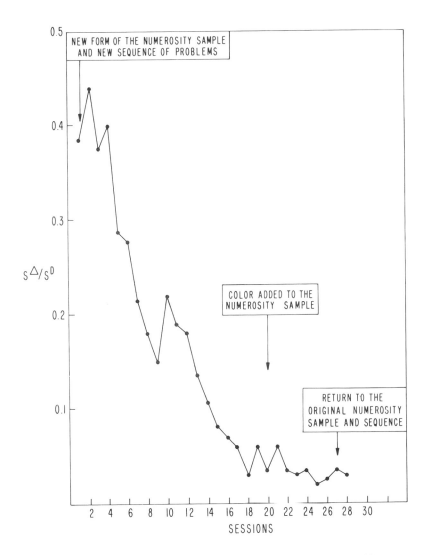

**Figure 6-8** Disruption of the matching-to-sample performance with numerosities 1, 2, and 3, when the spatial arrangement of the numerosity sample is altered.

every correct one. During the 20 or so sessions that were needed for the performance to return to the earlier level of accuracy, more than 20,000 unreinforced performances occurred, about the same as in the original development of the matching-to-sample performance before variations in the numerosity stimulus were introduced.

The interaction of the processes of stimulus control with those of intermittent reinforcement and extinction accounts for why performances involving highly abstract, conceptual discriminative control are so difficult to develop and maintain. Such is the case in science and mathematics where the performances are controlled by very abstract properties of the stimuli. Because so much extinction is necessary along the way of bringing the student's behavior under the discriminative stimuli defined by the science, such repertoires are sustained only under very special conditions. As we proceed from arithmetic to algebra, calculus, and higher mathematics, greater amounts of extinction are required to bring the performances under the control of the narrow range of circumstances where they can be reinforced.

## similarity between stimuli and the amount of extinction that occurs

More extinction and intermittent reinforcement occur in pigeon experiments during the development of differential discriminative control of a performance by an ellipse and circle than in the case with a red and green light. In colloquial terms we conclude that, for the pigeon, an ellipse is more similar to a circle than a red light is to a green one. Apart from the bird's genetic endowment, color is more likely to control the bird than shape because the pigeon's natural environment forms distinctions based on color more frequently than it does with subtle distinctions based on shape. On the other hand, the physical dimensions of the stimulus also need to be taken into account. The common language confuses the description of the physical differences between the stimuli and whether they control a performance differentially. We say that a red light is very different from a green one because the wavelengths of the lights are at some distance from each other in the visible spectrum. We also say that red is very different from green because very little extinction is required to bring a bird's performance under the differential control of the two stimuli. Where two stimuli exert very strong control over an individual's behavior, a great deal of extinction may be necessary before an operant performance will be emitted differentially under their discriminative control. A large amount of extinction and differential reinforcement occurs because the reinforcement of the performance in the presence of the one stimulus also increases its frequency in the presence of the other. Conversely, when a performance is not reinforced on one occasion, its frequency decreases when a similar stimulus is present.

Yet, there are situations where very small differences in the physical dimensions of a stimulus exert accurate and reliable control of a performance. Most readers have no difficulty in distinguishing, at a passing glance, an *o* from a *c,* even though the only difference is quite small. Similarly, in sight reading, the difference between *one* and *on*, *when* and *hen, train* and *strain,* and *rump* and *trump* is rarely unobserved. The control of behavior by such slight differences is often absolute. The jeweler in repairing a watch, the microbiologist in dissecting a cell, and the artist in observing nuances of color are accurately controlled by differences in sights and sounds that elude the untrained person. A large amount of extinction is needed to bring each of these performances under the control of subtle and small magnitude aspects of the relevant stimuli.

A change in the frequency of a performance in the presence of one stimulus because extinction or reinforcement has occurred in the presence of another is called *induction* or *stimulus generalization.* The amount of induction depends on the number of properties that the two stimuli share. For example, reinforcement in the presence of a small red triangle also establishes control by small figures, red objects, and shapes. Conversely, discontinuation of reinforcement in the presence of a large red square also weakens the control by the small red triangle. Each of the properties of the stimulus may have separate control of the bird's performance. The nonreinforcement when a bird pecks at a red square also reduces the tendency to peck at red triangles. The repeated alternation of the two stimuli, with the correlated differential reinforcement, eventually decreases the control by the other.

## developing control of a performance by stimuli which differ subtly

When a great deal of extinction is necessary to bring the bird's performance under discriminative control of a set of stimuli, we say they are very similar. During the development of control by very similar stimuli, the overall frequency of reinforcement may be very low because so much extinction is necessary. One way to maintain a high rate of reinforcement and avoid prolonged extinction is to pace the differences between stimuli to the rate of the development of their discriminative control. The least amount of intermittent reinforcement and extinction will occur if the stimuli correlated with nonreinforcement do not overlap those that occasion reinforcement. Under such circumstances, reinforcement will be frequent and highly intermittent schedules of reinforcement and prolonged extinction are prevented. When the performances come under discriminative control, it becomes possible to change them so that they overlap more. Thus, differential reinforcement of the performance is carried out in successive stages during which the stimuli become more similar. At each stage, the tendency to emit behavior when it will not be reinforced is not large enough to lead to highly intermittent schedules of reinforcement. (Applications of this process to problems in special education will made in Chapter 9.)

The problem of training a pigeon to peck differentially at a right triangle as opposed to other kinds of triangle of the same size is a way to elaborate the description of this process. The solution to the problem is to design a gradual program that can be carried out in several stages intermediate to the final repertoire. Faced with such fine differences from the start, a bird might never come under control of the difference, no matter how long the performance might be emitted alternately with and without reinforcement. The reinforcement of the peck could be controlled by the size of the triangle, the smaller or the larger angle, the orientation of the entire figure, or the length of any of the sides. So many properties of these two stimuli overlap that the differential reinforcement might shift the control from one property to the next, almost at random. Each of these properties that controlled a performance at one reinforcement might lead to its extinction on the next. Even if differential control over the performance were to develop, however, such large amounts of extinction would have occurred that the repertoire might be seriously weakened. If a triangle were paired with open rounded figures such as curved lines from the start, however, the bird's performance could readily come under the control of the two classes of stimuli. As a second step toward the final performance, the open rounded figures could be closed so that they would be a little more similar to the triangle. The amount of extinction that would occur as a result of closing the curved lines would be in proportion to how much the bird's behavior was controlled by any closed figure in contrast to other properties of the stimuli such as the absence of any angle or the curvature of the line.

After the bird was under the control of the closed figures, the curves could be squared up until the figures differed only in terms of the number of sides and the presence of acute angles. Once more, the number of unreinforced pecks that occurs depends on how many new properties of the triangle are shared by a rectangle as opposed to a rounded figure. Even this stage could be carried out slowly by squaring up the rounded figures a little at a time. With each kind of successive change in the stimulus, we would gradually limit the properties that controlled the bird's pecking until the two classes of stimuli overlapped completely except for the single critical one. At each stage the bird's behavior is under the perfect control of the two classes of stimuli. Each adjustment overlaps the reinforced and unreinforced stimuli so that relatively few nonreinforced performances occur. With such a procedure, it is possible to bring about very complex kinds of stimulus control, involving small subtle differences. Although very little unreinforced behaviors occur during any one stage, the total number of unreinforced performances needed to achieve the target repertoire may be very large. Nevertheless, there is an important advantage in the gradual and progressive development of complex stimulus control because it is possible to maintain a high frequency of reinforcement that will contribute to the persistence of the activity.

Of course, factors other than the program of stimulus sequences will influence the maintenance and efficacy of the process and these have been discussed earlier in the chapter and elsewhere in the book.

## a fading procedure for avoiding extinction during the development of stimulus control

A fading procedure provides another way to develop discriminative control by stimuli without engendering extinction.[2] In this procedure, the bird's behavior came under the differential control of red and green lights while virtually *all* pecks were reinforced. The experiment began with two stimuli that already controlled pecking differentially. One stimulus was the red color on the key, in the presence of which pecks were reinforced with food on a variable-interval schedule. The other was a dark key on which the bird almost never pecked and in whose presence pecks were never reinforced. In addition, the likelihood that the bird would peck the dark key was lessened even further by keeping it dark for only a few seconds.

The general plan of the experiment was to slowly fade the dark key to green. Before the dark key was faded to green, however, the first step was to slowly lengthen the period during which the key was dark. It was increased from 5 to 30 seconds. After the duration of the dark key met the criterion, a faint green light was projected on the previously dark key. To minimize the chance of a peck its duration was reduced to 5 seconds. The intensity of the brief green light was increased very slowly until it reached the maximum intensity. Throughout the progressive adjustment of the of the 5-second green light, the bird never pecked. The performance during the stimulus that occasioned reinforcement, the red key, occurred stably. The duration of the green light was then gradually increased and by the end of the session the bird was differentially controlled by a red and green light, each present for 90 to 180 seconds. The rate of pecking remained virtually zero during the green key light. The three stages described above were accomplished in the very first experimental session.

**results of the fading experiments** Comparisons among these fading conditions showed that large numbers of pecks occurred in the green light without the fading procedure. The experiment investigated which aspects of the fading procedure were the important contributors to the result. Figure 6-9 describes the results for variations of procedure designed to discover how to influence the development of stimulus control without engendering SΔ pecking. Each panel in the graph describes a separate procedure and the three bars in each panel describe the number of times each of three subjects pecked in the presence of the SΔ stimulus during the development of control by the red and green stimuli. The first panel, labeled *early progressive*, gives the results for the fading procedure described above. In the late progressive condition (third panel) the subjects were exposed to 24 sessions in which pecking was reinforced in the red light before the fading procedure was begun. The constant conditions were those where the SΔ stimulus was introduced at full intensity and duration either early or late in the experiment. Comparing the first two panels of the graph, early progressive and constant, with the last two panels, late progressive and constant, we see that introducing the differential reinforcement from the very start generates much less unreinforced behavior than either of the late procedures.

The results are most dramatic for the animals in the first procedure who were introduced to the green light by the fading procedure from the very start. These animals pecked the green key only 5 to 9 times during all of the experimental sessions and at the end showed perfect control by the red and green lights. The early introduction of the differential reinforcement, without the fading procedure produced some pecking in the green color. The number of pecks these birds made ranged from about 200 to

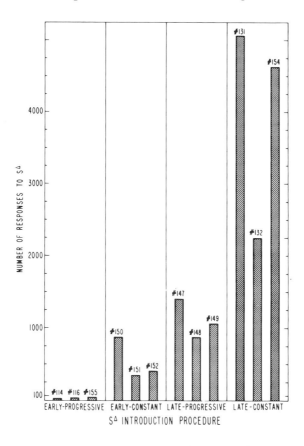

Figure 6-9    Results of the fading procedure.

900. In contrast, the fading procedure, when introduced after the bird had been reinforced for pecking in the red for 24 sessions produced much more inappropriate pecking. Finally, the absence of any adjustment in the schedule of the green light, coupled with an extended history of reinforcement before stimulus control was undertaken, produced the most unreinforced pecking of any of the procedures. In summary, the experiments show that it is necessary to have differential reinforcement from the very start as well as the progressive adjustment of the stimuli in order to reduce the amount of SΔ pecking. One bird never pecked the green key even once during the entire experiment and still acquired a repertoire with perfect differential control by the two stimuli.

In another experiment, it was shown that the same procedure could be used to transfer the control of a bird's behavior from a color to a geometric form without the bird ever pecking the inappropriate form or color.[3] Control was first developed by a red and green light with the fading procedure described above. When the birds were differentially controlled by the red and green lights of equal brightness, a vertical line was superimposed on the red key and a horizontal line on the green key. The intensity of both the red and green lights was then slowly faded. When the red and green lights were no longer detectable, the birds were under the control of the horizontal and vertical lines instead of the colors. During the entire procedure there were no instances where the birds pecked the key when the stimulus correlated with nonreinforcement was present. As in the previous experiment, the important aspect of the procedure was the slow transition in the stimuli, paced with their control of the bird's behavior.

In the original report by the psychologist who discovered the fading procedure it was suggested that one of the conditions for transferring control is that both stimuli already exert some control over the bird's behavior. Birds have highly developed visual repertoires and usually come to the experiment with a long history in which the color of objects in their environment have controlled their behavior. Birds are undoubtedly controlled by the color of grains and plants. In the first experiment where control was transferred from a dark to a green key, the bird was already differentially controlled by the dark key relative to the red color which occasioned reinforcement.

The transfer of control from the colors to the horizontal and vertical lines implies the same kind of preexisting control by the lines. It is not difficult to construct encounters in the bird's natural environment where straight lines have controlled operant performances. Straight lines are likely to control the bird's behavior as it avoids the edge of a wall or pokes its head through the bars of a cage. It seems reasonable to predict, however, that the behavior of laboratory animals is seldom occasioned by wavy lines and that a superimposition experiment in which the stimuli added to the colors were two kinds of wavy lines would not succeed.

# questions

1. Describe, in general terms, how the development of stimulus control inevitably leads to intermittent reinforcement.
2. Describe how bringing a performance under narrower control of some property of the stimulus already controlling it also results in intermittent reinforcement of the performance.
3. Give the criteria for determining how rapidly to change stimuli or to make other progressive adjustments during a procedure designed to increase the control by a certain property of a stimulus.
4. How is the amount of extinction that occurs during the development of stimulus control related to the similarity between the controlling stimuli.
5. Describe how a gradual program of stimulus changes may reduce the amount of nonreinforced behaviors that occur during the development of the discriminative control by stimuli.
6. Describe the procedure that was suggested for bringing a pigeon's behavior under the discriminative control of a right triangle as opposed to other kinds of triangles.
7. Describe the procedure for producing stimulus control by fading the stimuli. What was the difference between the results of the early-progressive and the late-progressive fading procedure.
8. Describe some conditions under which a fading procedure would be unsuccessful.

---

## part IV: how intermittent reinforcement and punishment influence the accuracy of stimulus control

### intermittent reinforcement of matching-to-sample

The matching-to-sample performance is particularly suited to studying how maintenance factors, such as the schedule of reinforcement, influence the control of the behavior by discriminative stimuli. It provides a baseline in which both the frequency of the behavior and the discriminative control of the unit performance can be measured at the same time. Thus, the frequency with which the bird matches-to-sample reflects the schedules of reinforcement maintaining the performance while each unit performance gives data about the accuracy with which the stimuli control its behavior.

To simultaneously study both the form and frequency of the matching-to-sample performance under intermittent reinforcement, we begin with a bird who is reinforced with food for matching colors. To distinguish pecks that occur in the $S^D$ and $S\Delta$ stimuli, a very brief time out, perhaps 0.5 seconds, occurs when the bird pecks at the nonmatching stimulus. To reinforce the performance intermittently, the magazine operation is withheld but each correct peck produces a brief light flash, normally accompanying the feeder operation, to serve as a conditioned reinforcer. When the schedule of reinforcement designates a food reinforcement, the next $S^D$ performance operates the food magazine. Thus, all reinforced pecks are followed by a brief flash of the magazine light but only occasional reinforcements include eating. The schedule of conditioned reinforcement is continuous because each performance is differentially reinforced by the conditioned reinforcer. The procedure has the advantage that each time the bird pecks correctly there is an immediate differential consequence even though food may not be delivered. As a result of such a procedure, it is possible to sustain thousands of matching-to-sample performances during a single experimental session, as with a single peck. Continuous reinforcement limits an experimental session to about 100 trials, since a day's food ration for a pigeon consists of 60–100 opportunities to eat. With an intermittent reinforcement schedule, however, several thousand matching-to-sample performances can be differentially reinforced using the same number of food reinforcements.

When we reinforce matching-to-sample on a fixed-ratio schedule, the result is roughly the same as with the fixed-ratio reinforcement of a single peck except that the bird cannot sustain as many pecks per reinforcement. Up to fixed-ratio values of approximately 35, the bird matches to sample immediately after reinforcement and sustains the performance as a continuous high rate until the next reinforcement. At higher values of the fixed-ratio schedule the bird pauses after reinforcement, with the length of the pause increasing as the fixed-ratio requirement is increased. Even without punishment of $S\Delta$ pecks, however, the accuracy is very high.[4] The birds fail to match 5 times or so out of each 100 matching-to-sample performances.

With interval schedules of reinforcement, however, the bird matches at chance levels of accuracy compared with the highly accurate performances that occurred with fixed-ratio reinforcement. In a fixed-interval schedule, the first correct matching-to-sample performance after the interval elapses operates the food magazine. Each correct match produces a flash of the food magazine lights and incorrect matches produce a brief time out, as with the fixed-ratio schedule. Despite the inaccuracy of the matching performance, the fixed-interval schedule produces a pattern of rate changes parallel to that which occurs with a single peck. On a 10-minute fixed-interval schedule, the bird pauses after reinforcement for a time and the rate of matching accelerates to about 0.5 or 0.75 matches per second. As is typical of interval schedules of reinforcement, the performance is well sustained despite infrequent reinforcement.

## a multiple schedule of matching to-sample

The magnitude and impact of the schedule of reinforcement on the accuracy of stimulus control is seen in its clearest form in a multiple schedule where it is possible to measure, within a single experimental hour and within the behavioral repertoire of one bird, the accuracy of the matching-to-sample performance under the two schedules. Figure 6-10 is a record of a matching-to-sample sequence reinforced on a 10-minute fixed-interval schedule when the lights behind the keys are steady and on a fixed-ratio schedule when it flickered.

The resulting performance is typical of a multiple schedule where the performance consists of single pecks except that the terminal rate the bird reaches at the end of the interval is somewhat lower. The reason for the lower rate is the time it takes the bird to complete a single matching-to-sample sequence. During the period when the key light is steady (the fixed-interval schedule) the bird pauses up to 7 or 8 minutes before the terminal rate is reached. In the fixed-ratio performance when the light is flickering, the bird begins matching-to-sample almost immediately and sustains the performance until the next reinforcement.

The difference in accuracy levels under the two schedules confirms the dramatic influence of intermittent reinforcement on the level of discriminative control. The result is shown in Figure 6-11 where $S\Delta/S^D$ refers to the ratio of unreinforced/reinforced matching-to-sample performances. When the food reinforcement depended on the number of matching

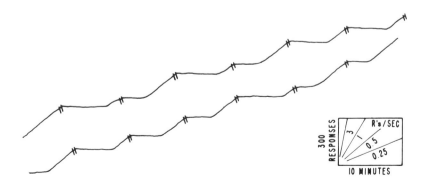

Figure 6-10    Multiple schedule of matching-to-sample.

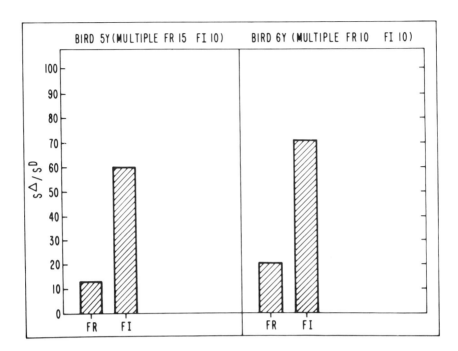

Figure 6-11

performances in the fixed-ratio schedule, the performance was relatively accurate. It pecked the nonmatching key approximately 12 times for every 100 times that the correct stimulus was chosen. On the fixed-interval schedule, on the other hand, the bird essentially took "pot luck." The control by the stimuli approximated what would occur were the bird pecking at random. A second pigeon in the experiment showed the same result: relatively accurate matching-to-sample in the fixed-ratio schedule and a random performance in the fixed-interval schedule.

One reason why the fixed-ratio schedule has a much lower error rate than the fixed-interval schedule is the way that the occurrence of errors influences the frequency of food delivery. If a bird is very accurate under a fixed-ratio schedule of reinforcement, the frequency of reinforcement will be very high since only correct performances count toward the fixed-ratio requirement. If the bird mismatches, the frequency of reinforcement will be reduced significantly. For example, if the bird is not controlled by the stimuli at all, essentially operating at a chance level, only half of the matching performances will count toward reinforcement and the frequency of food delivery will be substantially less than would be the case if pecks were emitted under the control of the stimuli. The bird would need to match-to-sample twice as many times as would be necessary if the matching were under the appropriate control by the stimuli. Such a difference in error level does not influence the frequency of reinforcement on a fixed-interval schedule, however. Since the first correct match emitted after the fixed-interval has elapsed is reinforced, even three errors in a row would postpone reinforcement only by a few seconds. On a fixed- interval schedule of 5 or 10 minutes, such a decrease in frequency of reinforcement would be negligible.

The effect of errors on the frequency of reinforcement accounts for some apparent discrepancies in the experimental literature. Investigators reported that birds matched-to-sample very accurately even though every correct performance was followed by food.[5] The experiments just cited, however, showed that accuracy of matching improved from chance levels at continuous reinforcement to high levels at higher fixed-ratio requirements. The discrepancy turned out to be a function of an inter-trial interval, a period of time out when all of the lights in the experimental chamber were turned off so as to interrupt the performance for a fixed period of time. With an inter-trial interval after each matching performance, an $S\Delta$ peck significantly reduced the overall frequency of food delivery.[6]

## intermittent reinforcement of a counting performance

A procedure with a chimpanzee where the complex performance that was studied was counting provides another example of how a reinforcement schedule based on the number of performances successfully completed contributes to the accuracy of the behavior.[7] Instead of the pigeon's matching-to-sample performance, a chimpanzee counts to three in this experiment. The procedure required the use of two keys. If the chimpanzee first pressed the left key 3 times, a subsequent press of the right key operated the food dispenser. If he failed to press the left key or pressed it 1, 2, or 4 times, pressing the right key led to a time out. After the time out he could try again. The performance was a chain in which the first performance was pressing the left key and the second performance was pressing the right key. The stimulus that reinforced the behavior on the left key and set the occasion for food reinforcement on the right key was pressing the left key 3 times. The chimpanzee's own behavior rather than an exteroceptive stimulus such as a sound or light was the event that reinforced the performance on the left key and provided the critical event that made possible the food reinforcement on the right key. The counting performance was reinforced on a fixed-ratio schedule by using a conditioned reinforcer in a manner parallel to that described for the pigeon in the matching-to-sample experiment. Pressing the right key after "counting 3" on the left key produced a brief tone. Pressing the right key inappropriately, produced a brief time out. On the fixed-ratio schedule, every $n$th correct counting performance operated the food dispenser as well as the conditioned reinforcer.

The result of the fixed-ratio reinforcement was a large decrease in the number of errors. Instead of 20 errors out of 100 trials, as occurred under continuous reinforcement, the error level under intermittent reinforcement fell to 2 out of 100. Possibly the reason why these fixed-ratio schedules, and the reset-procedure that will be described in the next section, decrease SΔ performances lies in the effect on the frequency of reinforcement. In these procedures, the frequency of food delivery falls markedly when the bird pecks the SΔ stimulus or the chimpanzee miscounts.

## punishment of SΔ performances by resetting the fixed-ratio or by time out

Another way to provide further pressure toward accurate control of an operant performance by discriminative stimuli is to reset the fixed-ratio requirement when an SΔ performance occurs. In that way food reinforcement can occur only if the bird completes the entire requirement without any SΔ pecks. If during a fixed-ratio 10 schedule an SΔ performance is emitted on the ninth time that it matched-to-sample, ten additional matching-to-sample performances would still be required for food delivery to occur. Adjustment of the fixed-ratio requirement to the bird's current level of stimulus control is required, however. If a bird is matching at a 95 percent level of accuracy, an error level that might occur on fixed-ratio schedule, the value of the fixed-ratio would need to be set below 20 if the resetting contingency is not to prevent the food reinforcement altogether. Thus, a requirement that would maintain a reasonable frequency of food delivery would be of the magnitude of 5 to 10 successively correct matches. As the reset procedure forces the error level lower, the fixed-ratio requirement could be increased. The increased requirement coupled with the reset by errors would, in turn force the error level even lower. In a pigeon experiment with matching-to-sample, error levels as low as 1 for each 1000 correct matches can be achieved.

Many chains of performances in the human work environment have a characteristic similar to resetting the fixed-ratio schedule. Such contingencies operate naturally in performances, such as a machinist following a complex blueprint while turning a piece on a lathe. The blue print is, of course, functionally analogous to the sample stimuli in the matching-to-sample procedure. The measurements of the piece with the micrometer and its visual inspection serve the function of the choice stimuli and the movements of the crank that turns the cutting tool into the metal function like the pigeon's peck. The machinist's performance is reinforced on a fixed-ratio schedule determined by the number of actions on the controls of the lathe required to complete the job. The correspondence between the dimensions of the metal piece being turned and the specifications on the blue print function as a conditioned reinforcer, much like the flash of the magazine stimuli in the pigeon experiment. When the machinist's performance occurs without appropriate control by the blueprint, an SΔ performance, the fixed-ratio requirement is effectively reset as in the pigeon experiment described above. If the error is large, the piece has to be discarded and the job started again. The completion of the piece, particularly if the machinist is on piecework pay, functions as the delivery of food in the pigeon matching-to-sample experiment.

An elementary school pupil doing long division faces a set of outcomes similar to those described for the machinist except that the "reset" occurs when the answer is checked by a review or verified by multiplication. The performance is writing a number, the conditioned reinforcer is the advance to the next stage of the division procedure, and the reinforcer equivalent to the food delivery is the verified completion of the long division. The set of numbers to be added has the function of the sample and the sum that is written, under their discriminative control, is like the peck to the side keys reinforced by the flash of the magazine lights in the matching-to-sample procedure. The typist working on a manuscript or a letter that needs to be typed without error exemplifies the same kind of reinforcement contingency. The performance is striking the keys of the typewriter under the discriminative control of the text that is being copied. The conditioned reinforcer is the line-by-line correspondence between the resulting copy and the text. The completion of the letter or a page of the manuscript is equivalent to the food delivery.

**Punishment by time out**  The time out described in the matching-to-sample procedure was a brief one whose effect is more of a differential consequence relative to the conditioned reinforcer than aversive properties that are derived from the postponement of positive reinforcement. Animal experiments in which SΔ performances in matching-to-sample were punished with varying durations of time out from the experiment, have provided some information on the general effects of such aversive control on the development of discriminative repertoire.[8] The experiments confirmed that brief time outs such as 1-second had little effect, apart from their function in regard to reinforcement, in suppressing SΔ pecking. Longer periods of time out from the experiment contributed to the accuracy of the bird's performance but when time outs reached values of 2 minutes, the by-products of the aversive control preempted the improvement in the accuracy of the performance. Overall rates of pecking were reduced severely as the punishment of errors reduced the bird's overall disposition to emit the behavior. In other words, the smaller magnitudes of punishment increased the accuracy of the performance by suppressing SΔ pecks but the larger magnitudes simply disrupted the entire repertoire without any differential benefit to accuracy.

# questions

1. Describe the procedure for intermittently reinforcing matching-to-sample.
2. How do fixed-ratio and fixed-interval schedules of matching-to-sample influence the accuracy with which the bird matches.
3. Describe the procedure for a multiple fixed-ratio, fixed-interval schedule of reinforcement of matching-to-sample.
4. Why does a fixed-ratio schedule produce higher levels of stimulus control than the fixed-interval schedule of matching-to-sample?
5. Describe the counting procedure. How was it intermittently reinforced and what was the effect on the accuracy of the performance?
6. What is the procedure for resetting a fixed-ratio schedule? How does this affect stimulus control?
7. Give some examples of highly differentiated performances in the human natural environment that are functionally parallel to that occurring when the fixed-ratio is reset in the animal experiment.
8. Describe the effect of the time out used as punishment for S performances.

# notes

[1] Ferster, C. B. and Hammer, C. E. Synthesizing the components of arithmetic behavior. Honig, W. (Ed.) *Operant behavior: Areas of research and application.* Englewood Cliffs, N.J.: Prentice-Hall, 1966.

[2] Terrace, H. S. Discrimination learning without errors. *Journal of the Experimental Analysis of Behavior* 6:1–27, 1963.

[3] Terrace, H.S. Errorless transfer of a discrimination across two continua. *Journal of the Experimental Analysis of Behavior* 6:223–232, 1963.

[4] When the fixed-ratio requirement is made larger—to values that produce pauses after reinforcement—accuracy falls. Thus, fixed-ratio schedules improve matching accuracy at optimal levels of maintenance.

[6] Thomas, J. R. Matching-to-sample accuracy on fixed-ratio schedules. *Journal of the Experimental Analysis of Behavior* 32:183–189, 1979.

[7] Ferster, C. B. Intermittent reinforcement of a complex response in a chimpanzee. *Journal of the Experimental Analysis of Behavior* 1:163–165, 1958.

[8] Ferster, C. B. and Appel, J. B. Punishment of SΔ responding in matching-to-sample by time out from positive reinforcement. *Journal of the Experimental Analysis of Behavior* 4:45–56, 1961.

# chaining and conditioned reinforcement

7

## study guide

This chapter begins by breaking down the performance of a pigeon peck-ing a key into the detailed component behaviors of approaching the key, pecking at it, moving to the food magazine and eating from it. The analysis describes how the light and sound of the feeder is the immediate conse-quence of pecking; the light and sound of the feeder designate the occa-sion when approaching the food dispenser will permit the subsequent chain of events leading to the swallowing of the grain. Simple chains are then analyzed in detail by constructing diagrams that make explicit the discriminative control of each of the component activities. Such analyses show how even as simple a performance as pecking a key may be de-scribed as a long sequence of individual performances each maintained by the stimulus it produces. Besides maintaining the preceding performance, each stimulus is correlated with the possibility of reinforcement of the next performance in the chain. Such analyses explain why and how it is necessary to construct chains from the end rather than from the begin-ning. The process of chaining is then illustrated with more complex behav-iors in longer sequences.

Money, attention, and approval are described as generalized rein-forcers and the differences between generalized reinforcers and simple conditioned reinforcers are explained. The concepts and methods of anal-ysis are then extended to complex human behavior and to other behav-ioral processes involving chains such as observing behaviors and delayed reinforcement. The apparent paradox of the operant reinforcement of reflexes and fixed-action patterns is resolved by describing how their eliciting stimuli may be part of a chain of operant behaviors.

Terms such as "the need for attention or approval", commonly used clinically and colloquially, point to chains of behavior maintained by generalized reinforcers.

## technical terms

chain
conditioned reinforcer($S^r$)
discriminative stimulus($S^D$)
fixed action pattern
generalized reinforcer

## outline

Part I: The Interrelation of Discriminative Stimuli and Conditioned Reinforcers in Chains of Behavior
The process of chaining
An example of a chain of performances in a dog
Diagramming chains of performances
Constructing chains of performances
Proving that the conditioned reinforcers in the chain control their respective performances
A complex chain of performances in a rat
Intermittent schedules of conditioned reinforcement

Part II: Analyzing Examples of Chains and Conditioned Reinforcers
Accidental conditioned reinforcement
Delayed reinforcement as a chain of behaviors
Chains that include reflexes and fixed-action patterns
The chaining of observing behavior
Chains of performances in normal growth and development
The varieties of consequences that can maintain chains of performances

Part III: Generalized Reinforcement
Money as a generalized reinforcer
Attention of the parent as a conditioned reinforcer
Special properties of the generalized reinforcer
Deprivation in human behavior

## the process of chaining

The processes of chaining, intermittent reinforcement, conditioned reinforcement, and stimulus control are all integral to each other. A simple way to illustrate the interaction of these processes is by observing an exercise with a rat: a chain of behaviors, such as pulling an overhead rope, is reinforced by a stimulus that designates on which occasions the rat's behavior of pressing the bar will operate the food dispenser. The detailed description of the chain of behaviors beginning with bar-pressing and ending with the eating of the food pellet will be postponed until the next section. But at this time, let us examine a simplified description of the exercise.

A reinforcer first needs to be created to establish the behavior of pulling the overhead rope as the first member of the sequence. A second requirement is that bar-pressing will have a low frequency until the behavior of pulling the overhead rope has occurred and has been reinforced. Otherwise, bar-pressing will preempt the less frequent rope-pulling performance.

Both of these purposes can be accomplished by bringing the bar-press —which is already in the rat's repertoire by food reinforcement—under the control of some arbitrary stimulus such as a light. To this end, a multiple continuous reinforcement-extinction schedule of reinforcement needs to be arranged. When the light is on, a bar-press operates the food dispenser. When the light is off, during the alternating two-minute intervals when extinction is scheduled, bar-pressing goes unreinforced. As was described in Chapter 6, bar-pressing soon occurs only when the light is on because of its consistent extinction on the one occasion and reinforcement on the other. When the key light is red for a fixed time following each food delivery, no pecks are reinforced. The schedule, in other words, is multiple fixed-ratio, extinction. With small fixed-ratio requirements, the bird will peck at a high sustained rate as soon as the green key light comes on and continue until reinforcement occurs after the fixed-number requirement is met. During the interval when the key light is red, pecking ceases. If a peck is now required for the red key light to change to green, we have arranged a chain where pecks at the red key are reinforced continuously by the appearance of the green key-light that, in turn, controls the fixed-ratio performance reinforced by the operation of the food dispenser. The appearance of pecking in the green light is evidence that there is a chain of behavior in which the first performance is maintained by a conditioned reinforcer.

Even more convincing evidence occurs when the schedule of reinforcement of the conditioned reinforcer (the green light) is altered. If we now arrange that the appearance of the light will occur as a result of the first peck after 5 minutes elapses (a 5-minute fixed-interval schedule) we will have established a chain of performances in which the two components are distinguished by the patterns of pecking engendered by the respective conditioned reinforcement schedules. The schedule of reinforcement of red-key pecks reinforced on a fixed-interval schedule by the appearance of the green light will produce a pause after reinforcement followed by a slow rate increase until it reaches a constant, moderate value a few minutes before a peck changes the color. In the red color, the rate increases immediately to a high, constant value that is maintained until the $n$th peck completes the fixed-ratio requirement. Thus the patterns of performance in the two components of the chain are additional evidence that they are maintained by two different reinforcers. Such a chain of performances is called *homogeneous* because the topography of the performance does not vary in the several components.

The control required to teach a rat to pull an overhead rope that turns on a light that, in turn, sets the occasion when pressing a lever will be reinforced by the operation of the food dispenser illustrates another kind of chain. The first step in developing such a chain is to reinforce bar-pressing under the discriminative control of a light. As soon as bar-pressing occurs reliably in the presence of the light and not in its absence, the light can be used to reinforce pulling on the rope. The first step is to turn off the light that controls bar-pressing. In the absence of the light, bar-pressing will not preempt pulling the rope. Possibly the unconditioned level of pulling the overhead rope will be so low that successive approximation is required. In that event, some item of behavior approximating pulling the rope can be selected and reinforced with the light that controls bar-pressing. The result will be an increase in frequency of that operant. Such an increase provides evidence that the light has acquired the properties of a conditioned reinforcer that can increase the frequency of an operant that produces it. Such a stimulus is called a *conditioned reinforcer* because it derives its reinforcing properties from the discriminative control it exerts over bar-pressing.

The reinforcer can then be applied repeatedly in behalf of successive approximation of the new performance because the chain of behaviors following the light will maintain its conditioned reinforcing properties. It is for this reason that the chain is constructed in the reverse of its natural order. Once the successive approximations of pulling the rope have proceeded to the point where the rat actually pulls the rope far enough to actuate the switch to which it is fastened, the performance will be stably

maintained because of the connection between the topographies of behavior that move the rope and the operation of the switch that turns on
the light.

## an example of a chain of performances
## in a dog

Many examples of conditioned reinforcement and chains of behavior
were mentioned in the preceding chapters. The clicker or "cricket" that
was used to train the dog to fetch a newspaper provides a useful example
of conditioned reinforcement and chaining. In the final performance that
was established, the cricket was sounded when the dog moved the required distance and direction. In the presence of the cricket the dog could
eat because the trainer put meat in the bowl whenever he sounded the
cricket. In the absence of the cricket, the performance of going to the
bowl was not reinforced and therefore had a low frequency as a result of
the extinction that had been carried on during training. The cricket was
the critical element in the chain of behaviors that was conditioned.
It increased the frequency of the performance it followed (conditioned
reinforcement) and it exerted discriminative control over the next
performance in the chain—approaching the food bowl. It had the
additional property that the higher frequency second performance (going to the food bowl) did not compete with the first performance that
required walking in a direction opposite to the food bowl. Magazine training was the critical procedure that reduced the approach to the food
bowl except in the presence of the cricket. It should be clear at this
point why "begging" should not be reinforced since such performances would compete with the lower frequency performances that were
being conditioned.

Once the clicker controls the approach to the food bowl, it becomes
possible to increase the frequency of any operant performance it follows.
The technical and precise use of reinforcement as a procedure for changing behavior and describing it in the complex environment derives from
understanding it as the stimulus change that occurs as the immediate
consequence of the performance. Chaining explains how organisms can
sustain operant behaviors when the event ultimately maintaining the
behavior occurs some time after it. It becomes clear that bar-pressing or
key-pecking are not reinforced by food but are part of a chain of performances that ultimately lead to food. Without a chain of performances to
take up the delay between the performance and the actual ingestion of
food it would not be possible to carry out procedures, such as successive
approximation or intermittent reinforcement, that require a precise relation between the performance and the change it effects.

## diagramming chains of performances

It is useful to represent a chain of performances, such as the behavior of the dog described previously, in a diagram (Figure 7-1) that emphasizes the essential events of the sequence. To reduce the diagram to a size concise enough for a summary, the performances and stimuli need to be abbreviated. The term $S^D$ had already been introduced in Chapter 6 as the abbreviation for a discriminative stimulus. The performances in the chain are designated by the symbol P. $S^r$ stands for the conditioned reinforcer maintaining the performance followed by the arrow. Since the same stimulus is the reinforcer for one performance and also the occasion for the reinforcement of the next one, its dual role is diagrammed by writing it twice in the same column. The chain consists of a sequence of operants each indicated by a 3-term contingency—[$S^D$·P——$S^r$]—linked to each other by the two-fold function of the conditioned reinforcer as a maintaining event for the performance that it follows and as a discriminative stimulus for the next operant in the chain. In the first line, the cricket is the reinforcer for the first performance as well as the discriminative stimulus that controls the second. In the second operant, moving to the food bowl under the discriminative control of the cricket is reinforced by the sight of the food. In the third operant, the sight of food is the discriminative stimulus that controls reaching down to bite, reinforced by the movement of the food from the bowl to the dog's mouth. The chain could have been extended in the diagram by indicating still another operant, chewing the food under the discriminative control of the presence of food in the dog's mouth reinforced by the increased contact between the saliva-moistened food and the sensory receptors in the dog's mouth. Thereafter, the chain blends into a sequence of reflex actions.

Even a pigeon pecking a key reinforced by food is actually producing a chain of performances and conditioned reinforcers of some complexity. The following text describes, with reference to Figure 7-2, the compo-

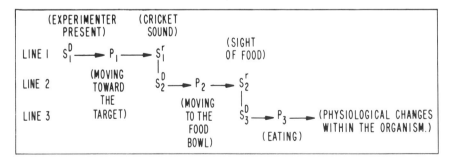

**Figure 7-1** Diagram of the chain of performances, reinforcers, and discriminative stimuli that occur when the dog's performance is reinforced with the cricket.

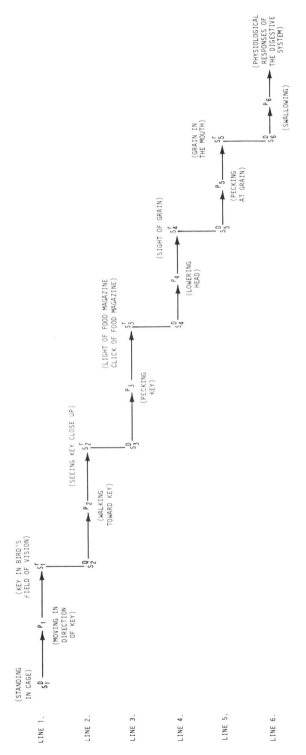

LINE 1.
$S_1^D$ (STANDING IN CAGE)
$P_1$ (MOVING IN DIRECTION OF KEY)
$S_1^r$ (KEY IN BIRD'S FIELD OF VISION)

LINE 2.
$S_2^D$
$P_2$ (WALKING TOWARD KEY)
$S_2^r$ (SEEING KEY CLOSE UP)

LINE 3.
$S_3^D$
$P_3$ (PECKING KEY)
$S_3^r$ (LIGHT OF FOOD MAGAZINE CLICK OF FOOD MAGAZINE)

LINE 4.
$S_4^D$
$P_4$ (LOWERING HEAD)
$S_4^r$ (SIGHT OF GRAIN)

LINE 5.
$S_5^D$
$P_5$ (PECKING AT GRAIN)
$S_5^r$ (GRAIN IN THE MOUTH)

LINE 6.
$S_6^D$
$P_6$ (SWALLOWING)
(PHYSIOLOGICAL RESPONSES OF THE DIGESTIVE SYSTEM)

Figure 7-2   Analyzing chains.

233

nents of the chain. Each performance is reinforced by a conditioned reinforcer under the control of the preceding discriminative stimulus and all are maintained by the ingestion of food.

*Line 1.* The chain begins with the bird standing in some unspecified position in the cage ($S^D_1$). From this position any movement of the head in the direction of the key ($P_1$) changes the visual stimulus ($S^r_1$). Those performances that bring the key into the bird's field of vision increase in frequency; those that do not are not reinforced and hence decrease in frequency. Notice the naturally maintained contingency between the performance and its reinforcer. So long as the next operant in the chain has a high frequency, the differential reinforcement of "looking at the key" will be virtually automatic.

*Line 2.* Walking toward the key ($P_2$) leads to seeing the key close up ($S^r_2$).

*Line 3.* When the bird's head is in front of the key ($S^D_3$), pecking the key ($P_3$) produces the light and sound that accompanies the food tray rising to a position where the grain is accessible ($S^r_4$).

*Line 4.* In the presence of the magazine light and the sound that accompanies it ($S^D_4$), lowering the head ($P_4$) to the hopper leads to the sight of grain ($S^r_4$).

*Line 5.* On the occasion of grain directly in front of its head ($S^D_5$), pecking at the grain ($P_5$) is followed by grain in the mouth ($S^r_5$).

*Line 6.* Grain in the mouth ($S^D_6$) is the occasion when swallowing ($P_6$) is reinforced by the subsequent chain of physiological and reflex responses of the digestive system.

**Summary** The first function of the conditioned reinforcers is to increase the frequency of those performances they follow: Grain in the mouth is a selective consequence of pecking at the grain; sight of the grain is a selective consequence of only those behaviors that bring the bird's head over the grain; the magazine light and sound occur only as a result of the bird striking the key with its beak; the sight of the key close up occurs as a result only of those movements that bring the bird closer to the key; and the sight of the key from a distance occurs as a result of those head movements that orient the bird's head toward the key.

The second function of the conditioned reinforcer is to determine the next performance in the chain that will lead to the next reinforcer. The unique significance of the conditioned reinforcer is that it is the circumstance that makes it possible for the bird to proceed to the next part of the chain: The sight of the key at a distance makes possible walking toward it; the sight of the key at close range is an occasion when pecking at the key can lead to the impact of the bird's beak on the key; and the occurrence of the magazine light and sound is an occasion when lowering the head can lead to the sight of grain. Each of these performances will be effective *only* on these occasions. When the bird is far from the key, pecking will not be able to occur with the required effect. Moving the head toward the food tray does not lead to the sight of food unless the magazine lights are on and the food magazine has sounded. Many inappropriate behaviors do, in fact, occur at various stages of training. For example, the bird may move toward the food magazine before the light and sound have been produced by pecking the key just like begging that may occur in the dog training procedure. The nonreinforcement of these inappropriate behaviors is the critical element, in large part responsible for the development of the control of the bird's behavior by the conditioned reinforcers and discriminative stimuli.

## constructing chains of performances

To construct a chain of behaviors by conditioning, we need to begin backwards, reinforcing the final performance first. The process is best illustrated by following the diagram in Figure 7-2 in the reverse order.

*Lines 6 and 5.* These are the final performances in the chain: Pecking at the grain ($P_5$) and swallowing it ($P_6$). Most birds have this performance already in their repertoire. A bird with normal experience of eating grain will consistently peck at the food and swallow it. It ordinarily will not peck and swallow when grain is not present. Although there appears to be a large phylogenetically determined component of "pecking at grain," there is ample opportunity in the natural environment to develop such control. Pecking at the ground or at pebbles resembling grain goes unreinforced and serves to bring the pecking behavior under the control of grain. If a food was used that was unfamiliar to the bird, it would probably have to be taught to eat it before the chaining procedure could be started. When the bird pecks at the grain or other food at a high frequency (under adequate deprivation) and does not peck in its absence, the sight of grain may then serve as a reinforcer ($S^r_4$) for the next earlier operant in the chain.

*Line 4.* To extend the chain the next step, the experimenter must arrange that the bird's approaching the food tray ($P_4$) will occur only if sound and light ($S^D_4$) occur. Thus, moving downward toward the feeder ($P_4$) is reinforced by the sight of food ($S^r_4$) only in the presence of the light and sound of the feeder ($S^D_4$). The food-magazine stimuli control the animal's approach because the food tray is kept out of sight and out of reach except when the magazine operation has occurred. When the bird approaches the magazine in the absence of the light, there is no access to the food tray and the performance goes unreinforced. Therefore, the frequency of approach to the food tray in the absence of light and sound soon falls to zero. When the food tray is raised periodically in the presence of the magazine stimuli, the performance of approaching the food tray is reinforced and the frequency of the performance on this occasion remains high.

*Line 3.* Now the light and sound of the magazine operation ($S^D_4$) may be used to reinforce ($S^r_3$) the next earlier performance, pecking the key ($P_3$). Any time the bird, standing in front of the key, moves its head toward the key, the experimenter manually operates the magazine. The experimenter must be certain that the conditioned reinforcer follows the exact performance whose frequency is to be increased. Because the magazine light ($S^D_4$) already controls the sequence of behaviors leading to the ingestion of food ($P_4$, $P_5$, $P_6$), it increases the frequency of pecking-like movements ($P_3$). By successive approximation the bird soon strikes the key ($P_3$), and the switch behind the key operates the feeder with its accompanying light and sound. Once the peck has been successively approximated to the point where it operates the switch behind the key, the performance is maintained by the connection between the performance and its reinforcer rather than requiring the arbitrary intervention of the experimenter.

*Lines 2 and 1.* At the start of the sequence, it is the physical properties of the cage that provide the reinforcers for walking from a distant part of the cage to a position in front of the key. The bird's position in relation to the key ($P_1$) and $P_2$) produces visual stimuli ($S^r_1$ and $S^r_2$) that determine whether or not the bird will peck. When the bird is standing some distance from the key, even pecking motions in the direction of the key do not result in impact on the key nor the sound of the feeder. In the immediate proximity of the key, however, movements of the head bring the key in near focus and occasionally moving the head in this direction results in striking the key and producing the magazine stimuli. Thus the visual stimulus of the key in relation to its distance from the bird controls the probability of pecking in the same way that the lights and sound of the magazine operation control the performance of reaching down to the tray for food. Once the visual stimuli from the key control pecking ($S^D_5$) they also serve as a differential reinforcer ($S^r_2$) for movements toward the key ($P_2$).

## proving that the conditioned reinforcers in the chain control their respective performances

To prove that each of these conditioned reinforcers is maintaining the performance it follows, we can break the chain at each of several places by altering the environment so that the reinforcer no longer follows the performance. The first place where the chain can be conveniently interrupted is after the bird pecks the key. This is the conventional extinction procedure used in many operant reinforcement experiments. The light and sound of the feeder ($S^r_3$) no longer follow pecking as before. Therefore, the bird does not move its head to the food tray since this performance is under the control of discriminative stimuli that are now missing. Instead, the bird will continue to peck at the key with decreasing frequency until the behavior ceases. If the bird was very well trained and the feeder operated quietly, it is possible that many hours could elapse before it would notice the presence of the grain.

The chain can be interrupted by removing the reinforcer ($S^r_4$) that follows movements of the head from the key down to the food tray ($P_4$). First we reconnect the food dispenser but cover the tray so that the bird can neither see nor reach the grain. Now when the bird pecks the key, the magazine light comes and the tray raises normally, but the bird cannot see the grain. The reinstatement of the magazine stimuli will also reinstate pecking and the other performances under its control. The bird will peck the key ($P_3$) and move toward the food tray ($P_4$) when the light comes on ($S^D_4$), but it cannot see or reach the grain. With the chain thus interrupted, the frequency of lowering the head as well as pecking the key will decrease in the manner that is typical after extinction.

The chain can now be broken a step closer to the final performance by covering the food tray with a glass rather than an opaque cover so that the bird can see the grain. Once again, the reinstated conditioned reinforcer will increase the frequency of the performance it controls (lowering the head) as well as all of the prior performances in the chain. The bird will peck at the key ($P_2$) move its head toward the feeder ($P_4$) and peck at the surface of the glass ($P_5$). The sequence of performances will be repeated, with declining frequency until they cease.

Finally, we could glue some grain firmly to the bottom of the food tray so the bird can reach it, grasp it with its beak, but not pry it loose so it can be swallowed. The conditioned reinforcer of the grain in the beak ($S^r_2$) will reinstate the performance it controlled (the bird will repeatedly grasp the grain). It will also begin pecking the key again, lower its head to the food tray, and peck at the grain until the frequency of the performance declines due to extinction.

Extensive instrumentation would be needed to alter the natural relation between other performances in the chain that have a direct, natural effect on the physical environment. For example, we could mount the key on a pivot so that it would swing away when a photo cell arrangement signalled the approach of the bird's beak to the key. Then, if the key swung out of reach as the bird pecked, we would have interrupted the chain at an even earlier component than the instances described above.

## a complex chain of performances in a rat

A demonstration carried out at Barnard College and Columbia University by Rosemary Pierrel and J. Gilmour Sherman[1] provides a vivid example of how behavioral principles contribute to the construction of complex chains of behavior. They trained a rat called Barnabus to perform a complicated series of acts that culminated in the rat pressing a bar reinforced by the delivery of food. Figure 7-3 illustrates the various performances that the rat carried out in sequence. Such sequences of activities or similar ones have been constructed by high school students once they have understood the principles of chaining and conditioned reinforcement. In principle, the procedure is no different than those involving pecking, bar-pressing, and pulling the overhead rope. The difference is in the complexity of the topographies of the component performances and the number of operants that are chained in sequence.

As above, the performances were established in the reverse order. Pressing a bar, followed by the receipt of a food pellet was the first performance that was conditioned. This established the sight of the lever as a conditioned reinforcer that reinforced the behavior of descending to the ground floor in the elevator. It would be a useful exercise to describe the rest of the chain in the manner that was presented in the preceding discussions.

Barnabus's performance exemplified a long complex chain of performances, held together in a fixed sequence by a large number of conditioned reinforcers including sounds, arbitrary stimuli, cues from the animal's own behavior, and visual and tactile aspects of the apparatus. Each performance, in turn, was shaped and maintained by its immediate and specific effect on the environment. All of the performances were under the control of food deprivation and the final parts of the chain leading to food. Each performance, because of the mechanical construction of the environment, produced the conditions that made the next performance possible. It was possible, however, for the rat to behave inappropriately at many points by leaping off the apparatus or attempting short cuts. The step-by-step construction of the chain backwards, establishing each performance under the control of the appropriate stimulus, made each performance occur in the appropriate sequence despite the rat's inclination to go directly to the food.

## intermittent schedules
## of conditioned reinforcement

A chimpanzee experiment performed by Dr. Kelleher illustrates how conditioned reinforcers can maintain performances under schedules of intermittent conditioned reinforcement in a manner somewhat parallel to chaining.[2] The conditioned reinforcer was a token that the chimpanzee could exchange for food. This was accomplished by installing a slot into which the token could be inserted to operate a food dispenser. After they successfully inserted poker chips into the slot, reinforced by food, chim-

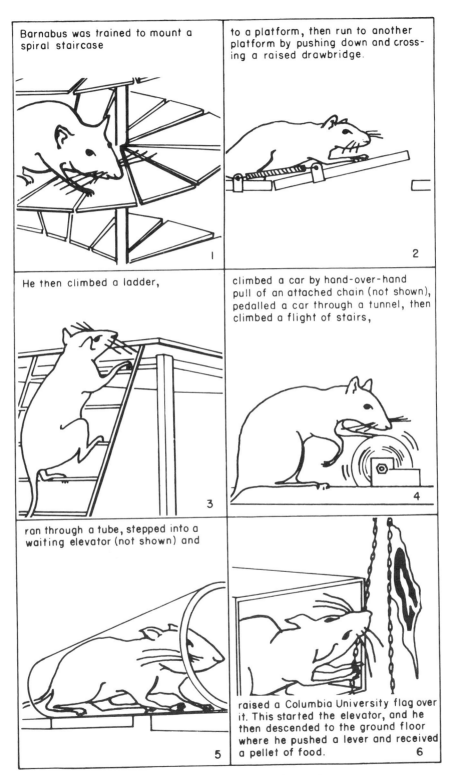

Figure 7-3  A complex chain of performances in a rat.    **239**

panzees pressed a key, a behavior reinforced by tokens. After they pressed the key reliably, the key-presses were reinforced intermittently by the tokens on a multiple schedule with fixed-ratio and fixed-interval components. In the presence of an orange light, the first performance after five minutes (fixed-interval) produced a token. In the presence of a green light, every twentieth press of the key produced a token (fixed-ratio). To minimize the association between the food and the tokens, the chimpanzees were not allowed to cash in their tokens for food immediately. A light over the token slot provided a means of delaying the time when the chimpanzee would cash them in. Only when the light was on did the insertion of a token operate the food dispenser. When the light was off, that performance went unreinforced. After the chimpanzee reliably inserted tokens only when the light was on over the token slot, the experimenter could arrange how long the animal had to carry its tokens before exchanging them. The cumulative record in Figure 7-4 depicts a performance when the chimpanzees were required to carry tokens for an hour before exchanging them. Each of the oblique marks on the cumulative record marks the delivery of a token. They were exchanged for food at the end of the record.

In general, the overall rate of key-pressing increased as the time to cash in the poker chips approached. The bursts of key-pressing that occurred at the approach of the time when the tokens could be cashed in for food appears to be an emotional effect. The performances under the multiple schedule of reinforcement were very much like what would have occurred had food been delivered each time rather than the token. The delivery of food depended on the number of such conditioned reinforcers that occurred, and the animal was introduced to the schedule gradually with the food first occurring after every second component of the multiple schedule. Finally, it occurred at the end of the session. Later experiments have shown that almost any stimulus, programmed on the same schedules, would maintain the performance stably.

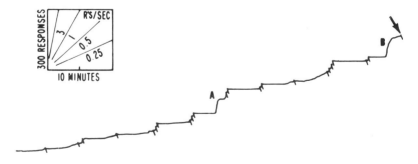

Figure 7-4

These experiments are a model of the way that intermittent reinforcement occurs in much of human behavior where the actual reinforcers are usually conditioned stimuli such as the token or a flash of the light on the key. Consider the behavior of a construction worker transferring a load of sand by wheelbarrow to the place on the construction site where it is being used. The final event maintaining the chain of behaviors is the sand in place in the new location. But the component activities are filling a wheelbarrow and transporting the sand. Prior to moving the full wheelbarrow full of sand to the new site, it is filled a shovel full at a time. Thus the full wheelbarrow is a conditioned reinforcer produced on a fixed-ratio schedule equal to the number of shovel fulls of dirt necessary to fill it. Even the movement of a single shovel full involves intermittent conditioned reinforcement. To remove a shovel full of sand the shovel has to be grasped, then raised, and placed in the wheelbarrow, and then turned to let the sand fall. Thus even without knowing what is the ultimate reinforcer maintaining the behavior, we can identify a long chain of behaviors intermittently reinforced by conditioned reinforcers.

Mostly the schedules are fixed-ratio. Shoveling sand into the wheelbarrow is reinforced on a fixed-ratio schedule by the wheelbarrow full of sand. Walking the wheelbarrow to the new location is also reinforced on a fixed-ratio schedule consisting of the number of steps to reach the location where the sand can be unloaded. Even a single shovel full of sand is a chain of behaviors even though the performances have varying topographies. Inserting the shovel into the sand pile is reinforced by its penetration. With the shovel in the sand, lifting it out is reinforced by the sand in place on the shovel; and moving the shovel full of sand allows it to be emptied in the wheelbarrow.

Peeling potatoes for dinner exemplifies the same kind of intermittent conditioned reinforcement. It takes a certain number of peeling motions to produce a potato that is ready for cooking. Each peeled potato is a reinforcer for a "second-order schedule" such as that described for the chimpanzee pressing a key reinforced by tokens that could be cashed in after a certain number had accumulated.

---

# questions

*1.* Describe a bird's pecking at a key as a chain of performances, each reinforced by a stimulus that follows it, and strengthened by the stimulus that precedes it. List each of the component performances.

2. Say why it is necessary to build a chain starting with the final performance.

3. Show how to prove that each stimulus in a chain is in fact the reinforcer maintaining the performance it follows.

4. Diagram Barnabus's chain and explain the functional relations between the component performances and the controlling stimuli. Use the following guide as the first step in the diagram.

| occasion (S$^D$) | performance (R) | reinforcer (S$^r$) |
| --- | --- | --- |
| Being at the bottom of spiral stairs | mounting the spiral staircase | reaching a platform |

## *part II: analyzing examples of chains and conditioned reinforcers*

### accidental conditioned reinforcement

Accidental reinforcement, introduced in Chapter 1, exemplified the fact that reinforcement was a temporal phenomenon. A reinforcing stimulus increased the frequency of a performance, willy-nilly, whether anyone intended it to do so or not. The phenomenon would of course also occur in chains of behavior and with performances maintained by reinforcers that were more remote from primary reinforcers than was the case with the examples discussed earlier of the accidental reinforcement of pecking. One situation where accidental reinforcement is an especially important occurrence is in the development of stimulus control, say in a multiple schedule with one component as extinction and the other continuous reinforcement. The point of contact between the performance and the conditioned reinforcer is at the end of the interval of time when the stimulus correlated with the extinction schedule is present. A peck, by chance, at the moment when the extinction period has ended and the stimulus is about to change would be reinforced as in a chain. Although the experimenter has programmed a schedule with extinction as the one component, the accidental connection between pecks in the extinction period and the appearance of the stimulus correlated with the schedule of continuous reinforcement by the food magazine alters it to a chain. Pecks in the presence of one key color are reinforced by the appearance of the other. Such accidental reinforcement may interfere with the development of differential stimulus control since pecking in the presence of the extinction stimulus will increase in frequency by accidental reinforcement rather than decrease as a result of extinction.

Such accidental reinforcement is prevented in animal experiments by extending the interval of the extinction stimulus every time the bird pecks near the end. This is a *dro* procedure with respect to the stimulus correlated with the food schedule. Since the appearance of the food-schedule stimulus is a conditioned reinforcer that will increase the frequency of any performance it follows, the *dro* schedule guarantees that it will follow some other behavior than pecking.

In such a situation accidental reinforcement is self-perpetuating. Once a peck is reinforced accidentally, the increased frequency of pecking at the end of the extinction period will make it more likely, the next time, that the bird will be pecking when the food-schedule stimulus appears.

## delayed reinforcement
## as a chain of behaviors

The phenomenon of accidental reinforcement also gives some clues as to the mechanism by which reinforcement is delayed. We ordinarily don't think of a chain of behaviors as a delay in reinforcement even though the ultimate reinforcer is delayed until a sequence of performances and discriminative stimuli occurs. We would speak of the reinforcement as delayed if there were no obvious or required performances that could be accounted for by a reinforcer supporting the performance. Thus, a delay in reinforcement would involve an interval of time between a performance and the conditioned reinforcer that followed it. An experiment, carried out some years ago with pigeons, illustrates the essential features of delayed reinforcement.[3] A pigeon's pecks at a lighted key were reinforced on a variable-interval schedule where the intervals between reinforcement averaged 1 minute. Reinforcement was delayed by turning off the lights in the box for 60 seconds between the peck that was to be reinforced and the operation of the food dispenser. Birds do not peck in the dark without special training so the blackout produced a 60-second delay between the peck and the operation of the food magazine that reinforced it. The birds could not sustain pecking under this condition of delay. The delay was then reduced to 1 second and increased gradually, paced with the bird's performance. It was increased only when the previous delay did not reduce the rate of pecking on the variable-interval reinforcement schedule. With such a result it seemed reasonable to suppose that some behavior was occurring during the period of darkened key that was accidentally reinforced by the operation of food magazine. In that event, the actual schedule would be a chain where the first component was a variable-interval schedule reinforced by the darkened key. The darkened key was a discriminative stimulus that controlled the performances accidentally reinforced on a fixed-interval schedule by the operation of a food dispenser. When the experimenters actually observed the bird, the hypothesized performances were, in fact, seen to occur. Each bird had acquired a distinctive topography of action that it sustained throughout the 60-second interval. As would be expected from the lack of any direct relation between the performance and the stimulus that increased its frequency, the topography of the performance was arbitrary. One bird turned in circles, another nodded in a corner, another waved its head from side to side, and so forth.

Performances in many sports offer examples of delayed reinforcement. The bowler, for example, is emitting a performance reinforced by the collision of the ball with the pins that occurs some seconds after the throw is complete. The bowler's gestures and postures, while the ball is rolling toward the pins, appears to have the same function as the pigeon's accidentally reinforced performances that took place during the delay interval. In tennis, even though the interval is not as long as in bowling, there is enough delay between the movement of the racket to the ball and the final destination of the ball so that the intervening interval is significant.

Such delay in reinforcement should not be confused with the ordinary discriminative control of behavior that can reduce the frequency of a performance to zero for indefinite periods of time without weakening it. For example, if a pigeon reached a stable performance on a multiple variable-interval, extinction schedule of reinforcement, the extinction stimulus could be used to interrupt the variable-interval performance and postpone the time at which a peck would be next reinforced without weakening the performance elsewhere. In fact, laboratory experiments with animals are started and stopped by presenting or withdrawing the discriminative stimulus that controls the reinforced behavior. Most human behavior is delayed in this latter sense, rather than by a delay between a performance and its consequence in the environment. The youngster who is told by his parent that he will receive the money earned for doing a chore several hours later when the parent has had an opportunity to make change is in a situation functionally parallel to the pigeon on the multiple schedule. The verbal statement that the child will be paid at a certain time later serves much like the time out in the pigeon experiment, although the verbal process by which the auditory stimulus controls the child's behavior is a complex one. The elements of such verbal processes will be considered in Chapter 10.

## chains that include reflexes and fixed-action patterns

A large emphasis was placed on the major differences between reflex and operant behavior by describing how they can have such different properties. Nevertheless, reflexes and operants can be connected to each other in important ways. One connection that was drawn in Chapter 2 concerned behaviors, such as sucking, whose topography was similar whether operant or reflex and which shifted their function in the normal course of development from reflex to operant. Another important connection was drawn in Chapter 4 where physiological and reflex actions occurred as a collateral effect of aversive stimuli. Still another connection between reflex and operant behavior occurs in chains of behavior in which an operant performance is reinforced because it produces a stimulus that is the conditioned or unconditioned stimulus that elicits a reflex. One example of such a chain is the case of actors who place an irritant in their eyes to produce tears that are a part of their role and that will influence the audience. Or, alternatively, they talk to themselves about sad events that are conditioned stimuli, already effective in their repertoire for eliciting tears. The latter case is an instructive example of the generic nature of the operant. The class of behaviors that defines the operant is those performances that have the effect of evoking a previously conditioned reflex. Thus, the production of tears will specifically and differentially reinforce those behaviors that effectively elicit the conditioned reflex. In other words, the elements of the person's latent potential repertoire are selectively reinforced by how they contribute to an emotional state that will produce tears.

It is important to distinguish the functional control of such crying, which has a generic connection with the operant performances that produce their eliciting conditioned stimulus, from the behavior of a cook peeling an onion for a meal. For the cook, the reinforcer for the behavior of peeling the onion is the progress toward completing the meal. The crying is collateral. Its relation to the cook's operant behavior, if any, is as an aversive stimulus that will reinforce turning the head away or any other item from the class of behaviors that will lessen the irritation to the eyes.

*Fixed-action patterns* of birds offer convenient examples of how reflexes and operant behavior may be connected in a chain and influence each other interdependently. As noted earlier, a fixed-action pattern present in the herring gull is the use of its long, curved beak to roll eggs that have fallen out of the nest back into the nest. Initially, the bird simply strikes at the eggs in a way that brings them toward it. The motion is a scooping one and there is no suggestion at the start that the movements are guided by their effectiveness in moving the eggs back to the nest. Later, however, the movements that contact the egg most securely and move it most efficiently in the required direction will increase in frequency and the others will decrease. The position of the egg as a releasing stimulus for the fixed-action pattern creates the reinforcer and the basis for the chain of behaviors that finally develops. Eventually, the performances of the beak against the eggs function in a chain of behaviors where the distance and direction of the egg from the nest are the discriminative stimuli that define the components. Such a chain would be a homogeneous one. A bird, in retrieving an egg, might repeatedly nudge it with the stereotyped scooping movements, take stock after it has moved some distance, and begin scooping movements again, now controlled by the new position of the egg relative to the nest.

Nest building is another example of phylogenetic and ontogenetic influences that are intertwined within a chain of behaviors controlled by operant principles. Why building a nest in the first place is reinforcing is answered in the animal's inherited history, including hormonal influences. But, given the particular species and hormonal influences, the actual building of the nest is determined by principles of operant reinforcement. The species determines *what* outcome is reinforcing and some of the forms of the behavior that are involved because the final effect maintaining the chain of events is the constructed nest. Each performance, however, is maintained by its immediate consequence and is connected to the next one in a chain of operant behaviors. Grasping a straw is reinforced by the change in its location from the ground to the bird's mouth. Turning in the direction of the to-be-constructed nest is reinforced by the sight of it and walking toward it is reinforced by its view, close up. The view of the nest close up is an occasion when inserting the straw can be reinforced by the increment in the nest. Even though the final component of the chain may be determined more by phylogenetic than ontogenetic variables, the preceding components obey operant principles of behavioral control. For a straw to be grasped, it needs to be approached from any direction where it appears and the pecking movement employed in picking it up will be different depending on the straw's orientation to the bird's body.

In the case of the infant's rooting reflex—turning the head when the infant's cheek is stimulated by the touch of the mother's breast—the reflex may be the first part of a chain of behaviors. The operant control of the movements of the head may not yet be developed while the performance of sucking has already shifted most of its function from reflex to operant. In that case, however, it cannot be considered properly as an operant chain because the control of the behavior is by the mother who must present the eliciting stimulus for the rooting reflex before the sequence of behaviors can begin.

*Imprinting*, originally described by Konrad Lorenz[4], is another situation in which a chain of operant behaviors is maintained by phylogenetically determined fixed-action pattern. He discovered that ducklings that normally follow their mothers within a day or two after they are hatched, also will follow another adult duck, or virtually any moving object, if it is present during the critical period of several hours immediately after the hatching. For the process of imprinting to become functional in the duck's life, almost all principles of operant reinforcement need to control its component activities. The imprinted animal or object needs to become a discriminative stimulus by differential reinforcement. Thus, when discriminative control is established, the duck will approach its parent when it is separated at some distance from it rather than another duck that is closer. Proximity to the parent needs to become a conditioned reinforcer because the reinforced chain of behaviors consists of walking to reduce the distance from the parent. Environmental obstacles between the duckling and its parent require the development of conditioned reinforcers to maintain the necessary adaptive patterns.

**Can reflexes be reinforced like operants?**    The chaining of reflexes and operants bears on whether reflexes may be conditioned like operants. For example, by monitoring a dog's blood pressure, food is given when it changes. If it can be altered by differential food reinforcement, then it provides evidence that physiological responses such as blood pressure would change as a result of operant reinforcement, rather than their control being limited to the laws of reflex action. Unfortunately, for purposes of a simple experiment, many kinds of operant activity, such as tensing one's muscles or exercising, can alter blood pressure. If one were to deliver food to a dog every time its blood pressure increased or decreased, it would not be possible to determine whether some operant performance were being reinforced in a chain by its effect on the reflex. For this reason, these experimenters have administered curare, a drug that inhibits muscle action to the extreme that the animals need to be artificially respirated. Unfortunately, the complications of such a drastic physiological intervention have cast more heat than light, and the results of these experiments are still in dispute.

**Biofeedback**    Recent attempts at the use of biofeedback for therapy involve chaining of operant and reflex behavior. If the state of relaxation of particular muscles is reflected in the skin resistance or the electromyographic voltage recorded on them, it has been suggested that persons may be taught to control the level of muscular tension by showing them a continuous record of their muscle voltages. Thus the galvanometer, which records the muscle voltage, becomes the reinforcer that maintains those behaviors that influence relaxation of these muscles. The principle is that a clear, amplified signal is much more discriminable than a person's unaided observation as to muscular state.

## the chaining of observing behavior

Paying attention to one particular feature of the environment or another is a performance of some complexity. At the simplest level, it involves performances such as turning the head, focusing the eyes, pointing to individual words of a text as one reads, or shining a light to increase the intensity of a visual stimulus such as a mechanical part one is repairing. Such behaviors are reinforced because they enhance the control by a discriminative stimulus that already controls some behavior that is stably maintained in the person's repertoire. As such, their overall function needs to be described as a member of a chain of behaviors. Laboratory experiments have provided a model for studying the properties of this kind of behavior and they will be useful in gaining some facility in thinking about the process.

One experiment, carried out by Dr. James G. Holland, studied human vigilance in a situation parallel to that encountered in a radar watch.[5] To measure the vigilance of an observer when the frequency of signals was very low, Dr. Holland instrumented the screen on which the signal appeared so that the subject needed to press a key to determine whether or not a signal had appeared on the screen. If the subject detected that a signal had appeared, he or she could report it by pressing a report key. In this way, the experiment could determine whether the subject was looking at the screen, and whether the subject detected a signal that had appeared. Holland called the first performance "observing behavior." The process of observing was carried forward in animal experiments by the same method.[6] The pigeon had two keys, one reinforced by food and the other reinforced by producing a stimulus on the food key that indicated when a peck would be reinforced and another that indicated when it would not. Thus, the pigeon could either take "pot luck"—with its pecks being reinforced on the unsignaled mixture of the fixed-interval and extinction schedules—or it could peck the observing key, reinforced by the production of stimuli on the food-key that converted its schedule to one with discriminative control: a multiple schedule with fixed-interval reinforcement when the one stimulus was present and with extinction in the second one. If the pigeon clarified the conditions of reinforcement on the food key by pecking the observing key, then it would peck on the food key only when the discriminative stimulus was present, and not at all during the stimulus that indicated extinction.

Clearly, the reinforcement of the observing behavior is by the discriminative control of the food-reinforced behavior. Its analysis suggests a chain of performances where the observing behavior, by clarifying the reinforcement conditions in the latter part of the chain, increases the frequency of reinforcement there and decreases the amount of unreinforced performances.[7] Much of educational development, particularly in science, has a parallel function. The verbal stimuli of biology, physics, and geology, once in the student's repertoire, provide opportunities to bring his or her behavior concerning the physical and biological environment under the control of stimuli that enhance the observation of them. Verbal clarification of this kind is crucial in normal growth and development and a focal point in the incapacities that psychotherapy is directed toward. One factor is the weakness of observing behaviors, reinforced by conditioned reinforcers, at the start of the chain because they are the greatest distance from the high frequency performances at the end of the chain. It is not surprising therefore, that observing behaviors are susceptible to disruption from aversive control and fail to emerge when the circumstances of the child's development are adverse. Also operative is the weakening effect of intermittent reinforcement . The observing behavior, say of the pigeon in the experiment described above, represents much intermittently reinforced behavior at the start of the chain that needs to be counterbalanced by the later reinforcement frequency and decrease in aversive stimuli. The whole process may be continuously self defeating if the lack of observing behavior weakens the individual's repertoire so that the maintenance of observing behavior is even less likely.

## chains of performances in normal growth and development

Consider a chain of performances where a child moves a chair across the room and uses it to climb to a cupboard to reach the key that will open it. This complicated sequence of behavior is linked together by critical stimuli that have the dual function of sustaining the performance they follow (conditioned reinforcement) and setting the occasion for the next performance (discriminative stimulus). Table 7-1 lists the component performances in the chain, each preceded by the occasion when it can be reinforced and followed by the change in the environment that is the reinforcer. The analysis of this chain is parallel to that presented in Part I except that the sequence of the performances and the topographies are more varied. As before, the construction of the unit performances described in the table emphasizes the double function of each stimulus.

**Table 7–1**   Component Performances in 2 Chain

| OCCASION | PERFORMANCE | CHANGE IN ENVIRONMENT |
|---|---|---|
| Chair located some distance from the cupboard | Pushing the chair | Chair located in front of the cupboard |
| Chair located in front of cupboard | Climbing on chair | Child standing on the chair |
| Child standing on the chair | Reaching for the key | Touching the key |
| Touching the key | Grasping the key | Key in hand |
| Key in hand | Climbing down from the chair | Standing on floor with key in hand |
| Standing on floor with key in hand | Walking to cupboard | Child located in front of the cupboard |
| Child located in front | Insert and turning key in lock | Door open |
| Door open | Reaching for candy | Candy in hand |

In the second line of the table, the child standing on the chair is the reinforcer that maintains the performance of climbing the chair. It is also, however, the occasion when the next performance—reaching for the key —may be reinforced by the next change in the environment-touching the key. The functional significance of the reinforcer, simultaneously serving as the discriminative stimulus controlling the next performance, may be appreciated by noting that reaching for the key on any other occasion does not lead to touching it. Only by standing on the chair, which puts the key within reach, can the reaching behavior be effective. The extinction of this performance when it is emitted inappropriately brings it under the control of the situation where it can be reinforced. The differential control by the occasions when a performance with a key is necessary is so extensive and consistent that we tend not to notice recurrent situations where someone tries to open a door that is always locked without using a key. Children sometimes reach for an object beyond reach, but we tend not to notice the occasional instances when adults do the same.

New chains of behavior are formed most rapidly during the second and third years of a child's development. Prior to the second year, the child's immobility limits new behaviors to those that can occur in a crib or playpen, or by influencing a parent who in turn engages the child in an interaction. As the child's mobility increases when it learns to crawl and walk, the range of potentially accessible reinforcers increases. Correspondingly, new behavioral repertoires are created through successvie approximation and chaining by these reinforcers. At first, the chains consist of performances that change the nonsocial world. Crawling and walking are the constituent elements of the earliest chains because the new locations support the child's behavior that could not occur if the child could not crawl. When a child crawls to an adult, it can tug at the adult's sleeve and induce the adult to pick her up. Or, if the child crawls toward a toy across the room, crawling is the first step in the chain of behaviors leading to play. Each new performance that emerges in the child's behavioral development makes possible extended chains of performances that in turn make possible new reinforcers. As soon as a child pushes a chair in place to climb on it and reach for a cookie, other objects in high places become potential reinforcers for climbing.

Even though a performance emerges in a chain, it still may develop by successive approximation. For example, the first time that a chair is pushed may be when it is very close to the table. Pushing the chair this small distance, climbing on the table, and taking the food, reinforces the chain of performances and the frequency of pushing the chair on subsequent, similar occasions will be higher. A carefully graded succession of experiences of this kind will occur naturally in a reactive environment. Successive approximation in chains is also illustrated by the development of a repertoire of handling large, bulky objects reinforced by their movement to a location where climbing on it will make possible reaching something. The optimal conditions for producing such a repertoire would where the furniture was light, easily lifted, and initially not too far from the required place. The ability to move heavier furniture over longer distances would emerge slowly after performances effective in moving ligher and smaller objects appeared. People who injure themselves lifting heavy objects improperly may be evidence of the failure of the person's environment to successively approximate these behaviors or the failure of the discriminative control of the lifting performance by the appearance of the object that is lifted.

The adult's physical environment provides myriad examples of chaining and conditioned reinforcement. Consider the number of discrete contingencies and performances that occur in the chain of performances involved in driving off in a car. If the car is in a garage, we walk to it, open the door, go through, move to the vicinity of the car door, place our hand on the door handle, press the latch, and pull the door open. Even placing the legs in the car followed by the change in position into the seat could be described as a chain of three or four discrete behaviors. Reaching for the key is reinforced by tactile contact with it, which is an occasion when it is possible to withdraw it from the pocket. With the key in hand it can be inserted into the ignition lock. With the key inserted in the ignition lock, it becomes possible to turn it so as to actuate the starter motor. Despite the smoothness and rapidity with which such a sequence is routinely carried out, the performances are controlled by the prior discriminative stimuli and reinforced by the change in the environment they effect.

## the varieties of consequences that can maintain chains of performances

Because so many behavior principles were discovered with simple operant performances of animals it might be thought that a behavioral view of human conduct implies that all human behavior is derived from primary consequences such as food or sex, and escape from physical harm. Such a view is encouraged by Freud's influential writings about the instinctual origins of the greater part of human behavior. Observation of the broad scope of human and animal behavior, however, does not support this view; nor do the views of later, psychoanalytically oriented writers. A wide variety of consequences have been observed to be effective reinforcers besides eating and sexual behavior.

**Fixed-action patterns**   The fixed-action patterns that have been discussed earlier in this chapter and in Chapter 2 present a boundary between reinforcers derived because they maintain the daily metabolic balance and those that maintain behavior independently of current, tangible deprivational factors. It seems highly probable that the puppy polecats' playful fighting with each other has its origins, phylogenetically, in its contribution to mating, later in the animal's life. Yet, no immediate metabolic change is maintaining it. Dogs commonly exhibit a combination of fixed-action patterns that mimic some biological or defensive function. For example, dogs "play" fighting each other, carry out the fixed-action patterns that occur when they actually fight, except that they never bite each other, their tails wag and the pattern might shift any moment to some other behavior, completely unrelated. Play has an obvious adaptive function in an organism's development. Yet, one could not say that behavior reinforced "playfully" is derived from some more general, underlying deprivation or metabolism. Much of the repertoire of children emerges from play where the component behaviors of the game have an important function in the child's later life but have limited consequences in its early development. Even the beginning repertoires emerging in play support chains of behavior indicating their independent effectiveness as a reinforcer. A youngster playing tennis, for example, will practice on a wall or swing the racket against a phantom ball, learn the rules of the game and how to keep score. These activities are maintained by conditioned reinforcement consisting of the increment in repertoire that permits more successful play during the actual game. The child, disposed to play with blocks, will ask a parent for them, search them out of a closet, and carry them to the play area. These are the performances reinforced because they produce the occasion when the blocks can be played with. The component activities of playing with the blocks are also chains of behavior where one performance produces the discriminative stimulus for the next. Placing blocks on one another is reinforced by the larger structure that emerges but the child's willingness, often, to tumble the tower and start again is evidence that the reinforcer is the "play" with the environment rather than the permanent use of the tower. Anthropologists have asserted that such chains of playful behavior are one of the major ways that the human infant acquires the complex repertoire that develops later.[8]

**Activity as a reinforcer**   There is considerable evidence that organisms are born with an innate disposition to engage in particular forms of activity and to be active generally. Human infants, for example, observed while drinking from bottles whose nipple openings were varied were restless and cried when they drank from a bottle with large openings in the nipple unless they were given an opportunity to suck the empty bottle.[9] Other infants who drank from a smaller opening in a nipple were satisfied with a lesser amount of milk. Probably some of the major aversive effects of time out, ostracism, restraint, and incarceration come from the activity limitations that are imposed. It seems reasonable to conclude from this and related studies that simple emission of certain kinds of activities is intrinsically reinforcing.

**Observing the environment as a reinforcer**   Butler's[10] experiments, involving measurements of the reinforcing effect of a view of the environment, shows a similar diversion of behavior from fundamental metabolic or defensive determination. Butler kept monkeys in the dark, unable to look out into the room where they lived, unless they pressed a key. He discovered that an opportunity to look around was an important event that could sustain large amounts of the monkey's behavior. In a related experiment, it was discovered that pigeons, restrained in a small space like the typical laboratory living cage, would peck in a sustained manner at a key if it were arranged that pecks on a fixed-ratio schedule would open the door to a large space.[11]

**Chaining of behavior by negative reinforcement**   The termination of an aversive stimulus is also a reinforcer that can serve to maintain performances in chains. Findley[12] has studied the process in animals and human subjects. One operant, on some schedule of reinforcement, for example fixed-ratio, is reinforced by terminating a stimulus that otherwise would have led to a shock being delivered. In experiments where the aversive stimulus is the withdrawal or postponement of positive reinforcement, an avoidance procedure is used. The fixed-ratio performance in the first member of the chain postpones an interruption by a time out stimulus, in the second—food-reinforced—member of the chain. Findley's experiment was analogous to many situations that occur naturally in the human environment. Consider, for example, the child who cleans up his room when threatened, punished, or nagged by a parent. No extended chains are involved when the aversive stimulus is applied, performance by performance, as the child cleans. In that case, the parent stands by, making continuous verbal threats of penalties and perhaps even punishes or imposes physical restraint when the child stops cleaning or leaves. No chain of behaviors is involved in such a situation since an aversive or conditioned aversive stimulus negatively reinforces each of the child's performances by postponing or withdrawing the stimulus.

An extended chain of performances is maintained, however, when the untidy room comes to function as a conditioned aversive stimulus through a history of aversive stimulation. The clean room serves as a conditioned negative reinforcer. The aversive consequences controlling the performances are temporally distant. The gap is bridged when the untidy room functions as conditioned aversive stimulus. The component activities of cleaning the room are part of a chain of behavior because each unit performance produces a conditioned negative reinforcer in the form of an increment in the room's cleanliness. The conditioned aversive properties of the untidy room share some of the characteristics of the generalized reinforcer that will be discussed in Part III of this chapter.

# questions

*1.* Describe how the natural ecology builds a chain such as walking to a chair, carrying it to the cupboard, climbing on it, reaching for the cookie jar, taking off the lid, reaching for a cookie, and finally eating it. The description should answer the following questions, How does the child (1) find his mouth when a cookie is in his hand, (2) pick up a cookie, (3) search for it, (4) get it out of the jar, and so to the end. You should carry out all of your descriptions using technical terms, specifying exact performances, and the occasions at which they are reinforced by specific stimuli in turn controlling specific performances.

*2.* In the example of the child climbing a chair, getting a key, and unlocking the cupboard, how do extinction and stimulus control influence the behavior of reaching for the key at an inappropriate part of the chain?

*3.* How does increased mobility during the second year increase the number of conditioned reinforcers which can sustain the child's behavior?

*4.* Describe how a child might learn to push a chair across a room. How does the natural environment arrange the reinforcer?

*5.* What makes a conditioned reinforcer such as money in a behavioral chain "sound"?

## part III: generalized reinforcement

### money as a generalized reinforcer

The conditioned reinforcers discussed so far control behavior so long as there is a level of deprivation relevant to the final reinforcer. The performances described for the rat, Barnabus, in Part I were maintained by the food pellet received as a result of pressing the lever at the end of the long sequence of operant performances. The rat's inclination to eat varied continuously as a function of its body weight and this in turn determined all of the performances in the chain.

The performances maintained by escape or avoidance of aversive stimuli have properties similar to those that are dependent on food deprivation. All of the cleaning activity described in Part II would cease as soon as the parents no longer applied corporal punishment, fines, or withdrawal of reinforcers when the room was dirty. The necessity of continuing the aversive control if the behavior is to be maintained is legendary, as conveyed by the aphorism "When the cat's away, the mice will play."

A generalized reinforcer is independent of these specific deprivations or aversive stimulation. Money, an important conditioned reinforcer in human affairs, serves as a convenient example of generalized reinforcement because so many of the contingencies from which it derives its function are explicit and observable. With money, a person may ask for food, shelter, amusement, goods such as clothes and automobiles. Without money, there is no possibility of these performances being reinforced. It will, therefore, reinforce any performances it follows as a result of its discriminative control of such important consequences as the click or sound of the food dispenser in the pigeon experiment. Receiving money differs from simpler kinds of conditioned reinforcement because the discriminative stimulus gets its property by setting the occasion for a variety of performances controlled by a variety of deprivations and reinforcers.

The child who sweeps the walk, receives money, walks to the store, and buys candy illustrates a chain of performances where money is a critical link. Table 7-2 specifies the operants in the chain in the form of the three-term contingency that is so central to their analysis. As with the example mentioned in Part II where a child moved a chair into position to climb for a cookie, any of the performances can occur inappropriately to the conditions where they can be reinforced. For example, many children will walk to the store without money and will look in the window. At some ages they might even ask the clerk to give them candy if the social pattern of the culture included verbal interactions with the clerk. In some communities the request would be frequently granted if the child were very young. Asking the parent for money also comes under the control of specific discriminative stimuli as a result of the child's history with the parent. Considerable differential reinforcement needs to occur before a child's behavior of asking for money comes under the control of the chores that the parents require.

### Special aspects of conditioned reinforcement in human behavior

In Part II of this chapter a distinction was made between delay in reinforcement as a brief time period between the performance and the consequence that is connected to it, and the interruption of the entire

**Table 7-2** Chained Performance Analyzed in Terms of a Three-Term Contingency

| OCCASION | PERFORMANCES | CONDITIONED REINFORCER |
|---|---|---|
| 1. Broom and dirty floor | Sweeping the floor | A clean floor |
| 2. A clean floor | Asking for money | Ten cents in hand |
| 3. Ten cents in hand | Walking to store | Standing in store with ten cents in hand |
| 4. Standing in store with ten cents in hand | "May I have a candy bar?" | Clerk holds out a candy bar |

chain by a "time out." It was possible, by special arrangement, to postpone the later parts of a chain as was done in the experiment where the chimpanzees had to hold their tokens until a light signaled when they could be cashed in for food. Such interrupted chains are more the rule than the exception in human behavior, particularly when reinforcements are mediated through the behavior of another person. The child who was paid to sweep the walk might not receive the money until several hours or even a day or more after completing the job. The verbal stimulus of promise to pay, by the parent, serves as the "time out" in the chain. The parent's verbal behavior is a stimulus that controls when the next performance in the chain of behaviors leading to the purchase of candy at the store can be executed. (The discussion of how a verbal stimulus that is present for a moment in time can exert discriminative control over performances that occur some hours later needs to be postponed until the next chapter, however.) The completion of the chain might be even further delayed in other situations as when the money is saved and spent the next day. Although the spending of the money is delayed, the reinforcement of the performance is not. The physical dimension of money, as the tokens in the chimpanzee experiment, allows it to be carried about easily so that it can control the behavior of another person, such as the shopkeeper, at any time that those performances could be carried out.

The same factors help to explain the pattern of reinforcement in job situations. It might be thought that a person paid monthly is engaging in performances reinforced on a fixed-interval schedule, where the interval is one month. Actually, the performance is likely to be a chain or a concurrent schedule. The daily performances are reinforced on fixed-ratio schedules by conditioned reinforcers. The salary reinforces taking the pay check on payday—a continuous reinforcement schedule. If the salary is to be part of a chain, then completion of a certain amount of work needs to be the occasion determining the receipt of the pay check. Such would be the case with piece work. More likely, however, even salary employment will include two concurrent schedules that are somewhat independent. Poor job performance may induce management to punish by firing or negatively reinforcing by threats. Many of the daily performances are likely to be reinforced on second-order schedules maintained by immediate reaction to the worker's production.

## attention of the parent as a conditioned reinforcer

Because the parent mediates the reinforcement of so many of the child's performances, her attention comes to serve as a generalized reinforcer. Different reinforcers are mediated by the parents at various stages of the child's development. For the infant, incapable of taking care of its most elementary needs, the parent's ministrations are mainly not contingent on the infant's performances. As the child matures, interactions occur, collateral to the feeding and physical care in which their performances reinforce each other in a chain. Even before the child starts to speak, still incapable of acting directly on the physical environment to sustain herself physiologically and defensively, she emits behavior reinforced by the influence on the parent. Crying, for example, changes its function from a fixed-action pattern or adjunctive behavior to a performance reinforced by inducing the parent to feed it, change a diaper, reduce the temperature of a bottle, or provide an opportunity for play. Later the child points or gestures to food, reinforced by the parent's compliance. Still later, verbal requests or demands induce the parent to open doors, tie its shoes, or transport it to another place. The amount of the child's behavior requiring the mediation of the parent increases at a rapid rate until school age. Then, the other juveniles, teachers, and neighbors take over the control of substantial amounts of the child's behavior.

Two important results follow from the way the parents mediate the reinforcement of so much of the child's repertoire. First, the parents' presence serves as a discriminative stimulus that controls many of the performances the child is inclined to emit. These performances, mediated by the parents' behavior, are reinforced in the parents' presence and not in their absence. Hence, they have a higher frequency when parents are present than when they are absent. Second, the attention of parents becomes a conditioned reinforcer that can increase the frequency of other performances and whose removal may be aversive. Only in the presence of the parent is the verbal performance, "May I have a cookie?" reinforced by the parent saying "Yes". The verbal stimulus "yes" is, in turn, a reinforcer because it is an occasion when the parent hands the child the cookie or permits him to open the cookie jar. The function of the parent's attention as a discriminative stimulus can be observed when children frequently say "Mom" with a rising inflection, reinforced by the mother's attention, indicated by her saying "Yes, what do you want?"

Because so much of human behavior depends on the intervention of another person, the attention of the listener becomes an especially salient conditioned reinforcer whose importance increases as persons other than the parents mediate reinforcement of substantial parts of the child's behavior. The importance of the attention of the listener as a reinforcer also follows from the evanescent character of verbal behavior, whether vocal or gestural. Since vocal behavior does little more than vibrate air, its effectiveness depends on a listener whose behavior will be influenced at the moment the stimuli occur. Because of this quality of verbal interactions, there is a natural differential reinforcement of the child-speaker depending on the features of the adult listener on those occasions when the child's speech is influential and when it is not. The physical dimensions of attention are difficult to specify exactly, but they include facial posture, the orientation of the head, the focus of the eyes, nods, and verbal statements such as "Yes, what do you want?". A greeting such as "Hello" tends to be a discriminative stimulus that occasions the probability that performances of a speaker will have an influence. Because "attention" is a discriminative stimulus that is a prerequisite for the control of almost any interpersonal interaction, it is a powerful reinforcer.

The most subtle dimensions of attention come to control the speaker. Most people are controlled discriminatively by a few degrees of focus of another person's eyes. It is common experience at social gatherings to notice that someone is no longer paying attention when the eyes are focused just a few degrees past the person who is speaking and to whom he is purportedly listening. The behaviors reinforced by parental attention are especially visible in children because they have not yet been punished or differentially reinforced for persistent demands for attention without regard for the other person's circumstances. A parent who is reading intently is not likely to be influenced by a child's request for a cookie. In that case, the child is likely to repeat the request or tug at the parent's clothing until the parent replies or reacts in a way that indicates "attending." Such an interaction describes the differential reinforcement that establishes the parent's attention as a discriminative stimulus and reinforcer.

Approval has properties very similar to attention. It too is an occasion when many performances have a higher likelihood of reinforcement than in its absence. Like attention, the physical dimensions of approval are difficult to specify, partly because they are subtle and partly because they may vary so much from person to person and in various cultures. We ask a favor of people more readily when they are smiling than when they are frowning. It is important, however, to view the physical dimensions of approval as derived from the contingencies of reinforcement that they prompt. Frequently, culturally standard forms of approval may be reversed as in situations where smiling becomes a performance reinforced by the special effects related to the conditions of the smiler, rather than the person observing the smile. Under certain circumstances, persons smile when they are about to withdraw reinforcers, negatively reinforced by the avoidance of counter control, and frown when they naturally engage the other person. Gambling is one such circumstance where the function of a smile and frown, signifying approval and disapproval, are reversed. The poker player who smiles is likely to be one who is about to withdraw reinforcers.

## special properties of the generalized reinforcer

The unique property of the generalized reinforcer is that it can reinforce many performances. The preceding discussion of a child's development illustrated how the function of a generalized reinforcer is a continuous process paced with the emergence of new performances under the control of new reinforcers. The infant, for example, may initially emit sounds like "mama" which set the occasion for the mother to pick up the child and give it the opportunity to feed, look at her face, or touch her. With the enlargement of the child's capability, through physical maturation and shaping by the environment, the mother's reaction to the child's vocalization sets the occasion for a much wider range of performances under the control of many different reinforcers. The multiple and varied kinds of reinforcers that are occasioned by generalized reinforcers are in contrast to the sound of the food magazine in the typical animal experiment that controls only one performance by one deprivation. Thus, the pigeon or dog reinforced with food will not engage in any of the performances when it is fully satiated. Conditioned reinforcers, such as attention, approval, money, or control over the physical environment remain effective as long as any of the reinforcers on which they are based is effective. It is difficult to imagine an individual so satiated in every area of deprivation that money or attention would not be an effective discriminative stimulus that would control some behavior.

Generalized reinforcement is likely to be a prominent feature wherever the control of a person's behavior involves social interactions because adult human activity so completely involves performances that require the mediation of another person. As will be seen in the next chapter, the very nature of verbal behavior is derived from such mediation because it functions in a chain where the change in the other person's behavior is the reinforcer. Thus, the failure of verbal behavior that occurs in some kinds of mental illness may be a symptom of an underlying deficit of interpersonally reinforced performances rather than a primary one. If the child's history in the social environment results in a deficit in performances and reinforcers that are mediated by the significant adults, the weakening of verbal behavior would be an inevitable by-product. A miscarriage of any or all of the major behavioral processes could contribute to such a loss of reinforcers. Chapter 8 will describe some of the ways that basic behavioral processes may be used to describe some major disturbances of human conduct.

## deprivation in human behavior

The deprivation factor in human behavior does not, at first, appear to be as clear-cut as in animal experiments. The apparent discrepancy occurs, even when generalized reinforcement is not specifically operative, because the chains contain more performances with varying topographies and longer time periods then in animals. The individual hailing a taxi to go to a restaurant is controlled by a level of food deprivation rather than deprivation in respect to taxis. Securing the taxi is an intermediate element in a chain of performances leading to an opportunity to eat at a restaurant. The absence of a taxi will strengthen many behaviors reinforced by its appearance, such as looking up and down the street, whistling, or telephoning. We would not ordinarily say that the person is deprived of taxis. The taxi is a conditioned reinforcer, because it makes possible the subsequent behavior in the chain. Food deprivation, however, is the primary condition that controls all of the components. The same argument holds for generalized reinforcers such as attention, affection, or intimacy. The approval, affection, or intimacy with family and friends are parts of chains of behaviors that avoid isolation and neglect, lead to cooperation in social and practical ventures, and allow play. Thus the important deprivations concern the activities subsequent to the attention or affection.

Everyday ways of talking about conditioned reinforcers sometimes obscure the properties of these events that are clearer in technical descriptions. One such colloquialism, "He has an excessive need for attention" especially obscures the actual events and the variables controlling them. It implies that attention and approval are reinforcers that maintain behavior intrinsically rather than as conditioned reinforcers in a chain of behaviors that produce other important consequences. People who might be said to have an excessive need for attention have not been deprived of attention or approval in the sense that an animal is deprived of food. What is actually observed is a high frequency of behaviors that lead to attention, though not necessarily approval, of other persons. Such a person is one who induces others constantly to comment on his clothes, who talks long after the attention of the audience is lost and who, as a student, asks interminable questions to which the answers are already known. Since such performances are not effective and often aversive to the audience, they are not likely to be maintained by positive reinforcement. Whatever the analysis turns out to be in a particular case (these behaviors are likely to be determined by very different factors from case to case) the basic fact is that the "asking for attention" performances have a high frequency. To understand this behavior functionally we need to know the function of the performances. The problem is like the one we face in understanding a report of a person who runs persistently. A topographical description does not tell us of the functional antecedents of the behavior—whether the runner is exercising, hurrying to a positively reinforcing situation, or escaping from an aversive stimulus.

Although the functional analysis of "attention-getting performances" is highly complex and varied, it will still be useful to indicate some hypothetical conditions that might maintain them. One possible function is negative reinforcement by the avoidance of isolation or nonsupport. A similar function occurs with the student who asks repeated questions whose answers he either knows or in which he has no interest. The aversive events being terminated are those associated with threatened criticism or loss of esteem.

The discussion of generalized reinforcement highlights its differences from control by negative reinforcement. Its essential property is that a particular level of deprivation that underlies any of the component reinforcers has little influence on the effectiveness of the reinforcer. In negative reinforcement, however, the aversive stimulus specifies the performance to be emitted so narrowly that its properties are diametrically opposite to those of generalized reinforcement. For example, once a performance terminates a bright light or cold wind, that reinforcer is, by definition, no longer operative. This narrow specification of the performance in aversive control is the reason why aversive control in social situations has such undesirable effects and leads to so much difficulty when used in interpersonal relations or in therapy. Nongeneralized reinforcers, whether based on positive or negative reinforcement, are those performances that will be emitted only under the special circumstances of the particular deprivation or the explicit aversive stimulus, in contrast to the more varied and flexible interaction with the environment that is possible with behaviors maintained by generalized reinforcement.

## questions

1. Describe how money functions as a conditioned reinforcer in a chain of performances, and how it differs from the simple conditioned reinforcers described before with animals.

2. Describe how attention comes to be a conditioned reinforcer for the child in his normal environment.

3. Say how attention is functionally parallel to money.

4. Explain why attention comes to have the particular physical dimensions that it usually has. For example, the orientation of the head is sometimes a dimension of attention.

5. Point to examples of human behavior from previous chapters in which attention was the major reinforcer involved.

6. Say in what ways a generalized reinforcer is different from simple conditioned reinforcers.

7. Explain why changing the environment is an event which acquires the properties of a conditioned reinforcer.

8. Give examples of whole chains of performances strengthened by a deprivation operation.

9. Say why we do not attribute a high disposition to look for a taxi on the way to a restaurant to a deprivation of taxis.

10. Reformulate the performance implied by the phrase "need for attention" into a functional analysis of a chain of performances.

# notes

[1] Pierrel, R. and Sherman, J. G. Barnabus, the rat with college training. *Brown Alumni Monthly,* Feb. 1963, 8–14.

[2] Kelleher, R. T. Conditioned reinforcement in chimpanzees. *Journal of Comparative and Physiological Psychology* 49:571–575, 1957.

[3] Ferster, C. B. Sustained behavior under delayed reinforcement. *Journal of Experimental Psychology* 45:208–214, 1953.

[4] Lorenz, K. *Studies in animal and human behavior,* Vol. 1. London: Methuen, 1935.

[5] Holland, J. G. Human vigilance. *Science* 128:61–67, 1958.

[6] Wycoff, L. B., Jr. The role of observing responses in discrimination learning. *Psychological Review*, 59:431–442, 1952.

[7] Several theories have been proposed to explain the mechanism by which the reinforcement of observing behavior is maintained (Fantino, 1979). One imparts the cause to conditioned reinforcement that is derived from the pairing of the discriminative stimuli (produced by the observing performances) with positive reinforcement (Nevin, 1973). A second theory accounts for the observing behavior by noting that primary reinforcement is delayed less when the performances are under discriminative control. (Taus & Hearst, 1970). A third theory deals with a reduction in uncertainty that occurs when the performances are under discriminative control (Jenkins & Boakes, 1973). The third hypothesis could be thought of as mentalistic since it is not clear whether the uncertainty is an inferred mental event or a description of reinforcement contingencies. Nevertheless, it suggests that observing performances, by allowing the performances to be emitted under discriminative control, reduce the total amount of unreinforced behavior that will be emitted.

Fantino, E. Conditioned reinforcement: Choice and information. In Honig, W. K. and Staddon, J.E.R. (Eds.) *Handbook of operant conditioning.* New York: Prentice-Hall, 1979.

Nevin, J. A. Conditioned reinforcement. In: Nevin, J. A. and Reynolds, G. S. (Eds.) *The study of behavior.* Glenview, III: Scott, Foresman, 1973.

Taus, S. E. and Hearst E. Effects of intertrial duration (blackout) on response rate to a positive stimulus. *Psychonomic Science* 5:265–267, 1970.

Jenkins, H. M. and Boakes, R. A. Observing stimulus sources that signal food or no food. *Journal of the Experimental Analysis of Behavior* 20:197–207, 1973.

[8] Vandenberg, B. Play and development from an anthropological perspective. *American Psychologist* 33:724–738, 1978.

[9] Ploog, D. Verhatensforschung und Psychiatrie. In Gruhle, H. W. and Jung, R. (Eds.) *Psychiatrie der Gegenwart.* Berlin: Springer, 1946.

[10] Butler, R. Exploration and related behavior: A new trend in animal research. *Journal of Individual Psychology, 14*, 111–120.

[11] Creed, T. L. and Ferster, C. B. Space as a reinforcer in a continuous free-operant environment. *Psychological Record* 22:161–167, 1972.

[12] Findley, J. An experimental outline for building and exploring multi-operant behavioral repertoires. *Journal of the Experimental Analysis of Behavior* (5, supplement): 113–166, 1962.

# 8

# stimulus control in verbal behavior

In this chapter, the principles by which stimuli control operant performances are extended to verbal communication. This is done by analyzing how the behavior of the listener is influenced by verbal stimuli produced by the speaker.

As in other kinds of operant behavior, the actual form of the behavior (its topography) is not so important as the change it effects in the environment. In the case of verbal behavior, this change occurs in the repertoire of the listener. The analysis of the vocal performance of the speaker, therefore, cannot be made simply in terms of the physical dimensions of the vocal performance or the description of the auditory stimulus. The chapter examines how textual stimuli, in reading, occasion a complex interaction with the individual's larger repertoire. The process is examined by describing how reading behaviors are developed educationally.

Performances that appear identical may be very different depending on the conditions that generate them. In colloquial language we refer to the speaker's *intention*. Technically, we talk about the variables that are responsible for the performance. An example is developed in which the word *toast*, emitted by the speaker, has very different functional significance depending upon whether it occurs as a result of a prior textual stimulus, an auditory vocal stimulus, a level of deprivation, or a nonverbal stimulus in the environment. The verbal stimulus differs from other kinds of stimuli because of the complexity of its dimensions, such as the order

**264**

of the words, the temporal spacing of accent, and the pitch changes of intonation. The control of the listener by all of the elements of the auditory or textual stimulus is analyzed in Part III in terms of the same basic processes by which any operant performance comes under the control of a stimulus.

Although verbal performances are operant behaviors that represent repertoires in a speaker or writer, verbal behavior is best analyzed in terms of the control these behaviors exert on the listener or reader. Verbal behavior, like other operant behavior, is fundamentally described by its unique effect on the environment that differentially reinforces it. In the case of speaking, this reinforcer is the influence on or the change in the behavior of the listener.

## technical terms

echoic
intraverbal
mand
tact
verbal behavior

## outline

Part I:   The Nature of Verbal Behavior
          The social nature of verbal behavior
          Verbal behavior as an operant
          Different modes of verbal behavior
          A refined definition of verbal behavior
          Verbal behavior as communication

Part
  II:    Functional Categories of Verbal Behavior
          A functional rather than a topographic description of verbal behavior
          The mand
          Echoic behavior
          Textual behavior
          Intraverbal behavior
          The tact

Part
  III:   Dynamic and Interactional Aspects of Verbal Behavior
          The expansion of the intraverbal repertoire from mand, echoic, textual, and tact performances
          The audience as a discriminative stimulus controlling the speaker's behavior
          meaning

## part I: the nature of verbal behavior

### the social nature of verbal behavior

Verbal behavior differs from other kinds of performances because it is not reinforced directly.[1] Rather, it produces a stimulus that influences the behavior of another person. The influence on the listener, in vocal behavior, can be an effective reinforcer for speaking even when there is no practical consequence supplied by the listener. The essential character of the process is the discriminative control of the listener's repertoire by the verbal stimuli presented by the speaker. The discriminative control of an operant performance that was presented in Chapter 6 is the major process underlying verbal interaction.

Figure 8-1 illustrates a simple interaction where stimuli produced by the speaker are reinforced by the behavior that they prompt in a listener. This episode, of a child asking the parent for toast, is minimally verbal because the reinforcer maintaining the child's verbal activity depends on food deprivation. Nevertheless, such an interaction is a useful place to begin because all the component events are observable and illustrate the social nature of verbal behavior.

The immediate change in the environment caused by the child's speech is the vibration of the air. That stimulus influences the parent because it is a discriminative stimulus that already controls some of her behavior. If seeing the child eat is a reinforcing event, then the child's speech simply provides the discriminative stimulus for the reinforcement of an existing performance. The same is true if the verbal stimulus "toast" is a conditioned aversive stimulus because the child had cried or otherwise acted aversively in past occasions when no cookie was given. In that case, the parent's behavior is negatively reinforced by terminating the child's crying. The essential properties of verbal behavior that are unique involve reinforcement by a change in the verbal behavior of the listener rather

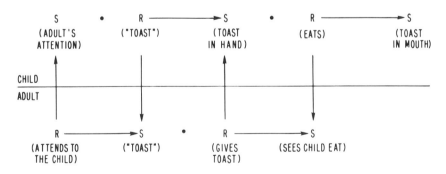

**Figure 8-1**  A simple verbal behavior interaction.

than a practical result, like the cookie in the example above. Categories of verbal behavior, to be described later, will be more illustrative of verbal interactions than these are because they are not limited by a practical result for the speaker.

## verbal behavior as an operant

The actual behavior of speaking is a complex integration of muscle movements of the mouth, tongue, lips, larynx, diaphragm, and chest. These movements are reinforced by the patterns and magnitudes of vibrating air that they produce. When we say that someone spoke a "word," what we know behaviorally is that the vocal muscles moved in such a way as to produce air vibrations prompting that verbal performance in a listener. But the reinforcement of the speaker's behavior would be considerably delayed if it were, in fact, reinforced by the change in the behavior of the listener. The sound produced by the vocal muscles is the only reinforcer that could produce such highly differentiated forms of vocal behavior.

It is because the speaker and listener are both within the same skin (the child can listen to himself speak) that the reaction of the listener can provide an instant, generically connected, reinforcer for speaking. We have only to observe the huge disruption in speech that occurs when hearing is anatomically damaged to appreciate how the sounds of speech reinforce the performances of speaking. Delaying speech electronically, using earphones, has the same drastic impact.

It is because the child is alternately speaker and listener that her repertoire as listener can instantly reinforce speaking and be its generic counterpart. The process occurs in its simplest form in the kind of verbal operant called *echoic behavior*. The behavior of the speaker as her or his own listener is the critical element in echoic behavior—the kind of verbal behavior that replicates, echoes, or imitates the sound that is heard. It is instructive to describe the acquisition of echoic behavior in three steps. The first requirement is a process whereby the person becomes an effective listener, perhaps even before he or she is a speaker. The requirement is stated more accurately in behavioral terms when we observe that the speech of adults influences a child as discriminative stimuli. These discriminative stimuli acquire control over operant performances because they define the occasions when the operants are reinforced and when they are not. Such discriminative control occurs when parents carry on a running comment to the child about their activities. For example, mothers commonly talk of their activities in the third person as they prepare a bottle, change a diaper or hold and play with the child: "Mommy will have your bottle in a few minutes—don't you fret;" "Mommy will be right back;" "Let Mommy warm this bottle for you;" At other times the mother might describe the child's activity saying, for example, "You're crying" or "You finally found your thumb." On other occasions the mother's appearance will be preceded by a sibling's statement, "Mom, the baby's up." Although we cannot say at what age the verbal stimulus "mama" or "bottle" function as discriminative stimuli, they will eventually control performances such as looking up and searching. The behavior prompted by "Daddy's coming" in a 15-month-old child will be very different from that controlled by "Here's Mom," because each represents a consistent pattern of reinforcement of different performances. The process can be best described by the three-term contingency that was introduced in Chapter 6, $S^D \cdot P \rightarrow S^r$. The speech sounds are the $S^D$, the performances might be turning the head or looking around, and the reinforcer is the sight of the person, followed, in turn, by interactions with the person. The voice tone of the parent predicts important events and therefore acquires discriminative properties in a way that is parallel to what occurs with structured speech. A tense worried parent might diaper roughly and feed insensitively to the child's participation. A preoccupied parent might delay feeding or diaper change, and the likelihood of play will be closely correlated with the voice and facial expression.

Once the sound patterns of the particular words and language function as discriminative stimuli, the second development can take place. Any sounds the child makes can now influence himself as listener in the same way that occurs when he hears the speech of others. Whereas, heretofore, the child only looked to the driveway when it heard "Dad" and to the other room when it heard "Mom," that differential reactivity can now be a reinforcer for the child's speech. If a child can distinguish between "Daddy," "Dotty," and "potty" when these stimuli are produced by another speaker, he will be able to be similarly controlled by the same sounds when he produces them himself. Furthermore, the sound of his own speech is a reinforcer that has a generic relation to the required performance, such as the relation between the balance of the ball on the seal's nose and the movements of its neck muscles.

Playing a musical instrument such as the violin illustrates the balance between speaker as her own listener and the outside listener. The actual performances are the movements of the bow and the pressure of the fingers on the strings. The reinforcer, generically connected to the performance, is the sound that results. But before the sounds can be effective reinforcers, the player needs to have performances that are under the discriminative control of the pitch and tone quality differences that she needs to produce. Such discriminative control arises in interactions with external listeners and the performances may be entirely verbal, of the form "That's right," "That's flat," "That's sharp," "That's a full tone quality." So, in playing the violin as in speech, the player as listener provides the immediate reinforcer for the movements that "play the violin."

The third stage of the process concerns the maintenance of the performance in the sense of its persistence. One kind of reinforcement of such a performance is practical as occurs when "cookie" is part of a chain of performances that eventually produces a cookie. The performance has a more verbal function by its echoic aspect, as will occur when the parent deliberately sets out to teach the child by saying "doll" in reply.

**A comparison of asking for cookie and replying echoically to the auditory stimulus "cookie"**  The reinforcement of the echoic performance, in the sense of the instant, immediate consequence of the performance, is identical with the examples where the verbal performances occurred because they brought a cookie or other practical consequences of the parent's attention. In both cases, the instant, immediate consequence that follows and shapes the performance is the sound it produces. But the nature of the operant, in the sense of the consequence ultimately maintaining it, is entirely different in the two cases. If the verbal performance "doll" occurs because the child is inclined to play with dolls and that performance in the past has induced the parent to supply a doll, the operant is aptly described as one controlled by a level of deprivation of the speaker. The reinforcer ultimately maintaining the behavior is the actual receipt of the doll. In the case where the child simply repeats what it has just heard, an echoic operant, the reinforcement is generalized because the performance is controlled largely by the prior stimulus, through the parent's approval acting as a representative of the particular language that is being spoken.

**The objective description of vocal behavior**  The most accurate description of the vocal performances in verbal behavior would be a record of the movements of the lips, tongue, diaphragm, chest muscles, and vocal chords, but the complexity of these interrelated muscle movements is so great and they are mostly inaccessible to direct observation. Any attempt to describe them is virtually unthinkable. Furthermore, our interest is in the sounds produced by the muscle movements rather than the movements themselves. The sounds produced by the vocal apparatus are accessible and could be measured by physical techniques, but these too, despite the objectivity and exactness of the physical measurements by a sound spectrograph, would be complex and voluminous. It is for this reason that the behavior of the listener is the most often used record of vocal behavior. The auditory stimulus that the listener produces, say in an echoic performance, may be only a rough copy of the original auditory stimulus because the nuances of accent, voice quality, and intonation will be lost. The record becomes more accurate if the listener is a trained mimic and can echo the auditory stimulus precisely. A listener trained in phonetic transcription may be even more precise in the reproduction of the auditory stimulus. All of the advantages of using a listener to record the behavior of the speaker are lost, however, if the recording detail is made finer by the use of a sound spectrograph.

These considerations are presented because of the confusion between speaker and listener that occurs in the ordinary ways of talking about vocal behavior as "words." The auditory vocal stimulus bridges the repertoire of the speaker and listener. For the speaker, the word is an auditory stimulus that results from the performances of the vocal musculature. For the listener, however, the same auditory stimulus causes the emission of the performance that had been previously conditioned. The meaning of the auditory stimulus, therefore, comes from the behavior it controls in the listener. This behavioral view of vocal stimuli makes it clear why "the meaning of a word" may be very different for the speaker than it is for the listener. The speaker as listener offers a complication. At one moment the control is exerted by variables of which the speaking is a function. At the next moment, the significance of one's speaking is the behavior it prompts in oneself as listener.

## different modes of verbal behavior

Ordinarily we think of verbal behavior as speaking, but vocal behavior is only one of the forms that it may take. Verbal behavior may also be gestures or the use of sign language. In the case of the deaf mute, the verbal performance is the movements of the fingers, and the function as listener is accomplished through the visual pattern of lip movements or the visual patterns produced on another "speaker's" fingers. Code through signal flags or sound signals transmitted electronically are also parallel to speaking and listening. The behavioral control between horse and rider is essentially verbal, with the rider's action on the reins equivalent to speaking, and the horse's response to the pressures of the reins on its back and through the bit in its mouth equivalent to the function of the listener.

**Textual behavior**    Verbal behavior is textual when the writer pro-duces stimuli with pen, pencil, or typewriter that in turn control similar performances in the reader as they did in the writer. Parallel to the listener and speaker in the vocal mode are the reader and writer in the textual mode. At its simplest level reading is the emission of a verbal performance under the point-to-point discriminative control of a textual stimulus.

The various modes of verbal behavior are functionally equivalent be-cause they are reinforced by the performances that they prompt in an-other person's repertoire rather than by a direct effect on the environment. When the sailor on the battleship waves the signal flags, the alterations in the positions of the flags produce only a minor change in the environment. The flags, however, control the behavior of the person who aims and fires the gun; or it controls the behavior of a pilot operating the controls of a large aircraft during landing; or the behavior of a person releasing a catapult. Because the alteration of the environment produced by the speaker's behavior is so slight, the major emphasis in the analysis of verbal behavior is the study of how the listener's behavior is increased or decreased in frequency by the stimuli produced by the speaker. The principle is carried in the aphorism, "Speak softly but carry a big stick." This is, of course, another way of saying that the previously conditioned behavior of the listener is the reinforcer that maintains and is the generic counterpart of the behavior of the speaker.

## a refined definition of verbal behavior

The difference between social behavior controlled by its influence on another person and verbal behavior is slight but crucially important. A person who drops a pellet into the food tray every time the rat presses the lever is in a social interaction where the behavior of each party is maintaining that of the other. The social character of the episode is conveyed by a cartoon showing a rat pressing a lever and saying, "Boy, have I got that guy conditioned! Every time I press the lever he drops a pellet of food." But there would be no advantage in describing such an interaction as verbal since it has no special characteristics apart from the separate reinforcement of each individual's performances. We come closer to a verbal situation in the interaction of a horse and rider.[2] Many of the horse's performances are already under the discriminative control of the pressures that the rider applies through the reins. The rider's performances, handling the reins, is reinforced by the direction and pace taken by the horse. The rider illustrates the function of the speaker and the horse that of the listener in verbal interactions that are vocal. The interaction between horse and rider is verbal because there is a language, already controlling the horse, that is tapped by the stimuli presented by the rider. It is for that reason that a trained horse's reactivity can differentially reinforce the appropriate behavior in the repertoire of a naive rider. The interaction would not be verbal, however, if the rider negatively reinforced "turning" or "stopping" by increasing the pressure of the bit in the horse's mouth to aversive magnitudes. Thus, it is to the special reactivity of the listener that we look for the defining characteristics of a verbal interaction. A language represents just such a reactivity because it specifies the listener's conditioning history that, in turn, specifies what performances of speaker will tap the listener's potential activity. In terms of the verbal development of a child, the language spoken by the parents functions as a large set of reinforcement contingencies that completely accounts for the child's emerging verbal behavior.

## verbal behavior as communication

A discussion of verbal behavior would not be complete without mention of the notion of communication, a concept that has wide usage in common language and in that view of language termed "information theory." "He communicates ideas clearly," "communication between them is difficult," "the communication of information," "the teacher communicates knowledge," and so forth, are some of the common expressions that occur colloquially. The term is not a productive one for a behavioral analysis, despite its wide usage, because it is a verb whose object is usually some mental or hypothetical entity such as ideas or information. Such terms, although they have a meaningful connotation, are less useful than a behavioral description because they obscure the details of a verbal interaction. The lecture is a commonly used vehicle for the transmission of knowledge and ideas and for that reason its analysis behaviorally will serve to illustrate how concepts of verbal behavior presented here provide an alternative to common-sense accounts of the same events.

The problem could be stated as follows: How can one person increase another's verbal repertoire by talking? In common-sense terms we think of the lecture as a way that one person communicates ideas to another. There is, however, the contradiction that nothing actually passes between the two people. Speaking is, after all, movements of the vocal musculature that vibrate the air. This movement of air can influence a listener only by increasing the frequency of existing performances. Therefore, for the lecturer to have any influence over the listener, there needs to be a repertoire in the listener that can be cued, triggered, or prompted by the air movements around his ears.

It is paradoxical that communication is perfect when the speaker and listener have identical repertoires. In that case, the speech sounds produced by the speaker can prompt their exact counterparts from the repertoire of the listener. But despite the perfect fit between the two repertoires, nothing is communicated in the common sense of the word. Paradoxically, when speaker and listener have entirely different repertoires, a circumstance where there is much to communicate, no influence at all is possible between them. In that case, the sounds made by the speaker cannot prompt any pre-existing behavior. Clearly, the middle ground, where the speaker and listener have a substantial portion of their repertoires in common, is the most useful one.

The range of circumstances when a speaker can influence a listener is surprisingly limited. To achieve the intended effect on the study the lecturer needs to tap three kinds of behaviors. Consider a teaching situation where the lecturer is telling the student that "magnesium is a metal." The first and simplest behavior, from a repertoire already established in the student, is the echoing of what has just been heard. The comparable form in the textual mode would be writing the same phrase. The second behavior that might be prompted is that of predication: affirming or asserting something about the subject of the sentence. Here, the word order, *"blank* is a *blank,"* is an instruction (discriminative stimulus) for saying about the first noun everything that can be said about the second: "Man is an animal," "three is a number," or "a carrot is a vegetable." You may say similar things of "man," "three," and "carrot" that you can say of "animals," "numbers," and "vegetables" respectively. Third, the predicate itself needs to be connected, intraverbally, to a broad range of performances. It is of no use for the student to say the same things about magnesium as about metals unless there is an extensive metals repertoire. The repertoire would consist of saying sentences such as: 1) metals form cations by the loss of one or more electrons from each atom; 2) they form basic oxides and hydroxides; 3) they conduct electricity; 4) they fuse and are malleable. If such behaviors already are potential items in the listener's repertoire that will be emitted if adequately prompted by discriminative stimuli, then we can expect the student to say about magnesium what we could say about metals. The increment in repertoire accomplished by the lecture in this case is a rearrangement of existing performances. Without these intraverbal connections to "metal," the instructional value of "magnesium is a metal" is limited. If the intraverbal performances are missing, the educational task of developing the missing intraverbal performances is too complex a task for a lecture mode. Or, to put the matter in another way, without the listener's intraverbal connections to metal, there is little basis for communication.

It may seem a paradox that the listener needs essentially the same repertoire as the lecturer if communication is to be effective. What then was communicated? Actually, an instruction was communicated—a rearrangement of existing verbal performances so that new combinations could occur. There are, of course, many other ways that the lecturer and student can interact in behalf of the task of increasing the student's repertoire. All of the ways that a speaker can influence a listener require that there be explicit behaviors already in the student's repertoire. Without them, speech is obviously just the movement of warm, moistened, vibrating air about the student's head.

Of course, lectures do often influence individuals in the audience, but it is important to specify which kinds of behaviors can be changed and under which conditions. Following are categories of influence that a lecturer may have upon an audience.

1.  The simplest reaction is the echoic performance described previously. The student listener repeats, vocally, exactly what the lecturer says, paced with the lecture. There is little significance to such echoic behavior since it exists only so long as the echoic stimulus is present. Unless its function shifts to other verbal operants, such as intraverbal behavior,[3] it could be described

as parroting. In the absence in the student's repertoire of a substantial amount of the behavior that the lecturer intends, the echoic performances will be evanescent. Furthermore, the pace of the stimulation from the lecture is such that any verbal process that might be possible for converting the echoic performance to intraverbal behavior would take too long compared with the pace of the lecture.

2. The lecturer may have emotional effects on the students as they laugh at funny anecdotes or hear a poignant tale. Such experiences may be rewarding in the sense that the students are likely to return next time, but there is no guarantee that they will even be able to repeat any of the stories.

3. The student and lecturer may have almost identical repertoires because their backgrounds are common, because the student is well prepared or because the lecturer has adjusted to the estimated repertoire of the student. The echoic reaction becomes a bridge between the two repertoires, prompting the intraverbal reactions in the student that correspond to those of the teacher. Such an interaction may be pleasurable, like the child at bedtime hearing a familiar story that he could almost tell independently, or it may be described as boring.

4. The student may try to overcome the evanescent nature of the spoken word by transcribing the entire lecture. This still leaves the requirement of interacting with the text so as to produce an intraverbal counterpart of the transcription. Note-taking may take a more productive form, however, when the student composes a note designed to produce the same effect on himself as the momentary effect of the lecture. By emitting behaviors that are discriminatively controlled by the speech of the lecturer the student effectively ties their repertoires together at the point of the verbal stimuli that have an effect that is in common. The process is subtle and cannot be observed overtly, but its existence seems a likely inference from the nature of the verbal processes that occur.

Considering the complexity of verbal transactions such as those described above and the limited conditions where they can be effective, it is surprising that there are times when listening is productive. The conditions when a verbal stimulus fails to create durable behavior in a listener are not limited to complicated experiences, such as a chemistry lecture. Communication often fails with simple language, the elements of which already influence the speaker in appropriate ways. Many persons have had the experience of asking directions and being told, "Go three blocks east, turn down Cantmiss Lane—there's a narrowing of the road as it curves off to the supermarket—and turn right at the third traffic light. You'll know it because it's a very busy intersection with a gas station." All of the behavior prompted by these verbal stimuli are potentially in the repertoire of the listener and they could be repeated one at a time. Yet, most people would not be able to follow them. The verbal stimuli might have been effective, however, as with the chemistry subject matter, if the traveler could already talk about the features of the neighborhood. Even when the behavior to be prompted is potentially in the listener's repertoire, a major difficulty of vocal interactions is the evanescence of the auditory stimulus. The text solves the problem of evanescence of the verbal stimulus, but, like the lecture, we cannot assume that saying the words from a text necessarily, of itself, will enlarge the student's intraverbal capacity.

Some of the reasons for giving and attending lectures may be found in other than enlargement of the student's intraverbal capacity. Some students come because of the emotional effects described above. Some come to avoid aversive consequences that follow from absence. Others, like the child with the fairy tale, come to hear a familiar discussion. Sometimes the lecture may bridge the repertoire of the lecturer and the student so that selected parts of the student's pre-existing repertoire are strengthened in unique combinations not likely to occur without the lecturer. The ideal relations for purposes of intellectual enlargement is similar to that of two people working together on an algebra problem or puzzle. They may approach the solution by essentially the same path, having similar intraverbal histories, but the one who emits the solution first becomes the speaker. The other is a well-prepared listener affected almost as strongly by the same controlling variable. The essential point is that the speaker does not build the repertoire in the listener. He can only prompt, modify, or rearrange verbal behavior already latent in the listener's repertoire. Thus, the interaction between the two was most productive when their repertoires were similar but not identical. The listener was well prepared for the speaker as evidenced by the fact that he would have said the same thing given another short period of time. The same point is illustrated by a skilled public speaker who gauges the repertoire of the audience and finds things to say that can prompt latent verbal behavior. A skilled conversationalist prompts and probes until the high frequency items in the other person's repertoire are tapped. Conversely, the lecturer often faces the task of talking to students whose repertoire he cannot probe so that it is problematical whether the verbal stimuli of the lecture will control enough of the student's behavior. A psychotherapist interprets a client's behavior when the client is very close to saying the same thing.

## questions

1. How does the interaction when a child asks for toast illustrate the social nature of verbal behavior? Why is it described as minimally verbal?

2. Why is the speaker's reaction to his or her own speech the reinforcer maintaining it even though the verbal behavior is social?

3. What are the necessary behavioral developments before a child can reply echoically?

*4.* How does playing a musical instrument illustrate how the discriminative control—by the music the player hears—provides the basis for the immediate reinforcer for playing?

*5.* Why are measurements of vocal muscles or a sound spectrograph not a workable way to record language objectively?

*6.* Describe how different modes of verbal behavior are equivalent.

*7.* Describe reading behaviorally at its simplest level.

*8.* Describe the "grain" of the control by elements of the textual stimulus of the reader's vocal performance.

*9.* How is the refined definition of verbal behavior different from a child getting food by crying?

*10.* Why is the interaction between horse and rider said to be verbal?

*11.* What are the disadvantages of a term such as "communication" compared with a behavioral description of the verbal interaction that is involved?

*12.* How does the interaction between lecturer and audience expose the difficulties inherent in concepts like communication?

*13.* What are the kinds of momentary influences that a lecturer can have on a listener?

*14.* Under what conditions can the listener overcome the evanescent aspects of the lecturer's influence?

---

## part II: functional categories of verbal behavior

### a functional rather than a topographic description of verbal behavior

Little is known about a verbal performance without knowledge of the kind of reinforcer or deprivation that generated it or the prior stimuli that control it. For example, the vocal performance "boy" may be controlled by a pleasant surprise in the sense of, "Isn't this grand?" It might be a command for a boy to appear. It could be a reply to a question, "What did you just say?" It could be a performance controlled by the text, *boy*. It could be a description of a person. When we talk about the meaning of a word, we generally refer to the variables of which a verbal performance is a function. Identical topographies of verbal performances, as in the examples above, are reinforced by very different outcomes. A functional analysis of a verbal performance is a close behavioral equivalent of the linguistic concepts of reference and meaning. To explore further examples, consider the various conditions that might control the emission of a performance such as "toast." In its simplest form, saying "toast" is controlled echoically when the child hears the parent say "toast" and repeats the same sound. Here, the control is in a prior auditory stimulus and the reinforcer generalized. If the child says "toast" in the presence of a text and there is some presumption that the vocal performance is controlled by it, we say he is reading. If he hears "toast" in the absence of a prior stimulus and the child has not eaten for some time, we would say that the performance occurs because it produces toast. When a piece of toast is present, the same performance may be discriminative of toast, in the same sense that presence of the mail carrier would be announced when mail is being delivered. The only immediate result in this last case is a stimulus that alters the parent's behavior, with little immediate consequence for the child.

Thus, virtually identical topographies of vocal behavior are instances of very different operant performances. When we hear a child say "toast," we can't be sure whether the child is reading, emitting an echoic operant, emitting a performance controlled by food deprivation, or announcing the presence or absence of toast. In practice, however, there are collateral properties of the verbal operant that correlate with its function. The child asking for toast might speak loudly or whine, be deprived of food, or be in a situation where food has been obtained in the past. When announcing the presence of a piece of toast, the pitch of the word is likely to start high and fall. If there were an immediately preceding auditory stimulus, we are likely to guess that the operant was echoic, particularly if the latency were short, there was no food deprivation, and no toast present. If we saw the child's eyes focus on a text, we would be fairly sure that the operant was textual, particulary if the performance lacked the dynamic quality of conversational speech.

Many homonyms in the English language are examples of the functional rather than the topographical control of vocal behavior. The word "pit," by itself might control a listener as a hole in the ground or as the inside of a fruit. "Well" may control the listener as a water hole or it may be emitted to describe a person who is not sick. The phrase "bank it" will control very different behavior in a house with a coal furnace when it is night time than it will in situations where there is talk about money. The effective control of the listener's behavior depends on the concurrent control by other stimuli, such as word order and context.

## the mand

The mand is a technical term describing a kind of verbal operant that has already been presented earlier as, for example, in the social interaction where the child asks a parent for toast.[4] The term has the connotations of demand or command, but the technical term is introduced to de-emphasize hypothetical inner states that are likely to be invoked as, for example, when we say, conversationally, that the child demanded food to get something to eat or that someone said "get out" because they were annoyed. By emphasizing the mand as an operant performance we have an opportunity to uncover and specify the details of its control by explicit variables that we can describe objectively.

As with all operant behavior, we need to take into account all three terms of the operant paradigm—the verbal performance, the stimuli preceding it that exert discriminative control over it, and the reinforcer maintaining it. The feature of the mand that distinguishes it from the other verbal operants that will be described in the next sections is that it names the reinforcer that maintains it and requires the presence of a related level of deprivation or aversive stimulation. We say "move over" when someone's proximity is aversive; the reinforcer is an increase in the distance. We say "pass the bread" when there is a sufficient level of food deprivation; the reinforcer is the emission of the behavior leading to its ingestion. Some examples of mands, set out below in relation to the three terms of the operant paradigm, illustrate its defining property.

| Discriminative Stimulus | Performance | Reinforcer |
|---|---|---|
| 1. Last forkful of beans | "More beans" | A helping of beans |
| 2. An arm lock | "Say you're sorry" | "I am sorry" |
| 3. A loud voice | "Stop shouting" | Quiet |
| 4. Baby with a marble | "Give it to me" | Baby without marble |
| 5. The presence of an unknown person | "What's your name?" | "Frank" |

Each of these mands specifies the consequence that will maintain its frequency (reinforce it). For item 1) the reinforcer is the receipt of food; for 2) it is the admission of regret; for 3) it is the cessation of the shouting; for 4) the removal of the marble; and for 5) it is the statement of the person's name. These performances would not occur if the person were not: 1) food deprived; 2) physically stressed; 3) aversively stimulated; 4) threatened with the possibility of the child's swallowing the marble; or 5) faced with the inconvenience of an unnamed person.

A useful distinction among various kinds of mands is made by considering what induces the listener to comply by providing the reinforcer indicated by the speaker's mand. We designate a mand as a command when the listener complies because the demanded performance is negatively reinforced by the removal of the threat posed by the speaker. When the reinforcement for the mand benefits the listener as well as the speaker, the mand has the form of advice: "If you got more sleep you would do better in your studies." When the listener's compliance to a mand is negatively reinforced by terminating an emotional state induced by the speaker, we call the mand an entreaty: "If you have an ounce of pity and a little bit of humanity, you would not press me for the payment of the debt now." The significance of these distinctions is the way that they clarify the variables that govern the behaviors of the speaker and listeners in a social interaction of this form.

By and large, the reinforcement of most mands occurs because the listener escapes aversive stimuli from the speaker by complying with the reinforcer specified by the speaker's mand. This follows naturally from the property of the mand as a performance whose reinforcer is relevant to the behavior of the speaker. It is for this reason that the listener's compliance needs to be negatively reinforced by aversive stimuli applied by the speaker. As we will see when we compare it to other verbal operants, the mand is only minimally verbal because it is so much determined by the level of deprivation or aversive stimulation of the speaker rather than by the verbal behavior that it prompts in the listener. But, on the other hand, mands like "move over" differ from practical operants such as pushing someone out of the way. However practical the ultimate consequences of the mand may be, the constraints on the performance are less than when the performance changes the environment directly. This is because the mand operates through the verbal repertoire of a listener. The less the listener controls the speaker, the fewer the constraints there are on the mand. One of the characteristics of psychoses and neuroses is that the speaker's control by the listener is reduced or distorted. This results in a high frequency of mands even though they are mostly emitted under circumstances where they cannot be reinforced. The same process occurs in everyday behavior when deprivation or aversive stimulation exceed those that occur typically. For example, a perspiring athlete says, "Gosh, I wish I had a glass of water," even though there is no water available in the vicinity and there is no possibility that his companion could supply it. A person late for work is often heard muttering, "Where *is* that bus?" The novel, *Portnoy's Complaint* by Phillip Roth presents a litany of mands emitted in the presence of a therapist even though the reinforcers specified by the mands could not possibly occur as, for example, when the patient complains about his upbringing by a deceased parent. The situation is similar when the mother of a soldier cries for the return of her son. These are called extended mands because they are extensions from other situations where similar mands are reinforced. The loosening of discriminative control in play leads to the same kind of extension of the mand when, for example, a child asks her doll to sit down or to pay attention. The extended mands occur in play because the frequency of the mand increases relative to the discriminative control inherent in the surrounding circumstances. It is in this sense that mands that occur in play represent a breakdown in discriminative control, as well as the other conditions that favor its extension.

Another kind of extended mand is exemplified by the football fan's "catch it" while watching a game or the dice player's "come seven." The process, different from the extensions described above, is accidental reinforcement that illustrated the temporal nature of reinforcement discussed in Chapter 1. These mands are called superstitious because, unlike the child and its doll or the thirsty athlete, reinforcement actually occurs. The outfielder does frequently catch the ball and a seven does sometimes appear after the dice player calls for it.

Because the mand is not a grammatical or formal unit, it may often occur in a covert form. That is, the behaviors that function as a mand may be discernible to an observer who is trained to describe the variables of which the performance is a function, even though the person emitting it may not be able to observe or state them. For example, the high frequency that a child looks at the candy set out on the table indicates a mand. Even though the child may never ask for it overtly or perhaps be unable to notice her inclination to eat it, the performance is a mand because it specifies the reinforcer and is controlled by the deprivation in respect to eating candy.

## echoic behavior

Echoic behavior has already been discussed in Part I to illustrate the way that sounds produced by the voice muscles were the reinforcers generically connected to the performances. The speaker as his or her own listener is especially important in echoic behavior. The effectiveness of this repertoire requires that the speaker be closely controlled by the differences between the auditory stimulus just heard and the one he or she has just produced. Such echoic performances are examples of the fine-grain repertoires discussed in Chapter 6, where there was a point-to-point correspondence between the discriminative stimulus and the performance it controlled. To the extent that the speaker can distinguish between auditory stimulus and the approximation produced, the correspondence produced will differentially reinforce the vocal performances necessary to reproduce the exact stimulus. Echoic behavior is verbal because its reinforcement is entirely a change in the verbal activity of the listener, unrelated to any immediate practical benefit to the speaker. Echoic behavior as it is generated educationally, formally and informally, is more to the purposes of the listener whose concern is in expanding the child's repertoire than it is for the child whose repertoire is expanded. The difference in function between echoic behavior and the mand, when both have the same topography, is critically important. When the child repeats the sound "candy" after hearing someone speak, the performance is echoic, and when "candy" is spoken because it has produced the actual foodstuff, it is a mand. In the first case, the echoic performance, the control is primarily in the prior stimulus, and the generalized reinforcer maintaining the performance does not encourage any special benefits for the speaker to influence it. "Candy" reinforced by the receipt of the foodstuff, however, will take any form that will be effective in inducing a listener to comply.

Even though echoic behavior reinforcement is generalized and the process is a verbal one, its emission may still have an important function for the speaker. When someone repeats what was just spoken, there is time to compose a reply. Repeating something is a way to overcome the evanescence of the verbal stimulus by prolonging it, and the point-to-point correspondence of the echoic performance with the prior stimulus that controls it discriminatively makes it more likely that the listener will be controlled by the details of the stimulus. Another consequence of echoic behavior is a reinforcer that maintains the behavior of the speaker. The listener's echoic performance is evidence that the speaker is having an influence and hence is akin to "attention" and other such generalized reinforcers. Echoic behavior is prominently reinforced in the child's early interaction with the parental environment because it is an important means of expanding the child's verbal repertoire. Once a child has a full echoic repertoire, virtually every verbal performance in the language is potentially available. To the extent that the child can distinguish between the echoic stimulus and the approximations to it that he produces vocally, the correspondence between the two will differentially reinforce the vocal behavior that is necessary to reproduce the exact stimulus. The process is yet another illustration of the generic nature of the performance defined by its reinforcer.

## textual behavior

Textual behavior refers to those verbal performances controlled by textual stimuli. The reader and the writer are parallel to the speaker and listener in the vocal mode. In the reader, the discriminative stimulus is textual and the performance is vocal. In transcription, the stimulus is vocal and the performance is textual.

Transcription—copying a text or writing what one hears—is usefully described in ways similar to echoic behavior. The difference is in the form of the performance and the kind of prior stimulus that controls it. The performance is writing and the prior stimulus is the text or voice that is being transcribed. The grain of the correspondence between the auditory stimulus and the performance it controls is necessarily not as fine in textual transcription as it would be in echoic behavior. The correspondence becomes very close, however, in phonetic transcription. Transcriptive textual behavior, thus defined, concerns the writer rather than the reader and is a minimally verbal process compared to the behavior that the reader exhibits. It is another indication of the relative importance of the listener in a verbal analysis relative to that of the speaker. Both echoic and textual behavior emphasize the control by the prior stimulus, the auditory stimulus that is repeated or the text that is copied, to the exclusion of the momentary states of deprivation or aversive stimulation influencing the speaker. As with echoic behavior, the instant immediate consequence of the transcriptive performance is important. In echoic behavior the immediate reinforcer was derived from existing discriminative control by the echoed sounds. In transcription, there is an additional step in a chain of performances. The auditory stimulus controls a textual performance, writing, reinforced by the physical appearance of the text produced by the pen or the typewriter. These, in turn, are discriminative stimuli that control a vocal performance, reading, that produces an auditory stimulus. Although the correspondence between the auditory stimulus and the one being transcribed ultimately maintains the transcription, the textual stimulus that appears is the reinforcer that is generically related to the transcribing performance.

**Reading**  In reading, the discriminative stimulus is textual and the performance is vocal. As with echoic and transcriptive behavior, the reinforcer is generalized. That is, the reinforcement of the vocal performance serves to restrict its control to the prior stimulus. Obviously, reading is a more complicated activity than simply the emission of a vocal counterpart of a textual stimulus because it interacts with other verbal functions, particularly intraverbal behavior. This more operational sense of reading will be discussed in a later section after intraverbal behavior has been described.

To teach a child to read, we need to assume that he already speaks the vocal behaviors he is to emit under the control of a text. The previously existing vocal performance changes its function when it comes under the discriminative control of the text, such as a letter, a word, or a phrase. At its simplest level, reading leaves no intraverbal residue. The vocal performances the child emits under the control of the vocal stimulus are not available in their absence. We say that such a reader does not understand what he is reading in the sense the performances prompted by the textual stimuli do not exert discriminative control over other related verbal behaviors already in his repertoire. Reading at this level has many properties in common with the echoic performances described above.

Reading is generally taught by either a "phonics" approach or a system with flash cards and a use of whole words right from the start. In the flash card approach, the teacher holds up a card containing a word or phrase printed in large letters. If the child says the word in the presence of the appropriate text, the performance is confirmed by the teacher. The reinforcement is generalized because the control that emerges is entirely by the textual stimulus rather than the child's inclination to say one thing or another. In the flash card procedure there is no guarantee that the separate articulatory components of the words are controlled by the corresponding parts of the textual stimuli. The beginning reader might read *has* and still not be able to read *as*. Or he might be able to read *hot* and *as* and still not be able to read *has*. Until this fine-grain relation between the textual stimulus and the vocal performance has developed, we do not say that the child is reading, even though a number of vocal performances are controlled by a number of texts. The development of a continuous repertoire in reading requires correspondence between discriminative stimulus and performance similar to that of echoic behavior. The same kind of differential reinforcement that was described in Chapter 6 in relation to drawing and driving is required. The phonics method may, however, develop control by details of the textual stimuli indirectly. Even though the control by *en* may never be explicit, it occurs in varying contexts such as *pen, fence, dent, tent,* and *hen* so that the control by this element may develop inductively. In that event, the student when faced with a new text, *rent,* will emit the appropriate vocal performance. The new textual stimulus would draw its control from past experiences where appropriate vocal performances were controlled by words that began with an *r*, like *rat* and *run,* and those words that contain *en,* as described above.

In contrast to the flash card method, the phonics or phono—visual approaches to reading are specifically designed to bring the beginning reader's vocal performance under the control of the details of the textual stimulus. For example, the child sees the letter and chooses the picture of the bat rather than a picture of a cat. As with the whole word method of teaching reading, the reinforcer is the confirmation of the choice by the teacher. Next, he might see the letter *c* and be required to choose the picture of the cat rather than the one of the bat. Thus, behaviorally, the phonics method may be seen as a way to bring performances under the control of elements of the textual stimulus that are smaller than the functional units. A student might be asked to underline the word that begins like *boy* when given a choice of the texts, *toy, boat,* and *joy.* Once the smallest element of the textual stimulus controls some performance discriminatively, the child can read words never seen before.

The process by which texts become discriminative stimuli-controlling vocal performances is made more explicit by a matching-to-sample procedure utilizing a teaching maching.[5], [6] The child sees a 5- x 8-inch card with a picture or a text in the upper part (the sample) and three stimuli across the bottom of the card (the choices). A piece of foil on the back of the card codes the correct choice and when the card is inserted into a simple machine, the correct choice is indicated by a signal light that comes on when the correct button is pushed. When the sample stimulus is auditory, it is presented by means of a strip of audio tape glued across the bottom of the card. The child inserts the card into an audio device[7] and then into the teaching machine. Figure 8-2 illustrates two types of cards that might be used. In the first card, the child hears "Where is the cat?" and pressing the button under the picture of the cat lights the indicator for a correct choice. The distinctions required become more verbal in the second card where the auditory stimulus is "Is this the word 'yes'?" (or "Is this the word 'no'?") and pushing the button under the appropriate text is reinforced. A more advanced card might have a picture of a girl sitting on a chair as the sample, and the texts below would require the student to choose between *the girl is sitting, the box is sitting,* and *the girl is standing.* Although the sample is pictorial, a vocal performance is likely to be involved since the picture will prompt a vocal performance thematically relevant to it.

Although the child is not reading in the explicit sense of emitting a vocal performance under the control of the text, the behavioral control that emerges is a large step to this repertoire because it establishes the details

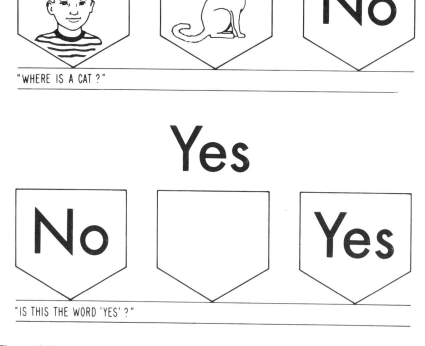

Figure 8-2

of the texts as discriminative stimuli. The fact that the child is pushing buttons rather than speaking is only a short step from reading the word. The "pointing performance" guarantees that the details of the text are controlling the student's behavior discriminatively. The step from reacting discriminatively to the texts in matching-to-sample to actual reading is accomplished by a simple test where the student is asked to read aloud the texts that were just reacted to discriminatively by pressing buttons. All of the elements of the required repertoire will have been established at this point. The child can emit the performances vocally and can point to the texts that correspond or do not correspond to the vocal form of the stimulus. The instruction to read provides a contingency for moving all of the previously developed components into reading.

An important advantage of such an explicit program for teaching reading is the possibility of avoiding excessive intermittent reinforcement and extinction by a gradual program of introducing stimulus differences paced with the discriminative control present at each stage. Texts can be chosen to correspond with the child's initial vocal repertoire and the distinctions required among textual stimuli programmed so that the requirement is only slightly more than what the novice reader has already achieved. With such an approach there is no need for the beginning reader ever to fail.

## intraverbal behavior

Intraverbal, like echoic and textual behavior, exemplifies the control of a verbal performance by a prior verbal stimulus in a chain of performances where the verbal stimulus reinforces the performance that produces it and sets the occasion for the next one. Rote phrases are ready examples of intraverbally determined performances: "quick as a wink," "fit as a fiddle," "I pledge allegiance to the flag. . . ." Like the other operants, the intraverbal differs from the mand because its form is minimally determined by the reinforcer maintaining it. It differs from echoic and textual behavior in that the prior controlling stimulus does not have any topographic relation to the intraverbal performance. "Four" in reply to "two plus two" is intraverbal behavior, as is most arithmetic and mathematics. Songs, memorized poems, and classroom activities involving lectures, books, term papers, and written examinations consist mainly of intraverbal behaviors. Most conversation consists of intraverbal sequences. In fact, the bulk of human vocal activity consists of chains of performances where the major determinant of each item is the preceding vocal stimulus in the speaker's own speech. The number of intraverbal relations in the repertoire of the adult speaker greatly exceeds the number of forms of performance because of the large number of combinations and permutations. Some intraverbal operants are composed of or share parts with others. Such an operant may be as small as a single speech sound, as in reciting the alphabet, or it may be composed of many words with grammatical tags, such as reciting a poem or composing a sentence freely. The classical word-association experiment where a subject is instructed to say all of the words except rhymes or repetitions that come to mind is a test of the intraverbal connections in that person's repertoire. Advertising illustrates the use of intraverbal sequences of behavior. The presumption is that once the intraverbal sequence is in the consumer's repertoire, any stimulus connected with the use of that product will prompt the sales ditty or slogan. The difficulty that some people experience when their recitation of a poem or memorized speech is interrupted is evidence of the chained nature of intraverbal behavior. In such cases the one reciting needs to return to an earlier part of the poem so that each part will be immediately preceded by the stimulus that controls it.

## the tact

The tact is described by the same three-term contingency that provided the descriptive framework for the other verbal operants that have been presented. In the presence of a ball and another person, the speaker says "That's a ball." The physical presence of the ball is the discriminative stimulus. The performance, topographically identical with the intraverbal, textual, or echoic versions, is the movement of the vocal apparatus that produces the sound. The term was introduced by Skinner[8] to differentiate this kind of performance from the mand, echoic, intraverbal, and textual behaviors that have already been introduced. The difference between the tact and echoic, textual, and intraverbal operants is in the nature of the prior, controlling, discriminative stimulus. It is nonverbal in the tact, auditory in echoic, verbal in intraverbal, and a written text in textual behavior. In common with these other forms, the tact differs from the mand because its control is predominantly through a prior stimulus rather than through deprivation or the reinforcer. In other words, its generalized mode of reinforcement allow the prior stimulus to control it exclusively.

Because the reinforcement of the tact is by the behavior it prompts in the listener, the tact may be profitably thought of as a bridge between speaker and listener. It lets the listener deal with the same object, much in the same way as does the speaker, even though he does not have access to the object. For example, if the tact "It's a ball" mentioned above occurred when a ball impacted on the outside wall of a house and someone asked "What was that?," the reinforcement of the tact is in its influence on the listener. There are two directions that such a tact might be useful to a listener. In either case its influence will be through existing intraverbals controlled by the stimulus "ball" already in the listener's repertoire. In the absence of the tact "ball," the listener might speak of many untoward events, such as damage to the building. In the presence of the tact, the listener could take effective action by going outside and asking the players to move their game elsewhere. The tact influences the repertoire of the listener by allowing him to act in respect to the "tacted object," verbally as well an nonverbally. One impact of such a tact is to limit the range of intraverbals that might otherwise be prompted in the listener's repertoire. Interpretations and other similar replies can have the same function when they occur in a psychotherapeutic interview. The interaction between the sentry in an observation post and the command center he reports to is another context for talking about the reinforcement of the tact. The sentry on the hill counts the approaching enemy troops and signals back to headquarters. The troop movements observed comprise discriminative stimulus controlling the tact the sentry will emit. The tact, a performance on the telegraph key, signal flags, or telephone, provides a verbal stimulus that prompts intraverbal behavior thematically relevant to the observations that had been made in the repertoire of the listener at the command post. As a result, the listener can talk about the troop movements almost as well as the observer. Based on these intraverbals, the listener at the command post prescribes action to be taken. The acknowledgement "Roger" serves as a conditioned reinforcer, like "Thank you," because it tends to be emitted when the listener has been influenced in a way that allows useful action.

**Distortions of the tact** The verbal community has a serious investment in having the tact controlled by the prior discriminative stimulus rather than by distorting influences, such as influencing the listener in order to achieve some special result for the speaker. When a performance is simultaneously controlled by the normal practice of the verbal community and a reinforcer derived from some area of deprivation in the speaker, we say that the tact is impure or distorted. The impurity refers to any factor that shifts the control of the performance away from the prior stimulus. The child who has not eaten for some time may report "It's almost six o'clock," while he might say "It is only 5:45" if a chore had to be performed by six o'clock. The control of the child's behavior by positive reinforcers related to his current level of deprivation or by negative reinforcement by aversive stimuli will make his announcements less reliable than if he were controlled solely by the prior stimulus. The child who says, "Johnny broke the ashtray" when she herself did it is emitting a vocal performance under the simultaneous control of two variables. An ashtray has been broken, and that is an event that can control a tact. But the person who broke the ashtray may be punished, so the behavior can take a form that will also avoid the aversive stimulus that may be forthcoming. If the performance were narrowly under the control of the actual event, the child would say "I broke the ashtray." The preaversive stimulus, the history of punishment and the relevant emotional state, reinforces "Johnny" instead of "I."

Scientific work is the area where the verbal community is especially attentive to whether some of the control of the tact is in the reinforcer maintaining it rather than in the prior stimulus. The scientific community requires the behavior of the speaker or writer of a scientific report be narrowly controlled by the actual event that is observed. Only if this is so can it be sure that someone observing the structure of a chromosome under the microscope is being controlled by the physical stimulus rather than some special effect that such a report might have on another person. In other words, the scientific community wants to be sure that someone else observing the same materials will make the same description no matter what the audience or the momentary condition of the observer. Even reinforcers nominally considered generalized, such as attention and praise, contribute to the impurity of the tact because they shift the control of the speaker's behavior away from the prior stimulus to influencing the audience. The oo's and ah's that the fisherman generates as he tells his story leads him to exaggerate the size of the fish. We state the same circumstances when we say colloquially that the fisherman exaggerates the size of the fish to impress his audience.

It is a useful exercise to distinguish between a lie and a tact that is impure. A lie is a negatively reinforced operant or a mand, depending on whether its function is to avoid aversive consequences or to produce an outcome relevant to the speaker's (liar's) level of deprivation. The child who gives an alibi, "I wasn't there," when he would be punished if he were, illustrates that the lie is a negatively reinforced operant. The child that tells the teacher incorrectly "My mother says it's okay for me to go on the trip" is emitting a mand that we colloquially label a lie. In the impure tact, the performance is still functionally that of a tact, except that the prior stimulus shares its control with the contaminating variable.

**Private events**  The stimuli that control some tacts are not public. The verbal performance "my tooth hurts" is a tact controlled by the events occurring in the tooth pulp. Such tacts become part of the speaker's repertoire because there are public accompaniments of the infected tooth that allow the verbal community to differentially reinforce the performance. The listener as a representative of the verbal community can develop such performances and differentially reinforce or punish them only on the basis of the public accompaniments of the private stimulus, since by definition no one other than the speaker can actually observe the private event. As a result, they are particularly subject to the kind of distortions described above as an impure tact. The proverbial statement of a headache by which a person escapes some social responsibility illustrates the complications posed by tacts controlled by private events. "I have a headache" may be a tact under the control of an inflammatory process within the skull, it may be simply a negatively reinforced operant that produces escape from an aversive social situation, or it might be an impure tact controlled partially by the prior stimulus within the skull and partially by the negative reinforcement from the declined social engagement.

**The relation between tacts and intraverbal behavior**  Intraverbal behavior may come into a person's repertoire first through reinforcement as a tact. If it is a tact, the performance "chair," mentioned above, is under the discriminative control of an actual chair. It quickly will assume a function in the intraverbal repertoire, however, as the performance is reinforced in conversation, particularly under the tension of questions: "Wasn't it thoughtful of grandma to buy a chair for your room?" "Too bad we don't have chairs here so everyone could sit down." Intraverbal performances are easily confused with tacts because their form is the same and because they both control the listener's behavior in useful ways. When someone says "John says that it is raining," such a performance is likely to be intraverbal because the controlling stimulus is a preceding verbal one and the actual nonverbal stimulus controlling the performance as a tact has occurred some time ago and in someone else's repertoire. Intraverbal performances tend to be confused with tacts because they serve a similar function for the listener who, in the presence of the intraverbal stimulus, can act appropriately. In the example above, the intraverbal provides a discriminative stimulus for the listener that prompts getting a rain coat, a performance that will be negatively reinforced by warding off rain. Instructions in textual form provide that same kind of function in interactions with other kinds of environments. The task of such a reader is to read the instructions to supplement existing intraverbal behaviors by the textual stimuli of the instruction and based on the intraverbal capability that results and be able to emit a performance that can be reinforced because it is under the control of the discriminative stimulus. For example, after reading a botany text, intraverbals that result might be of the form, "This plant propagates sexually, so I need to plant male and female forms." That intraverbal, in turn, is a discriminative stimulus that controls looking at the sex of the plant and selecting representatives of each sex. One of the major functions of intraverbal behavior, the main product of educational experiences, is verbal performances that bring the student's behavior under discriminative control of abstract and special properties of important parts of the environment. A tact under the control of the tooth of a gear, an abstract tact, provides a means of bringing the behavior of a listener under the control of that particular property of the nonverbal stimulus. Color, texture, and saturation are similar tacts by which we talk and think about visual situations. By and large, talking about the external environment is a means of noticing its important features, such as the beginning reader who points to the words one at a time to limit the control by neighboring texts that might interfere.

## questions

1. How do the various conditions controlling a performance like "toast" illustrate a functional as opposed to a topographic analysis of verbal behavior?
2. Give examples of homonyms as a functional rather than a topographic specification of a verbal performance.
3. Describe the mand as an operant.
4. What distinguishes mands that are designated commands, advice, and entreaty?
5. Discuss why the mand is minimally verbal.
6. What is an extended mand? Give some examples.
7. How does a superstitious mand differ from an extended mand?
8. Why is echoic behavior more verbal than the mand?
9. What are some situations that reinforce echoic performances?
10. How does transcription differ from echoic behavior? How is it similar?
11. Compare reading, transcription, and echoic behavior.
12. Describe how the teaching machine procedure brings the child's performance under the discriminative control of the fine-grain of the textual stimulus.
13. Describe the common features of the phonics method and the whole-word method of teaching reading that bring about the discriminative control by the details of the textual stimulus.
14. How is intraverbal behavior the same as echoic and textual behavior? How is it different?
15. How is the tact the same as echoic, textual, and intraverbal behavior? How is it different?
16. Why does the listener reinforce the speaker's "tacting"?
17. How can tacts be reinforced by their effect on the speaker as his own listener?
18. What is meant by a distorted tact? Give an example along with a functional analysis of it.

*19.* How would you distinguish between a distorted tact and a lie?

*20.* How do tacts under the control of private events differ from other tacts?

*21.* Why is it likely that intraverbal behavior may be confused with tacts?

---

## part III: dynamic and interactional aspects of verbal behavior

### the expansion of the intraverbal repertoire from mand, echoic, textual, and tact performances

The analysis of verbal behavior is complicated by the different functions that the same topography of performance can have. We have seen how identical performances can be echoic, intraverbal, tact, textual, or a mand depending on the controlling stimulus and its manner of reinforcement. Of these verbal categories, the intraverbal is the most prevalent. The intraverbal repertoire comes almost entirely from verbal performances controlled in other ways. A performance occurring initially as echoic or mand becomes intraverbal as a result of the special reinforcement practices of the verbal community. We need to understand how the verbal environment causes a shift in the control of these varied verbal operants to intraverbal behavior. The reason that the largest part of the normal verbal repertoire is intraverbal is that mand, echoic, and textual forms quickly shift their function under the tensions (reinforcement contingencies) supplied by the verbal community. The contribution of textual behavior to the intraverbal repertoire is especially important and needs to be discussed in a separate section.

A typical situation during early childhood, where new forms of verbal behavior are being developed, occurs when a barely verbal child emits nonverbal mands reinforced, say, by receipt of a cookie. At such an early stage of verbal development, echoic behavior is likely to already be in the repertoire, as described in the earlier parts of this chapter. The child whines, cries, and gestures (nonverbal mands) in the vicinity of the cookie and the parent says "Say cookie; you can have a cookie." With the slight delay in giving the child a cookie and the parent's more sensitive reactivity to the verbal over the nonverbal form of the mand, the performance "cookie" shifts from an echoic operant to a mand. By a parallel process, the same verbal form can shift to an intraverbal form in reaction to the parent's questions and discussions after the mand becomes verbal: "Have you eaten your cookie?" "Was the cookie good?" "Do you want another cookie?" Each of these intraverbal interactions indicates a parental verbal environment that is specially reactive to the emission of these previously mand and echoic forms as intraverbal behaviors.

The reinforcement of intraverbal behavior is not limited to the parent's reactivity to it. Intraverbal behavior provides discriminative stimuli that increase the frequency reinforcement of other performances in the child's repertoire because they clarify the environment in the manner described in Part II. Without an intraverbal repertoire, echoic performances would persist only as long as the discriminative stimulus controlling them were present. Thus, when a parent tells a child, "My purse is on the chair in the kitchen—bring it to me and I will give you a coin for buying ice cream," the possibility of these auditory stimuli controlling the performances of walking to the kitchen and looking for the purse depends on whether there are already performances in a child's intraverbal repertoire that could be prompted by the parent's instruction. The process of this conversion of function will be clearer in the next section when the shift from textual to intraverbal behavior will be discussed.

**Reading**   If there were no intraverbal repertoire, reading would be a limited, rote exercise of repeating a vocal form corresponding to the texts, of the kind we see when someone reads a language he doesn't speak or a text so unfamiliar that there is no residue in the absence of the text. The accomplished reader is engaged in a complex interaction between the performances prompted by the text and the related performances that increase in frequency from the intraverbal repertoire. For the most part, we can read intelligently only those texts that indicate verbal activities that we can already carry out. A biography, for example, is meaningful only if the reader can already talk about the political events of the period, other persons that are mentioned, and some issues that can be related to one's current life. On the other hand, a biography of a person that relates totally familiar events would be uninteresting because the intraverbals that would be prompted could have been emitted without the text. Some kinds of reading simply prompt behaviors already in the reader's repertoire without any other residue, as, for example, the kind of experience many readers have with an adventure story where the momentary reaction is the only product. A text does not, of itself or from its textual control of a vocal performance, add to the intraverbal repertoire. The conditions necessary for the transition of textual performances to intraverbal is illustrated at simple levels of reading by the teaching machine procedure, utilizing matching-to-sample that was described in Part II. If some reinforcer such as a token, money, or food is given for correct choices on the teaching machine, the child performs erratically and there is little residue. If, however, the tokens are given as a consequence of actually reading the words that had been the stimuli on the cards in the program, the result is active, fluent reading. Part of the process, of course, includes the differential reinforcement that occurs when a child cannot read the text that he had just studied through the matching-to-sample procedure and is told to go back and restudy the cards *so that he will be able to read them afterwards.* As with operant behavior generally, the reinforcer maintaining the study behavior determines how it will occur. The shift from reinforcement after pushing buttons to reinforcement after the actual vocal performance controlled by the text determines whether the behavior is reading or pushing buttons to get tokens.

The same shift in reinforcement contingency, as with the teaching machine example, occurs in the "speech procedure" used in individualized instruction.[9] Many students will read a portion of a textbook repeatedly without being able to talk about the themes or descriptions presented there. Behaviorally, it would be said that although the student was reading in the sense of emitting vocal performances corresponding to the text, there was no shift of the performances to the intraverbal repertoire. To accomplish this shift, there needs to be a contingency, after reading, that reacts differentially to the development of the required intraverbal behavior. One such contingency could be supplied by a "speech procedure" where the student is required to talk about what she has just studied to a listener, who without interrupting or prompting simply records whether the intraverbal residue evidenced in the speech is an adequate representation of the required repertoire. As a result of this differential reaction to the speech, the student's study behavior changes to a form that will produce the required vocal product. We cannot say exactly what the student does that produces the shift in the reading behavior, just as we could not say exactly what the pupil did while pushing the buttons in the matching-to-sample procedure to produce the shift to a vocal performance, or what the seal did with its neck muscles to keep the pressure of the ball on its nose. Some evidence of what occurs can be inferred by observing the change in the study behavior. The student who ordinarily would read passively, now stops frequently and is seen talking to herself, returning to portions of the text, and spending the larger part of her effort in actively speaking about what she is reading. These activities correspond to those of the pupil on the teaching machine when his finger hovers over each one of the buttons, his lips move in silent speech, and his eyes move back and forth between the three stimuli that are prompting his choice.

## the audience as a discriminative stimulus controlling the speaker's behavior

Since so much of a young child's behavior is reinforced through the intervention of other persons, their presence becomes an important discriminative stimulus. Crying, reinforced by influencing a parent to pick up the child, comes under the discriminative control of the parent's presence or absence. Babysitters often note a sudden decrease in crying as soon as the parents depart. The repertoire of most speakers contains a range of subdialects which are appropriate to different audiences. The child replies "yes" to a teacher and "uh huh" to his peer. The dialect used by the college teacher when discussing an academic subject is very different from that used when speaking to someone about baseball. We whisper when we go into the library and shout in the open field. These differing repertoires are the product of the reinforcement contingencies that occur in the different environments. Saying "uh huh" to the teacher is likely to be punished, and responding "yes" to a peer is likely to produce a reaction of jest that would interrupt the flow of the interaction. The form of speech used by adults with children and baby talk with infants are other examples of audience control. The infant is differentially reactive to high-pitched sounds and sharply rising inflections. Normal speech is less likely to alter the behavior of a young child than simplified, inflected forms. The differential reinforcement of the adult's speech, therefore, brings it under control of the particular listener whose reactivity is the reinforcer maintaining the speech.

The extensions of the mand, described in Part II of this chapter, exemplify the absence of control by an audience. In this case, the speaker's level of deprivation or aversive stimulation increased the performance's frequency so that it was emitted despite the absence of a listener who could comply with the speaker's demand. Examples included complaints like "I wish it would stop raining" or "Why doesn't he serve my food?" The child talking to its doll represents a similar lack of control of the performance by an effective audience. In the case of the child, in contrast to the extended mand, the normal developmental process provides the differential reinforcement that eventually weakens speech in the absence of an effective audience.

**The attention of the listener as an audience variable** Whether a person is an effective listener for a speaker depends on attentiveness. Only if a person is attentive can he or she be influenced. The pigeon experiment described in Chapter 6 shows the way that "attention" is a performance by which the subject allows or increases the control of its behavior by a discriminative stimulus. In that experiment, pecks at one key (the observing performance) produced stimuli that clarified the reinforcement contingencies on another key by which the pigeon's pecks were reinforced by food. We refer to the stimulus dimensions of these observing behaviors as the "attention" of the listener. The importance of the discriminative control by the listener's attention may be estimated from the very subtle aspects of the listener's appearance that control the speaker. One significant physical feature of the listener is his head orientation. More important with many listeners is the focus of the eyes. In general, the listener is being controlled by the speaker when his eyes focus on the details of the speaker's face. The magnitude of the stimuli are very small. At a distance of ten feet most people are differentially controlled by a shift in focus of the eye from near to far vision, from the body to the face, or even from the eyes to the chin. It is legendary at large parties that a person may stop talking when the focus of the listener's eye shifts from the speaker's face to a person just behind. This subtle discriminative control of the speaker's behavior by a stimulus change of such small magnitude comes about because of the consistent relation between the focus of the listener's eyes and his reactivity to the speaker's verbal behavior. Lecturers frequently come under very close control of the facial expressions of the audience and alter their speaking tone and content until the audience becomes attentive. This interactive process between speaker and audience is especially prominent in political speeches and the sermons of some religious denominations.

This close control of the speaker by the audience is an example of the two functions of a discriminative stimulus. Besides exerting discriminative control over the behavior of the speaker, it serves as a differential reinforcer for those kinds of speaking that bring about the attention of the listener. In other words, it is a conditioned reinforcer that has a generic relation to the behaviors that produce it. Further evidence of the large discriminative control exerted by attention is the high frequency of mands reinforced by the attention of the listener. More often than not, people begin a verbal interaction by speaking the listener's name. Only when the listener replies does the speaker start. Children are especially prone to repeat "Mom" or "Dad" and speak only when the parent replies, "Yes." Such performances are mands reinforced by the attention of the listener.

## meaning

The meaning of a word is different for the speaker than it is for the listener. For the speaker, the meaning of a vocal utterance is equivalent to the variables that control its emission. For the listener, the meaning of a verbal stimulus are the verbal performances, already in his repertoire, that it prompts. It is because the behavior of the speaker is shaped and maintained by its influence on the listener that we account for most verbal processes by studying the listener's characteristics.

**Intonation as a discriminative stimulus**   Despite the importance of articulation pattern, a large part of the control of the listener comes from the pitch and intonation changes of the verbal stimulus. The importance of these discriminative stimuli can be seen by the measures taken in texts to prompt them for the reader. Punctuation is frequently used by the writer to determine the intonation or pause pattern for the reader. In many cases, the reader will be misled without the discriminative control that would otherwise be provided by the intonational patterns of ordinary conversation. It is for this reason that public speakers familiarize themselves with their material sufficiently so that they can talk with only a few prompts from the text. In that case, the performance is intraverbal, resembling ordinary conversation since the audience controls the speaker's behavior rather than the text. Accent, intonation, pauses, and rhythm control the behavior of the listener in the same way as articulation patterns. Sarcasm, for example, is frequently conveyed by the intonation rather than the actual words or their order. The auditory stimulus "very nice," spoken with a high pitch and with inflection is an occasion when a listener is likely to be applauded. The same articulation pattern spoken without variation in tone is likely to precede the withdrawal of reinforcement. Sometimes questions are asked by intonation alone. For example, "the box is on the chair" spoken with a constant pitch usually is a stimulus that controls nonverbal action such as finding the box and picking it up. The same phrase with the pitch rising at the end is an occasion when a performance such as "Yes, it is" is reinforced.

The matching-to-sample procedure might be used to bring the behavior of a non-English listener under the control of the intonational patterns of English usage. One time the student hears "the box is on the table" and he chooses one of three buttons under a picture of a box on a table, a picture of a box under a table, or a text "Yes, it is." Pushing the button under the text is reinforced, while pushing the other buttons is not. If the auditory stimulus in "the box is under the table" with the voice rising during the last words, pressing the button under the text *No, it's not* is reinforced. When the auditory stimulus is the same statement pronounced evenly, pressing the button under the appropriate picture is reinforced. The differential reinforcement forces the student's reply under the discriminative control of the intonational pattern.

**Word order as a discriminative stimulus**   As with intonation, it is useful to show how the order of the words in an utterance serves as a discriminative stimulus by the use of the matching-to-sample teaching program. In the presence of the auditory stimulus, "The box is on the table," the subject sees two pictures, one with a small box on a table, the other with a small table on a large box. Pushing the button under the picture of the box on the table is reinforced, while pushing the other is not. On the next occasion, the auditory stimulus might be "The table is on the box." Reinforcement occurs when the button under the other picture is pressed. The verbal stimuli are identical except for the order of the words. We know that the subject is under the proper control of the order of the words if he or she chooses the picture appropriate to the word order. Highly inflected languages, such as Latin and German, use word endings instead of word order for the same kind of discriminative control.

**Discriminative control by grammar** Stimuli such as *on, under,* and *next to* exert discriminative control over the listener or reader in a manner like that exercised by word order. As in the previous categories, the differential control of the listener's behavior by stimuli, such as the preposition *on,* can be tested with the matching-to-sample procedure using special arrangements of boxes and tables in pictures. The subject hears a phrase and chooses among pictures of a box on a table, a box next to a table, and a box under a table. Reinforcement is differential depending whether the auditory stimulus is *on, under* or *next to.* When new stimuli are substituted for *box* and *table,* the abstract control of the listener's behavior by prepositions is demonstrated.

Frequently, different behavior is strengthened in the listener by the indefinite and definite articles *a* and *the,* even though the difference is very slight. For example, the sentence, "The box is on a table" controls a listener differently than the sentence "A box is on the table." The first sentence connotes that the box recently controlled the listener's behavior. In the second sentence there is no presumption that the box has recently controlled the listener, although there is a presumption that the table has. Examples of the differential reinforcement that is needed to bring about control of the listener of leader's behavior could be generated in a manner parallel to the previous examples.

## questions

1. Describe the events that are likely to occur when an echoic performance shifts its function to that of a mand.
2. Describe some conditions under which an echoic performance could change its function to intraverbal.
3. Describe how "operational reading" requires an interaction with the intraverbal repertoire.
4. Describe how the speech procedure used in classroom instruction brings about a shift in the control of a vocal performance from textual to intraverbal.
5. Give some examples of audience control and describe the reinforcement contingencies that bring the performances under the control of the specific audiences.

6. How does the extended mand exemplify the absence of discriminative control by an audience?

7. What are the stimulus dimensions of "attention"?

8. Why is "attention" described as an audience variable?

9. How do we speak of the meaning of a word behaviorally?

10. Give some examples of the way that intonation controls the behavior of the listener discriminatively.

11. Give some examples of the way that word order controls the behavior of the listener discriminatively.

12. Describe how the matching-to-sample procedure in a teaching machine could be used to bring the behavior of the listener under the control of grammar intonation or word order.

## notes

[1] This chapter is based largely on the concepts presented by B. F. Skinner in *Verbal behavior.* New York: Appleton-Century-Crofts, 1957.

[2] Ibid., pp. 224–226.

[3] Intraverbal behavior will be discussed in more detail in Parts II and III. For the present, intraverbal behavior can be thought of as sequences of verbal performances where each word controls the next as in a chain of performances.

[4] Skinner, Chapter 3.

[5] Rocha e Silva, M. I. and Ferster, C. B. An experiment in teaching a second language. Sonderdruck aus IRAL 4: 85–113, 1966.

[6] Cameron, J. L., Cameron, G. M., Fifer, W. P., Hardy, R. P, and Smith, S. A. Remedial reading: A psychoanalytic and operant approach. *British Journal of Medical Psychology* 45: 273–278, 1972.

[7] A Bell and Howell Master was the audio device used in the programs described in the second-language and reading programs described in notes 5 and 6.

[8] Skinner, B. F. *Verbal behavior.* New York: Appleton-Century-Crofts, 1957, Chapter 5.

[9] Ferster, C. B. Individualized instruction in a large introductory psychology college course. *Psychological Record* 18: 521–532, 1968.

# complex human conduct 9
# viewed from basic
# behavioral processes

**299**

Part V:
>    Aversive Control and Emotion
>    Growth and development
>    Education
>    Infantile autism
>    Self-control
>    Depression
>    Psychotherapy

---

## part I: introduction: how human conduct can be viewed from basic behavioral processes

The preceding chapters have described a general conceptual framework for talking about behavioral processes that were both phylogenetically general and useful for clarifying human conduct as it presents itself in social interactions. The general conceptual framework has been presented in five main categories of behavioral processes. How new behavior is acquired in an organism's repertoire was presented in Chapters 1–3; the influence of emotional variables and the side effects of aversive control were discussed in Chapter 4; the maintenance and persistence of behavior after it has become a part of the repertoire was presented in Chapter 5; how the environment comes to control operant performances because of its differential reinforcement in various situations was presented in Chapter 6; and how reinforcers emerge to bridge delays in reinforcement when chains or sequences of behavior are required to alter the environment was presented in Chapter 7.

Many investigators and practitioners have attempted to apply the principles of behavioral control that have been described. Some of these practical applications have been alluded to in the preceding chapters to exemplify the particular principle that was discussed. For example, the account of desensitization therapy in Chapter 4 was presented to focus attention on the interaction between operant and respondent conditioning. Other applications of operant conditioning principles to practical problems will be presented in Chapter 10 along with a critique of their basis in the principles of behavioral analysis.

For present purposes, it will be useful to understand some of the reasons why basic researchers have been so disposed to apply animal laboratory procedures as solutions to pressing human problems. For these researchers, the experience of shaping an animal's behavior with food is probably the most important source of this belief. This experience, shared by novice and professional alike, is a dramatic one. Contacting the animal only through a button that operates the food dispenser, the experimenter increases the frequency of a performance and shapes it into a new complex form, all in a matter of minutes. Although the demonstration is a standard laboratory technique, it has a strong clinical flavor because each subject is dealt with individually. The person operating the switch continually adjusts to the behavior of the animal, responding to its fine-grain details. Factors responsible for each animal's uniqueness are taken into account; none of these factors is considered too deviant to work with by the experimenter. The animal's behavior comes into existence and is shaped, moment-to-moment, as the animal operates the food magazine. A novice who carries out such a demonstration gains the conviction that the behavior of the animal is plastic and unlimited if the rules of arranging a properly reactive environment can be learned. It is not surprising that such an experimenter is disposed to apply this same degree of control to pressing human problems.

The concern of this chapter, however, will be in another direction than the literal applications of the animal laboratory technique to clinical directions or to the discovery of simple techniques of behavior modification. Perhaps the greatest utility of a science of human behavior is as a microscope that can expose the details of complex behavioral interactions and to clarify and communicate knowledge about human nature gained from practitioners of diverse theories. Alternatively, behavioral analysis will be used to complement knowledge gained in practical discovery and in other disciplines. In the long view, such use of behavioral knowledge may be more important than the discovery of practical methods. New methods of behavioral control emerge constantly through serendipity and through shaping by the practical involvement with the details of the problem. What is needed is an objective, communicable language that allows us to know in what way one treatment is different from another and exactly how it works. In that case there is the possibility of refining methods, and separating accidents and superstitions from effective methods.

The examples from child development that have been posed at various points in the text illustrate the complementarity between behavioral analysis and the specific subject-matter content of a discipline. We cannot expect that principles of behavior will expose or give information about the developmental stages that occur when the infant grows. These are the facts of developmental psychology that emerge from the direct study of the growing child by an observer steeped in the facts, methods, and objectives of the field study. Yet, behavioral analysis can play a part in the description and communication of these events. Behavioral descriptions of the growth and socialization patterns of the child expose details of the component behaviors so that they can be described in terms of the main categories of behavioral processes that have been outlined. In such an enterprise, the behavioral analysis provides a fine-grain communicable language that exposes details of the child's and parent's conduct that otherwise might not have been observable.

In this chapter, knowledge from child growth and development, education, the childhood psychoses, infantile autism, self-control, adult psychopathology such as depression, and the procedures of psychotherapy will be organized in terms of the five general modes of behavioral control described above.

In this chapter, the strategy is parallel to that carried out by Skinner in *Science and Human Behavior*[1] where he applied the concepts of the functional analysis of operant behavior to clarifying and communicating the kinds of human conduct that occur in government, religion, education, law, and psychotherapy.

## part II: reinforcement in human behaviors

### growth and development

Reinforcement, in the sense of shaping new forms of action, is a very visible part of the infant's development. At 1 month of age, the infant's repertoire consists primarily of reflexes—rooting in response to tactile pressure on the cheek, grasping an object pressed in the palm of the hand, blinking in response to a bright light, sucking in response to tactile pressure on the mucosal tissue of the lips, and swallowing in response to food in the mouth. There is also the moro reflex—an arching of the back and flinging of the arms in response to a sudden change—and reflexes such as gagging in response to liquid in the air passage; following an object visually; and crying. Operant behavior in the first days is minimal. By 3 months of age, the operant repertoire expands greatly. Head movements become operants reinforced as part of a chain of behaviors involving sucking and looking. Crying, as described in Chapter 2, becomes an operant reinforced by its influence on the parent and the movements of the hands are reinforced by their contact with the child's mouth and other objects. The rudiments of play begin when the infant makes sounds whose reinforcement is simply their effect on himself as listener, when the visual patterns produced by moving the hands in the field of vision increases the frequency of those movements, and when the movement of the hand over the bed clothes is reinforced by the tactile stimulation. The infant's neuromuscular development has not progressed to where these performances occur precisely but should the movement of the hand bring it into the field of vision, in contact with the mouth, or in touch with the fabric's texture, the performance persists because it is prolonged by the stimulus it produces. Such observations show that the infant's emerging competence occurs as a result of successive approximation by the "playful" as well as the biologically pressing consequences of its actions. A child who is nursing adequately will be seen to engage in many activities, collateral to feeding, that are reinforced independently. The infant might play with the nipple with its tongue and mouth and if its hands reach the breast or bottle the tactual stimulation may reinforce touching. The child will focus its eyes on the mother's face or follow the events when the mother interrupts the feeding to adjust the bottle or her position. The way that their bodies conform is another behavioral interaction collateral to feeding. Some of the reinforcers are negative as parent or child adjusts positions to relieve a tensed muscle. Others of the behaviors are reinforced by maximizing body contact between the two. It is hard to observe the small details of this interaction, but their generic effect on tension or their position with each other can be seen if one looks carefully. The interaction is of the same form as the balance on a bicycle as a reinforcer for "riding" or the speaker's discriminative reaction to his or her own speech as its generic counterpart.

With the child's neuromuscular immaturity, the range of performances from which the process of successive approximation can proceed becomes larger. The visual field of a child sitting up is larger than when it is lying in the crib; the interaction of hand movements with the child's mouth has a greater range when the neuromuscular development allows grasping of objects with the fingers. At 6 months most infants can move objects with their hands reliably. These movements can now be reinforced by getting them into the mouth. They also allow reinforcement by the tactile stimulation between the hand and the object that is grasped. The grasping of objects coupled with greater maturity of the neuromuscular control of the arms, allows an increased range of reinforcement by the visual effects of moving the grasped objects into the field of vision.

At 9 months, the infant can sit unaided and use the thumb and forefinger; at 1 year, the infant can crawl. By 3 or 4 years of age the child has acquired the gross forms of operant activities that constitute the bulk of its developmental repertoire. The child becomes verbally interactive with the social environment, locomotes efficiently, draws pictures, rides a bicycle, jumps rope and builds complicated forms with blocks and toys. Subsequent development involves more refinement, particulary in the verbal and discriminative repertoire, than the development of new forms of action.

Thus, the early development of the child is a complementary evolvement of the child's neuromuscular and central nervous system that is expressed as its operant interaction with the environment. The prominent influence of phylogenetic factors is seen in the constant developmental sequence that occurs across so many different cultures.[2] Yet, it does not seem accurate to describe the genetic factor as a cause of the behavior since the interaction of specific performances on the environment is the event that brings the behavior into being and shapes it into increasing complexity. When the interaction between parent and infant over feeding, warmth, freedom of movement, and elimination result in large levels of deprivation and aversive stimulation, these biologically urgent behaviors will preempt playful ones, like those mentioned earlier. Such preemption of nonbiologically urgent behaviors will result in a developmental deficit that will have a cumulative impact on the repertoire that emerges. Such deficits have been proposed as causal factors in mental illness as will be discussed in the sections that follow. Developmental psychologists have emphasized the importance of early mothering for normal development. The behavioral analysis of the details of the mother-child interaction give a view of how the actual repertoire emerges.

## education

A behavioral view of knowledge is the start for understanding educational activity. Behaviorally, knowledge is an ongoing activity rather than a specification of what is in a book or a syllabus. It is largely intraverbal, prompted by the individual's own thoughts, the speech of another person, or by a text. Thus, we are inclined to describe behavioral developments whose primary target is not intraverbal, such as learning a sport or a skill, as training rather than educational experiences.

The reinforcement of the intraverbal repertoires that constitute educational development is the best way to describe it. Educational reinforcement occurs in all the various ways that intraverbal behaviors provide the discriminative stimuli that allow a person to act in ways that produce other reinforcers. Reading signs, instructions or recipes are some of the obvious ways that intraverbal behaviors allow practical action. The required intraverbal behaviors are prompted by the sign, the recipe, or the instruction. In the educational activity preceding the practical reinforcement of these intraverbal behaviors, similar texts served to enlarge the student's intraverbal repertoire educationally. Intraverbal behavior serves in recreational and serious reading as a bridge between the verbal performances prompted by the text and the person's existing intraverbal repertoire. It is largely through textual activity that educational environments enlarge a student's verbal capacity.

Educational systems sometimes offer temporary reinforcers, often aversive, until the student has reached a stage where progress toward the complex target repertoire becomes a reinforcer of itself. For example, we give students personal attention, praise, and tokens or money in the case of programs for retarded or emotionally disturbed children. Conversely, we sometimes reinforce educational activity negatively, as when educational progress is maintained by threats of expulsion, incarceration, ridicule, or even corporal punishment. Such reinforcement suffers because there is no natural, generic connection between the study activity and the increment in repertoire it produces.

Teaching reading or a second language by the matching-to-example procedure described in Chapter 6 illustrates the difference between educational performance maintained by a contrived arbitrary reinforcer and a natural one such as progress toward the educational objective. The student sees a picture of a cat or hears the auditory stimulus "cat." Pressing the button under the text *cat* is reinforced. Pressing the button under the text *rat* is not. Even if we force an accurate performance by punishment of S performances or by the intermittent reinforcement procedures described in Chapter 6, there is little likelihood that the student will read the words that control his performance discriminatively. One way to establish progress toward the target repertoire as a reinforcer is to base the reinforcement on the actual repertoire that is desired. Instead of giving food or tokens or release from some aversive stimulation after the student completes the matching-to-sample task, the same reinforcers are given after the student actually reads the texts in the sense of emitting a vocal performance under the control of the text. The activity on the teaching machine then shifts to performances that develop actual vocal performances actively emitted under the control of the text. Whereas the student had been making choices rapidly, a new, subtle set of behaviors is reinforced by their connection with the actual reading that occurs after he studies.

## infantile autism

The repertoire of the autistic child and its etiology have been of special interest to behavioral psychologists because it represents such a profound deficit at such a young age in the most elementary operant behaviors. The child, often 3 years or younger, spends long parts of the day without activity, lying on the floor, staring vacantly, or sitting in one position, barely moving. When active, the performances are of a simple kind such as moving fingers in the visual field, touching a spot on a wall repeatedly, rubbing the hands, or swinging a door back and forth. These are activities that have little effect on the physical and particularly the social environment. Social behavior tends to be restricted, when present at all, to actions that affect others aversively, such as screaming in front of a door until someone opens it or screaming when someone attempts to take a shoe lace the child has been chewing all week. Such children are frequently mute, although sometimes nonvocal behavior such as tugging on a sleeve or gesturing occurs. Vocal behavior, when present, is only apparently verbal. It is usually echoic or intraverbal without any relation to the listener. Long chains of behavior are absent, as might be expected from the absence of simpler forms. With such an impoverished repertoire, discriminative and reinforcing control by attention, approval, money, or progress is absent. In a word, the autistic child has little potential for changing or being changed by the normal environment. Plausible organic causes have not been identified, although many speculate that they exist.[3] A child, however, may be retarded, brain damaged, and autistic.

Principles of operant reinforcement provide a framework for describing how the child's social milieu might have produced such gross deficiencies. Reinforcement and extinction are the main ways of creating or weakening operant behavior. Certain social situations inherently lead to large amounts of extinction. A mother may not answer a child because she is occupied on the telephone or with a book. Some environments are more extreme, producing extinction of large segments of the child's repertoire. A psychotic depressed parent, a drug addict, or an alcoholic will react to the child's actions infrequently. Sometimes apparently favorable environments turn out to have no reactivity contingent on the child's performances. A parent might talk to a child all day long but with few instances where the adult's activity had any connection to the child's repertoire except when the parent physically restrained the child from action. The role of aversive control, stimulus control, and schedules of reinforcement in the etiology of the deficits of infantile autism will be considered in Parts III, IV, and V.

## self-control

Negative reinforcement, the process basic to self-control was discussed in Chapter 3. There, the child biting the lips to prevent giggling and putting the hands behind the back to prevent reaching for fragile bric-a-brac were given as examples of negative reinforcement. In thinking about self-control of eating, the behavioral analysis begins with the simple observation, parallel to the child's inclination to play with the bric-a-brac, that putting food in the mouth is reinforced by its ingestion and digestion. But excessive eating results in weight gain that may be an aversive outcome for the individual. The various activities that might reduce the amount of eating would be negatively reinforced by preventing or escaping the overweight condition. These aversive outcomes are described as the ultimate aversive consequences of overeating because they are so delayed from the actual eating behaviors, especially compared with the immediate reinforcement that occurs with eating. Alcoholism is a similar example where hangover symptoms and the full impact of the social activity are delayed in comparison with the immediate effects of drinking. The practical development of the self-control performances requires taking into account four steps:

1. *Determining what variables influence eating.* Almost every known behavioral process is relevant. They include the effect of food deprivation, chaining, stimulus control, schedules of reinforcement, conditioned reflexes, and aversive control. Discussion of these avenues of control will be continued in the later sections of this chapter.

2. *Determining how these variables can be manipulated.* The task in this category is to find ways, within the person's existing repertoire, by which the variables of which eating is a function can be manipulated. One example would be the choice of food types so that they reinforce eating minimally but sufficiently to maintain its frequency.
3. *Identifying the ultimate aversive consequences of overeating.* Avoidance of the ultimate aversive consequences of overeating is the only reinforcer that can reinforce (negatively) the self-control behaviors. The development of these ultimate aversive consequences will be described in Part V of this chapter.
4. *Arranging the maintenance and successive approximation of the self-control.* Some of the required performances may be so far from the person's existing repertoire as to require successive approximation or other slow changes in the contingencies of reinforcement needed to build on an initially weak repertoire.

The analysis of self-control proposed here has advantages over descriptive terms such as "will power" because it exposes the frequencies of the constituent performances as the primary data that can be observed as new kinds of control are attempted.

## depression

The most obvious aspect of a depressed person's repertoire is a markedly reduced frequency of positively reinforced behaviors and an increase in the frequency of avoidance and escape. The frequency of a positively reinforced performance and its reinforcement are obviously related aspects of the same event. When eating or sexual activity are less reinforcing because of a depression in the frequency of the collateral performances, the individual's behavior in those areas is correspondingly reduced. Despite its diagnostic usefulness, a high frequency of bizarre or irrational behavior does not imply that it is strongly maintained. Even though the overall rate of speaking may be low, a depressed person may spend a large part of the day in simple activity such as hand wringing, pacing, doodling, or compulsively carrying some object about. A high frequency of such activities could occur by default of the rest of the repertoire.

The depressed person's complaints or requests for help are frequent and prominent almost to the exclusion of positively reinforced behavior. The depressed person repeatedly tells how badly he or she feels, talks about suicide, complains of the inadequacy of his or her own conduct, and complains of external circumstances, fatigue, and illness. These are, functionally, avoidance and escape behaviors. Many are extended mands, as defined in Chapter 8.

Suicide is, of course, the ultimate negatively reinforced operant and often a substantial risk in depression. But other negatively reinforced operants have undesirable consequences, too. Besides their significance for indicating aversive aspects of the depressed person's life experiences, these negatively reinforced activities also indicate a low frequency of positive reinforcement. Therapy ultimately has to deal with the missing positively reinforced behaviors. The avoidance and other aversively controlled effects are important, however, because they preempt the normal repertoire. It is questionable whether a person whose repertoire consisted solely of negatively reinforced performances could survive. The missing performances are potentially in a depressed person's repertoire. In the past, he or she has dressed, traveled to work, completed a job, and behaved interpersonally. The depressed and normal repertoires differ in the frequency of the various categories of activity.

The key to a behavioral description of depression is a functional description that includes the reinforcer maintaining the performance, as well as a specification of its topography. Thus, in response to the anxiousness induced by the sudden appearance of a particular visitor, one person might leave hurriedly, while another might begin to talk compulsively. Both are operant performances negatively reinforced by the aversive stimuli generated by the presence of the visitor.

## psychotherapy

There are many forms of psychotherapy but they have in common the employment of a professional whose task is to help bring about a change in the day-to-day life style and activity so as to reduce the amount of aversive control, to increase the proportion of the repertoire maintained by positive reinforcement and to achieve a stable state in the social environment.

Psychotherapy, with limited exceptions, is a verbal interaction between patient and therapist. Even though behavioral approaches to therapy attempt to use terms from behavioral theory in conceptualizing and talking to the patient, the actual events that occur are verbal behaviors by which they influence each other. Thus, we need to distinguish between the verbal behavior of a patient and therapist that is reinforced by its influence on each other and the events, elsewhere, that they are talking *about*. Viewed in this way, the events of psychotherapy, behaviors, reinforcers, and discriminative stimuli, are potentially objective observations that are accessible to both parties. The ways that such verbal repertoires can influence the patient's life elsewhere will be discussed in Part IV.

It is useful at the start to distinguish the task of psychotherapy from that of education. The behavioral processes differ even though each has components of the other. Psychotherapy makes no assumptions about the patient's initial repertoire. The therapist's task is to engage the patient's repertoire in any way that is possible and the relation between the patient's behavior and the influence on the therapist that maintains it is crucial. To the extent that the patient's speech is maintained by its influence on the trained-listener therapist, the behaviors reinforced in the differential interaction will be a model for activity elsewhere. The conversation may be about present or past events, but the actual interpersonal reinforcement is by the therapist's reactivity as listener. Educational tasks, on the other hand, rearrange existing repertoires. The behavioral changes are typically intraverbal and the reinforcers are typically generalized, often aversive, arbitrary, and without connection to the behavior that is developed. Clearly there are components of psychotherapy in education, and educational interventions in psychotherapy. The issue however is which is primary. Interpersonal influences between student and teacher may block the student's learning and the therapist sometimes can simply instruct a patient about his or her day-to-day conduct.

One exception to the verbal character of psychotherapy is in the treatment of a mute autistic child. Descriptions of therapeutic interactions with an autistic child give opportunities to use the concept of reinforcement in a complex natural interaction.[4]

Cutting paper with a pair of scissors is a simple example for showing how collateral support can create a durably reinforced performance. If a child has never used scissors before, there is no possibility of the performance being reinforced enough to increase its frequency. The reinforcer can be amplified, however, by providing enough collateral support for the performance that, despite the child's limited capability, it contributes to the success of the cutting movement. The therapist can stand behind the child with one hand behind each of his. In this position visual contact cannot prompt activities that might be prepotent over the newly developing scissor activity. The therapist's arms around the child reduce the possibility of the child walking away, another activity that would compete with scissor cutting. The child's fingers are put in the scissor, and the therapist's fingers control the child in such a way that the therapist can manipulate the child's fingers and at the same time the therapist can feel the slightest muscle movement. If the child operates the scissors to any degree, the therapist withholds his support in favor of the child's action. Such a procedure allows the slightest capability to be reinforced.

The performance is moving the blades with one hand while holding the paper with the other. The reinforcer is the separation of the paper into parts or the appearance of a hole. The therapist's support fades out as the child participates in the movement of the scissors. The therapist's role is a collateral one, allowing the child to achieve the reinforcing effect by supporting him. The reinforcer remains when the therapist leaves.

This interaction, although nonverbal, is therapeutic because it represents an increment in the repertoire of the child in a situation where the therapist is the person who facilitates the increased competence. The procedure is delicately paced with the child's capability. Little more is possible at such a primitive level of development. Such interpersonal control is a component of what clinicians describe as "relationship."

## questions

*1.* Describe how the psychotherapist's task differs from the teacher's.
*2.* Describe some problems encountered by students in controlling their own behavior.

## part III: the maintenance of behavior under intermittent reinforcement

### growth and development

Intermittent reinforcement is an important aspect of the various developmental periods of human life. In infancy simple activities emerge, continuously reinforced by their direct social and physical effects. Most of the infant's performances are continuously reinforced because they are connected to their reinforcers physically, as when the movements of the arm bring the hand in contact with the mouth or into the field of vision. The exception is crying, which frequently encounters variable-ratio reinforcement. The variable-ratio is defined by the parents' lassitude or preoccupation with matters that are prepotent over the behavior controlled by the child's cry.

The cumulative aversive impact of the crying increases the frequency of negatively reinforced compliance with the child's demand. Demand feeding schedules tend to prevent intermittent reinforcement of crying as do scheduled feedings. The latter is complicated, however, because crying is likely to be accidentally reinforced, in the manner described in Chapter 5, because the child is likely to be crying at the time when the feeding is scheduled. Alternatively, parents may not be able to control the emission of a performance that terminates the crying so that the result is equivalent to a combination of a fixed-time schedule and a variable-ratio. This is technically a tandem fixed-interval, variable-ratio schedule of reinforcement.

Chains of performances emerge in childhood. The child crawls to a toy, fills a container requiring a certain number of shovelfuls and makes a drawing that consists of an accumulation of lines by the marks of the crayon on the paper. These chains constitute a fixed-ratio schedule because completion of a picture requires a certain number of marks with the crayon. On the other hand, a conditioned reinforcer follows each mark in the sense of the second-order schedules described in Chapter 5. Such a performance, therefore, shares the properties of continuous reinforcement even though the maintaining reinforcer at the end of the chain occurs on an intermittent schedule.

It is the area of social interaction that produces the greatest intermittent reinforcement. Since many of the child's performances require some action of parents or others for their reinforcement, all of the factors in the other persons' lives which are beyond the child's control will determine a predominantly variable-ratio schedule of reinforcement—a schedule due to the child's persistence and the competing behavior of the person who is the mediating figure.

Behavior during the juvenile period tends to continue the patterns of childhood. Sports and play involve relatively continuous reinforcement, and social interactions are sufficiently uncomplicated that reinforcement is relatively predictable and stable. It is in preadolescence and adolescence that the major changes occur. The emergence of lust and more complex interpersonal patterns requires more sustained and demanding interaction with other persons. During this period social and work customs impose additional requirements. The adolescent needs to travel to a job and sustain work performances whose reinforcement may involve solely the pay received. Social interactions, in which the other persons heretofore had taken serious responsibility, now require specific behavior, as in sustaining small talk in a conversation. Money required for social interaction imposes the requirement of employment where performances are reinforced on fixed-ratio schedules, as compared with simply receiving an allowance heretofore. The sudden imposition of fixed-ratio requirements is an important factor in the stress and disruption typically experienced by adolescents. The process was seen in its basic form in Chapter 5 where the special conditions required for a successful transition to large fixed-ratio requirements were discussed. The sudden requirement of long chains of behavior imposes the same difficulty.

Adulthood is a period of fixed rather than variable-ratio reinforcement. By middle age, routines are relatively set with fixed-ratio schedules of reinforcement relatively predictable. Employment means driving some distance to work, packing a lunch, completing set tasks daily, maintaining the residence and its grounds. These are all fixed-ratio schedules whose ratio of performances becomes more fixed as time goes on. Behavior under such schedules of reinforcement are most susceptible to weakening, as will be discussed in treating the contribution of schedules of reinforcement to depression. Conversely, under optimal conditions these are the schedules that generate high sustained rates of activity. With old age there is a loss of reinforcers because of the decreased social interaction and lessened physical ability that precludes many sports and physically demanding work. As a result, there is a change in life style in the normal developmental pattern to activities involving small fixed-ratio schedules.

## education

Many educational activities have close parallels in the fixed-ratio reinforcement of matching-to-sample described earlier. They are fixed-ratio schedules because a minimum amount of activity is required to achieve an increase in repertoire. Long division illustrates the parallel. The performance "6" is reinforced in the presence of "2 X 3" but the performance "5" is reinforced in the presence of "2 + 3." Each of the performances in the long division is under narrow discriminative control and a certain number, the fixed ratio, is required to achieve a solution to the problem. The large amount of extinction that occurs during the intermediate stages when the arithmetic stimuli are gaining discriminative control represents a substantial and important source of intermittent reinforcement of the student's performance. With too high an S$\Delta$performance level, the size of the fixed-ratio requirement may be too large for the student to sustain continued participation in the learning.

**Transitions** Intermittent reinforcement is prominent in transitions such as arithmetic to algebra or calculus to higher mathematics. The maintenance of a student's behavior will depend on the disparity between the initial repertoire and the new requirement. The rote calculations of arithmetic allow continous reinforcement, or, at the extreme, small fixed-ratio schedules. With more advanced subject matters than arithmetic, trial solutions, long derivations, and complex calculations are required that result in a greater amount of activity per unit problem than the student had previously faced. Transitions are successful when the difficulty level increases by small increments, when the study task is defined in small parts in the manner of a second-order schedule, or by collateral support that reduces the overall amount of study required per unit of mastery. Students who do not have this intermediate experience are like the bird in Chapter 5 that is exposed to a large fixed-ratio schedule without being exposed to intermediate values paced with its sustained performance.

**Intermittent reinforcement from fading and other successive approximation procedures** In stimulus-programming-procedures,[5] a progression of stimulus differences produces a relatively error-free performance because the stimulus control is developed so gradually that S$\Delta$ performances rarely occur. While the main result may be a reduction in the number of unreinforced performances, the overall amount of behavior required per unit increment in the student's mastery may be increased. The difference is that in the programmed situation, conditioned reinforcers follow intermediate performances that are not present without the program. It is possible that the increase in the amount of behavior required for progress in competence would result in such a large fixed-ratio that the behavior would be weakened rather than being sustained by the gradual program of instruction. Students are likely to describe such a program as dull. Study competences by which students learn to arrange the study materials themselves are in the long run a better solution than programmed study materials because students can then adjust the amount of programmed support they require.

**Progress to a new repertoire as a reinforcer**   It is difficult to know what reinforcers are maintaining a student's behavior in dealing with a long text. It is reasonable to assume that some conditioned reinforcers, in the manner of a chain of performances, would need to occur if the performance is to be sustained for so long. The actual schedules of reinforcement will depend on the specific ways the study activity is carried out. The student who outlines and breaks the chapter into small parts is emitting performances reinforced on smaller fixed-ratios (second-order schedules) than the student who tackles an entire chapter. Studying the chapter becomes a chain of fixed-ratio schedules under discriminative control of the chapter outline.

## infantile autism

Intermittent reinforcement is critically involved in atavistic behaviors such as tantrums and self-mutilation that are so prominent in autism. Chapters 3 and 4 have described the process by which these behaviors, very aversive to the parent, may be reinforced and intensified by their attempts to escape. In addition, the reactivity of the depressed or alcoholic parent to the child varies widely. At the one extreme, the parent is hypersensitive to the child and at the other times so depressed that severe and sustained assault, verbal or physical, is the only way the parent is induced to action. The resulting variable-ratio schedule produces such a high rate and persistence, even during long periods without reinforcement (due to the characteristics of extinction after variable-ratio reinforcement), that the atavisms become a prominent part of the child's repertoire. The primitive behaviors are especially prominent during early childhood when the range of performance is expanding rapidly and new forms of behavior are successively approximated. Performances at this stage of development, newly formed and only approximately effective, will be especially disrupted by levels of intermittent reinforcement that could later be sustained. Along the same lines, the continuous requirement—as the child matures—that its behavior conform increasingly to the standards and forms of the social environment introduces another element of intermittency that makes the behavior most vulnerable to disruption. In a normal environment virtually all of the infant's behavior, except crying, is reinforced continuously. At 3 years of age, however, the child is expected to use the bathroom, stay clean, have the attention of the adult before speaking, use tableware, and so forth.

Although the infant's behavior is reinforced continuously for the most part, there are circumstances where important elements of even a very young infant's behavior may be reinforced on ratio schedules of reinforcement that may strain the performances. This would occur, for example, if a child were given a nipple with too large a flow and the mother kept it in the child's mouth no matter how the child turned or pushed against the nipple or attempted to squirm out of the parent's lap. A clinical case was reported where a parent of an autistic child reported that she believed the child had to finish its bottle each time and had kept the bottle in the child's mouth until it had all been ingested. The child's attempt to remove its mouth from the nipple resulted in a struggle that the parent won. A similar intermittent reinforcement of a negatively reinforced operant occurs when a parent is insensitive to the child's tension and relaxation while the parent is holding the child. The child's movements prompted by the aversive tensions of the parent's ineptness go unreinforced despite their persistence over long periods of time. Too small a nipple results in a fixed-ratio schedule of sucking that may weaken even a performance having as basic a biological base as feeding.

Once simple direct effects on the environment become a prominent part of the autistic child's repertoire, they preempt the development of more complex forms such as occur in chains of behavior maintained by generalized and social reinforcement. Social behavior and generalized reinforcement, because they require the mediation of other persons, are of necessity reinforced intermittently. Such intermittent reinforcement, along with the aversive control factors that will be presented in Part V, weakens positively reinforced performances in relation to the simple, direct effects on the environment continuously reinforced, that predominate in the autistic child's repertoire. While some atavistic activities, particularly self-mutilation, may be compulsive and insensitive to environmental control, they may also be controlled operant-wise in many cases, reinforced by influencing the parent.[6]

## self-control

Eating, except for the chain of gastrointestinal reflexes that occur after food is put in the mouth, is part of an operant chain of performances. At the extreme, the chain of behavior reinforced by eating may be quite extended as when someone dresses, leaves the house, walks to the store, enters, selects foods, pays the clerk, leaves the store, carries the food home, stores it, cooks and otherwise prepares it, sets the table, sits down, cuts the food with eating utensils, and places it in the mouth. Because the frequency of the final member of the chain depends on the overall length of the chain, the intermitency involved provides an avenue of self-control. By arranging that all of the foods require a certain amount of preparation, the tendency to eat can be reduced simply because the chain of performances leading to swallowing is lengthened. Keeping food out of frequently encountered places, shopping on a day-to-day basis (preferably when the disposition to eat is low), buying foods that are not edible without cooking, and placing food in inaccessible areas are techniques that weaken the disposition to eat by the intermittent reinforcement inherent in chains. In contrast to such long chains, eating is continuously and immediately reinforced by the stimuli that occur when food is placed in the mouth and swallowed. Many eaters are already carrying food to their mouth while swallowing the last forkful. An eating pattern where there is a pause after each forkful is placed in the mouth is a technique of control involving this variable.

The self-control performances are complex activities that need to be reinforced in approximations, beginning with a level of behavior already in the person's repertoire. The variables governing eating have to be assessed carefully so that the reinforcement for engaging in the self-control behaviors becomes highly likely and, ideally, continuous. To start with, therefore, items of self-control attempted are simple rearrangements of eating patterns carried out at normal deprivations before weight loss increases the disposition to eat. The kinds of self-control involving discriminative stimuli, to be described in Part IV, are themselves reinforced intermittently. They require that the person be exposed to a place a number of times without eating so that the discriminative control of the time and place is weakened by extinction. The development of this discriminative control is a fixed-ratio that requires the performance to be sustained long enough so that the reflexes and operants are weakened by extinction. The schedule of reinforcement is kept optimal by reducing the competing eating behaviors to a minimum. This is done by carrying out the exercises before loss of body weight has occurred.

## depression

A fixed-ratio schedule may, of itself, cause a decrease in the frequency of operantly reinforced behavior. While the schedule of reinforcement is only one of several factors, it would be surprising if it did not play an important part in the etiology of depression. The enormous influence of intermittent reinforcement was conveyed in Chapter 5 where large fixed-ratio schedules were described that produced long pauses after reinforcement that would result in starvation. Yet the same bird, when reinforced on a variable-ratio schedule requiring the same number of pecks per reinforcement, sustains its activity. This characteristic of ratio reinforcement schedules accounts for the large disruption often produced when people move from adolescence to maturity where the relation between work and its product is relatively fixed compared with the earlier period. The result is often seen as an abulia, such as displayed by the novelist who is unable to work for considerable periods of time after completing a previous book. Even when a casual observation of the person does not show obvious depression, the frequency of writing is clearly depressed. The high rates of performance on fixed-ratio schedules when the person is not in a pause, brings to mind the manic side of depression. The upwardly striving person could be thought of as one whose schedules of reinforcement are variable, sometimes requiring large amounts of activity per reinforcement and at other times requiring less. Such variable schedules are less likely to weaken behavior than those associated with a stable work situation. There, day in and day out, a constant amount of activity is required per unit effect on the environment. Arthur Miller's *Death of a Salesman* suggests such a depression.

## psychotherapy

The lowered frequency of some behavior from chaining and intermittent reinforcement may be an important factor in the emergence of new repertoires in psychotherapy. The events of daily life that are the subject of the patient's concern, can only be influenced by a chain of performances in which verbal behaviors, generated from the interaction with the therapist, are reinforced in the course of the patient's daily life when they are emitted intraverbally. The process is complex and subtle and even though we do not understand all of its details it seems inevitable that some performances need to be reinforced in the therapy interaction before they can be extended elsewhere.

The therapy interaction, of itself, has some of the characteristics of a variable-ratio schedule of reinforcement. The performance is the patient's speech about past life or present events to the therapist. The reinforcer, particularly at the start, is negative—the lessening of the patient's discomfort. The effect of the patient's talk on the therapist and on himself or herself as listener tends to be in proportion to the amount of talking. This relation generally holds even though exceptions come to mind where silence serves an important purpose. When therapy proceeds to the level of complexity of intraverbal interaction involved in "interpretation," we are dealing with performances that are reinforced because they generate intraverbal behaviors that "clarify" events between the therapeutic pair or in the patient's life elsewhere. In that case the chain of behaviors represents a level of intermittent reinforcement of a complexity such as that described earlier in the section on educational textual study.

# questions

*1.* Describe the relationship between schedules of reinforcement and the various developmental periods of human life.

*2.* Explain depression in terms of schedules of reinforcement.

## part IV: stimulus control

### growth and development

The child learns "distance" by the same process by which daylight comes to control moving the fingers in the field of vision. First there is a performance, reaching for a block, reinforced by tactual contact and the play that follows. The performance is reinforced when the block is within arm's reach and goes unreinforced when it is distant. The alternate reinforcement and extinction soon brings the performance of reaching under the control of "visual distance." The correlation between the discriminative stimulus and the reinforcement and nonreinforcement of the performance is so consistent that the discriminative control seems absolute. Yet, it is possible sometimes to observe very young children reaching for a block some 5 or 10 feet distant.

The discriminative control by the physical aspects of the parent's attention has been discussed in Chapter 7 in the context of the parent as a generalized reinforcer. The control of the adult verbal behavior by the physical aspects of attention has its roots in the infant's experience when performances are reinforced or not depending on the adult's appearance. A useful exercise for understanding how the processes of discriminative control serve in the developing relation between parent and child is to observe actual instances where the parent mediates the reinforcement of the child's performances. The process reaches its most subtle form when the dimension of attention is the focus of the eye. Because the control of a listener, when we speak, is so closely correlated with the focus of the eyes, a difference in only a few degrees exerts large control. Most speakers can distinguish between the focus of the listener's eyes when focus moves from the face to someone a few feet behind, and the corresponding loss of vocal behavior due to the missing audience usually follows.

**Enhanced stimulus control by fixed-ratio reinforcement** The conformation of walking or climbing stairs to the stimuli in the physical environment that control these performances is influenced by the requirements of its reinforcement schedule like the matching-to-sample and counting behaviors described in Chapter 6. Walking from one place to another or climbing stairs are examples of complex performances

where the reinforcement of the performance—reaching the destination—
is on a fixed-ratio schedule. The fixed-ratio schedule has a greater influence
on missteps, like the $S\Delta$ pecks in the matching-to-sample performance,
than would occur under continuous or variable-interval reinforcement.
Eating from a bowl with a spoon has the same properties as the preceding
examples. The performance of loading the spoon needs to be controlled
by its position relative to gravity and its movements in relation to the
child's arm and mouth. The reinforcer is the transfer of the food in the
bowl to the child's mouth and stomach, and its schedule of reinforcement
is fixed ratio because a certain number of movements is needed to empty
the bowl.

**Conditional discriminations**   Piaget's descriptions of children's
number concepts illustrate the behavioral concept of stimulus control set
out in Chapter 6. Piaget wrote:

> Let us lay down a row of eight red chips, equally spaced about an inch apart,
> and ask our small subjects to take from a box of blue chips as many chips as there
> are on the table. A child of five or younger will lay out blue chips to make a row
> exactly as long as the red row, but he will put the blue chips close together
> instead of spacing them. He believes the number is the same if the length of
> the row is the same. At six, children arrive at the second stage; these children
> will lay a blue chip opposite each red chip and obtain the correct number. But
> they have not necessarily acquired the concept of number itself. If we spread
> the red chips, spacing out the row more loosely, the six-year olds will think that
> the longer row has more chips, though we have not changed the number. At
> the age of six and a half or seven, children achieve the third stage: they know
> that, though we close up or space out one row of chips, the number is still the
> same as in the other.[7]

At issue is the aspect numerosity of the stimulus that controls the child's
statement of "more," "less," or "the same." Constructing a matching-to-
sample procedure for bringing these performances under the control of
the relevant stimulus would be a useful exercise toward a behavioral
description of the events that Piaget describes.

## teaching

Traditionally, teaching is mainly talking, whether in a lecture, tutorial,
or a discussion. A behavioral analysis of educational interactions needs to
clarify how talking to a student can increase the student's verbal competence. Explanations such as "transmitting ideas" do not contribute very
much to our understanding since speaking is, after all, a pattern of air
vibrations produced by the movement of the diaphragm and modulated
by the muscles of the vocal cords, jaw, and tongue. The movement of air
that results from speaking can only increase the listener's existing performances. Therefore, there needs to be an existing repertoire in the listener

that can be prompted by the speaker's sounds. This formulation, as noted earlier, points to the difficulties of concepts such as "communication." It is paradoxical that communication is perfect when speaker and listener have identical repertoires and not possible at all when their repertoires are entirely different and there is much to be communicated. Clearly, the middle ground, where the speaker can cause a rearrangement of listener's performances, is the most useful one.

When a lecture is effective, it bridges the repertoire of lecturer and audience so that selected parts of the listener's pre-existing repertoire are strengthened in unique combinations not likely to occur without the lecture.

The situation is extremely difficult when a teacher faces the task of lecturing to students whose intraverbal repertoires in the subject matter are unknown to him and with the assigned task of telling them about it. An aphorism by Goethe "You can only teach a student what he already knows" illustrates the difficulty. The task of a psychotherapist in interpreting a patient's behavior offers a related difficulty. Such an interpretation cannot be influential unless the patient is very close to saying the same thing on his own.

## infantile autism

A corrollary of the autistic child's minimal operant repertoire is the small influence on his repertoire by the features of the social and physical environment that control the normal child's repertoire so closely. The autistic child's minimal repertoire requires few distinctions for the primitive levels of reinforcement that maintain it. The lack of discriminative control prevents the development of chains of behavior and socially derived reinforcers such as attention, approval, praise, money and achievement.

### Sudden changes in the environment in the etiology of autism
The narrow control of the child's behavior by the parents, discriminatively, creates a potential for serious disruption. In infancy and childhood, the reinforcement of the child's performances are mediated so exclusively through the parent that a sudden change in environment can be debilitating. Consider the case where a mother did not interact with a child at all, delegating all of the care to a surrogate such as a "nanny," but remained in the environment. Thus, not only was the nanny the occasion when the child's performances would be effective but the mother, by also being present, becomes an S$\Delta$stimulus. The sudden departure of the nurse left the child totally without a repertoire and within two months the child became mute, incontinent, and had to be withdrawn from school with a classical diagnosis of autism. The difficulty was compounded by the history

of differential reinforcement where the child's performances went un-reinforced in the mother's presence and the failure of the mother to institute an environment reactive to the child's performances, probably for the same reason that the nurse was necessary in the first place.

**Reinstating verbal behavior in autistic children**   The failure of verbal behavior in autistic children is closely linked to low level of operant behavior and the consequent low disposition to influence others. If the most elementary kinds of stimulus control are absent from the autistic child's repertoire, verbal behavior is very unlikely because it depends on a generalized reinforcer as well as discriminative control of the child's performances by stimuli from an adult. Unless the child has some perfor-mances reinforced by their influence on other persons, there is no rein-forcer to sustain and shape speaking. In some cases there is evidence that complex verbal behaviors have existed in the disturbed child's repertoire. But it is enormously difficult to assess the child's perceptual and verbal capacity because the emission of operant behaviors are critical for deter-mining discriminative control. We may question whether the child even sees the adult unless there is some performance the continued reinforce-ment of which depends on some aspect of the adult's voice, presence, or facial expression. To develop speech in a mute child, therapeutically, the sequence of events has as its first step establishing the child as an effective listener for the speech of the adults with whom he or she interacts. The adult's speech must be a discriminative stimulus that is differentially corre-lated with the reinforcement of the child's various performances that the adult mediates. At this stage of development, there must be a large reper-toire of behaviors reinforced through the mediation of the adult. At such a point in development, the shift to speech as a way of influencing the adult is a relatively minor increment in repertoire. The reinforcement of vocal activity is significant, immediate, and important as compared with achieving the same consequences nonverbally. Contributing to the transi-tion from nonverbal to verbal social interactions is the function of the child as his or her own listener. Once the child can react discriminatively to the speech of the adults in the environment, the reinforcement of the child's own utterances by their effect on him or her as listener will be immediate.

## self-control

A frequent factor in the lack of self-control of eating may be the large range of circumstances where eating occurs. The disposition to eat could, therefore be reduced by narrowing the range of times and places. There are circumstances when even a determined eater will have a low disposi-tion to eat for periods of time simply because the environment is such that eating has not occurred there. Two kinds of behavior need to be brought under the control of a narrower range of stimuli than had controlled previously. One is the conditioned, elicited, reflex effects of food such as salivation, gastric secretion, and other responses of the gastrointestinal tract. The other involves operant behavior such as when a person, walks, talks, reaches, cooks, and so forth. The different properties of these classes of behavior, described in Chapter 2, need to be taken into account. The extinction of the conditioned alimentary reflexes is likely to be complete while the operant behaviors of eating still have a high potential frequency. The operant behaviors reinforced by food will increase in frequency continuously as the person loses weight even without any alimentary reflexes occurring.

The time of day is an important discriminative event controlling eating. With the individual who eats at regular intervals, gastric activity precedes these occasions closely and is absent at other times. The frequency of the operant aspects of eating also follow its temporal pattern although the parameters are different. A technique of self-control is to rigidly specify a temporal pattern of eating and find conditions for adhering to it. In the early stages of self-control, the development of a rigid temporal eating pattern would be carried out before any weight loss it attempted so that increased food deprivation from weight loss does not increase the disposition to eat beyond the beginning levels of self-control.

The actual characteristics of the eating situation may be used to control the disposition to eat. These stimuli are clearer and probably exert even larger control than the temporal pattern. For practical considerations, eating situations are chosen that occur infrequently in the person's normal routine. Nor should eating occur with other activities such as reading, because eating will acquire properties of a discriminative stimulus and increase the frequency of eating. Eating occasions can be emphasized by arranging very obvious stimuli, such as a set table with a table cloth or napkin of a particular color. Even a restriction in the range of foods eaten reduces the range of discriminative stimuli controlling eating.

Delimiting existing stimulus control of eating may take considerable time because: 1) the loss of control by a stimulus is a gradual process, requiring repeated exposure to the stimuli without reinforcement of the eating performance; and 2) it may be a long time before the individual encounters all of the situations in which he or she has eaten in the past. (The sudden temptation of the ex-smoker when meeting an old friend is an example.) Self-control developed under special diets (all protein, hard boiled eggs, and celery, etc.) will be difficult to maintain afterwards. The novel eating patterns and foodstuffs of a normal diet will be such a shift in controlling discriminative stimuli that the newly emerged self-control will be weakened. Hence, self-control performances need to be developed with foods and circumstances that are likely to be close to the eating pattern that is to be maintained.

## depression

The alternate reinforcement and extinction that is required to bring a performance under the discriminative control of a stimulus is the reason why close discriminative control of operant behavior may contribute to depression. Repertoires closely controlled by a discriminative stimulus are totally disrupted simply by its absence. The death of a close companion, for example, in effect removes performances from a person's repertoire. The impact of the death of a companion will be greater in the case of a reclusive person living alone with one companion because the *total* social repertoire is controlled by that person. The process is comparable to that described in Chapter 6 where it was possible to remove pecking from the bird's repertoire simply by changing the color of the key from green to red. The critical factor was the history of nonreinforcement of pecking in red that is comparable with the absence of any positively reinforced social activity with any other companion.

Physical changes from aging force a movement to new environments, performances, and reinforcers. Reduced sexual capacity is one change. Another is the capacity for physical exertion. Ironically, even eating becomes less possible because the decreased physical activity requires less food. Disease and physical incapacity may require a large shift in repertoire. Retirement imposes a drastic environmental change. Like the adolescent, the older person faces an environment where the previously reinforced repertoires, appropriate to the work environment, are no longer possible. A successful transition depends on whether the person has a sufficient repertoire to make contact with the new reactivities of the retirement environment. Depressions associated with changes such as those mentioned above are termed "reactive" clinically. These are in contrast to endogenous depressions, which will be discussed in Part V, stemming from the person's early history.

## psychotherapy

The crucial issue in psychotherapy, since it is primarily verbal, is how talking about past and present events to a trained listener can influence the person's life elsewhere.

**Stimulus control by the events with the therapist** If there were no discrepancy between what actually happened to a patient in daily living and the report of what happened, there would be no problem requiring therapy. If the patient can observe the therapist's conduct, how he or she has influenced it, and the reverse process, there has been progress toward making the same observations elsewhere. The therapist, as a trained listener who makes a functional analysis of the interaction, is in the position analogous to the violin teacher who can help the student to hear nuances of pitch that are at first audible only to the teacher.

**The intraverbal repertoire provides discriminative control else-where** There are practical benefits of an intraverbal repertoire that heightens observations of the patient's own behavior, that of others, and the interpersonal control. Without such a repertoire, there is little possibility of reducing either the amount of aversive control or the amount of intermittent reinforcement and extinction. The process is parallel to the occurrence of randon shocks in an animal experiment as compared with the effect of a preshock stimulus; or to an uncertain occurrence of a positive reinforcer as compared with clear events that set the occasion when the performance is reinforced and when extinction occurs. The absence of an adequate intraverbal repertoire produces emotional by-products, related to extinction and intermittent reinforcement, that we describe in every-day terms as loss, isolation, pain, abandonment, hopelessness, and despair. It is commonly observed, for example, that a patient, interrupted during therapy by frequent telephone calls, may not be able to talk about the complaint. The persistence and magnitude of the annoyance may be so large, however, as to eliminate almost all other interactions leaving talk about being bored, having nothing to say, or about quitting. Clearly there is an aversive event occurring that is influencing the patient but which is covert because there are no verbal performances about it in the patient's repertoire. Once there is intraverbal behavior having a point-to-point correspondence with the observation of the interruptions and the anger engendered by them, there is a possibility of ending the annoying prac-tices or accepting their necessity and deciding that they are worth putting up with. The alternative is a confused mixture of three factors: the pa-tient's observation of the interruption, the annoyance or anger at it, and a view of the therapist as the person who is responsible. On the other hand, the intraverbal behavior that emerges from interaction with the therapist is reinforced when it functions as "observing behavior" in the patient's day-to-day experience.

**Stimulus control in desensitization therapy** Although behavioral therapy by desensitization implies objective data about the events in the patient's life, the actual behaviors of the therapy are a verbal interaction about the events of the patient's life elsewhere and about the patient's state of relaxation. When the patient raises his hand when his state of relaxation is disturbed, the process that operates is that of differential reinforcement and stimulus control. The performance is raising the hand or reporting anxiousness verbally and the reinforcer is generalized, derived from the verbal interaction with the therapist. The discriminative stimulus is private, although muscle tension, voice quality, and even physi-ological changes give some collateral evidence. The sizes of the steps in the desensitization hierarchy is controlled by the patient and the variations are the equivalent of a program for teaching the patient to observe small changes in emotional disruption. Observing the aversive impact of the desensitization hierarchies is probably one of the most skillful aspects of behavior therapy.

The low frequency of verbal behavior, other than complaints, is a serious impediment to the improvement of the depressed person's limited, often distorted view of the world. Normally persistent verbal activity is important because observation of the day-to-day environment and the contingencies of reinforcement there depend in large part on an intraverbal repertoire that provides the relevant discriminative stimuli. It is in endogenous depressions, the causes of which are primarily in the early stages of the person's development, that the reduced verbal activity has a cumulative deficit. The lack of an intraverbal repertoire that can serve to control the person's day-to-day activities produces extinction and aversive control that contribute to the severity of the depression and in turn prevents the emergence of verbal activity that increases positive reinforcement and decreases aversive control.

The same facts are described by cognitive psychologists when they describe the depressed person as having a negative, limited, and unchanging view of the world. A limited view of the world refers to the absence of intraverbal repertoire that might allow the depressed person to adjust his or her performances to the variations in reinforcement conditions that occur from place to place and from time to time. The negative view of the world alludes to an increase in aversive situations because the stimuli preceding aversive events cannot be observed accurately. The unchanging view of the world refers to high-frequency, negatively reinforced behaviors that displace more playful or positively reinforced activities. The advantage of a behavioral description over the cognitive one is the clarity in objective events, performances, reinforcers, and discriminative stimuli that can be observed and defined accurately. Both points of view need to deal with the same facts.

## questions

1. Explain this statement—"You can only teach a student what he already knows."
2. How would you go about trying to reinstate speech in the child who became mute after his "nanny" left?
3. Why do some people regain almost all of their weight after dieting?

## growth and development

Aversive control and emotion tend to be connected because the withdrawal or absence of positive reinforcement has broad effects on an individual's repertoire beyond the specific performances. As was discussed in Chapter 3, the term emotion, behaviorally, is a word referring to those influences that extend beyond the specific performances involved, reinforced or not. Even though physiological responses may also occur and the verbal individual may "describe his feelings," the change in broad classes of operant behaviors provides the most objective and communicable account of emotional phenomena. The behavioral concept of emotion is illustrated by the new-born infant's persistent, fixed-action pattern crying elicited, say, by gastric distress or by long intervals of food deprivation. We talk about an emotional state in the sense that the elicited crying stops all other operant interactions that might otherwise occur with the parent or the physical environment.

The work of Bowlby[8] on the close attachment of the human infant to the mother and the drastic disruption that comes from the mother's loss, and Harlow's[9] studies of infants raised in isolation are useful introductions to the study of the extreme emotional effects that occur in early development derived from loss of reinforced behaviors. Related also are Seligman's[10] studies on learned helplessness. Bowlby observed that children under age 3, separated from their mothers, went through several stages of emotional disruption. First there was crying, tantrums, and hyperactivity; then depressed clinging to a familiar doll or article of clothing; and finally, an overall depression that Bowlby called despair. Should the mother return later, the child would turn its head and eyes away from her and refuse to interact with her as in the past.

The mother's absence is an aversive event because the bulk of the child's repertoire is reinforced through actions mediated by her. The crying, when the child is first separated from the mother, is a fixed-action pattern elicited by the aversive situation similar to the adjunctive behavior that is seen when animals undergo extinction or exposure to primary aversive stimuli.[11] Negative reinforcement is a second factor maintaining the crying because it was the predominant means by which the child induced the mother's attention. The persistence of the crying, even though the parent is absent, is like the extended mand described in Chapter 8. Its prolonged extinction, because of its emission where it cannot be reinforced, leads to depression because the performances most prominent in the child's life have been consistently unreinforced and with a secondary effect of blocking other, lower frequency behaviors.

The turning away from the parent even when she returns is evidence that she now functions as a conditioned aversive stimulus because of the withdrawal of reinforcers. The ultimate difficulty for the child is the arrest in development because the lack of a reactive environment prevents the shaping of the operant performances that would otherwise have been reinforced. The lack of these performances will, in turn, prevent the normal development of the perceptual repertoire since the control by the features of the environment follows from the differential reinforcement of operant performances depending on what stimulus is present. Harlow's social isolation of infant monkeys produced the same result experimentally.

A functional description of crying, sometimes as an operant subject to successive approximation and intermittent reinforcement or as a fixed-action pattern elicited by the withdrawal or loss of reinforcers, casts some light on the controversy about the proper parental attitude toward a child's crying. In one study it was found that children whose mothers responded promptly to their crying, cried less later.[12] The finding appeared to contradict the status of crying as an operant maintained by its influence on the mother.[13] The analysis of crying presented above in elaboration of the processes of successive approximation, intermittent reinforcement, and elicitation as a fixed-action pattern, helps to resolve the seeming paradox. Clearly there are conditions when parental reactions to crying increase its form and frequency, even to pathological magnitudes. These factors have been discussed in the sections about infantile autism. The issue is the same one that centered around whether an infant should be fed on demand or on a fixed schedule no matter how much it cries.

An immediate parental response to the child's crying is, of course, continuous reinforcement, as opposed to the variable-ratio schedule that occurs otherwise. The character of the behavior in extinction is very different under these two schedules, as was detailed in Chapter 5. Variable-ratio reinforcement generates extreme persistence that has an aversive impact that the parent may not be able to withstand without emitting an operant negatively reinforced by terminating it. Crying reinforced continuously does not have such persistence in extinction. Since crying is the major mode of the child's influence on the parent, its continuous reinforcement creates a repertoire that allows the parent to mediate the child's behavior, function as a generalized reinforcer, and still not rule out playful, nonbiologically important behaviors.

The profound extinction of such an important repertoire as crying has an outcome that shares many of the features of Seligman's "learned helplessness." Seligman restrained monkeys and dogs in a harness and exposed them to prolonged periods of electric shock. Although he did not measure the negatively reinforced operants that increased in frequency under the control of the shock, we can be sure that they occurred. It is certain that the dog engaged in many operant performances, derived from past situations where it had escaped aversive stimuli. These performances, basic to survival, were subjected to profound extinction because of the restraint by the harness. This deep level of extinction would appear to be the main factor responsible for the loss of repertoire, depression, and developmental retardation that resulted.

## education

Behavioral psychologists, perhaps because of their conviction about the efficacy of technical positive reinforcement have been critical of educatonal procedures based on aversive control. The theoretical basis of these criticisms is the same as for the objections to the use of aversive control in other areas: 1) the use of aversive stimuli to negatively reinforce study will generate counter control; the student will escape the aversive control by quitting; 2) the educational activity will cease as soon as the aversive consequences are no longer applied, thus the student loses his or her repertoire as soon as the examination is over if the performance were reinforced by avoidance of failure; 3) the by-products of aversive control will interfere with the very performances they are intended to reinforce; 4) knowledge maintained by an arbitrary relation to an aversive event will have different and less useful characteristics than that reinforced naturally by the increment in the student's competence and the advantageous use of the knowledge elsewhere. Aversively reinforced educational behavior is used, despite obvious disadvantages because, short of revolt, the educator can usually guarantee some level of participation and arbitrarily select what is to be learned without taking into account the relevance for the student's life.

The properties of arbitrary, aversively reinforced educational behavior are best highlighted by comparing them with natural, positively reinforced activity. With a generalized reinforcer such as an increment in verbal capacity, the performance is generically connected to the reinforcer maintaining it. It becomes possible for the student's study to be maintained by the way the new knowledge influences his life, practically or playfully. In contrast, the residue from study reinforced by avoiding a failing grade will be those behaviors specifically differentiated to pass the examination, whatever the productivity elsewhere. This is the sense in which we say that learning is for its own sake rather than to pass the course. One byproduct of the arbitrary relation between the study for an examination and the passing grade is the wide range of educationally nonproductive activities that may be reinforced, such as cheating, memorization, study of the professor's habits, and study of past examinations. All of these outcomes are related to the character of the examination as a reinforcer maintaining study behavior.

## infantile autism

The prominence of negatively reinforced, simple, atavistic forms of behavior is a corollary of the minimal behavioral development of the autistic child. These atavisms are either fixed-action patterns elicited by the aversive aspects of extinction and lack of positive reinforcement in the child's past development or they are operants, negatively reinforced because of their large aversive impact on the parent. The extreme aversiveness of the atavisms to the child's parents is the reason that they are reinforced so effectively. The depressed parent is likely to differentially reinforce extremes of atavistic behavior. At one extreme the parent may be hypersensitive to the child and at the other times so depressed that only extreme forms bordering on physical violence will produce a reaction. Under these conditions, topographies of action maximally aversive to the parent will be differentially reinforced and the level of the child's aversive control of the parent will escalate. The basic process has already been discussed in Part III of Chapter 3.

The direct and large scale social impact of tantrums, self destructive behavior, screaming, and crying prohibits further positive development and retards mature social interactions. While it is possible that extremes of corporal punishment or debilitating illnesses early in childhood may be important causal events in the autistic child's loss of repertoire, it is unlikely that such extreme deficits could be caused solely by suppression of the punished performances. Even when punishment is by physical trauma, it is likely that the more profound impact is the absence or withdrawal of interactions that are usually by-products. Also, the effectiveness of punishment depends as much on how well the punished behavior is maintained by the reinforcer maintaining it as it does on the magnitude of the aversive stimulus. The newly emerging repertoire of the infant is, therefore, especially vulnerable both to its aversive control and to the interference with its continued positive reinforcement. The emerging repertoire is especially vulnerable while it is being shaped and differentially reinforced because its reinforcement at that stage is especially intermittent.

Paradoxically, the autistic child's negatively reinforced operant behavior is likely to play a large part in the emergence of verbal behavior. Negatively reinforced operants, by their effect on the adult, are the basic constituents from which verbal interactions can develop because these simple, directly reinforced mands are such a prominent, high frequency part of the child's emerging social repertoire. The precursor to speech is some inclination to influence the behavior of those persons who support the child's behavior. If these persons have a verbal repertoire, then the verbal means of influence are reinforced even more directly than nonverbal means. The crucial step in the development of verbal behavior is the reinforcer mediated by those persons. Such reinforcement is immediate when it is negative and crucially important because it concerns so much of the child's repertoire. If these behaviors can be reliably reinforced, without the kind of differential reinforcement of extreme forms described above, they are an important avenue of verbal influence that is within the child's potential.

## self-control

Avoidance of the ultimate aversive consequences of uncontrolled eating is basic to the reinforcement of self-control performances. The problem arises because there is a lapse of time between eating and the weight gain that is experienced later. To overcome this lapse of time, a conditioned aversive stimulus is required that can occur at the time when there is a disposition to eat. The individual's own verbal behavior can serve the function of the conditioned aversive stimulus if it is an intraverbal repertoire that describes the long term, aversive consequences of overeating. It is not enough for the person to *know* the aversive effects of overeating for such performances may be weaker than the eating behavior and hence be preempted because of the strong, immediate reinforcement of the latter. Therefore, an extensive repertoire must be established so that the large intraverbal repertoire about the long range aversive consequences of overeating will persist even when there is a high level of food deprivation. By this process, certain foods, eating places, and times can acquire the properties of a conditioned aversive stimulus if they prompt the intraverbal performances about the long term aversive consequences. The difficulty is that these conditioned aversive stimuli may be suppressed by their own aversiveness, particularly before they negatively reinforce self-control effectively. The solution is to develop an extensive intraverbal repertoire, relevant to the factors in the person's own life, and to keep the level of food deprivation low enough so that the frequency of eating does not exceed the level of self-control that has emerged. When the self-control behaviors are effectively reinforced by avoiding the long-term aversive consequences of overeating, it becomes possible to tolerate a larger intraverbal repertoire about the ultimate aversive consequences of overeating. The process is the same as in a chain of performances where a rat presses a bar reinforced by a mild shock that is a discriminative stimulus that sets the occasion when another performance produces a reinforcer. By beginning with very mild shocks, it becomes possible to construct a chain of performances where a strong shock controls the next operant in the chain rather than negatively reinforcing a performance that removes it. Since the actual aversive effects of being overweight are largely individual matters that vary widely from person to person, some format such as group discussion is needed to generate them. It would be a reasonable prediction that a person would talk about the actual aversive impact of being overweight in increasing detail as performances, effective in self-control, developed.

## depression

The repertoire of the depressed person, like the autistic child, consists of a preponderance of negatively reinforced operants, mands, over positively reinforced behavior. These tend to be predominantly in the form of the extended mand described in Chapter 8: "I feel awful." "Why does everything turn out so badly?" "I am so unhappy." "Nothing is going right for me." "I have nothing to live for." The complaints are in the form of telling how badly one feels, and about crying, fatigue, illness, and loneliness. High frequencies of agitated activities such as hand wringing, pacing, or compulsive talking serve a function similar to complaints because they mask (by prepotency and hence escape and avoidance) other aversive conditions such as silence, inactivity, or anxiety-producing activities. Were more effective methods of avoiding aversive situations available to the depressed person, these methods would be prepotent over these simple forms.

The aversive and positive aspects of the depressed person are interrelated. A repertoire that efficiently avoids aversive stimuli may still lack sufficient positively reinforced activities. Conversely, the aversively maintained behavior of some depressed persons may come from the absence of positively reinforced behavior or a sudden reduction in it. Therefore, although the extreme distress and aversively motivated behavior need to be the first point of contact in therapy, the long-range objective includes a concern for the positively reinforced behaviors that are missing, as discussed earlier in this chapter.

**Anger turned inward or self-punishment**    A common attribute of depressed persons is a high frequency of self-critical remarks. Such behaviors result from blend of two kinds of negative reinforcement. The first part is the child's performances when they act aversively on the parent, as a reaction to a withdrawal of attention or personal support, or even basic care. This is the mand described earlier and it may or may not overtly specify the reinforcer that is the mand's objective. Such a situation might arise with a parent who feeds a child unsatisfactorily and whose disruption by the aversiveness of the child's crying further prevents satisfactory feeding. When the force and frequency of the mand (or extended mand) reaches large magnitudes, we call it rage. The second area of negative reinforcement occurs because such aggressive action is often punished reciprocally by the parent's withdrawal of attention and even by corporal punishment. Such punishment will increase the frequency of the very behaviors the parent intends to terminate. Besides increasing the frequency of the child's mands for personal interaction, such punishment differentially reinforces the aggressive behavior toward a topography that avoids punishment. The result is a less overt form of the punished behaviors. At the extreme, the mands may be suppressed into completely covert forms so that neither parent nor child can talk about them. Although the child's aggressive activity has the possibility of correcting the imbalance by informing the other person about what is lacking, the result is as likely to be catastrophic. Aversive control in response to loss is likely to produce counter control that implicitly reinforces the covert rather than overt form of aggressive action. It is a paradox, similar to the analysis of the nagging and teasing episode of Chapter 4, that the parent differentially reinforces those activities in the child that are sufficiently aversive to keep them fighting but of a form of which neither one may be overtly aware. The one part of the interaction consists of aggressive actions toward the person, causing isolation, loss, or absence of personal relation (an extended mand). The other operant is a performance of a form that avoids the parental counter control. The blend that results from these two conflicting contingencies is a class of operants that has, at once, the quality of attack and blame and are also in a covert form that does not expose it to the extreme aversive counter control that it would otherwise engender.

Not only do such self-aggressive behaviors constitute some of the main diagnostic indicators of clinical depression, they also are a significant area of ongoing behavior that displace, albeit somewhat covertly, the highly differentiated verbal activities that are maintained by generalized reinforcement.

## psychotherapy

Two tasks facing the psychotherapist in the day-to-day interaction with a patient are: 1) an understanding of the thrust of his talk by appreciating the variables of which it is a function; and 2) keeping those behaviors that produce aversive stimuli that will disrupt the interaction between them to a minimum. The first factor, already discussed in Part 1 of this chapter and in Chapter 8, describes the relation between the therapist's reactivity as listener and the increment from it in intraverbal repertoire that benefits the patient. This factor is an example of Skinner's "refined" definition of verbal behavior, where the reinforcer is the immediate influence on the listener, verbally, rather than some later, practical action mediated by the listener. The management of the disruptive effects of aversive stimuli also contributes to this first factor, if talking to the therapist is negatively reinforced by a reduction in disruptive aversive control.

The management of the level of aversive control of the patient's behavior occurs in two ways. The first way, like the heirarchy in desensitization therapy (see Chapter 10), is being careful not to prompt verbal behavior that will have disruptive aversive effects. Like the disruption by a preaversive stimulus (Chapter 4, Part V) intraverbal behavior vaguely correlated with aversive events in the patient's life will suppress ongoing operant behavior. Or it will negatively reinforce avoidance and escape in the form of anxious "chit-chat," drowsiness, forgetting, or even not returning to the "painful" situation. A second way that the aversive disruption of the patient's behavior is lessened by the therapist is by stimulus control through the intraverbal repertoire developed in therapy. In that event, the control by the aversive stimulus is limited to the actual situation where the behavior is occurring and where it can be influenced in place of a pervading continous effect.

## questions

1. Explain why a child will turn away from its mother when she returns from a vacation.
2. Explain why we say learning should be for its own sake.
3. Why do depressed people frequently make self-critical remarks?

## notes

[1]Skinner, B. F. *Science and human behavior.* New York: Macmillan, 1953.

[2]Kagan, J. Family experience and the child's development. *American Psychologist* 34: 886–891, 1979.

[3]Rimland, B. *Infantile autism.* New York: Appleton-Century-Crofts, 1964.

[4]Ferster, C. B. Transition from animal laboratory to clinic. *Psychological Record* 17: 145–150, 1967.

[5]For example, see the fading procedures described in Part III of Chapter 6.

[6]Lovaas, O. I., Freitag, G., Gold, V., and Kassorla, I. Experimental studies in childhood schizophrenia: Analysis of self-destructive behavior. *Journal of Experimental Child Psychology* 2: 67, 1965.

[7]Piaget, J. How children form mathematical concepts. *Scientific American.*

[8]Bowlby, J. Grief and mourning in infancy and early childhood. *Psychoanalytic Study of the Child* 15: 19–52, 1960.

[9]Harlow, H. F., Dodsworth, R. O., and Harlow, M. K. Total isolation in monkeys. *Proceedings of the National Academy of Science* 54: 90–97, 1965.

[10]Seligman, M. E. P. and Maier, S. F. Failure to escape traumatic shock. *Journal of Experimental Psychology* 74: 1–9, 1967.

[11]Azrin, N. H., Hutchinson, R. R., and Hake, D. F. Extinction induced aggression. *Journal of the Experimental Analysis of Behavior* 9: 191–204, 1966.

[12]Bell, S. M. and Ainsworth, M.D.S. Infant crying and maternal responsiveness. *Child Development* 43: 1171–1190, 1972.

[13]Gewirtz, J. L. and Boyd, E. Does maternal responding imply reduced infant crying? A critique of the 1972 Bell and Ainsworth report. *Child Development* 48: 1200–1207, 1977

# 10

# applications of behavior principles to practical problems

In Chapter 9, we discussed how behavior principles can be applied to human experiences; the function of the behavioral analysis was to complement discoveries about human conduct with an objective description of the same facts. The purpose was to make the observation and formulation of these facts more communicable and understandable than they would be otherwise.

The applications of behavioral principles dealt with in this chapter are more direct and practical than the theoretical elaborations of Chapter 9. Part I describes some of the ways that animal procedures have been used as practical techniques in industry and in the military. The operant reinforcement baselines with animals also have provided means for studying a number of conditions, including the behavioral effects of drugs, brain function in behavior, and models of alcoholism and drug addiction. Experiments using the procedures and processes described in Chapter 6 have provided techniques for using animals to study issues in psychophysics that heretofore could only be investigated with people.

In Part II, the non-therapeutic applications of operant conditioning procedures to the practical solution of human problems are described. These problem areas include delinquency, the training and management of retarded children, classroom misconduct, traffic control, and dyslexia.

In Part III, therapies derived from behavioral principles are described. These include desensitization therapy, biofeedback, and token procedures. These procedures will be exposed to a behavioral analysis such as that carried out in Chapter 9.

---

# outline

The modern development of methods for investigating the individual behavior of organisms has led to a variety of practical results at both the animal and human levels. Some are highly specific and some are general in nature, as will be seen in the examples given here. All of them can be considered as the consequence, more or less immediate and direct, of laboratory science.

---

## part I: applying animal laboratory procedures

### pigeons as pill inspectors

Procedures similar to matching-to-sample were used for training pigeons to inspect a line of drug capsules and to reject defective ones. A pigeon's potential visual acuity far exceeds the gross differences between a perfect and defective capsule, therefore the task was within the birds' capabilities. Although the application "worked," it was ultimately never installed because it did not seem advisable to have animals so prominent in the production of drugs for human use. However, the procedure is important to study as an example of a potential application. The procedure is shown graphically in Figure 10-1.[1]

The bird compared each pill to be inspected with a standard sample and pecked one key if it matched and a second key it if didn't. The standard pill was fixed in position behind the key. A line of pills passed across the same key one at a time. Some were perfect, and some were defective. In the training procedure all the capsules on the inspection line were coded by an electrical switch, so that the bird's peck on key 1 could be reinforced when it matched the standard and on key 2 when there was a defect. The bird is most likely to look at the pills if it is required to peck them. Hence the procedure entailed a chain of performances, each to be completed before the next could be carried out. When the bird pecked at the sample window, the lights behind the keys below it were illuminated. Then, the bird could register, by pecking the appropriate key, whether the production capsule matched or mismatched the standard. Each time the bird completed a trial, the assembly line moved to the next pill. With this procedure the bird's pecking soon came under the control of the pill's identity with the standard sample.

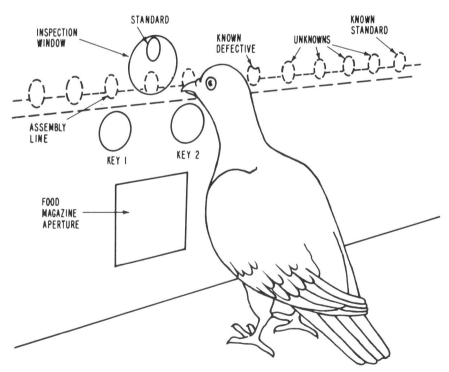

Figure 10-1    A diagram of the pill inspection apparatus.

One of the problems to be solved in the practical extenstion of the procedure was how to differentially reinforce when the defective capsules were not coded. If all of the pills were pre-coded, the bird wouldn't be needed as an inspector. Verhave solved the problem by inserting, at a certain frequency, pills that he knew were defective or perfect. Either reinforcement or time out was delivered on these occasions. The bird had no way of knowing which pills resulted in reinforcement or punishment since this was determined by a switch on the assembly line that was not visible. Thus every reinforcement was correlated with the acceptance of a perfect pill and every punishment was correlated with the acceptance of an imperfect one. Defective capsules were planted with sufficient frequency for providing adequate differential reinforcement to maintain control of the bird's behavior by the capsules and to keep it at the task.

## pigeons as observers of military targets

An experiment was carried out for the United States Army to develop a procedure for pigeons to identify human figures embedded in a complex photograph (Herrnstein and Loveland).[2] If pigeons could be trained to react to the abstract property of a stimulus, such as "human," they could perform many field functions such as sending back signals whenever a particular kind of person or weapon appeared; these tasks were previously carried out by soldiers. The task is similar to that of the pigeon pill inspector described in the preceding section.

The phrase "identify the presence or absence of human" refers to a performance under the control of an abstract property of a stimulus. The defining property of a human does not exist in any one stimulus. It is the common property of a class of stimuli as distinguished from another class that does not have the critical property. The complex photograph, in which the human is a very small part, contributes to the control by the abstract property of the stimulus by the differential reinforcement it provides.

After the birds were magazine-trained and conditioned to peck the key, in the way that has been described in Chapter 1, the key was illuminated by pictures projected by 35 mm color slides. 1200 different slides were available and, during any one session, 81 could be projected automatically as part of the stimulus-control procedure. In each experimental session, half the photographs had a human figure. The human figures appeared in complex contexts, many obscured by trees, automobiles or windows. Even the people varied in appearance from clothed, semi-nude, nude, children, men, women, and so forth. Pecks at scenes with people operated the food magazine on a one-minute, variable-interval schedule of reinforcement. Other pecks went unreinforced. The slides changed randomly every minute.

The first indication of whether the bird's peck is being controlled by the presence of a human figure was a difference in the rate of pecking when a figure was present and when it was absent. Figure 10-2 shows that the bird's pecks were in fact controlled by the presence or absence of a human figure. Each point is the rate of pecking for an entire experimental session. The open circles represent the rate of pecking when the picture contained a person and the closed circles show the rate when it did not. There were only four instances where the rate of pecking at pictures without people was above 0.3 pecks per second whereas in 43 other cases in the presence of a person, the rate was between 0.3 pecks per second and 1 peck per second. In most of the sessions, the rate of pecking without people was below 0.2 and there were many sessions with even lower rates.

The bridge between the control of the pigeon's behavior by this abstract property of the stimuli and human conceptual behavior is a long one even though the basic stimulus-control process is identical. Such kinds of stimulus control in human behavior occur mostly with verbal perfor-

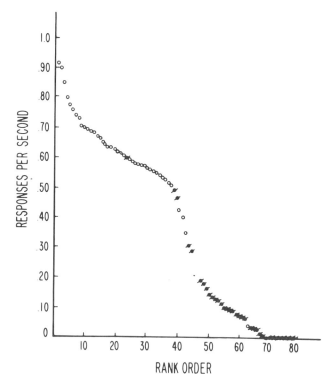

Figure 10-2   Rate of pecking in the presence of each picture as a function of the rank order of the rate. Open circles represent pictures containing people; closed circles, pierced by a line, pictures without people.

mances, such as the abstract tacts and intraverbal behaviors that were described in Chapter 8. The great accuracy and consistency of the human performance in this situation is due to an intraverbal repertoire that has a point-to-point control by the small details of the picture.

**World War II experiment on animals as military observers** The experiment described above followed the general format first developed by Skinner during World War II when he proposed that pigeons be used to guide bombs toward targets. Concentrating more on the practical aspects of the system, since the development was proposed as a wartime measure, Skinner dealt with all the issues of control of the bird's pecking by abstract properties of the target stimuli.[3] As with the later experiment, the bird pecked at the target that was projected on the key. In the military application, the bird would view the actual scene in front of the falling bomb. Pecks at the target were reinforced with food and this performance, through transducers, altered the course of the bomb appropriately as the target moved from the center of the key because the bomb was off course. The birds were trained to follow a variety of land and sea targets and to neglect irrelevant features of the complex field.

Skinner's procedure for training the birds to peck at special targets such as ships at sea in various forms, distances, and contexts, involved the same issues of control by an abstract property of a stimulus as later replicated by Herrnstein and Loveland.

## psychophysics

Psychophysics, the study of sensory capacities such as the threshold of vision or hearing, has traditionally been studied with human subjects who indicated verbally whether they could detect the presence of absence of a stimulus or the difference between two stimuli that differed in varying degrees. The relevant concepts have been the *threshold* of the stimulus or the *just noticeable difference* between stimuli. The traditional psychophysical methods have relied on the subjects' verbal behaviors. These, as described in Chapter 8, are tacts under the control of a light presented at the subject's eye or a sound presented at the ear. The task of psychophysical investigations is to determine the relation between a stimulus that is precisely specified and the correspondingly defined performances under the discriminative control of that stimulus.

The processes of discriminative control described in Chapter 6 have led to laboratory procedures where animals such as pigeons have been the subjects in psychophysical studies. The starting point is a performance, such as pecking, that is under the discriminative control of the light or sound. Thus, the occurrence of a peck under the discriminative control of the stimulus of a given intensity or frequency is the functional equivalent of human verbal performances such as "I can see it," or "the two stimuli are of the same wavelength," or "the two stimuli are of different wavelengths."

The general method of using pigeon operant conditioning to study psychophysical problems is illustrated by a procedure in which a pigeon pecks at one of two keys depending on whether the stimuli there are the same or different.[4] The wavelength of the light on each of the keys is the same or different from trial-to-trial and when the colors are different the magnitude of the difference also varies from trial-to-trial. The general form of the procedure is the same as in the pill-inspection procedure described earlier except that the experimenter precisely controlled the wavelength of the light that is projected on the key. The absolute magnitude of the wavelength and the difference in wavelength between the stimuli on the two keys could then be described as a function of their discriminative control over the bird's pecks. As a result, wavelength generalization curves were drawn and just noticeable differences read from them.

A more complex kind of discriminative control is used to determine a pigeon's threshold to light intensity. The procedure is best described by Figure 10-3, the diagram of the apparatus that is used to present the stimuli and correspondingly reinforce the bird's pecks discriminatively.[5] Most of the diagram concerns the control of the light's intensity. The optical wedge blocks light to a degree that depends upon its thickness, and is moved up and down with a motor. Pecks at the triangular key are reinforced when the key is dark. Pecks at the round key decrease the intensity of the light by lowering the optical wedge a small amount. Whenever a peck is reinforced, the shutter blocks the light completely so that there is a firm correlation between the reinforced peck and a dark key. Pecks at the triangular key also increase the intensity of the light by driving the wedge in the upward direction. Pecks on the circular key decrease the intensity of the light. Thus a peck at the round key is equivalent to the performance of a person saying "I see it." The darkened key, as a discriminative stimulus that controls when a peck operates the feeder, is the reinforcer that maintains pecking on the round key. Each peck is reinforced by a dimming of the light until it is sufficiently dim that the low intensity prompts a peck on the triangular key. Reinforcement of pecks on the darkened round key by the food magazine are always preceded by the shutter closing so that the performance is controlled by total darkness. At other times, the intensity of the light will oscillate around the value where the bird no longer sees it. By the use of this method, it has been possible to study psychophysical phenomena such as dark adaptation, heretofore possible only with human subjects. The method was originally devised in research on the threshold of hearing and has subsequently been used to investigate other sensory modalities and dimensions.[6]

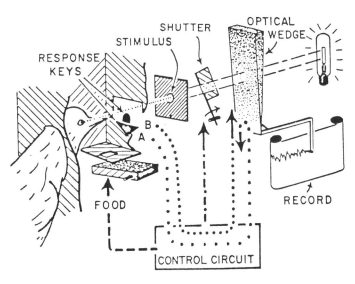

Figure 10-3 A schematic picture of the threshold tracking apparatus. (From Blough, 1958).

## psychopharmacology

The laboratory procedures of pigeons' pecking, reinforced on intermittent schedules, have provided baselines for evaluating the behavioral effects of drugs. These studies have provided much useful information relevant to the wide use of tranquilizing drugs in the treatment of mental illness, and the recent concerns about the behavioral effects of toxic by-products of chemical substances. The laboratory procedures have provided models of the basic behavioral processes—reinforcement and the maintenance of behavior, positive and aversive control, discriminative control, and emotion. Furthermore, the ability to maintain an easily repeatable, topographically stable performance such as a pigeon's peck over a period of time has provided a sensitive baseline that has been used to reflect the time course of action and the degree of frequency increases or decreases that are caused by the drug action.

An experiment examining the effects of phenobarbital on a pigeon's performance on a multiple fixed-ratio, fixed-interval schedule is a useful place to begin because this schedule has already been described in Chapter 5. A multiple schedule is especially apt for the study of the behavioral effects of drugs because the drug action may be seen in two very different kinds of behavior at the same time. As the experiments to be described will show, the behavioral effects of psychotropic drugs are different depending very much on the process that is controlling the animal's behavior. Figure 10-4 is a cumulative record of the baseline performance from which the effects of the drug were studied.

The fixed-ratio and fixed-interval schedules that are the components of the multiple schedule change after every 2 fixed intervals and after every 10 fixed ratios, rather than the simple alternation that was described in Chapter 5. The multiple schedule has the advantage that the behavioral control inherent in the performances under the two schedules is so differ-

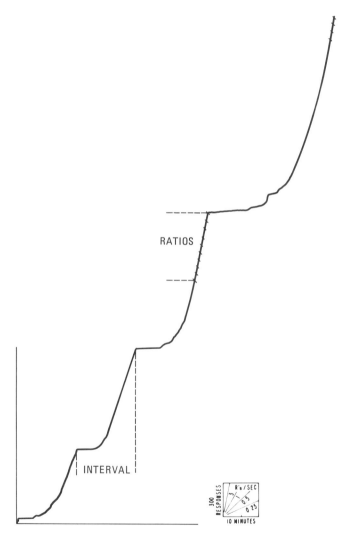

**Figure 10-4** The performance of a pigeon on a multiple fixed-ratio, fixed-interval schedule that served as a baseline to determine the behavioral effects of phenobarbital.

ent. Figure 10-5 shows the performance of a bird that had been injected with 30 milligrams of phenobarbital and tested at various intervals subsequently. By this means it was possible to measure the time course of the drug effect.

Record A, showing an interval and ten fixed-ratio segments, shows that the drug has affected the two kinds of performances differentially. When the stimulus present controls the fixed-interval schedule performance, pecking is completely suppressed. The pecking on the fixed-ratio schedule is much disrupted but in the main the bird continues pecking. At record B, taken 24 hours after the drug injection, the fixed-ratio performance is normal, but the fixed-interval pattern of a pause followed by an accelleration to a moderate rate is lost, replaced by sustained pecking throughout the 10-minute interval. In record C, 30 hours after injection, the fixed-interval performance has recovered only slightly and it is not until 48 hours after the phenobarbital injection, Record D, that the performance returns to normal. Various drugs produce different patterns of behavioral changes depending on whether the effect is examined on the fixed-ratio or fixed-interval schedule. Amphetamines tend to increase the rate of pecking on the fixed-interval schedule by large magnitudes without affecting the fixed-ratio except at very high doses.

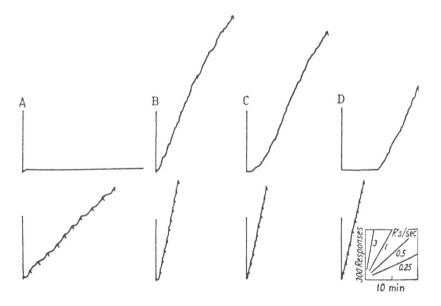

Figure 10-5    The effects of phenobarbital on performance at various time intervals after injection. The upper series shows the selected interval and the lower series shows the 10 ratios. The interval above each sequence of ratios is from the same standard run. Symbols: A=18 hours, B=24 hours, C=36 hours, and D=48 hours after injection.

Not only does the schedule of reinforcement determine a drug's action, the nature of the reinforcer and the behavioral history are equally influential. Figure 10-6 describes an experiment showing how a history of punishment can alter the behavioral effects of amphetamine. The squirrel monkey's performance is pressing a key, reinforced on a 5-minute, fixed-interval schedule by food. The left panel shows little effect from small doses of the drug and substantial reductions in overall rate from the larger doses. The monkeys were then given a brief experience with a shock avoidance schedule, returned to the fixed-interval performance until the original performance was recovered and tested once again with the same doses of amphetamine. Now the lever-pressing, reinforced on the same 5-minute fixed-interval schedule, shows large increases in the rate of responding simply as a result of the previous history.[7] Thus, the greater effect of the drug after the history of avoidance was determined by the fact

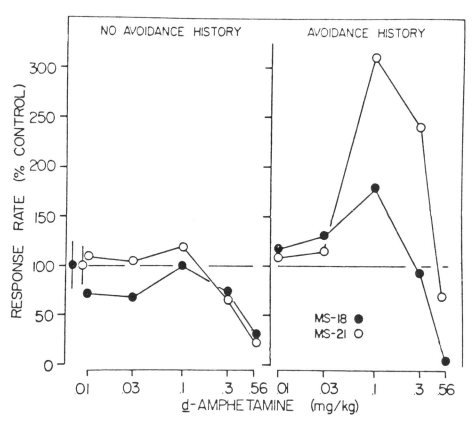

**Figure 10-6**   Effects of *d*-amphetamine sulfate on punished responding of two squirrel monkeys before and after exposure to an avoidance or shock-postponement schedule. Control points ±1 S.E. are indicated on the left.

that the rate of shock avoidance performances increases under the influence of amphetamine.

Such experiments have been of practical use in behavioral evaluation of psychotropic drugs. The laboratories of many pharmaceutical companies employ techniques of this kind in their evaluation and testing of new drugs. The stability and objectivity of the baseline makes it possible to measure the effects of varying doses of a drug in an individual subject. Because the intermittently reinforced free operant is emitted continuously over time, the baseline reflects the onset and duration of the drug action. Such experiments relate the drug effects to the basic behavioral processes that have been the theme of the preceding chapters.

## drug addiction

Operant-conditioning experiments have been applied to the phenomena surrounding drug dependence. The impetus for these studies has come from the debilitating social, psychological, and medical consequences that appear when people become addicted. Drug dependence is defined, pharmacologically, as an increased tolerance for the drug, cocaine or morphine for example, that requires increasingly large doses to achieve the reinforcing effect and to prevent the onset of withdrawal symptoms. Animals such as rats or monkeys are addicted by giving them increasingly large doses over a period of time. Animal conditioning procedures, using a free operant such as pressing a lever, have provided a ready means of studying addiction if the performance of an addicted animal is reinforced by the infusion of the drug on some schedule of reinforcement.[8] In the typical animal experiment, a catheter is permanently implanted in a vein, the animal is partially restrained and the device that pumps the blood into the blood vessels is automatically operated.

A large number of experiments have shown how a free-operant performance is maintained stably when it is reinforced on some intermittent schedule, such as fixed-interval or fixed-ratio, by the infusion of a drug such as morphine. Since the morphine also produces a general systemic depressive effect on the animal's ongoing operant behavior as well as drug-reinforced performance, the experimental technique that evolved programmed a time out after reinforcement during which the systemic drug effect could dissipate. The performances that were recorded in these experiments were indistinguishable from those maintained by food reinforcement such as were presented in Chapter 5.

Behavioral studies have uncovered neurochemical mediators of drug reinforcement. One line of research with these laboratory models of human addiction explored narcotic antagonists, such as methadone for heroin addiction and antibuse for alcohol, based on neurochemical mediators of drug reinforcement. These are evaluated behaviorally by maintaining an operant performance reinforced by the drug and investigating whether the effect can be interrupted by giving a biochemical compound that blocks the action of the addicting drug. Some compounds, like antibuse, make the previously addicting drug aversive.

The availability of a performance, maintained by the infusion of drugs such as morphine, has made it possible for investigators to study whether the reinforcing properties of the drug come from its action as a positive reinforcer or because of the prevention of withdrawal symptoms. Such experiments reinforce an operant performance without first addicting the animal. It was discovered that it was possible to maintain performances reinforced by morphine when the doses were low enough so that addiction did not occur. The experiments showed that doses of morphine, not high enough to produce withdrawal symptoms in its absence, still continued to maintain the drug-reinforced performance.

Another important application of animal conditioning experiments, with drugs as reinforcers, determined a drug's potential, pre-clinically, for producing dependence. Animal screening procedures, where a performance is reinforced by the test compound, provide a pre-clinical basis for assessing its potential for abuse.

Conditioned drug effects are an important variable in drug abuse. In human situations, the actual drug administration occurs after a long chain of events of obtaining money, buying the drug, and preparing it for its injection. The stimuli preceding the actual drug effect have the potential of assuming discriminative control over the drug effects and may be powerful influences on persons undergoing drug withdrawal. The issues are the same as those described for the discriminative control of eating as an avenue of self-control. An experiment showed how stimuli associated with the administration of an opiate acquired the ability to elicit many of its physiological and behavioral effects. Addicted animals pressed a lever reinforced by food and shock avoidance in the presence of one stimulus. In the presence of another stimulus, the performance was reinforced by morphine. The effect of withdrawal, therefore, could be seen as a disruption of the food and shock-reinforced performances. When previously addicted animals were given a saline injection in place of the morphine, the disruptive effects of the morphine withdrawal were averted. The experiment thus demonstrated that the injection, per se, had acquired some of the properties of the drug.

## questions

*1.*  Describe the procedure used to train the pigeon to select defective capsules.

2. Describe the critical part of the procedure that was responsible for bringing pecking under the control of human figures.

3. Explain why the effects of morphine withdrawal were avoided when addicted animals were given saline instead of morphine.

## part II: applications to human behavior

### vigilance

Many work situations require that a person engaged in a monotonous perceptual task be continuously alert and vigilant. The prototype of such a demanding situation is the radar operator monitoring a screen for infrequently appearing targets that need to be identified consistently and accurately. In general, radar operators experience a decreased vigilance as their watch progresses. The observing response, described in the related animal experiment reported in Chapter 7, provides a way to maintain these behaviors by schedules of intermittent reinforcement that produce sustained rates of observing performances. These experimentally developed notions were demonstrated practically in human experiments where the radar operator's observing performances were "externalized" by establishing an explicit operant performance (pressing a key) that had the same function as turning the head, focusing the eyes, and the other aspects of "attention."[9] The analogue to the radar watch in these experiments consisted of reporting when a needle was deflected from its normal position. But the position of the needle could be seen only when the operator pressed a key that produced a brief illumination of the otherwise darkened screen. When the operator observed a deflection, he registered the appearance of the target by pressing a "report" key. His task was to report every time a target appeared.

The experimenter then reinforced the observing performances on various schedules of reinforcement. Figure 10-7 shows the result of fixed-interval reinforcement when the first press of the observing key after the elapsed interval, exposed a deflection of the target needle. The data shows clearly that the observing behavior was reinforced by the uncovering of the target and maintained appropriately to its schedule of reinforcement. Other schedules of reinforcement produced their typical patterns of emission of the observing performance. A variable-interval schedule of reinforcement would be used in practical applications of these findings to maintain a constant, substantial frequency of observation. In order to keep the operator alert when no real signals appear on the screen, "fake" signals may be projected on the screen and when detected by the operator are revealed as test signals.

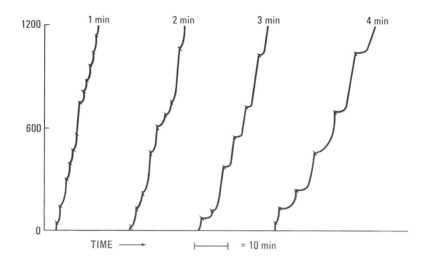

Figure 10-7   Cumulative response records for 1– , 2– , 3– , and 4–minute fixed-interval schedules of pointer deflections. Detections are indicated by lines cutting across the records.

The simple effect of a schedule of reinforcement on observing behavior that was discovered in these experiments obviates the need for mentalistic and hypothetical explanations such as "vigilance is an excitatory state opposed by an inhibitory one." Other explanations, equally mentalistic and diverting from the variables that actually control the performance, focus on the operator's "expectancy" to account for his vigilance. Clearly, the details of how the observing behavior is maintained by its schedule of reinforcement is a more direct and practical explanation. Problems similar to the radar watch occur in many important situations such as long distance driving, assembly line inspection (such as the pigeon or human pill inspector described in Part I), forest watches, or serving as engineer on a train.

## reading

The matching-to-sample procedure introduced in Chapter 6 was used in a practical application to teach reading to children with learning disabilities. A teaching machine provided the child's main interaction with the teaching materials, although the related interactions with the teaching staff were important in the definition of the reinforcement procedures. A 5- X 8-inch card like that shown in Figure 10-8 is first inserted into a special tape recorder that plays the phrase or sentence indicated in the figure. The phrase is recorded on a strip of audio tape pasted across the face of the card. The child then inserts the card into a teaching machine and selects the choice appropriate to the recording that he has just heard. A piece of foil on the back of the card keys the correct response. In this case the button under the middle window with the picture of the cat corresponds to the vocal stimulus "Where is the cat?" and produces a tone indicating that the choice was correct. Figure 10-8 illustrates teaching material at beginning levels, perhaps even pre-reading.

Subsequent cards require the reader to choose texts of increasing complexity and to make increasingly finer distinctions. One card might require the reader to choose between the texts *cat* and *rat* when the vocal stimulus he hears is "cat." A phonics card would present an auditory stimulus "What word rhymes with cat?" and require the reader to choose between the texts *bat* and *bag.* A more advanced card might have a text *animal* as the sample and require the child to choose from the texts *chair, dog,* and *baseball.* The performance is a functional part of reading because it brings the student's performances under the point-to-point control of the details of the textual stimulus. Actual reading of course requires a vocal performance under the point-to-point correspondence of the text. To accomplish this shift, the teaching procedure extended the reinforcement of the reading activities to a later interview with a teacher. Depending on the level at which the child is reading, a text is chosen that is amplified by a set of teaching cards along the lines of those described above. When the pupil finishes studying the card on the teaching machine he would meet with a teacher or teacher aide who listened to her read the text aloud. If the pupil reads successfully, she goes on. If not, the pupil needs to review the cards on the teaching machine in preparation to reading them aloud later again. Thus, the function of the teaching-machine procedure is to bring some performance under the discriminative control of the details of the textual and vocal stimulus and the function of the speech afterwards is to shift the repertoire from the control of a nonverbal performance to the control of the vocal performances corresponding to the text. Since reading (see Chapter 8) is the emission of a vocal performance under the discriminative control of a text, the conversion from the teaching machine repertoire to that required by the inter-

"WHERE IS A CAT ?"

Figure 10-8    An example of teaching machine card.

view can occur easily if the required vocal performances are in the pupil's intraverbal repertoire.

An application of this approach was made to the task of teaching children and adults with learning disabilities to read.[10] Since the interaction with the teaching assistant is the final event in the chain of study activity, the assistant's mode of action was as critical as the programming of the teaching machine cards to produce a graded, relatively error-free progress through the course of instruction. The teaching assistant who runs the session has the responsibility for monitoring the pupils as they carry out their study and to watch for evidence of strain that might come from too rapid an increase in the level of difficulty of the teaching materials. In general, the assistant avoids telling the pupils they are wrong and avoids paying direct attention to them when they are disruptive or inactive. Teaching-machine cards are prepared to develop reading of a page of text. When the child has worked his way through the sequence of teaching-machine cards necessary to develop a vocabulary, word attack, phonics, and comprehension to the required level, he reads the page or sections of it to the teaching assistant. Should a child stumble over a word or fail to grasp one, the assistant responds along the lines, "That's almost right; try again." The assistant coaches slightly but not in a pedagogical style. If the difficulty continues, the pupil is given the teaching machine cards relevant to that part of the text. Although in these experiments a play period at the end of the session is usually arranged to help to maintain participation in the program, the reinforcement of the study behavior is best described by the increase in repertoire that results. The chain of events from working on the teaching machine to reading to the teaching assistant is crucial. In the early experiments with programmed reading instruction, pupils were given tokens as direct consequence of operating the teaching machines and the result was sloppy, uneven performances even though progress toward reading was made. By giving the tokens after the child read the texts from the book and returning the child to the teaching machines when he could not, the performance became more closely controlled by the teaching maching program. The pupils could be seen to talk to themselves and to hesitate before pressing one of the buttons. Such a result is another example of a reinforcement that is arbitrary in the one case and generically related to its reinforcer in the other.

The issues discussed in Chapter 6 for programming the development of control by a stimulus over a performance so as to keep the level of S Δ performances to a minimum are important in the design of the sequence of the program. In this way, the performances are continuously reinforced and the aversive effects of extinction are avoided.

## retardation

Problems with institutionalized retarded children have proved especially amenable to applications of behavioral principles because the task of establishing the needed repertoires is largely educational. Staffs are largely untrained and behavioral training programs have provided a remedy by which a reactive educational environment can be substituted for the limited custodial care that occurs so predominantly and which has exaggerated these children's deficiencies. A case study illustrates how behavioral principles permit the training of the regular staff of these institutions so that the children can be taught self-care performances.

One case concerns a 14-year-old retarded adolescent girl, institutionalized most of her life, who did not walk or feed herself without assistance from the staff.[11] The application began with the behavioral observations that the staff made no attempts to encourage the girl to feed herself. To the contrary, she got special notice when she crawled to take food from other children. Eating is a particularly apt performance to train staff with, since the reinforcer is so explicitly and generically connected with the repertoire that is desired. Thus, work on self-feeding began. The use of utensils was reinforced in successive approximations. The staff member gave a bite of food contingent on the girl's looking at the spoon, then pointing to it, and finally touching and grasping it. Within 5 days the child was eating unassisted. As a result of this increment in repertoire she could take her meals at a table with other children and the social interactions that followed were a collateral benefit. With the expanded experience socially, the approval and attention of staff members and peers increased and interaction with staff over toilet training and walking became possible because of the generalized reinforcement that became operative.

Most research and training procedures in institutions for retarded children have dealt with self-care skills such as toilet training, feeding, dressing, grooming, and elimination of aggressive and self-destructive activities. Successive approximation, the reinforcement of specific performances and the maintenance of optimal frequencies of reinforcement are the main ingredients in all the programs that have proved successful. The impact of behavioral training procedures is as valuable to the staff members who learn to apply them as to the retarded children who are trained. When the staff members have affirmative experiences of changing a child's behavior, their participation and interaction with the children increases. The increased interaction with the children creates the potential of generalized reinforcement by the attention and the involvement of the staff.

The reinforcers are often arbitrary. Although food was generically related to the self-feeding program, it has no such relation to eliminating feces on a toilet—a performance often reinforced with food. Its mediation by the staff, however, who need to interact sensitively and in detail with the child in order to administer the program, produces an interaction in which there is an increase in the frequency of many operants, and many occasions when the adult is a discriminative stimulus who sets the occasion for the reinforcement of the child's performance. The result is a reactive environment for both staff and children that increases progressively to the limits of the child's potential. Each increment in repertoire involving the mediation of the staff member creates the potential of an increasingly effective conditioned reinforcer. Token reinforcement systems, to be described in the next section, have been another kind of application of behavioral methods to educating and managing retarded children.

## token economies

As discussed in earlier chapters, token economies are a practical attempt to engineer a conditioned reinforcer that can be given immediately following a performance whose frequency is to be increased. In its barest form, it is the star system that has been commonly used in elementary schools. The stars and tokens, like money, are established as reinforcers because they are discriminative stimuli that allow reinforcement of other behaviors such as participating in an outing, seeing a movie, viewing TV, receiving a meal or a preferred food, or an opportunity to help the teacher.

Token economy programs have most often been applied in institutional settings with retarded persons, prisoners, adolescent delinquents, and psychotic patients. In many token programs for patients in mental hospitals, tokens are given for taking part in work assignments, self-care activities, and participation in social and group-therapy events.[12,13] The outcomes of token economies on the behaviors that are targeted have been evaluated objectively in many of the situations where they have been applied. Typically, token programs produce a substantial increase in the targeted behavior and typically the experiments prove that the tokens were the responsible factor because the performances cease when the tokens are no longer given. There is no evidence, however, that success of the programs include long-term, sustained rehabilitation in the absence of the token procedures in the natural environment. To the contrary, the predominant evidence is that almost all investigations that have collected follow-up data report that the performances are lost when the arbitrary reinforcer maintaining it is discontinued.[14] Indeed, it would be surprising if the behaviors reinforced by tokens persisted in their absence. This implication is present in the typical "ABA" design used to evaluate behavioral targets reinforced by tokens. The reinforcement by the token is proven by the disappearance of the target performance when the token procedure is interrupted and by its reappearance when it is reinstated.[15] The generalization of performances from an arbitrary environment to other places where the person may live is a crucial question to be answered if the goal of token economies is taken to be the maintenance of the targeted performances. The concept of the operant as a unit in which the performance and its reinforcer are integral and generically connected suggests that the way to enlarge a repertoire, practically, is to find reinforcers that are intrinsically (generically) related to their performances. The reinforcement by the immediate consequences of the behavior is, of course, derived from the context of the person's overall repertoire and the natural environment in which he lives. Both concepts involve conditioned reinforcement but the one is arbitrary while the other is derived from an ongoing, naturally maintained repertoire.

**Benefits of the token economy**    Even if the token economy does not create a behavioral repertoire that can be sustained outside of the institution it is still a major achievement because it creates a more humane style of living than would otherwise be possible with chronic psychotic or severely retarded persons. Another benefit, independent of the target behaviors that might be generated, is collateral to the stated goal of the token procedure. The collateral result comes from enhanced observation and the sensitivity of the staff to the patient as by-products of defining a target performance and attending to the patient in detail so as to be able to reinforce it. Not only does the staff need to observe the patient in more detail than would be necessary without the token program, the patient observes the staff more closely because their activities are now discriminative stimuli that set the occasion for reinforcers. Despite the implication of an objective, impersonal criterion for the interaction between patient and staff, it is inevitable that many interpersonal interactions will arise over the tokens that would not have occurred otherwise. In common speech we would say that they get to know each other better and treat each other more personally. The staff's observations of the individual patient will extend beyond the target behaviors to many details of conduct that need to be observed because of the increased overall level of interaction between them.

An example from an attempt to apply a token reinforcement procedure for the treatment of delinquent adolescent provides an occasion for thinking about the limitations that are present with the arbitrary application of tokens. The institution cared for delinquent girls who cut deep wounds on their arms and legs—a practice known as "carving."[16] An attempt to rehabilitate the girls had the paradoxical effect of increasing the amount of carving when a token program was introduced. The staff speculated that the tokens and the contingencies backed up by tokens did not have a close enough connection to the target behavior. They surmised that the more important target repertoire involved the inmates' responsibility for managing their own affairs. Presumably, the self-mutilation was the only way these girls could exert counter control on the staff in opposition to the token economy that had been imposed. Acting on this premise, they allowed the inmates to participate actively in formulating a behavioral control program of their own and told them that they would no longer try to prevent the self-mutilation. When the inmates took control over their lives by designing the rules for the modification of their own behaviors, the variable responsible for the self-destructive behaviors, vandalism, and aggression no longer operated. A collateral result was the modification of token procedure that was adopted by group consensus.

## contingency management in community affairs, education, and special education

A behavioral view of many community and educational practices has resulted in practical rearrangements that have solved important social problems. The term contingency management[17] is exemplified by the following selected cases, which illustrate the way that restructuring the contingencies of reinforcement in the educational or ongoing environment has improved otherwise maladaptive behaviors.

A number of explicit experiments have established the obvious fact that consumers reduced their consumption of electricity when they saved money thereby and were given point-to-point feedback about the savings and the conservation.[18] Experiments in job training programs show that the trainees' performance depend on the reinforcement contingencies inherent in the job environment. Behavior analysts, observing that participants worked in a desultory manner, altered the pay schedule so that attendance credit and hence pay were given in proportion to the work produced. The result was an increase in the work product. The process involved in the increased productivity is similar to the increase in accuracy of matching-to-sample and counting when the performances were reinforced on ratio rather than interval schedules (Chapter 6).

One behavioral analyst was able to eliminate lateness by paying a 16-cent bonus when workers arrived on time. The effect on the worker's behavior was out of proportion to the amount of money given and indicates the complexity involved in specifying when and how and why a consequence of a performance may be an effective reinforcer.

A program for modifying the behavior of drivers, referred by the courts for traffic violations involving drunk driving, proved successful with young offenders without a long history of alcoholism.[19] The program involved the elements of self-control training along the lines of those described in Chapter 8. The training included identifying the aversive consequences of drinking, educational development of an intraverbal repertoire about them, and training in behavioral analysis, teaching the drivers how to observe the functional control of their own behavior.

Hyperactive and otherwise disruptive children in special educational classrooms have been the subject of contingency management procedures in which teachers are trained to use their attention as reinforcers.[20] There is an exaggerated tendency for the teacher to react especially when children are disruptive, inattentive and idle. Classroom experiments have shown that such attention reinforces the unwanted conduct. Conversely, when teachers, through special training, or prompting by a trained observer, react differentially and affirmatively to the desired behavior, its frequency increases and disruptive performances decrease. The natural reactivity of the teacher to the disruptive, annoying behavior exemplifies one of the reasons for the predisposition to the use of aversive control that was discussed in Chapter 4.

Token economies applied toward rehabilitating delinquent adolescents in residential settings have focused on inadequate social learning histories and inadequate academic and vocational skills as the major problems to be solved. Not only have these programs been highly successful in rehabilitating delinquent youths with histories of arrest and school failure, but they have been able to objectively measure the youngsters' progress and to evaluate the contribution of the individual elements of the rehabilitation program. One such program, called Achievement Place,[21] in operation for a number of years, combines a token economy with a social structure led by "teaching-parents" who were trained in behavioral analysis. The targets of the program are the development of peer and parent relationships, self government, and skill development. Tokens are given for grooming, chores, job participation, reading, homework, grades and collaborating with the staff in practical management tasks. Tokens are taken away for aggressive behavior, disorderliness, poor manners, tardiness, cheating, poor grammar, and poor grooming. The individual house where the youths live functions like a normal family's, led by the teaching-parents. Residents attend public school, have time for individual activities in the afternoon, help prepare meals, and care for the house. An evening meeting is a chance to discuss the rules and structure of the token system and the running of the house. The token economy functions like a power source, engaging the youths and staff with each other and enabling discussions of the governance of the token program and other matters of concern for daily living.

## influencing behavior by increasing the detail and frequency of observation

The maintenance of observing behavior was discussed in these terms in Chapter 6. Evidence is accumulating of the practical benefits that accrue when people monitor their activities. Experimenters who attempted to secure a baseline for experimental studies by having subjects or patients monitor the frequency of the target behaviors were surprised to discover that in the course of monitoring their activity, they changed it. One investigator reported that smoking patterns, monitored as the first step in an experiment aimed at investigating ways to control them, changed simply as a result of being monitored.[22] A similar effect was implicit in the discussion in Chapter 8 of self-control of eating.

The savings by residents mentioned earlier, who monitored their day-to-day consumption of electricity, followed directly from observations of their electric meters. Another investigator reduced the number of safety hazards present in an industrial plant simply by a procedure through which supervisors were given information about hazardous conditions in their departments.[23] In the absence of such data, which could have been obtained directly by the supervisors, the hazardous situations were ignored. Another experiment[24] increased the amount of interaction between staff and children in an institution for the mentally retarded when staff members were asked to keep a record of their interactions.

## university teaching

The personalized system of instruction, sometimes described as the "Keller Plan," has been an important and influential application of behavioral principles to teaching.[25] It provides a method of instruction in which students proceed through the course at their own pace and in which lectures are used inspirationally and motivationally rather than as a way to create the target repertoire; there were perhaps four or five lectures in a semester. The course objective is broken down into study units each of which the student needs to pass at a high level of mastery before going on to the next. No penalities are imposed for partial success, but another opportunity to pass is given. Tests are graded immediately by proctors, usually students who have completed the course in an earlier semester. Thus, the course can be conceived as a chain of operants, each on a fixed-ratio schedule, reinforced by the completion of the course. Each study unit is designed so that the fixed-ratio schedules involved can be maintained by the student. Less is required in the early units so that the fixed-ratio strain (Chapter 5) can be avoided and the sequence of increasing fixed-ratio requirements can be arranged so that the course "shapes" the required persistence. The student studies when inclined to engage the course material rather on a fixed, pre-determined schedule or under the intense aversive pressure of an imminent examination.

Another version of a programmed college course utilized a remedial procedure in place of self-pacing.[26] In this course, a massive enterprise involving almost 1000 students in many sections, there were weekly 1-hour class meetings for 10 weeks during which objective quizzes were given. Answers were discussed in class immediately after the test and the grades posted the next day. Students who passed a quiz at less than 90% level did not receive credit but could make up failed tests during the final 5 weeks that were devoted to remediation. The final examination provided another means of demonstrating competence by which students who had not completed the entire course during the preceding 10-week period could raise their grades. This procedure shares some of the elements of the normal classroom method; it takes its behavioristic slant from the immediate response to the student quizzes, the high frequency of quizzes that require daily study, and the sensitivity of the course structure toward remediation for students who do not conform to the structure at the beginning or who otherwise have difficulty.

Application of the concept of how verbal behavior is reinforced (Chapter 8) stimulated a variation in the course procedure that emphasized a definition of the target of the course of instruction that was different than that of the course described above. In that procedure, there was a formal requirement that one student speaks to another, without benefit of the text, about a 10–15 page study unit just completed.[27] Because the student speaks in detail, and without prompting from the text, concerning a short section of about 3000 words, there is a fine-grain relation between the speaking performance and the study behavior that preceded. The core process was described in Chapter 8 under the topic of how performances emitted under the control of a text can change in function to intraverbals. The speech, to another student, is the reinforcer that maintains the shift of textual behavior to intraverbal. Reading is a complex activity that can produce residues at many different levels of complexity beginning with a rote recitation. The speech is a reinforcer that defines the subtle complex forms of study interaction with a text that produces the required verbal fluency. In other words, the speech is the change in the student's behavior that is generically related to the study activity with a text that produces such a residue. One advantage of the speech over a written test derives from the great speed at which speech can occur as compared with writing. Because of the practical limitations of writing, the test needs to sample the potential productions from textual study with the consequent possibility that the sampling character of the test will define the student's study behavior too arbitrarily. The speech on the other hand deals with the entire textual target of the course.

## questions

1. Describe the benefits of a token economy.
2. Explain the limitations of a token economy.
3. What advantages are derived by students speaking to each other rather than to an instructor?

## the difference between psychotherapy and education

The oft-stated premise of behavioral therapies is that they are treatments deduced from the laws of learning. Implied in the organization of this chapter is a somewhat different view that emphasizes the distinction between psychotherapy and educational changes rather than behavioral and nonbehavioral methods. The task of behavioral analysis that is put forward here is that of first, uncovering the actual events that the therapist observes and reacts to, and next, describing the interaction behaviorally. The task is the same whether the technique is behavioral, psychodynamic, or client-centered.

Part II covered the practical ways of behavioral control that seemed aptly described as educational. In all of the examples there, it is implied that reinforcers are at hand or can be contrived to create and maintain the target behaviors that are desired. Where the maintenance of the behavior is the primary problem, as in vigilance, the enterprise simply involves environmental engineering. In the other types of behavior modification described in Part II, existing or contrived reinforcers are applied, usually in an educational setting, to successively approximate items of conduct from the person's existing repertoire. In applications with token reinforcement, direct observation determines which performances are to be approximated. In verbal-educational ventures, the targets tend to be determined by texts. In all of these cases, the teaching task is a technical one of fading, successive approximation, maintenance of behavior under intermittent reinforcement, the efficient development of discriminative control, and the management of competing behaviors. An underlying assumption is that there is a clear target repertoire and effective reinforcers relevant to the target that can be manipulated. For retarded children, some of the benefits come from shaping and maintaining simple activities such as dressing, feeding, and grooming by constructing a stable environment structured like a token economy. Some performances, once established, act naturally on the normal environment already accessible to the child and are maintained without further intervention. Walking, for example, once in the child's repertoire, will be reinforced automatically so long as changes in the child's position set the occasion for the reinforcement of other behavior. Most behavioral developments, however, require that the reinforcing environment be maintained artificially. Institutionalized psychotic patients, with few exceptions, have dressed, combed their hair, washed, or done some kind of work at one time or another. In the token economy these performances are maintained by a token system of reinforcement to substitute for the reinforcers that maintain such behavior in the normal interaction between the person and his available social and physical environment.

There are important differences between the educational procedures described in Part II (and characterized above) and psychotherapy.[28] In psychotherapy, the missing repertoires are those that are maintained by an interaction between persons. In such an interaction, the behavior of one person is reinforced because it influences another's behavior. By this definition, psychotherapy is primarily verbal and is characterized by situations where the reinforcer needs to arise from the verbal influence of one person on another during the therapy interaction. The absence of a reinforcer, generically related to the interactional repertoires, defines the behavioral deficits to be remedied by psychotherapy. The rehabilitation program for delinquent youths described earlier contains both kinds of behavioral control. The token economy and the performances that are targeted such as grooming, self-care, school participation, and deportment are clearly educational. The development of relationships with peers and teaching parents is more aptly characterized as therapeutic than educational because the potential reinforcers are derived from the target repertoire itself. In the development of a relationship it is not possible to separate the target repertoire from the reinforcer sustaining it. The laws of behavior govern both the educational and psychotherapeutic interactions so the difference between them has to do with the nature of the interaction rather than the terms used to describe it. Insofar as interpersonal relations comprise the bulk of the behavior of most people, the primary task of therapy would be to influence this class of behavior.

Because of the changing views of recent years, the behavioral analysis that follows is a necessary introduction to the exposition of behavior therapy. As originally formulated, behavior therapy could be applied in a manner similar to any other educational procedure.[29] More recently, however, behavior therapists have moved toward a broader definition of their therapy that includes the nature of the interaction between patient and therapist.[30] Like the behavioral analysis of the token program for delinquent youths, we can expect that behavior therapy will turn out to have educational as well as therapeutic components.

## systematic desensitization

Systematic desensitization has been mentioned in Chapter 4 to illustrate the way aversive control can have systemic effects on an individual's repertoire. This widely used therapeutic procedure is applied primarily to disorders that come from specific fears. Its application to problems such as drug addiction, alcoholism, speech disorders, sexual problems, uncontrolled anger, insomnia, motion sickness, and nightmares assumes that these manifestations are a symptom of anxiety produced by some underlying phobic stimulus. Thus, if the anxiety were eliminated, it would not produce stuttering, insomnia, or cause the person to drink. The therapy assumes that there is no underlying deficit in the person's operant repertoire so that extinction of the conditioned aversive concommitents of operant behavior eliminates the anxiety and thereby the disruptive effect on the person's repertoire. Therefore, desensitization therapy is not recommended where the anxiety arises from a lack of basic repertoire. An extreme deficit in interpersonal behavior may have very aversive by-products that lead to high levels of fearfulness or anxiety. Desensitization is not deemed to be appropriate in these cases because the anxiety is a by-product of the isolation caused by the lack of interpersonal competence. Sexual problems, which at first glance appear to be candidates for desensitization therapy, may lead to the conclusion that the person is not capable of satisfactory relations with the person of the opposite sex in other important interactions when examined in detail.

Deep relaxation training is a crucial element in the desensitization procedure. It has been reported in its own right as a treatment for disturbances such as migraine or high blood pressure. The theory, originally proposed by Wolpe, was called reciprocal inhibition between the state of relaxation and the disruptive effects of anxiety. Wolpe argued that anxiety might inhibit the person's relaxation or, conversely, the relaxation might inhibit the anxiety. A behavioral analysis of the therapy procedure will reveal other properties of the behavioral control that is involved, however, and such an analysis, derived from the principles set forth in the preceding chapters, will be presented in the next section.

Although systematic desensitization, in theory, appears to be a fairly objective and potentially automatic procedure, behavior therapists are reporting interest in many of the issues that are of concern to therapists of other theoretical positions. The determination of patients deemed suitable for behavior therapy implies a clinical judgment based on the interview and the response to the relaxation procedure. The relaxation procedure is commonly described as the first step in establishing rapport and trust with the patient. The discussion with the patient about the events of the preceding days is a potentially therapeutic aspect of the interaction. The actual conduct of the therapy requires a careful monitoring and interaction with the patient in which sensitive judgments about the patient need to be made. For example, the report that some patients may selectively remember only parts of the scene that they are visualizing in the therapy appears to be close to the psychodynamic therapist's accounts of repression and denial. The importance of interpersonal control between patient and therapist, called "relationship and transference" by the psychodynamic therapist, is seen in the behavior therapist's caveat to the beginner that there is a danger of accepting the patient's reports of "no anxiety" uncritically because the patient's report may be negatively reinforced by the therapist's reaction.

*Evaluation of desensitization procedures as psychotherapy* is difficult because: 1) once started, treatment needs to conform to the patient's needs rather than the requirements of the experiment; 2) selection of patients and characterizing them objectively and validly offers difficult problems; 3) students, in so-called "analogue therapy" whose complaints simulate those of patients are commonly used; 4) it is difficult to equate the effectiveness of therapists who use different kinds of procedures; and 5) there may be bias in the criterion for selecting patients that is either implicit in the background conditions of the study or an explicit part of the methodology.

As a result, there are claims and counter claims about the efficacy of desensitization therapy. Some attribute almost total effectiveness for desensitization therapy across a wide spectrum of disturbances compared with no treatment or treatment by conventional psychotherapy.[31] Viewing the same data, others find such a lack of consistency and serious methodological flaws that they conclude that valid conclusions cannot be drawn and that definitive research is not possible.[32] Despite the disagreement, the mass of case reports by clinicians doing desensitization therapy leave no doubt that it is effective in eliminating or reducing anxiety in some situations and with some kinds of patients. The situation is the same with the formal, experimental evaluation of conventional psychotherapy where evidence presented about psychotherapy with children asserts that it is no more effective than no treatment.[33] There, too, the finding is questioned by a critical evaluation of the research.[34] And there, too, case reports and the experience of individual therapists persist in producing a consensus that is effective enough to justify its continued application.

*The theory of desensitization therapy,* as counter conditioning or reciprocal inhibition, appeals to behavioral processes and events that are speculative and hypothetical. Anxiety is an effect on the overall operant repertoire rather than a response. We are misled by the parallel systems of reflexes and operant repertoire changes that were described in Chapter 4. If we are to analyze behavioral desensitization "behaviorally" we need to describe the actual behaviors that are involved and put them in the context of the basic behavioral processes that govern them.

**In a behavioral analysis of desensitization therapy**    One can be sure that a procedure such as desensitization therapy would result in extinction of conditioned reflex effects of past aversive control. The relaxed state of the patient guarantees that the conditioned reflexes evoked are not severe enough to negatively reinforce some operant that prevents exposure to the stimulus. It is hard to imagine that such extinction, by itself, would not be ameliorative. Nevertheless, the view that desensitization is simply an extinction of conditioned aversive stimuli and conditioned reflexes appears to be an oversimplification of the therapy processes. The additional complexity derives from the complexity of the interaction that the therapist and patient engage in during the various components of the desensitization procedure.

One way to view the therapy interaction is a very active process in which the patient has almost total control of the interaction with the therapist, despite the fixed format of the therapy. The patient is allowed to take control over the actions that lessen or increase the level of anxiousness, and also learns ways of doing so. At all times the patient can pace involvement in the task and in the interactions.[35] This characteristic is of a therapeutic rather than an educational interaction because the sensitive, point-to-point relation with the therapist's involvement is so crucial.

Perhaps the most clinical aspect of the desensitization therapy is the way that the interaction with the therapist provides tension for reinforcing verbal performances controlled discriminatively by heretofore unobserved events within the patient's skin. Slight disturbances in the patient's relaxation give collateral evidence that both patient and therapist can observe, thereby allowing the therapist to reinforce tacts under the discriminative control of the private events that come from the conditioned aversive stimuli of the desensitization hierarchy. Both patient and therapist are commenting on the same event—the therapist, through the collateral evidence of the patient's anxiety, and the patient through direct contact with the private stimulus. For the most part the performance that is reinforced is a nonvocal performance such as raising the finger, and we would expect that the discriminative control of this performance would become increasingly precise. It would also be predictable that such tacts would eventually function as intraverbal performances as the events of the desensitization procedure are discussed and as the therapist is especially attentive to reports of similar events outside of therapy. The emergence of tacts under control of states of anxiety allows the patient to emit performances elsewhere than in the therapy hour and to observe anxiousness there as well. The complex process, that we cannot describe without the detailed data of the individual case, is how the tact emitted in the presence of a fearful situation, such as one involving an employer, may eventually lead to intraverbals. Clearly the talk to the therapist that generates intraverbals related to the daily events discussed is part of this "observing repertoire."

## flooding, response prevention, punishment
## of self-destructive behavior, and
## food-reinforcement of speech

The reader who has some familiarity with the literature published on behavior therapy will notice that response prevention, use of shock to suppress self-destructive behavior of psychotic children, and aversion therapy have not been discussed in any detail. Although these topics are normally found in books designated as behavior therapy, if included here they would have been presented in Part II. In general, they tend to be procedures in which the reinforcer is applied to a performance targeted by the therapist rather than performances maintained by their intrinsic effect in the interaction with the therapist. While the results reported in the literature are suggestive of possible benefit, they are, for the most part unevaluated.

Response prevention is derived from the notion that the extinction of conditioned reflexes associated with phobias or compulsive behaviors does not occur because the conditioned aversive stimulus very quickly negatively reinforces any operant that removes or escapes it. Therefore, extinction can never occur because the conditioned stimulus never is present long enough. If the patient can be forced into prolonged contact with the aversive stimulus, it is reasoned, extinction of the reflexes can occur. The proponents of desensitization therapy are careful to point out that the therapy is indicated when the disability is largely a result of the phobic disturbance rather than an underlying deficit in interpersonal competence. Although it is conceivable that there might be obsessive or compulsive persons whose disability is solely a product of some past phobic experience, it seems more likely that the anxiety and aversively maintained performances are a by-product of a deficient past history including inadequate interpersonal repertoires. From the perspective of possible products of therapy, the shift to flooding and response prevention, rather than the more fine-grained interaction of desensitization therapy, takes away the possible therapeutic developments that were described in the previous section.

The use of shock to suppress self-destructive behavior has been justified as a way to prevent the extreme injury that psychotic children may cause themselves. The proponents of such interventions also argue that the extreme persistence of the self-destructive behavior prevents the development of other activities that would be more socially productive for the child.[36] Fortunately, therapeutic alternatives are possible, involving equally behavioral approaches. One general format for treating such problems is for a therapist with some positive relation to the child to restrain the child manually by holding the child and reinforcing alternative actions by the release of the restraint, coupled with play or some other positive interaction.

Attempts to reinforce speech of mute autistic children have, in general, failed because the reinforcer generically related to speech is the influence the child may have on another person. Until the autistic child is inclined to influence another person, there is no basis for functional verbal behavior. The details of the process, in normal development, were described in Chapter 8. Such a development can be simulated in therapy if the child is emitting a wide range of performances reinforced by a wide range of reinforcers that are mediated by the therapist or other staff members. At some point, speech becomes just another component of such a repertoire, and will emerge as soon as the speech of others control his behavior discriminatively in the course of their interaction.

# questions

1. Explain the difference between psychotherapy and educational procedures.
2. Describe desensitization therapy.

# notes

[1]. Verhave, T. The pigeon as a quality-control inspector. *American Psychologist* 21: 109–115, 1966.

[2]. Herrnstein, R. J. and Loveland, D. H. Complex visual concept in the pigeon. *Science* 146: 549–550, 1964.

[3] Skinner, B. F. Pigeon in a pelican. In: *Cumulative record.* New York: Appleton-Century-Crofts, 1959.

[4] Honig, W. K. Discrimination, generalization and transfer on the basis of stimulus differences. In: Mostofsky, D. I. (Ed.) *Stimulus generalization.* Stanford: Stanford University Press, 1965.

[5] Blough, D. S. A method for obtaining psychophysical thresholds from the pigeon. *Journal of the Experimental Analysis of Behavior,* 1: 31–43, 1958.

[6] Bekesy, G. von. A new audiometer. *Acta-oto-laryn,* 35: 411– 422, 1947.

[7] Barrett, J. E. Behavioral pharmacology. *Trends in Pharmacological Science* 1: 215–218, 1980.

[8] Johanson, C. Drugs as reinforcers. In: Blackman, E. I., and Sanger, D. J. (Eds.) *Contemporary research in behavioral pharmacology.* New York: Plenum Press, 1978.

9 Holland, J. G. Human vigilance. *Science* 128: 61–67, 1958.

10 Cameron, J. L. Borst, C., Fifer, W. P., La Vigne, T. L., and Smith, S. A. Remedial reading: A psychoanalytic and operant approach. *British Journal of Medical Psychology* 45: 273–278, 1972. Cameron, J. L., Cameron, G. M., Fifer, W. P., Hardy, R. P., and Smith, S. A Group process in an individualized learning situation. *British Journal of Psychology* 47: 265–272, 1974.

11 Whiteney, L. R. and Barnard, K. I. Operant learning theory and nursing care of the retarded child. *Mental Retardation* 4: 26–29, 1966.

12 Allyon, T. and Azrin, N. H. *The token economy.* New York: Appleton-Century-Crofts, 1968.

13 Atthowe, J. M. and Krasner, L. A. A preliminary report on the application of contingent reinforcement procedures. *Journal of Abnormal Psychology* 23: 37–43, 1968.

14 Leveine, F. M. and Fasnacht, G. Tokens may lead to token learning. *American Psychologist* pp.: 816–818, 1974.

15 The same issue is phrased mentallistically by alluding to a person's perception of what is causing the behavior. Social psychologists speak of a person's attribution of the cause of his or her behavior. When the attribution theorist states that reinforcing study or reading with tangible reinforcers reduces the intrinsic satisfaction that such study can potentially have, she or he is alluding to the same issue as the behaviorist who points to the requirement that a performance be described functionally rather than topographically. Thus, the student who does homework or reading because of the consequences intrinsic to the effect of the performance on her existing repertoire is emitting an operant that is very different from the same topography of action reinforced by the receipt of a token. In fact, as was described in Chapter 1 in regard to bar-pressing and key-pecking, the operant is more usefully defined by its reinforcer than by its form.

16 Ross, R. R. and McKay, B. *Self-mutilation.* Lexington, Mass: Lexington Books, 1979.

17 The term "contingency management" and the various examples follow the discussion by Rimm, C. C. and Master, J. C. *Behavior Therapy.* New York: Academic Press, 1979.

18 Winnett, R. A., Neale, M. S., and Grier, H. C. Effects of self-monitoring and feedback on residential electricity consumption. *Journal of Applied Behavior Analysis* 12:173–184, 1979.

19 Lovibond, S. H. Use of behavior modification in the reductions of alchohol-related road accidents. In: Thompson, T. and Dockens, W. S. (Eds.) *Applications of behavior modification.* New York: Academic Press, 1975.

20 Madsen, C. H., Becker, W. C., and Thomas, D. R. Rules, praise and ignoring. Elements of elementary classroom control. *Journal of Applied Behavioral Analysis* 1: 139–150, 1968.

21 Wolf, M. M., Phillips, E. L., Fixsen, D. L., Braukman, C. J. et al, Achievement place: The teaching-family model. *Child Care Quarterly* 5:92–103, 1976.

22 McFall, R. M. Effects of self-monitoring on normal smoking behavior. *Journal of Consulting and Clinical Psychology* 35: 135–142, 1979.

[23] Sulzer-Azaroff, B. and De Santamaria, M. C. Industrial safety through performance feedback. *Journal of Applied Behavior Analysis* 13:287–295, 1980.

[24] Burg, M. M., Reid, D. H., and Lattimore, J. Use of a self-recording and supervision program to change institutional staff behavior. *Journal of Applied Behavior Analysis* 12: 363–375. 1979.

[25] Keller, F. S. *Summers and Sabbaticals.* Champain, Ill:Research Press, 1977.

[26] Mallot, R. W. and Hartlep, P. *Contingency management in education,* 2nd ed. Kalamazoo, Mich: Behavioradelia, 1979.

[27] Ferster, C. B. Individualized instruction in a large introductory psychology course. *The Psychological Record* 18:521–532, 1968.

[28] The same distinction was enunciated by Keehn, J. D. and Webster, C. D. Behavior therapy and behavior modification. *The Canadian Psychologist* No. 1, 1969. They describe behavior modification as an S. R. S paradigm (educational) and behavior therapy as an S–O–R paradigm (psychotherapy).

[29] Wolpe, J. *Psychotherapy by reciprocal inhibition.* Stanford: Stanford University Press, 1958.

[30] Lazarus, A. A. Has behavior therapy outlived its usefulness? *American Psychologist* 32:550–554, 1977.

[31] O'Leary, D. K. and Wilson, G. T. *Behavior therapy.* Englewood Cliffs, N.J.: Prentice-Hall, 1975.

[32] Meyer, V. The impact of research on the clinical application of behavior therapy. In: Thompson, T. and Dockens, W. S. III (Eds.) *Applications of behavior therapy.* New York: Academic Press, 1975.

[33] Levitt, E. E. The results of psychotherapy with children: An evaluation. *Journal of Consulting Psychology* 21: 189–196, 1957.

[34] Meltzoff, J. and Kornreich, M. *Research in psychotherapy.* New York: Atherton Press, 1970.

[35] Goldfried, M. R. Toward delineation of therapeutic change principles. *American Psychologist* 35: 991–999, 1980.

[36] Bucher, B. and Lovaas, O. I. Use of aversive stimulation in behavior modification. In: Jones, M. R. (Ed.) *Miami Symposium on the prediction of behavior, 1967: Aversive stimulation.* Coral Gables, Fla: University of Miami Press, 1968.

# glossary of technical terms

**Abstract control by a stimulus**   The property of a stimulus that controls operant behavior may not be found in a single stimulus only, but in many. The size, the shape, or the color of an object, for example, may be the controlling factor. The property, it might be said, is "abstracted out." In such cases, we speak of *abstract control.*

**Abulia**   *Abulia* is a non-technical term describing an organism whose performances are occurring at a low frequency because the number of performances required for reinforcement is too high. Abulia is often treated as a loss of "will power," an inability to act, or an ability to make decisions.

**Accidental reinforcement**   *Accidental reinforcement* describes a coincidence of a performance and a reinforcer. Even though there is no contingent relationship between the organism's performance and the reinforcer, there is still an increase in frequency of performance. In accidental reinforcement, the form of the behavior that is reinforced is not fixed in advance. Accidental reinforcement is synonymous with adventitious reinforcement.

**Adjustable stimulus**   An *adjustable stimulus* is one which an animal may change with its own behavior. An adjustable stimulus is used in the procedure wherein a bird may increase the length of a line by pecking at one key and decrease the length by pecking at another.

**Adventitious reinforcement**   See *accidental reinforcement.*

**Anxiety**   *Anxiety* is a descriptive term that refers to changes in performance produced by aversive or preaversive stimuli. These changes include a decrease in the frequency of many operant performances that might have occurred in the absence of the preaversive stimulus. They also include an increase in the frequency of performances which in the past have terminated or reduced the magnitude or broad classes of behavior in the individual's repertoire. Because many performances are altered, we speak of anxiety as a *state* of the organism.

**Arbitrary reinforcer**   An *arbitrary reinforcer* is one that the effectiveness of which requires the direct intervention of a second person. The reinforcer is generally related to conditions of deprivation of the controller rather than the individual to be controlled. Arbitrary reinforcement frequently involves the use of aversive control. A critical feature of such reinforcement is that its use specifies a rather narrow and limited repertoire for the organism, which discourages flexibility of performance. The use of arbitrary reinforcers tends to limit performances to the specific conditions present, rather than to other circumstances of the natural environment.

**Aversive stimulus**  A stimulus the termination of which increases the frequency of a performance is called an *aversive* stimulus. The increase in frequency is said to be through *negative reinforcement.* An aversive stimulus that increases the frequency of performance through its termination is called a *negative reinforcer.* An electric shock or a loud noise may decrease the frequency of the performance it follows (punishment); it may elicit reflexes (unconditioned stimulus); or it may alter the frequency of many operant performances of the ongoing repertoire (anxiety or emotion).

**Avoidance behavior**  *Avoidance* describes a performance which increases in frequency because it postpones the appearance of an aversive stimulus. In the classical laboratory experiment, a rat postpones an electric shock for a brief interval each time it presses the lever. If the rat presses the lever often enough, it avoids the electric shock. Avoidance is to be contrasted with escape, wherein the performance actually terminates the aversive stimulus.

**Baseline**  *Baseline* usually indicates a stable performance from which the effects of an experimental variable can be observed. The use of baseline suggests that the performance is recoverable after some experimental operation.

**Chain**  A *chain* is said to exist when one performance produces the conditions which make the next one possible. The stimulus linking the two performances serves both as a conditioned reinforcer, maintaining the topography and frequency of the first performance, and acts as a stimulus for the second.

**Conditioned reinforcer**  The actual reinforcer maintaining the frequency of a performance is the stimulus immediately following it. In the case of the pigeon, the reinforcement for pecking is the sound and light accompanying the operation of the food magazine. These stimuli in turn set the occasion on which the pigeon may go to the feeder and eat.

**Conditioned response**  A *conditioned response* is the change in the organism's behavior elicited by a conditioned stimulus. In a reflex, the buzzer (conditioned stimulus), which precedes food in the dog's mouth (unconditioned stimulus), comes to elicit salivation (conditioned response) after a sufficient number of pairings.

**Conditioned stimulus**  A stimulus which acquires the property of eliciting a previously unconditioned response is called a *conditioned stimulus.* A buzzer (conditioned stimulus) which initially has little influence on blood pressure (unconditioned response) comes to elicit changes in blood pressure (conditioned response) when it is paired with an electric shock (unconditioned stimulus). The complete event is called a *conditioned reflex.*

**Conditioned suppression**  The presentation of a conditioned aversive stimulus, such as a buzzer, when an animal is performing on some schedule of reinforcement —for example, fixed interval—often results in a decrease in the rate of performance. This decrease in the rate of performance in the presence of the aversive stimulus is called *conditioned suppression.*

**Conditioning**  The term *conditioning* is used to describe both operant and respondent behavior. It refers to a change in the frequency of form of the organism's behavior as a result of the influence of the environment. In operant conditioning the frequency of a performance changes as an organism interacts with the environment. In respondent conditioning, a neutral stimulus comes to elicit a response as a result of pairing it with an unconditioned stimulus.

**Contingency of reinforcement** The circumstances under which a specified performance will or will not be followed by specified reinforcers. The *contingency of reinforcement* specifies the relationship between a performance and its outcome.

**Continuous reinforcement** *Continuous reinforcement* is a schedule of reinforcement in which each performance is followed by the reinforcer. Continuous is distinguished from *intermittent* reinforcement, which refers to schedules of reinforcement in which some performances go unreinforced.

**Control** The term *control* expresses the functional relation between a performance and the variable of which it is a function. Thus we say, "A performance is under the control of a level of deprivation," is synonymous with, "A performance is a function of a level of deprivation," or, "A performance changes with changes in level of deprivation."

**Cumulative record** The *cumulative record,* used in operant experiments, is a graphic record which emphasizes the rate of performance or its frequency. In a cumulative record, a recording pen moves along the abscissa with passage of time and along the ordinate with each occurrence of a performance. Thus the rate of the performance is demonstrated by the slope of the curve.

**Dependent variable** In behavioral science, the *dependent variable* is usually the behavior of an organism which changes as a function of environmental change (the *independent* variable).

**Deprivation** A *deprivation* is an experimental operation designed to increase the effectiveness of a particular reinforcer. Thus an animal may be deprived of food or water for a specified period of time, if the food or water is desired for use as a reinforcer in a given experiment.

**Differential reinforcement** The occurrence of a reinforcement on selected occasions after one topography (form) of a performance, as opposed to another topography, is called *differential reinforcement.* For example, one may differentially reinforce performances that exert great force upon a lever as opposed to performances that operate it lightly.

**Discrimination** *Discrimination* refers to the control of an operant performance by a discriminative stimulus. Thus, discrimination has occurred when the discriminative stimulus controls the frequency of an operant performance. In this book, we talk about a stimulus controlling a performance rather than the organism discriminating (perceiving) a stimulus or stating that discrimination has occurred.

**Discriminative stimulus ($S^D$)** A *discriminative stimulus* is the particular occasion on which a performance is reinforced, in contrast with other occasions (stimuli) on which this performance is not reinforced. The term has the connotations of the common language term *to discriminate* or *to distinguish between stimuli.* The common-language term, however, refers to the state of the organism that discriminates rather than to the technical properties of a stimulus in the environment.

**Elicit** The term *elicit* refers to reflexes where the unconditioned response bears a one-to-one relationship to the unconditioned stimulus. Because the unconditioned stimulus determines both the form and occurrence of the unconditioned response, we speak of the unconditioned response as being *elicited* rather than *emitted* as in the case of the operant.

**Emit**  We speak of operant behavior as *emitted* because the main variable controlling the frequency of the performance is the way in which the performance changes the environment. The emitted nature of operant behavior is to be contrasted with the elicited nature of reflex behavior. In operant behavior the main emphasis is on the stimulus which follows the performance in contrast with reflex behavior where the main emphasis is on the stimulus which precedes the response and elicits or evokes it. Because operant behavior is emitted, it has the quality of "purposiveness,"in contrast with the highly determined nature of the reflex.

**Emotion**  *Emotion* is a state of the organism in which the form and frequency of several items of behavior in the ongoing operant repertoire are altered. The term *emotion,* as it is classically used, has the disadvantage of referring to an inner state which usually cannot be observed. The term *emotional stimulus* overcomes some of these difficulties because it describes a stimulus which alters many ongoing performances in the organism's repertoire other than those directly affected by reinforcement or extinction.

**Environmental control of behavior**  *Environmental control of behavior* refers to the changes in the frequency of operant performances produced by the presence or absence of discriminative stimuli.

**Escape**  The term *escape* describes a relation between a performance and an aversive stimulus in which the performance terminates the aversive stimulus. Escape is to be contrasted with avoidance, where the aversive stimulus does not occur at all as long as the avoidance performance continues to postpone it.

**Experimental space**  The enclosure in which an operant conditioning experiment is carried out and in which a simple, easily repeatable performance can be reinforced and measured is referred to as an *experimental space.* An experimental space in which there is a lever that a rat can press, or a key that a pigeon can peck, is frequently referred to as a *Skinner Box* because it was first developed by B. F. Skinner.

**Extinction**  *Extinction* refers to a procedure in which reinforcement of a previously reinforced operant performance is discontinued. Thus, if a performance has previously occurred with a certain frequency because it has produced food, we describe the procedure as extinction when the performance is no longer followed by food. The use of the term here is specifically limited to the procedure of discontinuing reinforcement. The usual and most prominent effect of extinction is to decrease the frequency of a performance. Thus the effect of extinction on the organism's performance occurs as a result of each unreinforced emission of the performance. If the animal has no opportunity to engage in the behavior, then the term *extinction* is inappropriate. When a previously conditioned performance is extinguished (no longer reinforced), it generally occurs initially with high frequency and then falls continuously until its rate reaches near zero. Occasionally, the rate of a performance may actually increase (although temporarily) when the performance is no longer reinforced. Such cases make it even more important to use the term *extinction* to describe the procedure of discontinuing reinforcement rather than as a description of a change in the animal's performance. Otherwise, we would be in the unfortunate position of saying, "The performance was extinguished, but it did not extinguish." *Respondent extinction* involves the presentation of the conditioned stimulus without the subsequent presentation of the unconditioned stimulus.

**Fading procedure**  *Fading* is a term used to describe a procedure for gradually changing a stimulus controlling an organism's performance to another stimulus.

For example, consider a pigeon that pecks at a green key and not a red one. If a cross is superimposed on the green key and the green color is faded out, the new stimulus will control the bird's behavior without the occurrence of any reinforced pecking. This is functionally the same procedure that Dr. Sherman used with the mute psychotic man in Chapter Four, Part I.

*Fading,* disregarding the common usage of the term, does not always refer to the disappearance of a stimulus. Sometimes in a fading procedure a stimulus begins at a low value and is increased in magnitude. Consider, for example, a case where a pigeon pecks (and is reinforced) when the key is red, but not when it is dark. The control by the dark key may be shifted to a green key by first projecting a faint green light on the dark key and then gradually increasing the intensity. If the rate of change of the stimuli is properly paced with the organism's behavior, the control may be shifted from one stimulus to another without any instances of the bird's pecking inappropriately.

**Fine-grain repertoire**   A *fine-grain repertoire* refers to an operant performance which changes under the control of small variations in the stimulus. Examples of this are drawing from copy or steering a car. The phrase, "point-to-point correspondence between changes in a stimulus and the corresponding changes in a performance," refers to a fine-grain repertoire.

**Fixed-interval schedule**   In a *fixed-interval schedule* of reinforcement, the first performance that occurs after a fixed period of time elapses is reinforced. The interval of time is measured from the preceding reinforcement. Thus, on an *FI* 5 schedule, reinforcement is given after the first performance that the animal emits at least five minutes after the preceding reinforcement.

**Fixed-ratio schedule**   In a *fixed-ratio schedule* of reinforcement a fixed number of performances (counted from the preceding reinforcement) are required for reinforcement. Thus on an *FR* 50 schedule, the fiftieth performance after the preceding reinforcement produces the next reinforcement. The term *ratio* refers to the ratio of performances required for each reinforcement.

**Generalized reinforcer**   The *generalized reinforcer* is a type of conditioned reinforcer the effectiveness of which does not depend upon a single kind of deprivation. Many different performances may be reinforced by a generalized reinforcer. Money is a generalized reinforcer for most persons.

**Incompatible performance**   A performance is *incompatible* with another when it is impossible for both performances to occur at the same time. Thus the behavior of clasping the hands behind the back is incompatible with reaching for an object on a table.

**Independent variable**   In behavioral science the *independent variable* usually refers to events in the environment which the experimenter can manipulate and of which the behavior of the organism (the dependent variable) is a function.

**Intermittent reinforcement**   *Intermittent reinforcement* occurs when reinforcement is omitted following some emissions of an operant performance. The various ways in which reinforcement may be intermittent are varied in different schedules of reinforcement.

**Key**   A hinged plate which produces an electrical pulse when moved is called a *key.* In experiments with pigeons, a translucent disc at a convenient height on the wall of the experimental box is frequently used as a key. When a pigeon pecks this disc, the movement operates an electrical switch. A spring returns the hinged plate to the unoperated position. In experiments with rats, a horizontal bar, parallel to the wall of the experimental space, closes the switch against the pressure of a light spring.

The specific design and construction of the key varies, depending upon the organism operating it. The term *key* has come to be a generic term, synonymous with manipulanda, foot treadle, or lever. A performance frequently recorded in the performance of a monkey or a chimpanzee is that of pressing a toggle switch similar to the key used on a telephone switchboard. All these devices have the advantage that the relationship between the performances and their effect on the food dispenser may be objectively and accurately specified on automatic recorders. Experiments with performances which do not involve the operation of a switch (such as head raising in the pigeon) are much more difficult to define and require personal judgment as to when the performance conforms to a criterion which defines a class of performances objectively.

**Latency**   *Latency* refers to the interval between a stimulus and the organism's behavior which is controlled by it. In the case of a reflex, the latency may be the interval between a conditioned stimulus and the conditioned response. In the case of operant behavior, latency may refer to the interval between the appearance of a discriminative stimulus and the operant performance it controls.

**Limited hold**   On various interval schedules of intermittent reinforcement, the reinforcer is made available after a certain period of time, but it is not delivered until a performance occurs. *Limited hold* is a time period during which the scheduled reinforcer is kept available but is not delivered until a performance occurs. If the performance does not occur during the limited-hold interval, the scheduled availability of reinforcement is terminated. For example, in a fixed-interval schedule of reinforcement where the reinforcer is made available after 150 seconds have elapsed, the reinforcer might be available for a period of 15 seconds after the 150-second interval. If no performance occurs during the 15-second, limited-hold interval, the availability of reinforcement is terminated, and a new 150-second interval must elapse before reinforcement is made available again.

**Magazine**   The term *magazine* refers to a mechanical device containing a supply of food which can be delivered in small portions to the organism.

**Magnitude (of the stimulus and the response in a reflex)**   The *magnitude* of the stimulus and response has unique importance for the reflex because it is the most important dimension of the reflex. In general, the major effect of reflex conditioning is on the magnitude of the response. In a similar way, the magnitude of the stimulus controls the magnitude of the response very closely. In operant behavior the magnitude as well as the form of the performance is arbitrary and depends upon what performances are selectively reinforced.

**Matching-to-sample**   *Matching-to-sample* is a procedure in which the choice of a stimulus that matches a sample stimulus is followed by a reinforcer. Typically, in the matching-to-sample procedure, the organism touches a key on which the sample stimulus appears. The performance on the sample stimulus is reinforced by the appearance of two stimuli on two other keys. One of these stimuli corresponds to the sample. The final reinforcement occurs if the organism chooses the key on which the stimulus corresponding to the sample stimulus appears. A time-out or the reappearance of the sample stimulus occurs if the organism chooses the key which does not correspond to the sample.

**Multiple schedule**   A *multiple schedule* is a combination of several schedules of reinforcement, each of which is accompanied by a characteristic stimulus. For example, in the presence of a red light, key pecking is reinforced on a fixed-ratio schedule; and in the presence of a green light, key pecking is reinforced on a fixed-interval schedule.

**Natural reinforcement**   A *natural reinforcer* is one to be found in the everyday (natural) environment of the individual. The effectiveness of a natural reinforcer is maintained by its presence in everyday circumstances and because it does not depend on the intervention of a second person. The use of *natural reinforcement* encourages a wide, flexible range of performances. Natural reinforcement begins with the current repertoire of the individual—not with some arbitrary form of a performance that is shaped and determined by the controller.

**Negative reinforcement**   *Negative reinforcement* refers to an operant performance whose frequency increases because it has terminated an aversive stimulus. Both negative and positive reinforcement increase the frequency of a performance. In the case of negative reinforcement, the increase comes about because of the termination of the stimulus, while in the case of positive reinforcement, the increase occurs as a result of the presentation of a reinforcing stimulus. In this book, *negative reinforcement* is not used in the sense of punishment.

**Neutral stimulus**   The term *neutral stimulus* is used in the description of conditioned reflexes to indicate that the stimulus which is to be established as a conditioned stimulus did not initially evoke or elicit the unconditioned response. Such a neutral stimulus, however, may not be neutral in respect to other aspects of the organism's repertoire.

**Ontogenetic history**   The *ontogenetic history* refers to the individual organism's experience in its interaction with the environment. The result of such ontogenetic experiences may produce unique behaviors in each individual because the environments generating the performances are different for each individual.

**Operant behavior**   *Operant behavior* refers to those performances which are increased in frequency by operant reinforcement. Operant performances are to be contrasted with reflexes, when the environment elicits a change within the organism. In general, an operant refers to a class of behaviors rather than a single performance. Thus, an operant performance might designate a specific instance of a performance while an operant designates a class of performances maintained by a common reinforcer. When we say, for example, "The food magazine reinforced a whole class of performances which had the common property of moving the treadle far enough to operate the electrical switch," we are expressing the concept of a class of operants. Colloquially, we could speak of these treadle performances as feeder-operating behaviors. A similar connotation is carried by the expression, "attention-getting behaviors." The performance is actually defined by the reinforcer it produces.

**Pavlovian conditioning**   The term *Pavlovian conditioning* is synonymous with reflex or respondent conditioning. It refers to pairing a neutral stimulus with an unconditioned stimulus. Eventually the neutral stimulus (now called a conditioned stimulus) comes to elicit a response as a result of the previous pairings.

**Performance**   The behaviors that change or operate on the environment are called operant *performances*. Operant behavior refers to those performances that are increased in frequency by reinforcement. Any given operant performance usually refers to a class of behaviors rather than to a single performance. An operant is a class of behavior because a variety of performances could all produce the same reinforcer. The performance is usually defined by the reinforcer that it produces.

**Phylogenetic history**  *Phylogenetic history* refers to the evolutionary history of the species in which the survival of individuals with particular genetic features produces a selection of behavior patterns. Thus, the inheritance of a given species is determined by the evolutionary history in which other kinds of animals did not survive, rather than in the ontogenetic experience of the organism.

**Point-to-point relation between a stimulus and a performance**  See *fine-grain repertoire.*

**Probability of a performance**  The probability that a performance will be emitted within a specified interval is inferred by observing its frequency of occurrence under comparable conditions. *Probability of a performance,* a statistical term, has some of the connotations of "disposition to perform" or "an animal's inclination to engage in a performance." In almost every case it is possible to substitute "frequency of a performance" for "probability of a performance."

**Property of a stimulus**  *Property of a stimulus* refers to a single dimension of the stimulus which may control a performance differentially from other dimensions of the stimulus. Thus, a stimulus might be described as a large, red, right triangle, and a performance may be reinforced in respect to only one property of the figure, such as its size. See *abstract control by a stimulus.*

**Punishment**  *Punishment* describes a procedure in which an operant performance is followed by an aversive stimulus. Punishment, therefore, is usually an interaction between a performance maintained by positive or negative reinforcement and an aversive stimulus.

**Reflex**  A *reflex* is a relationship between an eliciting stimulus and an elicited response such as the contraction of the pupil of the eye as a result of shining light on it, the jerk of the knee as a result of tapping the patellar tendon, the excretion of sweat as a result of warm air, or the constriction of blood vessels in response to a loud noise. The reflex describes both the behavior of the organism (response) and its environment (stimulus). Thus, the patellar reflex is a description of what happens when the patellar tendon is struck with a hammer. For purposes of analysis, it is convenient to describe the two events separately: the hammer blow to the tendon, which is the stimulus, and the subsequent contraction of the muscle, which is the response. The temporal relation is reversed in operant conditioning, in which the performance is followed by a reinforcing stimulus which then increases the frequency of the behavior. Such separate descriptions of the performance and the environment emphasize the differences between operant and respondent behavior.

**Reinforce**  To *reinforce* is to follow a performance with a reinforcing stimulus. Such a procedure may or may not increase the frequency of the performance, depending upon collateral conditions.

**Reinforcement**  When a stimulus follows a performance, *reinforcement* has occurred.

**Reinforcement contingency**  See *contingency of reinforcement.*

**Reinforcer**  The *reinforcer,* or the *reinforcing stimulus,* is the event which increases the frequency of the performance it follows. A reinforcing stimulus may also have other effects on behavior. One of these is the elicitation of an unconditioned response in a reflex.

**Reinforcing stimulus**  See *reinforcer.*

**Repertoire**  The term *repertoire* is used to indicate the total number of latent performances which the organism may emit under the various conditions present in its environment and as a result of its past history.

**Respondent**  See *reflex*.

**Response**  The use of the term *response* has been limited in this text to the reflex. Operant behaviors are designated as performances. Other writers, however, use the term *response* interchangeably with operant and reflex behavior.

**Sample**  See *matching-to-sample*.

**Satiation**  *Satiation* refers to the procedure of feeding an animal and is to be contrasted with deprivation, the procedure of withholding food. The effectiveness of food as a reinforcer increases with deprivation and decreases with satiation. Some writers, however, use the term *satiation* to refer to the change that occurs in an organism's performance when a large amount of food has been ingested.

**Schedule of reinforcement**  When the reinforcement of an operant performance occurs intermittently, the particular schedule by which reinforcement occurs is termed a *schedule of reinforcement* (such as fixed-ratio, fixed-interval, variable-interval, and variable-ratio schedules of reinforcement).

**Self-control**  *Self-control* occurs when an organism produces a change in the environment which in turn alters the frequency of some performances in its own repertoire. Thus, the dieter who stores peanuts and candy in an inaccessible place is engaging in a performance which changes the environment so that the frequency of eating peanuts and candy is reduced. The reinforcement of the self-control behavior is negative in this case because it prevents overeating, which has aversive consequences for the dieter.

**S-delta (S$^\Delta$)**  An *S-delta* represents the particular occasion on which a performance will not be reinforced, in contrast to other occasions (discriminative stimuli) during which the performance will be reinforced.

**Slope**  The *slope* of a cumulative record refers to the tangent of the angle the record forms with the abscissa. Where the rate of the performance is changing, the slope of the record at any point is given by the tangent to the curve at that point. The slope of the cumulative record is equivalent to the rate of emission of the performance.

**Stable state**  A schedule of reinforcement does not usually produce its final result until it has been in effect for a definite period of time. When the reinforcement conditions are kept constant the performance stabilizes and occurs in a repeated pattern. Such a condition is referred to as a *stable state* and implies that the performance will continue unchanged if the same reinforcement schedule is continued.

**Stimulus**  A *stimulus* is any physical event or condition, including the organism's own behavior. A stimulus may have many different functional relations to an organism's repertoire. It may be an eliciting stimulus for a response in a reflex. It may serve as a discriminative stimulus which precedes an operant performance. It may be a conditioned reinforcer or a primary reinforcer which follows an operant performance and increases its frequency. It may be an aversive stimulus whose termination increases the frequency of an operant performance. Finally, it may have no demonstrable effect on the organism's repertoire.

**Stimulus control**  *Stimulus control* refers to a differential form or frequency of a performance in the presence of one stimulus which is not evident in the presence of another.

**Strain**  *Strain* is a term used to describe the decreased frequency of a performance that occurs when the performance is reinforced on a large fixed-ratio schedule. Under most conditions, strain occurs between long periods during which the performance does not occur at all and periods when there are bursts of the performance at high rates. The term *abulia* is also used as a synonym for strain.

**Successive approximation**  *Successive approximation* is used to condition a performance which is not currently in the organism's repertoire. Some performance which is an approximation to the desired behavior and which the organism is already emitting is first reinforced. Thereafter, reinforcement occurs after those performances which are in the direction of the desired performance. Conversely, performances which are most distant from the desired behavior go unreinforced.

**Superstitious behavior**  When a performance is changed or maintained because of an accidental relationship between the performances and reinforcers, the resulting performances are referred to as *superstitious behavior.* Thus, when a reinforcer is delivered every minute, independent of what performance the animal is emitting, we may observe the animal to emit a certain stereotyped behavior after this procedure has been followed for a while. This behavior is called superstitious behavior, because it has no actual effect on the delivery or nondelivery of the reinforcer.

**Threshold**  The term *threshold* has been used in the text to refer to the magnitude of an eliciting stimulus which is just sufficient to elicit the reflex. The term *threshold* is widely used in the literature of experimental psychology in relation to the stimulus control of operant behavior.

**Token**  A *token* is used as a conditioned reinforcer. It is usually a metal or plastic disc which an organism (usually one with an opposing thumb and forefinger such as a man or chimpanzee) can carry around and exchange for privileges, food, or other items.

**Transition state**  When an organism is changed from one schedule of reinforcement—for example, fixed-ratio—to another schedule of reinforcement—for example, fixed-interval—there is a period of time during which the response rate is not typical of what one would expect on either schedule. The behavior emitted during this time and before the final performance on the new schedule of reinforcement is reached is referred to as a *transition state.*

**Unconditioned response**  An *unconditioned response* (reflex behavior) is the behavior elicited by an unconditioned stimulus. Such behavior frequently influences the internal economy of the organism. The form is usually determined by the organism's phylogenetic history.

**Variable-ratio reinforcement**  *Variable-ratio reinforcement* is a schedule of intermittent reinforcement in which reinforcement follows after a variable number of performances. The schedule is specified by the average number of performances required for reinforcement. Thus, *variable ratio 10 (VR* 10) means that ten performances on the average are required for each reinforcement.

# index

## A

Abstract property of a stimulus:
  complex control by, 201–4, 337–39
  control by, 199–201
  extraction due to, 210–13
Abulia, 145, 146, 316
Acceleration, 156
Accidental reinforcement:
  of avoidance behavior, 34–35, 86–87
  contingencies of, 11–12
  in human behavior, 33–35
  in interval schedules, 12, 182, 310
  preventing, in experiments, 242
Activity, as reinforcer, 252
Adaptation, 42
Adolescence, 311, 316
Adulthood, 311–12
Anger, 45, 79, 114, 115, 128, 330–31
Animal laboratory procedures:
  apparatus, 24–26
  conditioning a pigeon, 4–6, 24–27
  cumulative recorder, 153–54
  practical applications of, 335–46
Anxiety (see Systematic desensitization)
Approval behavior, 258–59, 269
Atavistic behaviors, in autism, 313–14, 328
Attention:
  as audience variable, 294–95
  as conditioned reinforcer, 256–58
  as discriminative stimulus, 293–95
Attention-getting behavior, 260–61
Autistic children (See Infantile autism)

Autonomic nervous system, 44, 50
Autoshaping, 68–69
Aversive control (see also Systematic desensitization)
  arbitrary, 130–36, 138
  aspects in positive reinforcement, 130–31
  benign vs. malignant forms, 129–30
  by-products, 106–18, 126–27, 128–29, 180–81, 225, 327–28
  contributing to depression, 330–31
  disruption of behavior from, 48, 121, 248, 328
  in education, 126, 131–33, 304, 305, 327–28
  and emotion, 325–32
  extinction substituted for, 127–42
  in infantile autism, 100–102, 139–41, 328–29
  in interactions between persons, 94–102
  in parent and child interaction, 94–98, 180–81, 325–26, 331
  in playground activities, 98–100
  positive reinforcement substituted for, 127–42, 138–39, 180–81
  psychotherapy involving, 100–102, 308, 331–32
  in self-control, 329–30
  somatic by-products of, 117–18
Aversive stimuli:
  accidental reinforcement with, 34–35, 86–87
  conditioned, 75–78, 86, 326
  derived, 75–84
  disruptive effects of, 48, 121, 248, 328

**377**

# S